GOVERNORS STATE UNIVERSITY LIBRARY

3 1611 00047 9326

W9-CKM-348

WITHDRAWN

Issues and Research in Special Education

Volume 1

GOVERNORS STATE UNIVERSITY
UNIVERSITY PARK
IL 60466

ISSUES AND RESEARCH IN SPECIAL EDUCATION

Volume 1

EDITED BY

Robert Gaylord-Ross

TEACHERS COLLEGE PRESS

Teachers College, Columbia University
New York and London

LC 3981 .I87 v. 1

261306

Issues and research in
special education

Published by Teachers College Press, 1234 Amsterdam Avenue, New York, NY 10027

Copyright © 1990 by Teachers College, Columbia University

All rights reserved. No part of this publication may be reproduced or transmitted in any form
or by any means, electronic or mechanical, including photocopy, or any information storage
and retrieval system, without permission from the publisher.

ISBN 0-8077-2994-9

Printed on acid-free paper

Manufactured in the United States of America

97 96 95 94 93 92 91 90   8 7 6 5 4 3 2 1

Contents

Series Editor's Preface

This first volume of *Issues and Research in Special Education*, a new addition to the Teachers College Press Special Education Series, represents our commitment to address the changing nature of special education. Teachers, parents, and communities are grappling with newer conceptions of what constitutes best practice; for example, we see movement from sheltered workshops to supported work, from group homes to family-scale living arrangements, from segregated public school classes to regular classroom placements, and so on. Theses changes compel professionals and parents to make decisions based on solid information.

We are committed to reporting the latest research in important areas of special education and to do so by describing the nature of the inquiry process in each area. How one goes about studying a particular problem may be just as valuable as the specific results obtained. After all, our field is in a state of flux and we hope to capture newer ways of studying persons, programs, and issues. The authors whose work appears in this volume emphasize research on specific groupings of persons with disabilities and on pivotal issues reflecting recent policy initiatives. Thus, this volume contains chapters on adolescents with deafness *and* the integration of students with severe and profound disabilities, to cite just two examples.

We envision publishing new volumes on a regular basis, since there is no shortage of important issues in need of careful analysis. With leadership from the editor, Robert Gaylord-Ross, we expect to continue to identify researchers and practitioners who are enthusiastic about their work and who value a scholarly approach to the study of educational change.

Peter Knoblock, Ph.D.
Special Education Series Editor

Foreword

Advancing a professional knowledge base requires interpreting and integrating new findings with prior knowledge and current practice. The contribution of research to professional practice is rarely achieved as a result of a single study. The advancement of theory, hypotheses, and applications occurs as research findings accumulate in a manner providing empirical and conceptual support for, or rejection of, problem representations and relationships.

Research and practice are often guided by implicit beliefs that link premises, inferences, and conclusions into explanatory or predictive models. The syntheses presented in this volume of Issues and Research in Special Education make these underlying assumptions explicit and examine the nature and extent of the empirical support upon which they are built. The chapters capture the progression of inquiry and methodological and application advancements characterizing the research knowledge base associated with each topic.

The research reviewed in this volume examines critical components underlying the professional practice of those providing early intervention, special education, and related services to infants, toddlers, children, and youth with disabilities. These chapters focus attention, provide direction, and identify critical features to be considered in the design or delivery of interventions and instruction.

Professional practice is based upon a knowledge base that incorporates both research and craft wisdom. The influence of a professional knowledge base upon practice and advancement is as dependent upon the questions being generated as it is on the findings produced. The contribution of theory and conceptual models arises as much from their power to generate questions as from their explanatory or predictive strength. These reviews make explicit the questions that underlie and have contributed to the research and practices presented in these chapters. The authors, based on their syntheses, have identified unanswered questions and remaining issues as a means of suggesting direction for future inquiry.

The reviews contribute to the understanding of current issues because of their effort to describe, explain, compare, align, and, where possible, integrate research findings. Understanding of the dimensions, progression, disjunctures, and competing positions associated with the issues addressed in this volume is enhanced by grouping the discussion in the reflective thought and experiences of researchers and service providers. This volume is designed to advance how professionals think about approaches to special education issues, design interventions, and consider the effectiveness of current and emerging practices.

Martin Kaufman
Director, Division of Innovation and Development
Office of Special Education Programs
United States Department of Education

Introduction

Special education is a field that attempts to deliver quality educational services to students with disabilities. It is thus an "applied" field. It does not purport as psychology might, to delineate the personality dynamics of individuals with learning disabilities. Rather, it might, for example, design a teacher-parent instructional program to enhance persistence and self-sufficiency in the personality of the learning disabled child. In this light, "applied" should not be viewed as inferior to "pure" science. Indeed, successful interventions may create new portrayals of the personality or cognitive characteristics of the disabled individual. For example, the severely disabled adult who successfully works in a nonsheltered setting and befriends nondisabled coworkers will probably be characterized quite differently than the person who attends a sheltered workshop. Educational interventions that increase disabled individuals' skill attainment and proficiency in challenging environments will undoubtedly change how the pure sciences define a particular disability. Hence, applied efforts might both drive and underlie purer scientific advances.

Its importance as a catalyst notwithstanding, applied research will likely continue to be viewed as a stepchild to and something lesser than pure research. This problem is particularly acute in the field of special education. Its methods of inquiry have been adopted almost entirely from other disciplines, most notably psychology. The experimental designs, sampling procedures, and so forth, are drawn directly from social science research, which was primarily influenced by experimental psychology. More recently, there has been a heightened interest in ethnographic and anthropological approaches to studying disabled students. While these research methods have led to advances in the field, the question still remains whether a research model endemic to special education will emerge. It may be asking too much to expect an applied field to generate a new model for research. Yet if the quality and contributions of an applied science are to increase, one might hope for a unique research methodology to emerge.

This biennial series, in which this book is the first volume, seeks to contribute to that end. By reviewing research on contemporary topics in special education, the series will help to advance conceptual or theoretical models that will not only further the state of our research but also influence policy for the education of students with disabilities. This series should serve as a reference for educators and other professionals. It might also provide texts for a graduate course in special education research.

Despite special education's current dependence on other disciplines for its research methodology, there is one area where innovation characterizes the field. Historically, special education has advanced and implemented a number of models to provide instruction for students with disabilities: for example, mainstreaming models for learning disabled students or integration models for severely disabled students. Special education research has often been consumed with evaluating the efficacy of such models. The "program," in a sense, is the global independent variable. More refined research may attempt to identify the critical causal components of the intervention. At times, rather elegant methodologies unfold as the investigator pursues a career line of research, studying, for example, parent–child interactions of delinquent youth.

Thus, the state of the art for special education research in the near future may not be the emergence of a new research method. Rather, cumulative data bases may emerge that indicate the differential impact of educational interventions and models. One excellent way of organizing this information relies on a "quasi-judicial" focus. As it states, quasi-judicial inquiry applies a courtroom-based mode whereby the investigator (lawyer) offers many sources of evidence (multiple measure data) to make a case. Ultimately, the judge and jury (editor and peer reviewers) will decide guilt or innocence (was the intervention successful?). The appeal of the quasi-judicial method is that many research methods (quantitative and qualitative) may be compiled and synthesized to reach a particular conclusion. There is no one way, or single methodology, to attain truth. Thus, an article or book may include information from a group design as well as individual case studies.

Chapter 1 in this volume by Switzky and Heal directly addresses the issue of research methodology in special education. They first describe and comment on the set of research principles advanced by Campbell and Stanley (1966). Here is an example of a methodological advance that did emerge from educational researchers. Switzky and Heal then report a line of research that studied the personality characteristics of mentally retarded individuals. Switzky and Heal examine this line of research in terms of the Campbell and Stanley criteria and offer the reader a feel for the strengths and weaknesses of this enlightening line of work. Switzky and Heal present their work applying single case designs to a severely disabled population. Single case designs have emerged from behavioristic research (Baer,

Wolf, & Risley, 1968). The designs establish internal validity as they sequentially modify a number of behaviors. Single case designs are particularly appealing in works with low-incidence populations, e.g., hearing impaired. The heterogeneity of these populations often precludes the use of group sampling. Individually graphed data may often lead to a better understanding of student characteristics and intervention efficacy. Single case designs are well suited to evaluate interventions in naturalistic settings; i.e., those contexts that may take much effort to obtain experimental control.

Perhaps part of the difficulty in advancing special education research is the dual roles that investigators must often play. That is, in its effort to upgrade services, all professionals (including researchers) in some capacity become advocates for some particular cause or program. Advocacy advances a value system. While advocating, investigators are primarily political and emotional. The search for truth and the notion of value-free science are secondary. While advocacy and research do not necessarily conflict, it is not uncommon for advocates to value research only when it supports their findings. For individual investigators, their tendencies to be advocates may guide their selection of hypothesis and data, as well as lead them to make tenuous conclusions that extrapolate well beyond the extant data.

The science–values controversy will never be fully resolved. All investigators impose some set of values or sentiments within their research efforts. The notion of a fully value-free social science is a myth. It is up to researchers to be aware of their own values and monitor and edit them accordingly. Just as there are controls for experimental confounds, there might be checks for values permeation into research. A most common intersection of values in special education research is found in studies evaluating a new or old program dealing with integration. Let us assume that the research was done at a time when most disabled students were placed in special classrooms and that it was found that a special class produces no better educational effects than a regular class. A conservative interpretation of the data could be that until there was evidence of superiority in the regular placement, students should remain in the special class. Such logic places an implicit value in the status quo, and does not consider the alternative; namely, that if there is no difference, why not place the student in the regular class? The latter position could be expanded by drawing on the value of least restrictive environment; that is, if there is no difference between programs, then the more integrated one would be favored. The main point to be made in this discussion is that all research questions contain some value. The researcher cannot deny these values, but must be aware of them and include them in designing and interpreting research.

Along those lines, each volume in this series will have chapters that address controversial topics in the special education field with an advocacy and value base. The authors attempt to clarify these values and issues and then cite and interpret related research. When possible, the authors point out whether a particular intervention has proven effective or not. In addition, they seek to advance conceptual or theoretical positions to synthesize a particular area of inquiry.

An example of an issue that has perplexed the special education field for many years is whether to place a student in a completely segregated or wholly integrated setting, or some mixture of the two. Since the passage of Public Law 94-142, the least restrictive environment mandate has led to the progressive inclusion of disabled students in regular education settings. Yet there is still much debate related to the extent of that inclusion. The Regular Education Initiative would place disabled students in regular classes for the complete school day. There would be no special education classes, and certainly no special schools. Such a radical integration plan cries out for convincing data to determine its effectiveness versus that of more traditional special education programs.

Historically, the most complete studies of social integration have appeared in early childhood programs. Richard Shores (1987), William Bricker, and their colleagues at George Peabody College monitored the rates of social interaction between disabled and nondisabled preschoolers. In this volume Chapter 2, by Filler and Olson, reviews the evaluation of early childhood programs. The data base from the multiplicity of these programs enables investigators to conduct statistical meta-analyses to evaluate treatment effectiveness across a number of studies. Chapter 2 reviews this research as well as other relevant topics like family dynamics.

Probably the greatest acceleration of service provision in the field has been for students with severe disabilities. P.L. 94-142 introduced the zero-rejection notion that all children, no matter how severe their disabilities, would be provided a free public education. In Chapter 3 Halvorsen and Sailor document this development and provide an encyclopedic catalogue of social integration tactics that work. Their review reflects the growing interest in the establishment of social support networks in the school and community.

Vocational special education represents another area of substantive growth toward integration. Historically, most disabled persons were not considered capable of being employed. In fact, the current high rate of unemployment of disabled adults reflects this belief, or self-fulfilling prophecy. During recent years, however, there has been a rapid growth in the vocational training of disabled youth. First with mildly handicapped students, and more recently with severely disabled students, there has been an adoption of community-based vocational training (work experience). Subsequent transition programs have planned for employment and independent living in adulthood. In Chapter 4 Siegel, Park, Gumpel, Ford, Tappe, and Gaylord-Ross review the many advances in vocational special education. It gives particular attention to the large number of follow-up studies which have monitored school-to-work transition and evaluated the efficacy of vocational training programs.

Language delay is an almost universal characteristic of disabled children. A wide variety of speech therapies have been used to remediate language delays. Reichle, Mizuko, Doss, Sigafoos, Benson, and Bykowsky in Chapter 5 provide an overview of speech disorders and their treatment. Their focus overlaps with the social skills–training approach of the integration literature in their emphasis on social communication and pragmatic intent. The authors also stress the functions of communication in their review of aberrant behavior and communication-based interventions.

Chapter 6, by Bullis, Freeburg, Bull, and Sendelbaugh, on hearing impairments reviews literature dealing with this specific disability. Besides presenting relevant information about the characteristics of hearing impairments the authors advance a bold model of deafness and cultural difference. The issues for the integration of deaf persons appear to be more complex than for other disability groups. Deaf persons have asserted their need to cluster within the support groups of other deaf persons. Thus, a balance must be struck between integrative and cloistering forces. The model of Bullis et al. elegantly reflects this balance.

Interestingly, assessment often dominated the early period of special education. There was much interest in diagnosing the student and identifying cognitive and motor deficits. But over time assessment has become, in some ways, a dinosaur that has outlived its purpose. Standardized tests often give few guidelines for the teacher to develop curriculum. A new approach, that of dynamic assessment is only now emerging. Dynamic assessment attempts to uncover the process the individual uses in thinking and performing. Originated and developed abroad by Vygotsky (1978), dynamic assessment has had particular appeal for school psychologists attempting to complete culture-fair assessments. In Chapter 7 Rothman and Semmel describe the foundations of dynamic assessment and show how it has been translated into experimental reading research by Brown, Campione, and their colleagues (e.g., Palincsar & Brown, 1984).

The chapters in this book address a wide span of topics in dealing with disability, educational models, and research methodology. In spite of its limitations, the special education field can be proud of its accomplishments in terms of cumulative data bases and productive interventions. Whether a new research paradigm will emerge from within special education will

ISSUES AND RESEARCH IN SPECIAL EDUCATION

Volume 1

CHAPTER 1

Research Methods in Special Education

HARVEY N. SWITZKY
LAIRD W. HEAL

Special education, like general education, is currently undergoing a test of confidence. Blue-ribbon federal panels, as well as scholars both inside and outside the profession, are examining the procedures and methods (and the assumptions that undergird them) that govern how handicapped children and adults are cared for, trained, and educated in school-based settings, community environments, and worksites (*Briefs of the AACTE*, 1987; *Educating Students*, 1987; McKinney & Hocutt, 1988; *OSERS News in Print*, 1987; Reynolds, Wang, & Walberg, 1987; Wang, Reynolds, & Walberg, 1986). The pressures brought by parents and advocates for handicapped persons, combined with special educators' own enthusiasm to train and teach *all* handicapped children and adults, no matter how impaired, have sometimes caused the profession to go beyond its limited store of knowledge based on scientific research methods. Special education professionals have been treading too long on the "thin ice" of expediency, allowing themselves to be stranded by the practical necessities and emotional realities of educating and training handicapped children and adults; they need to move as quickly as possible to the solid shore, and to take time to examine the "bedrock" of scientific research methods and techniques that can be applied to solve very difficult problems in special education. It was in accordance with these goals that this chapter was written.

This discussion of methodology begins with global comprehension and proceeds toward increasingly specific case studies of methodological applications. The first of the three major sections integrates all the senses in which research is judged valid:

1. Correct testing of *a priori* hypotheses (internal validity)
2. Representative sampling of the people, settings, and observations about which research proposes to provide information (external validity)

3. Use of measures that are credible indices of the investigated constructs (measurement validity)
4. Demonstration of relevance to real-world questions (social validity)

The second section features the specific examination of three experiments in special education curriculum according to the standards of these four validities. The third section provides an even more specific anatomy of the pursuit of the construct validity of a single construct, motivational orientation.

GENERAL RESEARCH AND DESIGN ISSUES

There are many fine books that delve in great detail into the application of scientific research and design issues for students of the social sciences and educational psychology (Borg & Gall, 1983; Gage & Berliner, 1984). They should be consulted by readers who wish to go beyond the ideas presented here, which are limited by the demands of this chapter and the idiosyncrasies of the authors.

Science begins with the observation and recording of empirical events that are then organized and reasoned with in order to establish empirical and theoretically consistent regularities, which are initially called hypotheses. The clever scientist deduces implications from these hypotheses and then attempts to invent experiments to test their generalizability and the "truth" of his or her logic.

Research methodologies (Campbell & Stanley, 1966) evaluate research designs and the scientific enterprise in terms of two broad concerns: *internal validity*—the extent to which "true" inferences can be drawn regarding the participants, settings, measures, and conditions investigated—and *external validity,* the extent to which experimental results will generalize to other participants (*population validity*), other environs (*ecological validity*), and other measures (*referent generality*) beyond those that were actually studied (see Bracht & Glass, 1968; Campbell & Stanley, 1966; Cook & Campbell, 1979; Kratochwill, 1978; Sidman, 1969; Snow, 1974). Another concern of research methodologists (e.g., Crocker & Algina, 1986) is with the *validity of measurement,* the extent to which measures of dependent variables accurately reflect the constructs, concepts, or events that they are presumed to assess. The newest concern of some research methodologists (Kazdin, 1982; Rusch, Schutz, & Heal, 1983) is with *social validity,* the extent to which the goals and outcomes of a scientific study meet the relevant needs of the consumers of the research: If research on socially important issues is to be viewed as valid, it must necessarily be supported by evidence that the participants and other consumers who have a vested interest in the research view it as relevant to their needs.

Internal Validity

Internal validity refers to the extent to which "true" empirically based inferences support a tentative hypotheses about the relationship between a variation in the environment (the independent variable) and result or effect of that variation (the dependent variable). In the simplest "true experiment," the two values of the independent variable are defined by the assignment of participants *randomly* either to an experimental group (which receives the critical intervention) or to a control group (which does not receive the critical intervention). Random assignment of participants to experimental conditions is necessary for the internal validity of scientific research methods. Research studies in special education employing random assignment of participants to experimental conditions are rare. Most research studies in special education are variants of "quasi-experimental designs" in which the independent variable is manipulated by sampling groups of participants from different populations. Unfortunately, in these designs experimental and control groups may differ on many unknown and known dimensions besides their difference on the independent variable.

There are numerous threats to internal validity that have been identified by Campbell and Stanley (1966), Cook and Campbell (1979), and Heal and Fujiura (1984); these threats are summarized in the sections that follow.

Selection bias. The differential selection of participants in one experimental condition compared to the other is called *selection bias*. Control strategies may include random assignment of subjects to experimental and control conditions, assessment of the extent of equivalence of intact groups, and matching of groups on critical parameters.

History. Other concomitant events may covary with the experimental intervention and thus compromise the validity of the research. These events may be *extrinsic* to the research design (i.e., collateral events that are independent of the experimental intervention) or *intrinsic* to the research design (i.e., collateral events that are correlated with the experimental intervention—multiple treatment effects). A special type of intrinsic historical contaminant is *differential loss of participants*, or *attrition*, in one experimental condition compared to the other.

Maturation. Maturation effects occur when collateral events, such as growth, degeneration, warm-up, and fatigue, affect the dependent variable regardless of the intervention.

Measurement effects. Biases in the measurement of the dependent variable can create the impression of an effect due to the experimental intervention when in reality none exists. These effects include contaminants such as *biased testers* or observers and the participants' *reaction to assessment*. Also, *floor* or *ceiling effects* exist when the range of measurement is constrained so that the true performance of a high-scoring participant is underestimated or that of a low-scoring participant is overestimated.

Regression to the true score. Regression is the statistical drift of scores on an unreliable measure and is manifested by the statistical tendency for individuals with extreme scores on one occasion to achieve more nearly average scores on subsequent occasions.

External Validity

External validity refers to the extent to which conclusions based on a sample of observations from a unique group of participants in a unique setting may be generalized to a broader population of participants and settings, and to a broader sample of measures. External validity has the following components:

Population validity. When special education research studies are done with one sample of exceptional persons, practitioners may question whether the results generated in one study are appropriate or useful for their particular exceptional individuals. Questions of this sort have to do with population validity. Key concerns are defining the population, locating all its members, and sampling representatively from the members who have been located. Population validity is fundamental to the scientific method applied to the problems of special education practices. If the population under study cannot be well defined, if the defined members cannot be found, or if the selection of participants is biased, then the degree of generalizability of the results to other exceptional populations is suspect.

Ecological validity. When special education research studies are done in one particular setting (i.e., classroom, workshop, restaurant, or laboratory), practitioners may question whether the results generated in these unique settings are appropriate or useful in their particular setting. A scientific research study has ecological validity to the extent that its findings can be applied and generalized to different physical settings, to different laboratory settings, to different temporal settings, and to different social settings. The demands made on researchers are to sample from the populations of places, times, and social demands without bias or differential error, until they are assured that the target behavior of their studies occurs in their targeted settings but not in non-targeted settings.

Referent generality. Special education researchers need also to attend to the sampling of dependent measures, or what Snow (1974) calls *referent generality*. Just as participants and settings are sampled from those possible, so dependent variables (i.e., responses, test scores, observations, ratings, effects, and impacts) are sampled from an array of direct and remote referents. Control strategies may include testing the subjects directly in a variety of settings and asking the subjects' friends, relatives, and teachers to document changes and conditions under which changes occur and do not occur in subjects. These concerns lead us to the next area, where questions regarding measurement issues are analyzed in greater detail.

Validity of Measurement

Measurement is fundamental to all scientific enterprises. To employ a construct in science one must operationally define it in measurement terms that are valid, that is, in terms of events that can be observed and recorded (Bridgeman, 1927). The topic of validity of measurement can be divided into five areas: reliability, face validity, content validity, empirical validity, and construct validity.

Reliability. This area refers to the consistency or stability of measuring the same variable on two or more occasions. There are three kinds of reliability that may be relevant for special education research:

1. *Internal consistency reliability*—the extent to which the various items on a test or scale tend to agree with one another. Control strategies include the use of item analysis procedures to eliminate any items that correlate negatively or negligibly with the others. The recommended index, coefficient alpha (Cronbach, 1951), equals the average of all possible split-half correlations among the items on an instrument.
2. *Inter-rater agreement*—the stability of ratings among raters or judges of the attribute being assessed. Indices of inter-rater agreement include the intraclass correlation, Robinson's *a* (Robinson, 1957), if the variables are measured on an interval scale, or Cohen's Kappa (Cohen, 1968), which indexes percentage agreement for categorical data. Both

of these indices correct for chance agreement if one or both raters guess at their subject's score.

3. *Test-retest reliability*—the repeatability of a measure over time. The primary index of test-retest reliability is Pearson's r as a coefficient of stability.

Modern test theory has led to the development of a more inclusive approach, *generalizability theory* (Berk, 1979; Crocker & Algina, 1986; Cronbach, Gleser, Nanda, & Rajaratnam, 1972; Suen & Ary, 1989), which indexes reliability using analysis of variance techniques that generate the proportion of variance that can be attributed to each source of measurement "error" (e.g., time, raters, settings, etc.).

These four kinds of reliability measurement are sensitive to different kinds of measurement error. Test-retest reliability assesses errors due to time-related changes in participants—the extent to which scores vary simply with the passage of time. Inter-rater agreement assesses errors due to individual differences in raters' perceptions—the extent to which different observers of the same event vary in their report of their observations. Internal consistency reliability assesses errors due to variations in the tester's sampling of items from the content domain of the test—the extent to which scores reflect a vague multidimensional set of items used to index a unidimensional construct. Generalizability theory attempts to identify the variability due to each source of measurement error.

Content validity.   The extent to which items adequately represent a performance domain or construct of specific interest is called *content validity.* Although content validity resembles referent generality, content validity involves sampling items from a multidimensional domain, whereas referent generality involves sampling measures that are expected to index a *single construct* or conceptual *dimension.* Some indices proposed to assess content validity include (Crocker & Algina, 1986):

1. Percentage of items matched to objectives
2. Percentage of items matched to objectives with high "importance ratings"
3. Correlations between the importance weighting of objectives and the number of items measuring those objectives (Klein & Kosecoff, 1975)
4. Index of item-objective congruence (Rovinelli & Hambleton, 1977)
5. Percentage of objectives not assessed by any of the items

Face validity. Similar, but not identical, to content validity, face validity refers to the extent to which items appear to measure a construct in a way that is meaningful to the researcher.

Empirical validity. The extent to which a measure predicts some criterion that itself has plausibility as an index of the construct being measured is called empirical validity.

Construct validity. A test is said to have construct validity to the extent it has both content validity and empirical validity; that is, its items are representative of the content domain being measured, and it consistently predicts criterion behaviors that are associated with a proposed construct according to some theoretical position. To be useful a construct must be defined on two levels (Lord & Novick, 1968). First, it must be operationally (or semantically) defined, usually by specifying the procedures used to measure the construct. Second, a construct requires definition by the postulation of specific relationships between measures of the construct with (a) measures of other constructs in the theoretical system, and (b) measures of specific real-world criteria. Thus the operational definition of a construct is not enough; the meaningfulness or importance of the construct must also be made explicit through a description of how it is related to other variables.

Procedures for determining construct validity are (Crocker & Algina, 1986):

1. Correlations between a measure of the construct and designated criterion variables. If the strength of the relationship were weak, this would constitute evidence against construct validity.
2. Differentiation between groups differing on the measured attribute. Failure to find expected differences would raise doubts concerning construct validity. However, possible explanations that need to be ruled out include failure of the theory underlying the construct, inadequacy of the instrument for measuring the construct, or failure of the empirical treatment, if any.
3. Factor analysis to determine whether item responses "cluster" together in patterns predictable or reasonable in light of the theoretical structure of the construct of interest. Variations in responses to items that form a cluster can be attributed to variation among subjects on a common underlying factor. Such a factor, which is not itself directly observable, can be considered a construct suggested by this particular set of empirical observations. The issue is whether the constructs, empirically de-

fined through factor analysis, correspond to the theoretical constructs that the test developer hypothesized in developing the test. The critical issue is whether the subtests or tests, which are supposed to measure the same construct, are empirically identified as measuring a common factor.

4. Multitrait multimethod (Campbell & Fiske, 1959). This technique features the assessment of two or more traits by two or more methods. Using one sample of subjects, measurements are obtained on each construct by each method, and correlations between each pair of measures are then computed. Evidence of construct validity of the measure is obtained when measures of a construct have high intercorrelations among themselves (convergent validity) but low intercorrelations with measures of the other constructs being assessed (discriminant validity).

5. Applications of generalizability theory (Kane, 1982) can determine whether observations for an individual are invariant over different methods of measurement through analysis components.

Validity of measurement issues are usually ignored, misunderstood, or misapplied by special education researchers. This problem is so large and so pervasive that one wonders: If the products and conclusions of special education researchers were rigorously evaluated in terms of validity-of-measurement concerns, how much of our knowledge regarding special education procedures, instructional strategies, and interventions would be sufficiently free of error to be of practical use?

CASE STUDIES OF CURRICULUM RESEARCH

Three cases were selected to exemplify the features of research validity that were described above. These three studies were selected because they were examples of empirical research into widely varying curricula (receptive language, reading words, and community adaptation skills), and served as examples for many facets of design validity. The first case (Heal, Colson, & Gross, 1984) featured a large-group experiment to evaluate a curriculum for preparing severely handicapped secondary school participants for postschool living. Participants were randomly assigned to control and experimental conditions. The second case (Orelove, 1982) studied the learning of one-syllable words by 12 moderately mentally retarded subjects who served as their own controls in a small-n study. Some words were presented directly to the subjects, and others were presented incidentally. The third case studied the facilitation of learning receptive vocabulary through sign language by four severely retarded subjects. Kohl, Karlan, and Heal (1979) used a design (subjects repeated in conditions) similar to Orelove's, except that learning conditions were counterbalanced in a Latin square.

Summaries of these three studies are given immediately below. Following the summaries is a discussion of the features of these studies that enhanced or limited their validity as empirical research in special education.

Case Summaries

Heal, L. W., Colson, L. S., and Gross, J. C. (1984). Heal, Colson, and Gross (1984) evaluated skill acquisition by secondary-level severely mentally handicapped participants on functional community and living skills (e.g., grocery shopping, ordering a restaurant meal). Participants were trained on 12 tasks in generic ("natural") settings according to a behavioral analysis of the curriculum tasks that divided them into systematic teaching and error-correction procedures. The evaluation of learning was done using a "cross-group, cross-over," true-experiment design, described as follows. Each year, six tasks were paired for apparent difficulty and randomly assigned to Task Set 1 or Task Set 2. Available participants were randomly assigned to be trained on one set or the other in the fall of 1978. Participants were then pretested on all tasks, trained on their assigned tasks, and posttested, again on all tasks. Logically and structurally, this design is a true experiment in that each group served as a *randomly constituted control group* for the other on half of the tasks. In the spring of 1979, the tasks were interchanged; thus, over the course of two semesters, all participants were trained on all tasks, and each participant served as a control subject on half the tasks in the fall and on the other half in the spring. The same procedure was followed for the 1979–80 school year.

For each year an analysis of variance was done using a $2 \times 2 \times 2$ cross-group cross-over design, where the three factors were groups, task sets (with three tasks per set), and semesters. The results of this analysis for the first year's data indicated that groups gained significantly more from pretest to posttest on those skills that were trained than on those skills that were not trained, $F(1,26) = 27.68$, p < .001. This finding was qualified by an interaction of training (vs. no training) by individual tasks within sets, $F(4,104) = 4.64$, p < .002. Thus, training was more effective for some tasks than for others. In order to analyze the training effect for each task, an analysis of covariance was completed for each task for each semester in each of the two years. The adjusted means (plotted in Figure 1.1)

FIGURE 1.1. Adjusted means from the analysis of covariance completed for the fall and spring semesters of the two project years for trained and untrained subjects

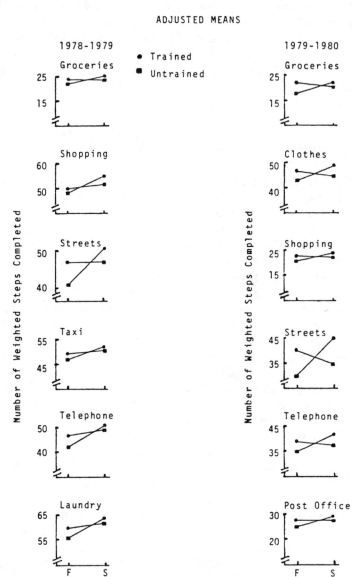

ADJUSTED MEANS

Note: For each graph the lines join the means of particular groups of participants from the cross-over design; each group was trained on the task one semester but not the other. For all six tasks of both semesters of both years, the trained group performed better than did the untrained group. From Heal et al. (1984), with permission of the American Association on Mental Retardation.

of the trained group surpassed those of the untrained group on all 24 tasks. The difference was statistically significant in 16 of the 24 comparisons of the tasks.

Orelove, F. P. (1982). Orelove (1982) taught six pairs of moderately or severely mentally handicapped residents in a large, 60-bed intermediate-use facility for developmentally disabled adults to read one-syllable sight words that had been carefully selected from cooking recipes and printed on flash cards. Sixty words were selected at random from those that participants imitated but failed to read orally on a flash card pretest. The 60 words were randomly divided into 12 five-word sets. Participants were taught in pairs. One five-word set was randomly assigned to each participant in each of the six participant pairs as words to be directly taught in each of the four training phases. Words directly taught to one participant in a pair served simultaneously as words incidentally presented to the other participant in the pair and vice versa. The four remaining word sets for each pair served as their control lists in the four training phases. Following each pair's training session, participants were tested on their five directly taught words, their five incidentally presented words, and their five untrained control words. Training was conducted in four phases. Phases I and III were *simple direct instruction,* which consisted of one-to-one instruction in the presence of another participant. Phase II was *task components,* in which the trainer prompted both participants to attend to the trainer at the beginning of every trial ("Everybody, watch me." "Look at this word."). Phase IV was *"vicarious" reinforcement,* in which the participant receiving direct instruction was reinforced for each correct oral response with a reward that had been previously shown to be rewarding to both participants in the pair. Results (Figure 1.2) showed that participants learned their own directly taught words, $F(1,6) = 66.38$, $p < .001$, and, to a lesser but significant extent, words directed to their peers (i.e., incidentally presented), $F(1,6) = 17.39$, $p < .01$. The amount of incidental learning was apparently unaffected by the trainer's prompting (task components; Phase II) or vicarious reinforcement (Phase IV). Maintenance probes showed that participants maintained correct responses for both directly taught and incidentally presented items.

Kohl, F. L., Karlan, G. R., and Heal, L. W. (1979). Kohl, Karlan, and Heal (1979) examined the facilitation of the acquisition of instruction-following behavior when spoken instructions were paired with manual signs. Participants were four severely handicapped participants who resided in a pediatric nursing school for mentally and physically impaired

FIGURE 1.2. Percentage of words read aloud correctly from flashcard prompts on five-word sets

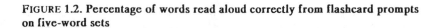

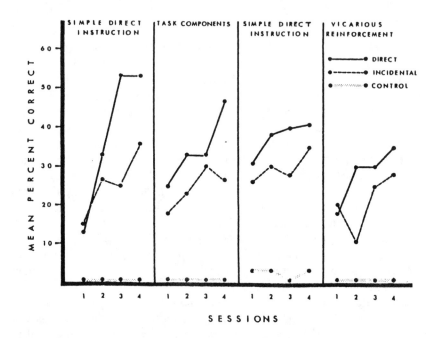

Note: Word sets were taught directly, presented indirectly as they were taught to another participant, or not taught at all ("control") during four instructional phases: simple direct instruction, task components (i.e., teacher prompting for attention), and vicarious reinforcement (reward available only to the directly instructed participant). Performance was 0% on all words on a pretest before the first simple direct instruction session. From Orelove (1979), with his permission.

children. Training materials consisted of 18 stereometric objects that were found in the students' classrooms or bedrooms.

Each participant was pretested individually on their knowledge of objects (nouns), actions (verbs), and relations (prepositions). First, the instructor placed four objects on the table and named one object that the participant sitting beside her was to touch (e.g., "P, touch book"). The procedure was repeated twice for each of 34 objects. Following this object-discrimination testing, the instructor placed one object on the table and asked the participant to perform a specific action with the object (e.g., "P, shake."). The procedure was repeated twice for each of 20 actions. Next, the instructor placed two randomly chosen objects on the table and asked the participant to place an object in a specific location (e.g., "P, put the cup

in the box."). The procedure was repeated twice for each of 10 prepositions.

Two types of instructions were used. Type I consisted of verb-noun
constructions (e.g., lift car, fold sock). Type II consisted of the following:
"Put"-noun-preposition-article-noun (e.g., put block in the cup). From
those actions (verbs) to which all participants responded correctly on the
receptive pretest, 20 Type I instructions were generated. In order to determine Type I instructions to be used for receptive training, the instructor
placed four objects on the table and asked the participant sitting beside her
to perform each of the 20 Type I instructions that had been generated. The
procedure was repeated twice for each instruction. Responses were recorded according to the accuracy of each sentence element; a participant
could select the correct object, perform the correct action, do both, or do
neither. From those instructions to which all participants responded correctly on the object discriminations but incorrectly on the actions, six Type
I instructions were chosen. From those prepositions to which all participants responded incorrectly and from those objects to which all participants responded correctly on the receptive pretest, 15 Type II instructions
were generated. Objects (both direct objects and objects of the prepositions) were selected that were different from those used in the six Type
I instructions. The same procedures were used as with the selection for
Type I.

After the instructions had been generated, participants were trained.
In each of three training phases (made up of five training sessions of 40
trials each), participants were assigned to one of the three instructional
conditions.

1. *Complete Signing* (CS): Manual signs were paired with spoken instructions in a one-to-one correspondence to each word.
2. *Partial Signing* (PS): Manual signs were paired only with key spoken words. Verbs in Type I instructions were paired with their respective signs; prepositions and direct objects (the second noun) in
   Type II instructions were paired with their respective signs.
3. *No Signing* (NS): Spoken instructions were not paired with signs.

These conditions were counterbalanced in a repeated measure 3 × 3 Latin
square, so that each condition was given first, second, or third to one participant or another. This is an old, well-known technique arising from the
early agricultural analysis of variance research designs, which could be
adopted in more behavioral research, especially that in which several conditions are administered to the same subjects.

Instruction consisted of the least obtrusive variation of the following procedures: (1) speaking and/or signing the instruction, depending on the instructional condition (CS, PS, or NS), (b) modeling the correct response, and/or (c) guiding the participant through the instructed actions. Each response was followed by Kohl's praise. Credit was given only when a correct response followed the instruction (a) without additional assistance (b or c).

Reliability measures were taken once every three or four sessions for every participant. The reliability was determined by having a second observer observe training and score the student's responses as incorrect (i.e., assisted) or correct. Reliability was computed by the formula: $100 \times$ number of agreements $\div$ (number of agreements + number of disagreements). All reliability scores exceeded 86% for all instruction types.

As shown in Figure 1.3, for all four participants the number of correctly completed instructions was greater for the instructional conditions in which manual signs were paired with spoken instructions (either complete, $F(1,2) = 21.10$, $p < .05$, or partial signing, $F(1,2) = 16.8$, $p < .1$), than for the non-signing control condition.

Validity Issues

Table 1.1 lists as rows the types of design validity described above in the first part of this chapter, and as columns (a) a description of each validity type, (b) suggested general control strategies for each type, (c) features of Heal et al. (1984) that relate to each type, (d) features of Orelove (1982) that relate to each, and (e) features of Kohl et al. (1979) that relate to each type. Several features of this table merit emphasis.

Internal validity. Although experimental research tends to suffer when examined according to the standards of external validity, it fares much better under the standards of internal validity. These three experiments were exemplary in many ways. By using random assignment of subjects to intervention and control conditions, Heal et al. (1984) avoided many of the pitfalls of group comparison designs. By using subjects as their own controls, both Orelove (1982) and Kohl et al. (1979) were able to eliminate individual differences as a possible explanation for differences among conditions. The discussion of internal validity follows the types listed in Table 1.1.

Selection bias was logically avoided in all three studies: by random assignment in Heal et al. (1984) and by comparing participants with themselves in the other two.

Text continues on p. 24.

FIGURE 1.3. Number of instructions completed correctly by subjects 1-4 in each of three instructional conditions

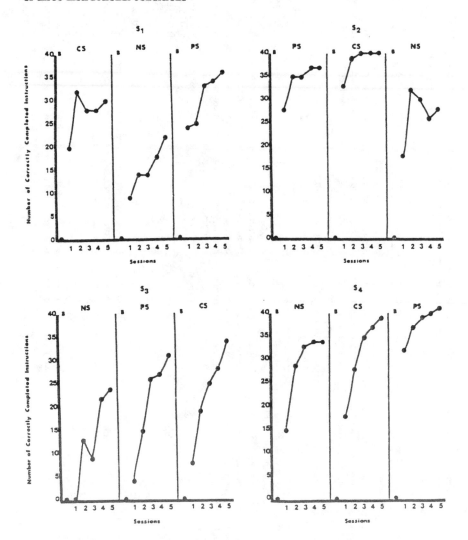

Note: Instructional conditions were: Pairing of all spoken words and their signs (CS); pairing of principal spoken words and their signs (PS); and spoken instruction only, with no signs (NS). The number of instructions completed correctly during the one-session baseline prior to training, indicated by a "B," was 0 for every subject in every condition. Participants 1-3 comprise a Latin square design for instruction conditions, and participant 4 provides counterbalancing (with participant 3) of CS and PS conditions after NS training. From Kohl et al. (1979), with permission of the Association for Persons with Severe Handicaps (TASH).

TABLE 1.1. Strategies for Improving the Validity of Special Education Research from Three Studies Selected for Review

			STUDIES SELECTED FOR REVIEW		
Type of Validity	Description	Control Strategy	Heal, Colson, & Gross (1984)	Orelove (1982)	Kohl, Karlan, & Heal (1979)
I. INTERNAL VALIDITY					
A. Selection Bias	More promising cases are selected for the experimental group than for the control group.	Randomly assign subjects to experimental and control conditions; compare intact groups to assess their similarity.	Subjects were randomly assigned to conditions; thus selection factors were randomized.	Subjects were compared with themselves—perfect control.	Subjects were compared with themselves—perfect control.
B. History	Unpredictable events occur coincidentally with the intervention.	Disentangle events and time.			
1. Collateral Events Extrinsic to Research Design	Collateral events are external to the intervention.	Include a "proximal" control group in design; this control group must experience the same history as the experimental group.	Control and intervention conditions occurred and were evaluated at the same times.	Intentional and incidental conditions occurred in the same sessions and were evaluated simultaneously.	Intervention order was counterbalanced in a Latin square, so the intervention effects were orthogonal to systematic changes from session to session. This balance held between, not within subjects.
2. Collateral Events Intrinsic to Research Design	Collateral events occur inadvertently with the intervention; "Multiple treatment interference."	Define treatment carefully. Partition treatment into setting and intervention components; employ blinded intervenors who have no vested interest in the outcome of the experiment.	Several control and intervention conditions were evaluated at the same time in the same subjects. Any multiple treatment facilitation would affect all conditions equally.	Validity threatened: Control was minimal. The incidental and intentional conditions may have facilitated or interfered with each other.	Validity threatened: The conditions were carefully defined, but given by a single experimenter, who may have enriched some conditions in unspecified ways.

TABLE 1.1. Continued

Type of Validity	Description	Control Strategy	Heal, Colson, & Gross (1984)	Orelove (1982)	Kohl, Karlan, & Heal (1979)
3. Attrition	Loss of subjects due to mortality, upward mobility.	Include various attrition results as scale dependent variable; replace lost subjects by preselected, matched substitutes; compare attrited and surviving groups on pretest(s) to assess similarity.	Validity threatened: Cases who may have been lost through absenteeism.	No attrition, and because subjects were controls, attrition would have had minimal effect on the validity of the study.	No attrition, and because subjects were used as attrition would have had minimal effect on the validity of the study.
C. Maturation	Growth, degeneration, warm-up, and/or fatigue impact on the dependent variable(s) regardless of any intervention.	Include a randomly constituted control group whose extraexperimental experiences are comparable to those of the experimental group.	The same subjects were used in both control and experimental conditions.	Because intervention and control conditions were given simultaneously to the same subjects, their maturation logically influenced both conditions equally.	Maturation, which was confounded with sessions and independent of treatments (Latins) was, like extrinsic history (see B-1), orthogonal to intervention effects.
D. Measurement	Measurement of the dependent variable(s) creates the illusion of an intervention effect where none exists in reality.				
1. Reaction to Assessment	Responsiveness to the intervention is catalyzed by testing or observation.	Omit pretests for all or a random half of all study groups; use unobtrusive measures, especially before and during intervention.	*All Three Studies:* Criterion referenced tests assured that assessment and training demanded the same skills. Reaction to assessment in the control condition was thus the learning baseline for the experimental condition.		

TABLE 1.1. *Continued*

			STUDIES SELECTED FOR REVIEW		
Type of Validity	*Description*	*Control Strategy*	*Heal, Colson, & Gross (1984)*	*Orelove (1982)*	*Kohl, Karlan, & Heal (1979)*
2. Biased Testers or Observers	Examiners whose scores are based on information other than that provided by the subject.	Employ "blinded" subjects and observers, who know only what they are measuring, not what scores are expected.	Testers were "blinded" substitute teachers.	Validity threatened: The experimenter did all training, and knew its purpose.	Validity threatened: The experimenter did all training, and knew its purpose.
3. Floor or Ceiling Effects	The range of a measure is constrained so that the performance of a high-scoring subject is underestimated or that of a low scoring subject is overestimated.	Employ measures whose ranges extend well above and below the levels that occur in the subjects of study.	Validity threatened: Scores ranged from 60% to 97% task steps correctly completed, with scores >90% on 6 of the 48 tasks on pretests and on 24 of the 48 on posttests.	Validity threatened: Scores ranged from ½% correct to 53% correct on probes for intervention words and from 0% to 2½% on control words.	Validity threatened by both floor and ceiling effects: Percent correct rose rapidly from 0% to over 90% in 5 of the 12 subject by conditions combinations.
E. Regression to True Scores	The statistical tendency for individuals with extreme scores on one occasion to achieve more nearly average scores on subsequent occasions.	Assign subjects randomly to groups. Never select subjects on the basis of scores that are higher (or lower) than those expected in a random sample from the same population.	Significant gains were shown on all measures, but some regression was possible.	Validity might be questioned because all subjects scored zero correct on a pretest. Some might well have scored above zero on a second pretest.	Validity might be questioned because all subjects scored zero correct on a pretest. Some might well have scored above zero on a second pretest.

TABLE 1.1. *Continued*

Type of Validity	Description	Control Strategy	Heal, Colson, & Gross (1984)	Orelove (1982)	Kohl, Karlan, & Heal (1979)
II. EXTERNAL VALIDITY					
A. Population Validity	The experimental subjects are typical members of the population of subjects to which the research is claimed to apply; i.e., the results can reasonably be generalized to the population from which the subjects were drawn.	Randomly select subjects from a defined population. Haphazard selection from an ill-defined population is less satisfactory. Convenience sampling accompanied by arguments that the subjects are typical is not at all satisfactory.	All members of the secondary school severely handicapped class participated, although some were excluded from data analyses.	Validity threatened: Twelve residents of an intermediate care nursing facility were carefully selected.	Validity threatened: Four residents of a pediatric school nursing facility were carefully selected.
B. Ecological Validity	The experimental setting is typical of all settings in which the experimental procedures might be applied; i.e., the results can reasonably be generalized to a broad array of settings.	Perform the experiment in the setting(s) where findings are expected to be applied. This might imply that a population of settings should be defined and experimental settings randomly selected from it.	Training and testing was done in generic community settings.	Validity threatened: Small classrooms; one facility.	Validity threatened: Small classrooms; one facility.
C. Referent Generality	The assessments of the experimental outcome are sufficiently diverse to assure that the measured attribute is indexed by an adequate array of assessments.	Use several assessment approaches: Test subjects directly; ask subjects' friends and relatives to document changes; observe changes in subjects in a variety of settings; document conditions under which changes do not occur; etc.	Task analyses were carefully developed from several teachers' repertories. Several sites were used for most tasks. Several teachers and examiners were used.	Validity threatened: Words were presented on one set of flash cards by one experimenter.	Validity threatened: Words and signs were taught by one set of materials and one examiner.

TABLE 1.1. *Continued*

			STUDIES SELECTED FOR REVIEW		
Type of Validity	*Description*	*Control Strategy*	*Heal, Colson, & Gross (1984)*	*Orelove (1982)*	*Kohl, Karlan, & Heal (1979)*
III. MEASUREMENT VALIDITY					
A. Reliability					
1. Internal Consistency	High correlations among test items, indicating that measurement is of a single attribute.	Use item analysis procedures to eliminate any item that correlates negatively or negligibly with the others. Index with Cronbach's alpha.	Not reported. Criterion-referenced instruments were not amenable to internal consistency assessment.	Available but not reported.	Available but not reported.
2. Interobserver Agreement	Agreement among observers on the correct score to assign the subject for each performance.	Have a "blinded" (i.e., uninformed) observer complete assessments and compare them with those of the experimenter. Index with Cohen's kappa.	Pearson's r's ranged from .88 to .99 on the 12 tasks that were studied.	Kappa exceeded .60 on 115 of the 122 situations for which it was calculated (Kappa of .60 = % agreement of .80).	Percent agreement between two observers exceed 86% on all learning and probe trials. Kappa was not reported.
3. Test-retest Reliability	Stability of subjects' scores over time.	Retest subjects, using same procedures that were used in their first test, after a period of time that is sufficient for them to forget particular responses but too short for them to change extensively regarding the measured attribute. Index with Pearson's r.	Available because of the repeated testing but not reported.	Available because of the repeated testing but not reported.	Available because of the repeated testing but not reported.

20

TABLE 1.1. *Continued*

Type of Validity	Description	Control Strategy	Heal, Colson, & Gross (1984)	Orelove (1982)	Kohl, Karlan, & Heal (1979)
B. Face Validity	Investigators and readers find the measures used to be credible operationalizations of the attribute being measured.	Have consumers and subject populations examine, evaluate, and modify measures.	Measures were steps taken on the criterion-referenced task analyses.	Percent correct responses has compelling face validity as a learning measure.	Percent correct responses has compelling face validity as a learning measure.
C. Content Validity	The selected items are a representative sample from the universe that comprises the attribute being measured.	Identify systematically all the properties included in and excluded from the attribute; then select a representative sample of these properties as items on the measure.	Moderate validity. The instructed tasks were those most commonly nominated by parents and teachers.	All available 120 items (words) were screened, but only 60 that were completely unknown to the subjects were used in training.	Minimal validity. There was no evidence that the items used were representative of the universe of useful words for this population.
D. Empirical Validity	Correlation of the measure with an established index of the attribute being measured.	Correlate the measure with an established index or see if it discriminates between groups who are presumed to differ on the measured attribute.	No effort.	No effort.	No effort.
E. Construct Validity	A correlation of the target measure with other indices of the construct (trait) being measured.	Correlate the measure with an established index or see if it discriminates between groups who are presumed to differ on the measured construct.	No effort.	No effort.	No effort.

21

TABLE 1.1. *Continued*

Type of Validity	Description	Control Strategy	Heal, Colson, & Gross (1984)	Orelove (1982)	Kohl, Karlan, & Heal (1979)
			STUDIES SELECTED FOR REVIEW		
IV. SOCIAL VALIDITY					
A. Empirical Comparison	The goals, procedures, and outcomes for the experimental population are consonant with those practiced in the standard population, i.e., the one into which the experimental group aspires to be integrated.	Observe the practices of the standard population and select outcome goals, intervention procedures, and standards of performance for the experimental population that are consonant with standard practices.			Presumed—learning to follow instructions involving familiar objects, actions, and relationships.
1. Goals			Standard generic adult tasks.	Words to be learned were taken from those that appear in standard cooking recipes.	
2. Procedures			Standard settings dictated procedures.	"Standard" tutored flash card procedure.	Validity threatened: Procedures (sign learning) not standard.
3. Outcomes			Task analyses terminated in standard adult performance.	Validity threatened: Words were not read in cooking recipes.	Validity threatened: Results (learning sign language) not standard.

TABLE 1.1. Continued

Type of Validity	Description	Control Strategy	Heal, Colson, & Gross (1984)	Orelove (1982)	Kohl, Karlan, & Heal (1979)
B. Subjective Evaluation	The goals, procedures and outcomes for the experimental population are appropriate in the eyes of those who have a vested interest in their well-being.	Question individuals in the experimental population or their advocates to determine that the goals, procedures, and outcomes are appropriate.			
1. Goals			Tasks to be taught were taken from a thorough inventory of the environmental demands by master teachers.	Words to be learned were taken from those that appear in standard cooking recipes.	Words and signs were everyday nouns, verbs and prepositions. Nouns were names of objects found in the subjects' bedrooms and classrooms.
2. Procedures			Parents, teachers were consulted.	Standard instructions passed the scrutiny of the agency and University Research Ethics Review Boards.	Standard instructions passed the scrutiny of the agency and University Research Ethics Review Board.
3. Outcomes			Task analyses terminated in standard performance.	Validity threatened: Words were not read in the context of cooking recipes.	Validity threatened: Results (learning sign language) not standard.

23

In considering historical threats to interval validity, it is important to clarify the distinction between extrinsic and intrinsic historical concomitants of treatment interventions. *Extrinsic concomitants* are those that are correlated with the occurrence of the intervention but are external to the experimental situation. Examples include epidemics of influenza, changes of school administration, and stock market crashes. They are of special concern in time series experiments and repeated measure studies like those of Orelove (1982) and Kohl et al. (1979). In the present case these extrinsic components were presumably controlled because the training and assessment associated with different conditions (direct vs. incidental presentations) occurred simultaneously (Orelove) or were counterbalanced in different subjects over time (Kohl et al. used a Latin square to counterbalance intervention order in three of their four subjects). *Intrinsic historical concomitants* of interventions are those that occur inside or within the experimental situation. For example, the pitch of an experimenter's voice might change as he or she goes from an experimental to a control condition. The noises of an apparatus may be different when a reward is accessible. It is very challenging to control for these intrinsic historical concomitants, especially in applied research, for which the experimenter typically knows the intervention very well and develops large repertoires of non-explicit communication with the subjects. This threat to internal validity is, by definition, *uncontrolled by random assignment* of participants to experimental and control groups! This threat to internal validity was controlled to some extent in the Heal et al. study by having participants tested by substitute teachers, who were not involved in the training and were unaware of which subjects had been given which interventions. Furthermore, because intervention conditions and control conditions were evaluated in the same subject, any cross-task facilitation should have affected control conditions as much as experimental conditions. The studies of Orelove and Kohl et al. were susceptible to invalidation because authors trained and tested their own participants and could have given subtle discouragement on test trials having control words. With regard to *attrition,* Orelove (1982) and Kohl et al. (1979) had no problem because they lost no participants. However, Heal et al. (1984) lost 5 of their 35 cases because they were "inappropriate," and they had more losses on some of their tasks due to absenteeism. These lost participants may very well have been atypical.

Maturation was well controlled in different ways in the three studies. The cross-over design of Heal et al. and also the repeated measures design of Orelove assured that the maturation of control participants and experimental participants was equated or (for Orelove) identical. In the Kohl et al. study, maturation was controlled between, not within, participants, because the order of conditions was counterbalanced in a Latin square (for three of the four participants).

Turning to *measurement effects,* it is noteworthy that the use of criterion referenced tests eliminates *reactiveness to assessment* as a concern in comparing experimental and control conditions. The reason for this is that assessment, learning, and training become very similar, and any learning on the part of the control group becomes a baseline for the learning of the experimental group. Thus, as long as there is no ceiling on this baseline, any extra learning associated with the intervention will be reflected in the comparison of the two groups. *Floor and ceiling effects* were tolerable in these studies. The high posttest performance of the participants in Heal et al. (1984) exposes the problem generic to criterion-referenced instruments—complete mastery is the expected outcome. Kohl et al. (1979) may also have had a ceiling problem, since very rapid learning by their participants resulted in a 90% correct performance in 5 of 12 condition combinations by their fifth (final) session. Perhaps this rapid learning masked differences among conditions. Turning to possible floor effects, both Orelove (1982) and Kohl et al. used training materials only if subjects scored 0% correct using them on a pretest. This severe floor completely masked the distribution of knowledge that subjects had before the experiment began.

Regression to true scores is a pervasive, yet often misunderstood problem in experimental research. When subjects are selected on the basis of pretest scores, one must always be concerned that subsequent (posttest) scores will regress toward the mean of the population from which the subjects have been drawn. Thus, although gains were shown on all measures in the Heal et al. (1984) study, it is possible that some gains were due in part to suppressed pretest scores because of the strangeness of the examiner, the situation, the setting, the test instructions, or other factors. Orelove (1982) and Kohl et al. (1979) had a different problem. Because all subjects scored 0 correct on the pretest for all training items, some might have scored well above 0 had a second pretest been administered. Orelove eliminated (controlled) this possibility by randomly assigning 20 of his 60 words to each subject as untrained control words. Repeated tests on these words showed virtually 0 performance throughout the course of his experiment.

External validity. External validity is the Achilles' heel of much experimental research, especially research in the applied behavioral analysis tradition. The studies both of Orelove (1982) and of Kohl et al. (1979) offered little that would give the reader confidence in generalizing their results to a broader population of subjects than those studied, to an array of settings beyond the small classrooms in which the experiments were conducted, or to other approaches to the evaluation of what subjects had learned. While Heal et al. (1984) have a better claim to the generalizability of their results, their study, too, was far from ideal. Although their population included 30 of the 35 members of a large joint agreement district in suburban Chicago, one must wonder how well their results would generalize to inner city or to rural classrooms. Similarly, while training and testing was done in a variety of generic community settings, one must wonder how well the participants would perform in strange communities, in the inner city, or in rural settings. On the other hand, it is admirable that 12 different community living skills were trained using task analyses developed from several different teachers' repertoires. Furthermore, their ecological validity was increased by the use of different sites for testing the same tasks, and the use of different teachers and examiners on different occasions. One would expect that an unfamiliar teacher in an unfamiliar setting would find these participants performing near the same levels as they had during the experiment.

Validity and reliability of measurement.   These three case studies were all flawed in their attention to the *reliability* of their assessment instruments. Errors were made in both omission and selection. In terms of omission, only inter-observer reliabilities were reported; none of the studies reported test-retest or internal consistency reliabilities. Estimating internal consistency is somewhat incompatible with criterion referenced measures (see Heal et al., 1984), since ideally items are all passed up to a particular level of performance and then failed thereafter. Guttman scaling analysis (e.g., Nie, Hull, Jenkins, Steinbrenner, & Bent, 1972) would give a better indication of the extent to which a scale approaches this type of consistency than would Cronbach's alpha. Heal et al. (1984) made no reference to internal consistency. Measures used by Orelove (1982) and by Kohl et al. (1979) were both amenable to internal consistency assessment, but it was not done. All three papers reported their inter-observer agreements, all with procedures that were credibly objective with credibly disinterested reliability assessors. However, only Orelove reported inter-observer agreement using Cohen's kappa, the statistic of choice for this type of reliability.

Validity of measurement is, in the last analysis, realized only through the "expert's" imprimatur. Either the measure, or the criterion with which it is correlated, or both, must be declared by fiat to be an operationalization of the attribute being indexed. Some attributes, like "performing an instruction" or "reading a word from a flash card," are easily observed, and the validity of their measures is seldom questioned. However, abstract attributes, like "ability to order a restaurant meal," are more challenging to operationalize. Nevertheless, the dependent variables of all three of the case studies reviewed here were concrete and credible operations for the attributes they purported to measure.

Social validity. While this research appeared to be socially valid, these authors tended not to make an explicit examination of their goals, procedures, and outcomes to determine whether these met the test of *empirical comparison* to target populations with whom they would have their special populations integrate or of a conscious *subjective evaluation* by the peers and advocates of the experimental populations. Nevertheless, the social validity of these three experiments appears to be potentially adequate. Heal et al. (1984), in particular, undertook a conscious inventory of the tasks that would be required by their secondary participants when they entered adult, post-secondary roles. Orelove's (1982) selection of material was also interesting in that his words were taken from ordinary cooking recipes as a project in a special teacher education course. The selection of materials, and procedures used by Kohl et al. (1979) were taken from the subjects' natural environment.

Conclusion

The purpose of this second section was to evaluate some specific experiments in special education in order to provide conceptual analyses using the validity taxonomy. The results of these experiments were more-or-less credible because they met most of the internal, external, measurement, and social validity standards.

The next section examines an even more specific series of studies whose primary focus is on the establishment of the validity of a specific motivational construct: internal vs. external motivation orientation. The studies in this series demonstrate the intertwining of content validity and empirical validity in the establishment of construct validity.

CASE STUDIES OF RESEARCH ON INDIVIDUAL DIFFERENCES IN MOTIVATION AND PERSONALITY: THE SEARCH FOR CONSTRUCT VALIDITY

Several studies were selected to illustrate the research validity of a line of studies investigating the variance in learning and performance of exceptional and ordinary learners in terms of their individual differences in personality characteristics and motivational states. The major function of this section is to elucidate the research problems involved in demonstrating *construct validity,* that is, the extent to which a measure has both content and empirical validity. To demonstrate that a measure has construct validity, evidence is usually assembled through a series of steps, as follows (Crocker & Algina, 1986):

1. Formulate hypotheses about how those who differ on the construct are expected to differ on demographic characteristics, performance criteria, or measures of other constructs whose relationship to the performance criteria has already been validated. These hypotheses should be based on an explicitly stated theory that underlies the construct and provides its definitional elaboration.
2. Select (or develop) a measurement instrument whose items assess behaviors that are specific, concrete manifestations of the construct.
3. Gather empirical data that will permit the hypothesized relationships to be tested.
4. Determine if the data are consistent with the hypotheses and consider the extent to which the observed findings could be explained by rival theories or alternative explanations (and eliminate these if possible).

We will draw from the studies of Haywood and Switzky, which investigated the relationships between one set of individual difference characteristics, referred to as "task-intrinsic motivation," and the behavior effectiveness of mentally retarded and non-retarded persons (Haywood & Burke, 1977; Haywood, Meyers, & Switzky, 1982; Haywood & Switzky, 1986, in press; Switzky & Haywood, 1984; Switzky & Schultz, 1988). For Haywood and Switzky, motivational orientation is a learned personality trait by which persons are characterized in terms of the incentives that are effective in motivating their behavior, whether task-intrinsic or task-extrinsic. Persons who characteristically seek their principal satisfactions by concentrating on task-intrinsic factors (e.g., responsibility, challenge, creativity, opportunities to learn, and task achievement) are referred to as *intrinsically motivated* (IM). Those who tend instead to avoid dissatisfaction by concentrating on the ease, comfort, safety, security, health, and practicality aspects of the environment (i.e., task-extrinsic factors) are referred to as *extrinsically motivated* (EM). While all persons respond to both kinds of incentive, it is the relative balance between the two sources of motivation—the relative number of situations in which one is likely to be motivated by task-intrinsic versus task-extrinsic factors—that constitutes a stable and measurable personality trait.

According to their theoretical model (Haywood & Burke, 1977; Haywood & Switzky, 1986, in press; Switzky & Haywood, 1984; Switzky &

Schultz, 1988), persons who have an IM orientation should work harder on a task, prefer not to be paid off for their work with task-extrinsic rewards, and persist on tasks longer than predominantly EM persons. Additionally, IM persons should learn more efficiently in academic situations than EM persons who are matched with them on age, sex, and IQ. These expected differences in performance between IM and EM persons are due to differences in their internal self-system characteristics. IM persons appear to be dominated more by internal, cognitive, self-regulatory processes, whereas EM persons appear to be dominated by external, environmental influences. Additionally, IM persons appear to have a more strongly developed internal reinforcement system, whereas EM persons have a more strongly developed external reinforcement system. We have selected a series of experiments that test these predictions and refine the constructs of internal and external motivation for mentally retarded individuals.

Research on individual difference characteristics such as intrinsic motivation in exceptional learners is potentially extremely important in the field of special education, and not enough has been carried out. In order to insure optimal educational opportunities for individual learners, it is necessary to identify the critically important effects of motivational variables that influence learning so that appropriate and effective educational strategies for teaching this diverse student population may evolve. The summaries of studies on motivational variables that follow are arranged chronologically, beginning with the earliest. Following the summaries of research, we will discuss aspects of these studies that enhance or limit their internal, external, measurement, and social validity. We shall focus especially on the construct validity of the motivational orientation concept.

Case Summaries

Haywood, H. C. (1968a). The purpose of this study was to describe some of the motivational structures in overachieving and underachieving elementary school children across three levels of intelligence. Preliminary versions of motivational orientation theory (Haywood, 1964) suggested that such personality and motivational factors may influence learning more strongly in mentally retarded than in intellectually average or above-average persons, since a sufficiently high level of intelligence could overcome an inefficient motivational structure in common learning situations. This early study is an example of *ex post facto* research.

Ex post facto research is systematic empirical inquiry in which the scientist does not have direct control of independent variables because their manifestations have already occurred or because they are inherently not manipulable. Inferences about relations among variables are made, without direct intervention, from concomitant variation of independent and dependent variables (Kerlinger, 1973, p. 379).

The Haywood (1968a) study was based on the premise that when age, sex, and IQ are controlled, overachievers and underachievers in school learning will differ in motivational orientation, with overachievers being relatively more intrinsically motivated and relatively less extrinsically motivated. The general strategy of the study was to select a group of overachievers and a group of underachievers in each of the three scholastic areas of reading, spelling, and arithmetic, and then to compare the groups according to their scores on personality tests of motivational orientation.

A longitudinal sample of 5,000 10-year-old children from Toronto, Canada, who had scores on a group IQ test and on the *Metropolitan Achievement Test* (MAT) were studied. The sample was initially divided into 5-point IQ ranges comprising an overall range from 63 to 154. For each IQ range, the mean and standard deviation of scores on the MAT were computed in each of the areas of reading, spelling, and arithmetic, and z-scores were determined. Overachievement was defined as a positive z-score of at least $+1.00$ with respect to a participant's own 5-point IQ group. Underachievement was similarly defined as a negative z-score of at least -1.00. Thus, psychometric intelligence was held constant within the definition of overachievement and underachievement. A random sample of participants was obtained from the larger population such that 25 overachievers and 25 underachievers were obtained at three separate IQ levels: 65–80; 95–109; and over 120. The sampling process paid no attention to the school locations of the individual participants; therefore the 150 participants were drawn from 75 different schools. The motivational orientation of the participants was determined by the *Choice-Motivator Scale* (Haywood, 1966). Children were tested in small groups, and those who did not seem to understand the testing procedure in the group situation were tested individually. A multiple-choice version of the *Choice-Motivator Scale* was used, consisting of 20 pairs of vocational titles. For each pair, the participants were told to assume that they could be or do anything they might wish, then to indicate (by underlining) which of the two activities or vocations they would rather do or be. Then they were asked to give the reason for their choice. Choices were not scored, but the reasons given for the choices were scored according to a standard manifest-content-analysis procedure. Based on previous factor analyses (Kahoe, 1966a, 1966b), five IM reasons and five EM reasons were presented as follows:

1. I could learn something new.
2. I could make more money.

3. It would be good for my health.
4. It would be safer.
5. I like to take responsibility.
6. It would be easier.
7. I would like to make beautiful things.
8. I would like working to achieve a goal.
9. I like to see how well I can do at something.
10. I'd never be out of work—could always get a job.

Reasons 1, 5, 7, 8, and 9 were scored as IM responses. Reasons 2, 3, 4, 6, and 10 were scored as EM responses. Reasons could be written out by the respondent or told to and written out by the examiner. This multiple-choice version assured a standard number of scorable responses and raised the interscorer agreement to 100%.

Three scores were derived for each individual. The IM score was the total number of responses in the IM category, while the EM score was the number scored in the EM category. A difference score (D), used for the principal analyses, was the sum of IM responses minus the sum of EM responses. Thus a positive D score indicated a majority of IM reasons, while a negative D score indicated a majority of EM reasons. Separate statistical analyses were done on the D scores for the independent samples of overachievers and underachievers in reading, in spelling, and in arithmetic. Haywood (1966) found that the scores were roughly normally distributed, that the educable mentally retarded (EMR) children in the study (IQs 65–80) were able to understand and respond to the items, that there were quite acceptable internal consistency coefficients, generally in the 80s, and test-retest reliability over a 2-week period varied between .79 and .85.

Figure 1.4 presents the mean Choice-Motivator Scale difference scores of overachievers and underachievers in reading, spelling, and arithmetic by intelligence levels. This figure shows that scores become relatively more IM as IQ increases, especially in the underachievers. It is also apparent that there is no overlap in motivational scores between overachievers and underachievers (except in the superior-intelligence group in arithmetic) and that overachievers are consistently more intrinsically motivated than are underachievers.

Separate two-way analyses of variance (IQ by Achievement Levels) were computed for the three scholastic areas. The analyses revealed a significant main effect of IQ levels in reading, $F(2,144) = 4.80$, p < .02, and in arithmetic, $F(2,144) = 5.06$, p < .01, but not in spelling. Achievement levels yielded significant effects in all three areas, p < .01. There were nonsignificant differences in motivational orientation between overachievers and underachievers in the superior IQ groups. In both the average and

FIGURE 1.4. Relative intrinsic and extrinsic motivational orientations of 10-year-old scholastic overachievers and underachievers in reading, spelling, and arithmetic

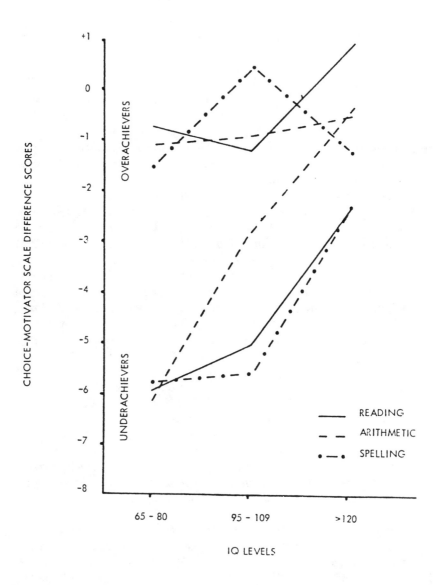

Source: Haywood (1968a), with permission of the American Association on Mental Deficiency

EMR groups, the overachievers on the spelling and arithmetic subtests were more IM than were the underachievers, the effects intensifying as intelligence levels were lowered, $F(2,144) = 3.3$, p $< .05$.

Overachievers summed across groups were found to be relatively more IM than underachievers in all three academic areas (reading, spelling, and arithmetic). The differences in motivational orientation between overachievers and underachievers were largest in the educable mentally retarded range (IQs 65–80) and smallest in the superior range (IQs 120 and above). The tentative conclusion from this study is that overachievers tend to be motivated to a greater extent by factors inherent in the performance of tasks, while underachievers tend to be motivated more by factors extrinsic to the task, such as the ease, safety, comfort, and security aspects of the environment.

Haywood, H. C. (1968b). In this cross-validating *ex post facto* study, 400 10-year-old schoolchildren in Toronto, Canada, were drawn from the large sample of 5,000 used in Haywood (1968a). Children were sampled randomly from each of the IQ ranges as in the Haywood (1968a) study (i.e., superior, average and educable mentally retarded), with age and sex held constant. They were then given the multiple-choice version of the *Choice-Motivator Scale* as described in Haywood (1968a) and grouped into high IM and high EM participants, representing the highest 35 scores and lowest 35 scores in each IQ range, yielding a total sample of 210 participants (Haywood, 1966). The scores of these participants on the *Metropolitan Achievement Text* (MAT) in the areas of reading, spelling, and arithmetic were computed and compared within each IQ range. The achievement scores of students were expressed as standard scores with a mean of 50 and a standard deviation of 10. MAT standard scores, available on these children for each of their first three years in school, are presented in Figure 1.5.

The achievement curves as a function of time appeared to be almost straight lines. Motivational orientation had little effect on the school achievement scores of children in the superior range of intelligence (IQs greater than 120) in any of the three school years. Motivational orientation made a sizable difference in school achievement scores for the average and educable mentally retarded (EMR) groups. In all three achievement areas, IM children were achieving at a significantly higher level than EM children with age, sex, and IQ held constant. For example, individual differences in motivational orientation were associated with 0% of the variance using eta-squared in achievement scores of the intellectually superior students, but such differences were associated with 10% of the variance using eta-squared of the intellectually average, and up to 30% of the variance using eta-squared of the EMR group. On the average, the IM children in the

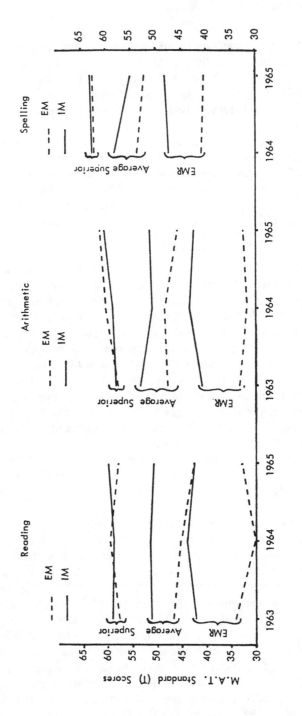

FIGURE 1.5. Metropolitan Achievement Test standard scores over 3 years of IM (solid) and EM (broken lines) children

Source: Haywood (1968b), with permission of the International Association for the Scientific Study of Mental Deficiency

34

average-IQ and EMR groups had achievement test scores about one full school year higher than those of the EM children in the same IQ group. The achievement of the IM EMR children was not different from that of the EM average-IQ children. Thus, there was evidence (a) that intrinsic motivation is associated with higher school achievement, (b) that the effects of individual differences in motivational orientation appear to be greater as IQ declines, and (c) that the effects of these motivational differences appear as early as the 6th year of life.

The next series of studies builds from these earlier studies and other studies conducted over the subsequent 17 years. The two studies to be presented in detail are *true experimental* designs rather than ex post facto studies. In true experimental designs, the scientist can randomly assign participants to the experimental groups that constitute the categorical independent variable. Concomitant variation of independent and dependent variables supports the inference that the independent variable, defined by the presence or absence of direct intervention, is causally responsible for performance change in the dependent variable.

Haywood, H. C., and Switzky, H. N. (1985). The purpose of this study was to extend these earlier conceptions of IM and EM motivational orientations to the area of self-regulation of behavior vs. externally imposed regulation. Haywood and Switzky's conceptual analyses of motivational orientation (MO) (Haywood & Switzky, 1986, in press) as well as those of Bandura (1969, 1978) on self-regulation, suggested that individual differences in MO may be central to the ability to direct one's behavior independently and to derive satisfaction from doing so. The ability to regulate one's own behavior rather than being dependent on others for direction is critical to the postinstitutional adjustment and community living skills of retarded persons (Edgerton, Bollinger, & Herr, 1984). In addition, the facilitation of learning that is intrinsically motivating and free from external-controlling teacher practices and extrinsic motivational control is viewed by many (Bruner, 1962; deCharms, 1976; Switzky & Haywood, 1984) as the ideal model for education. The major principles guiding this paper were (a) that self-regulation is extremely important to the ability of retarded persons to adjust to relatively independent living and learning, and (b) that the response of retarded persons to expectations of self-regulation or to expectations of external imposition of regulation depends upon individual differences in task-intrinsic motivation.

In this study, Haywood and Switzky operationalized Bandura's (1969, 1978) concept of self-reinforcement, reasoning that relatively IM persons may employ self-monitored reinforcement systems that make them less dependent on external reinforcement conditions, whereas relatively EM persons may be motivated by external reinforcement systems. Thus, EM persons should be differentially more responsive than are IM persons to social reinforcement and consequently should show more efficient learning under such task-extrinsic incentives. When task-extrinsic incentives are presented noncontingently, EM persons should not show any changes in performance, whereas IM persons (who are more sensitive to task-intrinsic incentives and who are more likely to reinforce their own behavior) may show changes in performance in spite of the absence of contingent reinforcement. The idea that IM persons have a more strongly developed self-reinforcement system whereas EM persons have a more strongly developed external reinforcement system proved useful for understanding some previously collected data that will be briefly mentioned here, and also generated some newer theoretical conceptions and research studies.

Haywood and Weaver (1967) showed, in a true experiment (with regard to experimental conditions but not with regard to motivational state), that the performance of mildly retarded adolescents and young adults on a simple motor task consisting of hole-punching on a teaching-machine answer sheet varied with the motivational orientation of the individuals and the reinforcement incentives. Mildly retarded adolescents varying in motivational orientation could perform the task for either a task-intrinsic incentive (e.g., the opportunity to work on a more interesting motor-task) or a task-extrinsic incentive (e.g., 1 cent or 10 cents per trial). EM persons performed most vigorously under a task-extrinsic (money reward) incentive, and less well under a task-intrinsic incentive such as the opportunity to work on a more interesting task. IM persons showed just the opposite behavior, giving the best performance when offered the opportunity to do a more interesting task, and performing least well under the money reward incentive. In the no-reward control condition where participants were instructed to punch as many holes as they could, IM persons performed more vigorously than did EM persons.

Haywood and Switzky (1975), in a true experiment (with regard to experimental conditions but not motivational state), found it was possible to condition the verbal expression of motivation in IM and EM non-retarded school-age children by the use of contingent verbal social reinforcement ("Good!") of statements that were counter to or supportive of the individual's own motivational orientation. Given a Taffel-type task with statements that had been judged to be IM or EM printed on index cards, participants were instructed to look at pairs of cards presented simultaneously, and to choose one of the two in each pair to read aloud.

Participants in all contingent reinforcement groups learned to discriminate IM from EM statements, with extrinsically motivated participants demonstrating slightly more efficient learning, suggesting that the task-extrinsic verbal social reinforcement was more effective for them than for the intrinsically motivated participants. In a non-contingent, random-reinforcement (Control) condition where the IM or EM response statements were reinforced half the time, IM participants increased their rate of IM verbalizations in spite of the lack of consistent external verbal social reinforcement, whereas EM participants failed to show any significant changes over trial blocks.

In a very seminal paper, Switzky and Haywood (1974), using a true experimental design regarding experimental conditions, showed that in order to predict performance under different reinforcement operations in 160 nonretarded school children in Grades 2 through 5, it was necessary to consider: (a) the internal or external control of the reinforcers, (b) individual differences in motivational orientation, and (c) the relative strengths of an individual's self-monitored and externally imposed reinforcements. Bandura and Perloff (1967) had compared the motor performance of children under self-monitored and externally imposed reinforcement and found no differences between the two conditions. Both reinforcement conditions sustained responsivity, whereas the control conditions did not. Adding the dimension of individual differences in motivational orientation, Switzky and Haywood (1974) divided their participants into IM and EM samples and gave them the Bandura and Perloff task. They found a dramatic interaction between the reinforcement conditions and the motivational orientations of the participants: IM children worked harder, set leaner schedules of reinforcement, and maintained their performance longer than did EM children under self-monitored reinforcement conditions; by contrast, EM children performed more vigorously and maintained their performance longer under conditions of externally imposed reinforcement. These relationships are illustrated in Figure 1.6.

The Haywood and Switzky (1985) study, a true experiment regarding conditions, was designed as an analogue of the Bandura and Perloff motor task extending the Switzky and Haywood (1974) study to the work behavior of mildly retarded adults. The Haywood and Switzky (1985) study was designed to get evidence on the relative efficacy of self-monitored and externally imposed reinforcement for IM and EM retarded persons, specifically with response to their performance in work-related tasks. It was expected that because IM persons have a more highly developed self-reinforcement system than do EM persons, the IM persons would maintain their performance under conditions of minimal external support. EM persons, on the other hand, were expected to be more responsive to and

FIGURE 1.6. **Number of wheel-cranking responses (an index of "vigor and persistence of behavior") as a function of motivational orientation and reinforcement conditions**

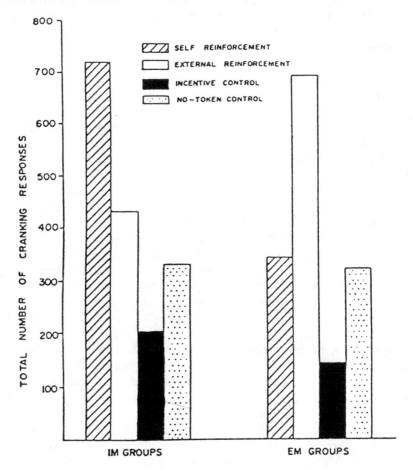

Note: Reinforcement conditions were: self-monitored, externally imposed, incentive control, and no-token control. From Switzky & Haywood (1974), with permission of the American Association on Mental Deficiency.

dependent upon the operation of externally imposed reinforcement. Specifically, it was expected that under conditions in which they set their own performance standards and reinforcement schedules, IM retarded persons would set a higher standard for their performance, maintain their work longer, and set a leaner schedule of reinforcement than would EM persons. By contrast, a condition in which performance standards and reinforcement schedules were imposed externally should be more effective for EM persons than for IM persons in maintaining work. Finally, we expected that under a no-reinforcement control condition, IM persons would show more sustained work than would EM persons.

The participants were 72 mildly retarded adults (30 men, 42 women) residing in a community-based intermediate care facility. They were divided into two groups constituting the top (intrinsically motivated) and the bottom (extrinsically motivated) quartiles of the frequency distribution of scores of 144 potential participants on a scale of intrinsic motivation, the Picture Motivation Scale (Kunca & Haywood, 1969). Their mean age was 40 years (SD = 13.52), and their mean IQ was 69 (SD = 7.80). Participants were assigned randomly to three conditions: self-regulated reinforcement, externally imposed reinforcement, and no-token control. Participants in the external-reinforcement group were matched individually to participants in the self-regulation group by sex, age, motivational orientation, and, in a yoked manner, schedule of reinforcement. Those in the control group were matched for sex, age, and motivational orientation with participants in the self-regulation group.

Kunca and Haywood (1969) developed the Picture Motivation Scale specifically for persons with mild handicaps, though it can be used as well by nonhandicapped children. This instrument is used to measure the degree to which an individual is intrinsically or extrinsically motivated in terms of the learned personality trait of motivational orientation. It replaced the Choice Motivator Scale (Haywood, 1968a, b) because it was easier to use for children and persons of low mental age. In the Picture Motivation Scale, each item is a pair of pictures of people engaged in different activities, vocations, or endeavors, determined to be qualitatively either extrinsic or intrinsic. For each of 20 pictures illustrating an intrinsically motivated activity (e.g., opportunity to learn, challenge, intense psychological satisfaction, responsibility) or an extrinsically motivated activity (e.g., opportunity for safety, ease, comfort, security), the participant is asked which of the two they would prefer to do. Each activity is described while the participant looks at the pair of pictures, then the participant chooses between the two activities. The pictures help to overcome a position bias in low mental age (MA) and retarded persons in which they tended to choose the second of two named activities. In addition, in this scale, choice is combined with a reason for choice (e.g., "Here is a picture of an astronaut going to the moon [point]. Here is someone watching him go [point]. I want to know if you would rather do something exciting like being an astronaut or if you would rather stay on earth so you would be sure not to get hurt"). The final score used to classify the participant as IM or EM was the number of IM choices out of the 20 pairs. The Picture

Motivation Scale is useful for participants from a mental age of 3 years up to adolescence and has acceptable test-retest reliability coefficients, generally in the 80s for both long and short intervals (e.g., Kunca & Haywood, 1969; Miller, Haywood & Gimon, 1975; Switzky, 1988; Switzky & Schultz, 1988). These studies show that the Picture Motivation Scale yields a roughly normal distribution of scores down to about mental age 3 years, and that this distribution tends to become skewed (i.e., higher frequencies of intrinsic responses) with increasing chronological and mental age up to middle adolescence. It has been shown that intrinsic motivation orientation is an increasing function of chronological age, mental age, and social class (Call, 1968; Gambro & Switzky, 1988; Haywood, 1971; Haywood & Switzky, 1986; Switzky, 1985). Item analyses on ordinary children and retarded children and adults (Call, 1968; Haywood, 1971; Haywood & Switzky, 1986; Kunca & Haywood, 1969) identified which of the items on the Picture Motivation Scale were most effective in differentiating IM from Em oriented persons.

In the Haywood and Switzky (1985) study, the motivational orientation of each mentally retarded participant was individually assessed using the Picture Motivation Scale. Participants in the top and bottom quartiles of the frequency distribution of 144 potential participants were classified as IM (mean of 8.26 IM responses) and as EM (mean of 3.90 IM responses) in orientation. Respondents whose scores fell into second and third quartiles were not examined further in this study.

All participants were given a work task consisting of placing a single flat or lock washer into each compartment of seven 18-compartment boxes placed side by side in a row. Work goals were set by placing a washer in the end-most compartment they intended to reach. Participants in the self-regulation condition set their own work goals, and after reaching the work goals, determined the number of tokens they should get for their work. They also determined how long they would work. Tokens were exchanged for prizes at the end of the experimental session. Selections made by the self-regulation participants were imposed on participants in the external-reinforcement condition. In the control condition, the experimenter set the work goals, participants worked as long as they wished with no indication of "pay" for their work, and were given a prize at the end.

The study consisted of a 2 (motivational orientation) × 3 (condition) factorial design with 7 women and 5 men in each of 6 cells. The principal dependent variable was the number of compartments filled (a measure of performance maintenance or task persistence). The analysis of variance revealed a main effect of motivational orientation, $F(1,66) = 13.7$, $p < .01$. IM mentally retarded participants worked harder (mean of 118 compartments filled) than did EM mentally retarded participants (mean of

80 compartments filled), confirming previous research with nonretarded school-aged children (Switzky & Haywood, 1974). In addition, there was an interaction of condition and motivational orientation, $F(2,66) = 9.97$, $p < .001$, the focus of principal interest in this study, which is illustrated in Figure 1.7. In both the self-regulation and control conditions, IM mentally retarded participants filled more compartments than did EM mentally retarded participants, while IM and EM mentally retarded participants did not differ significantly under the external-reinforcement condition. IM participants also filled more of the compartments under the self-regulation condition than they did under the external-reinforcement condition. A higher level of intrinsic motivation was associated with more self-regulatory behavior than was a lower level of intrinsic motivation, repli-

FIGURE 1.7. **Work performance of IM and EM mildly retarded adults as a function of regulatory conditions**

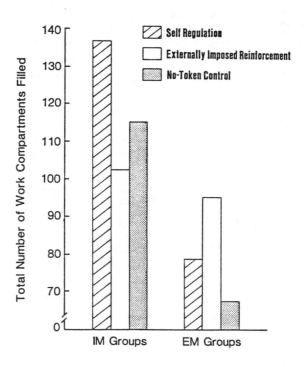

Note: Regulatory conditions were: self-regulation, externally imposed reinforcement, and no-token control. From Haywood & Switzky (1985), with permission of the American Association on Mental Deficiency.

cating the Switzky and Haywood (1974) finding with nonretarded children and the Haywood and Weaver (1967) findings with mentally retarded adults.

Switzky, H. N., and Haywood, H. C. (1985a). In this next study with mildly retarded adults, cited in Haywood and Switzky (1986), the purpose was to investigate the effects of internal self-influences and the role of external environmental influences in a retarded person's self-regulatory behavior. External environmental influences—such as stringent, variable, and lenient demand conditions; instructional sets; performance standards; and schedules of self-reinforcement—were varied. The participants were 60 mentally retarded adults (30 men and 30 women) residing in community-based intermediate care facilities. Their mean age was 37.3 years (SD = 11.2) and their mean IQ was 66.4 (SD = 14.9). They were divided into two groups constituting the top (IM) and bottom (EM) halves of scores on the Picture Motivation Scale. The IM participants' mean was 8.8 IM responses, whereas the EM participants' mean was 3.8 IM responses. IM and EM participants were randomly assigned to three conditions of self-reinforcement task demands: stringent (instructed to set very high work goals, instructed to work as hard and fast as they could, experimenter modeled a lean schedule of reinforcement), variable (given choice of high or low work goal, and experimenter modeled a schedule of reinforcement proportional in richness to the work goal chosen, i.e., more tokens for higher goals), or lenient (instructed to set low work goals, experimenter modeled a rich schedule of reinforcement). A task was constructed varying in seven levels of difficulty, ranging from 3 to 9 lines of geometric figures arranged randomly on a page. The seven sheets of geometric figures containing random combinations of squares, trapezoids, and heptagons were arranged in sequence from easy (3 lines) to difficult (9 lines) in front of the participants. The performance task was to cross out a geometric shape matching one initially crossed out on each sheet.

All participants were told to perform the task to get tokens that could be exchanged for prizes; the more tokens the better the prize. After reaching their work goals they could pay themselves as many tokens from a nearby container as they thought their work had been worth. Dependent variables were (a) number of figures canceled (i.e., total work behavior across trials); (b) average number of figures canceled (i.e., average work behavior across trials [work standard]); (c) percentage of modeled standard (i.e., goal chosen as a percentage of the goal modeled by the experimenter); (d) schedule of reinforcement (i.e., items of work accomplished divided by the number of tokens paid to self); and (e) percentage of modeled schedule of reinforcement (i.e., schedule of reinforcement as a percentage of the schedule of reinforcement modeled by the experimenter). The dependent variables were analyzed individually in terms of a 2 (motivational orientation) × 3 (instructional demands) factorial design with 10 participants in each of 6 cells.

Since internal self-influences interact with external environmental influences in determining behavior, it was expected that IM mildly retarded persons residing in quasi-institutional settings would perform more vigorously than EM persons under all imposed conditions. This was because IM persons have a more highly developed self-reinforcement system and also as strongly developed an external reinforcement system as do EM persons. IM persons were expected to work harder, set a higher performance standard, and set a leaner schedule of reinforcement compared to EM persons.

Results indicated that both external-environmental conditions (i.e., task demand conditions) and internal-self characteristics (i.e., motivational orientation) had significant effects on performance. Participants in the stringent demand condition worked harder, set higher goals, and arranged leaner schedules of reinforcement than did those in the lenient demand condition. Intrinsically motivated participants also worked harder, set higher goals, and arranged leaner schedules than did EM participants in all demand conditions. Further, IM participants chose a higher goal than had been demonstrated to them (in the lenient demand condition, the only reasonable comparison for this variable) and also arranged a leaner schedule of self-reinforcement over all demand conditions than had been demonstrated to them, while EM participants either copied the schedule set by the experimenter or set richer ones. Differences between IM and EM participants were most pronounced in the lenient demand condition, suggesting that motivational orientation will lead to the most divergent performances in situations where there is least external support and guidance. Figure 1.8 presents the percentage of the modeled work standard selected by IM and EM participants as a function of the three task demands, illustrating again the familiar interaction of individual differences in motivational orientation with source of reinforcement.

The authors concluded that internal self-system characteristics interact with external demand characteristics of the environment to reveal substantial individual differences in patterns of self-reward behavior, and further, that these studies provide data quite consistent with Bandura's (1969, 1978) concept of the self-system as well as their own previous theories and research on motivational orientation. Switzky and Haywood (1985b), cited in Haywood and Switzky (1986), and Gambro and Switzky (1988), extended this series of studies to young normally developing children vary-

FIGURE 1.8. Percentage of modeled work standard chosen by IM and EM mildly retarded adults as a function of task demand characteristics

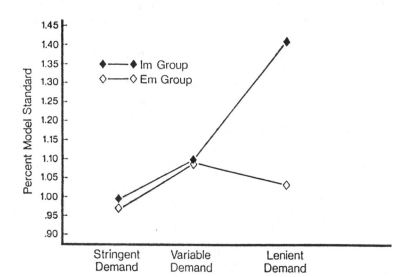

Note: Task demand characteristics were: stringent, variable, and lenient. From Switzky & Haywood (1985a), with permission of Academic Press.

ing in age between 4 and 6 years, using the same paradigm, and have replicated these effects. All together, these studies provide good cross-validation and construct validity for the motivational orientation concept concerning the effects of internal self-influences and the role of external environmental influences on the self-regulatory behavior of young children and adult mentally retarded populations.

Validity Issues

Table 1.2 (pp. 64–81 at the end of this chapter) features as rows a list of the types of design validity, and as columns (a) a description of each validity type, (b) suggested general control strategies for each type, (c) features of Haywood (1968a), (d) features of Haywood (1968b), (e) features of Haywood and Switzky (1985), and (f) features of Switzky and Haywood (1985a) that relate to each type of validity issue.

Internal validity. The four experiments differ in terms of their design characteristics. The studies of Haywood (1968a, b) are examples of *ex post* *facto* research, whereas the studies of Haywood and Switzky (1985) and Switzky and Haywood (1985a) are examples of *true experimental* research. *Ex post facto* research is systematic empirical inquiry in which the scientist does not have *direct control* of the independent variables because their manifestations have already occurred or because they are inherently not manipulable. Inferences about the relationships among the variables are made, without direct intervention, from concomitant variations of independent and dependent variables to demonstrate some kind of empirical validity (Kerlinger, 1973). In *true experimental* research, scientists use the principle of randomization and active manipulation of the independent variables to observe the effects on the dependent variables. *Ex post facto* research has the major inherent weakness of lack of control of the independent variables.

In the Haywood (1968a, b) studies there are numerous *potential* threats to internal validity, i.e., other known or unknown variables that correlate with the "manipulated" variable(s) could be the "real basis" of the observed relationships. These *potential* threats to internal validity include *selection bias, extrinsic historical events, intrinsic historical events, attrition, maturation, reaction to assessment, biased testers, floor or ceiling effects,* and *regression to the true score.* The Haywood (1968a, b) studies, however, show good *empirical validity* (refer to Table 1.2). Providing significant relationships among variables does not demonstrate proof for one's favored hypothesis implying casual connections among sets of variables, because alternative competing hypotheses have not been ruled out. One can, however, "confirm" and "disconfirm" hypotheses under study by showing that alternative plausible hypotheses are or are not supported—what Platt (1964) termed "strong inference." Chamberlin (1965) describes a "method of working multiple hypotheses" and outlines how the investigator's own "intellectual affections" can be guarded against.

> The effort is to bring up into view every rational explanation of new phenomena and to develop every tenable hypothesis respecting their cause and history. The investigator thus becomes the parent of a family hypotheses; and, by his parental relation to all, he is forbidden to fasten his affection unduly upon any one. (p. 756).

It is possible also to control statistically for the operation of competing independent-variable hypotheses on the dependent variables (Joreskog & Sorbom, 1979; Pedhazur, 1982). The methods of testing alternative hypotheses logically or statistically are some of the ways to "control" the independent variables of such research. Lacking the possibilities of randomization and manipulation, *ex post facto* researchers must be very sensitive to alternative-hypothesis testing possibilities.

The studies of Haywood (1968a, b) are not totally worthless as examples of scientific research. Many *ex post facto* studies are done in the early stages of research endeavors that lead to *true experimental* research designs and the search for construct validation. To demonstrate construct validity, a whole line of research conducted over many years needs to be carefully evaluated.

Haywood's (1968a, b) early *ex post facto* studies concerning the effect of intrinsic and extrinsic motivation on academic achievement in three ranges of IQ were constructed on very well conceived hypotheses concerning the operation of motivational orientation, IQ, and academic achievement, and they featured very explicit theory-based predictions. Care was taken to sample very carefully from a well-defined population of underachieving and overachieving school children using randomization and matching techniques as much as possible *to reduce confounding selection biases. Unpredictable historical events* that could have occurred coincidentally with the intervention are possible but unlikely. *Differential loss of participants* from groups was possible but unlikely. *Differential maturational effects* confounded with level of intelligence could not be ruled out in these early studies as the true causes of the empirical effects. *Differential reactivity to assessment* in these early studies was also confounded with experimental manipulations. It is unlikely that the internal validity of these experiments is undermined by *biased testers. Floor and ceiling effects* would have operated against the hypotheses that were empirically supported and can be ruled out as important competing hypotheses. Similarly, *regression to true score effects* would have operated against the manifested empirical effects.

The limitations of *ex post facto* research are numerous and include: (a) the inability of the researcher to manipulate independent variables, (b) the inability of the researcher to randomize groups, and (c) the risk of improper interpretations due to lack of adequate "controls." Researchers who are forced to use *ex post facto* designs need well-conceived theories to guide their investigations in order to minimize spurious predicted relationships. *Ex post facto* research that is conducted without considered hypotheses and well thought out predictions—research in which data are just collected and then analyzed with canned statistical packages and interpreted—are very dangerous in their power to mislead because they capitalize on error and chance relationships. *Post factum* explanations do not lend themselves to nullifiability because they are so flexible. Whatever the observations, new interpretations can always be found to "fit the facts" (Merton, 1949, pp. 90–91). One wonders how much of current special education research falls under suspicion because of these concerns?

The studies of Haywood and Switzky (1985) and Switzky and Haywood (1985a) were *true experimental* designs that used the principles of randomization and active manipulations of the independent variables relating to experimental interventions to observe the effects on the dependent variables. Of course, motivational status was not randomized: Such a design would require that subjects be randomized and then be trained to respond characteristically as internally or externally motivated. Nevertheless, in terms of the interventions, *selection bias* confounding was minimized because of the use of randomization and matching procedures. *Confounded historical events* were minimized because experimental and control groups experienced the same history of intervention and the experimenters were blind to the MO of the participants. *Attrition* effects were minimized as much as possible. There was no differential loss of participants due to lack of cooperation of participants in the experimental conditions. *Maturational* confounds were controlled by matching and randomization procedures. *Reaction to assessment* was similarly controlled. The effects due to *biased testers* were minimal. The use of the Picture Motivation Scale had no apparent *ceiling or floor* limitations. *Regression to the true score* effects on the Picture Motivation Scale, if they operated, would work against the expected predictions. The *true experimental* studies reported here appear to have excellent internal validity.

External validity. The studies reported here fell short on external validity concerns, as do the vast majority of studies in special and regular education. This is because it takes a great deal of research time and effort to demonstrate even minimal degrees of research exportability of phenomena in special education research. The practitioner is usually left to the subjective biases of "experts" who come up with lists of so-called "best-practices" or "state-of-the-art programs." Taken one at a time, the studies reported here vary considerably in *population validity.* The Haywood (1968a, b) studies may be limited to the teaching practices and populations that existed in Toronto, Canada, schools of the 1960s. The studies of Haywood and Switzky (1985) and Switzky and Haywood (1985a) may apply only to adult mentally retarded populations residing in intermediate-care facilities in rural northern Illinois. Only careful replication of the research interventions and the very careful definition of the populations studied will lead to better population validity. Questions of population validity are most serious concerns in contemporary special education research and practice (Switzky & Haywood, 1984; Switzky & Haywood, 1985c; Switzky, Haywood, & Rotatori, 1982). In terms of *ecological validity,* all the studies reported here fall short. However, an attempt was made in the Haywood and Switzky (1985) study to make the experimental work task simulate a sheltered workshop environment for retarded adults. However, no test was made to see if the work behavior of participants was similar to their behavior in sheltered workshop settings. The contrived task (marking geometric forms on a sheet of paper) used in the Switzky and Haywood (1985a) study may have limited ecological validity for more realistic settings in the community, work environment, or school. Only further research will demonstrate ecological validity. In terms of *referent generality,* an attempt was made in all the studies reported to build a case for the referent generality of the motivational orientation construct.

Measurement validity. In all the studies presented, considerable effort was devoted to different aspects of measurement validity in both the Choice-Motivator Scale and the Picture Motivation Scale. Initial attempts were made to assess *internal consistency, test-retest,* and *inter-rater agreement reliabilities,* although much more work needs to be done. Attempts were made to assess *face* and *content validity* using classical item analysis procedures (Crocker & Algina, 1986; Ghiselli, Campbell, & Zedeck, 1981), but additional studies need to be undertaken. In terms of *empirical validity,* all the studies showed substantial correlation of subjects' MO with performance criteria.

Reviewing the search Haywood and Switzky have made to demonstrate *construct validity* of their MO concept, we necessarily go beyond the four studies reviewed in Table 1.2. The search for construct validation in current educational psychology and special education research is very much like the search for the Holy Grail undertaken by the knights of King Arthur's round table. Both may turn into ultimate lifetime quests fraught with danger, temptations, and frustrations because the ultimate goal, if it is in fact attainable at all, may nevertheless always remain slightly out of reach.

To demonstrate construct validity the following conditions must be met:

1. The construct must be operationally defined, and a measurement instrument that consists of items representing behaviors that are specific, concrete manifestations of the construct must be developed.
2. The theoretical model underlying the construct must be explicitly defined, and its relationship to other theoretical constructs in the model must be clarified.
3. The relationship of the construct to measures of real-life criteria must be made explicit.

4. Hypotheses concerning both individuals who differ on the construct and differences on demographic characteristics, performance criteria, or operational measures of other theoretically important constructs that have already been validated must be made clear and must be based on an explicitly stated theory.
5. Empirical data must be gathered to test the hypothesized relationships.
6. It must be determined if the empirical results are consistent or inconsistent with *a priori* hypotheses and if the empirical findings could more readily be due to the operation of competing theories. These competing theories should be logically and empirically eliminated to the extent possible.

The studies of Haywood and Switzky reviewed here do make a fair case for the construct validity of the motivational orientation (MO) construct. MO was operationalized in terms of scores obtained on psychometric measures of motivational orientation, the earlier Choice-Motivator Scale and the more recently developed Picture Motivation Scale. Considerable effort went into determining the psychometric characteristics, classical measurement reliability, and referent generality of the two measures, although much work has to be continued, especially on the psychometric characteristics of the Picture Motivation Scale, the operational measure of MO used with mentally retarded samples and young children. Even if the psychometric instruments were infallibly reliable, their construct validity would be in jeopardy unless hypothesized relations based on an explicit theoretical model were supported by empirical data sets. If correlations between measures of the construct and designated criterion variables were nonsignificant or very low, or in the inappropriate direction and strength, this would provide *prima-facie* and *bona fide* evidence against construct validity. Additionally, if differentiations between groups who supposedly differ on the measured attribute failed to materialize, this, too, would raise serious doubts concerning construct validity. Thus the empirical validation of construct validity is deemed both necessary and sufficient to make one's case.

In terms of future directions concerning demonstrating construct validity of the MO concept, additional time must be spent examining the factor structure of the psychometric instruments, and more modern approaches must be utilized, based on item-response theory, causal modeling, and generalizability theory, especially in classroom, workshop, and community settings having more ecological validity (Brennan, 1983; Jackson & Borgata, 1981; Kane, 1982). Few studies have looked at the influence of intrinsic and extrinsic motivation in classrooms, work settings, or other community-based settings with mentally retarded populations (Switzky & Schultz, 1988), and thus there is a very strong need to expand research to these environments to demonstrate the construct validity of the MO concept in the context of more applied research questions and issues.

There have been few attempts to discover how intrinsic and extrinsic motivational orientations develop in mentally retarded children, how to facilitate the development of the IM orientation, or how to convert EM-oriented persons into IM-oriented persons (Switzky, 1987). These more global research concerns apply most strongly in demonstrating the construct validity of the MO concept.

Social validity.   The social validity of the motivation-orientation research reported is feasible in the sense that the ultimate goal of the research has been to identify crucial individual difference characteristics so that practitioners may develop optimal educational environments to facilitate learning, performance, and independent self-regulation of behavior in mentally retarded persons—that is, to make mentally retarded persons function more like ordinary persons. One of the themes of the research was to make empirical comparisons between mentally retarded and ordinary persons as regards the operation of internal self-system characteristics (MO) and external environmental demand characteristics. This design provides *de facto* evidence of empirical-comparison social validity, especially regarding procedures and outcomes (see Section IV.A in Table 1.2). However, no explicit evaluation of social validity was made regarding the goals of this line of research. The social validity of this research needs to be evaluated, as it will be when the context of research moves into classroom, work, and community-based settings.

Future Directions

Research on intrinsic and extrinsic motivation in exceptional populations is an underdeveloped area of inquiry in special education research (Haywood & Switzky, 1986, in press; Switzky, 1987; Switzky & Schultz, 1988), but a few studies do exist (Connell & Ryan, 1984; Deci & Chandler, 1986; Gottfried, 1982; Silon & Harter, 1985). In regular education, the interest paid to the effects of intrinsic and extrinsic motivation is massive (Ames & Ames, 1984, 1986; Brophy, 1983; Corno & Mandinach, 1983; McCombs, 1983; Paris, Olson, & Stevenson, 1983). More recently educational researchers have paid more attention to the determinants of self-regulation in exceptional populations (Covington, 1987; Paris & Oka, 1986; Paris, Jacobs, & Cross, 1987), and to the thesis that motivational variables may be the key to activate general strategy knowledge, and strategy use in exceptional populations (Borkowski & Kurtz, 1987). New research on motivational processes in exceptional populations needs to concentrate on tying together the various existing motivational models and their relationship to motivational orientation: how it develops in exceptional populations, and how it interacts with environmental and other internal self-processes to determine learning and performance (Haywood & Switzky, 1986, in press; Switzky, 1987; Switzky & Schultz, 1988).

Finally, while Haywood and Switzky have used true experiment, random-assignment designs with regard to conditions, IM and EM levels have been studied only as traits, never as motivational "states" that are amenable to intervention, as their theory suggests. We are overdue for an experiment that has individuals assigned randomly to groups who are then given IM or EM experiences that modify their motivational states.

FRONTIERS FOR RESEARCH METHODOLOGY IN SPECIAL EDUCATION

The preceding analysis of research validity has many implications for research methodology in special education. These will be presented under the topics of research validity that have appeared throughout the paper.

Internal Validity

Methodologists in social science have placed the greatest emphasis on internal validity, but errors of logic still abound. One of the errors often made by applied scientists is their neglect, or sometimes inappropriate application, of statistical procedures intended to help them with their decision making and communication. The studies above show that powerful statistical procedures are available even though the number of participants studied may be small. These procedures provide a common set of rules for decision making in social science research, thereby assuring a universal standard for social scientists and the practitioners who apply their findings.

Despite its many weaknesses, much *ex post facto* research must be done because many research problems in special education do not lend themselves easily to experimental inquiry. Controlled inquiry is possible, but true experimentation involving randomization methods may not be possible. Special education researchers need to be mindful of the following advice (Kerlinger, 1973):

1. Ignore the results of any *ex post facto* study that does not test hypotheses.

2. Be highly skeptical of any *ex post facto* study that tests only one hypothesis and disregards the testing of alternative "negative" hypotheses. Researchers should predict significant relations and nonsignificant relations, whenever possible.

In non-experimental research it is possible to resort to a variety of statistical controls in lieu of randomization. The analysis of covariance has long been employed to this end.

More recently several creative research techniques have evolved in the social sciences to study causal relationships in *ex post facto* research (Asher, 1983; Berry, 1984; Goldberger & Duncan, 1973; Joreskog & Sorbom, 1979, 1984; Kenny, 1979; Kenny & Campbell, 1984; Pedhazur, 1982). Researchers who attempt causal analysis use the multivariate techniques of path analysis (Pedhazur, 1982), cross-lagged panel correlation (Kenny, 1979; Kenny & Campbell, 1984), and the structural equation modeling method known as LISREL (the linear structural relations method of Joreskog & Sorbom, 1979). These evaluate and standardize regression coefficients among a set of variables to test suggestions of causal linkages based on empirical knowledge, theoretical formulations and assumptions, and logical analyses. Path analysis (Pedhazur, 1982) is the *a priori* arrangement of variables into interacting, co-acting, and causal chains that can be evaluated by a set of regression equations that have been uniquely constrained to be congruent with the *a priori* arrangement. Beta coefficients, which are standardized in the same way as correlation coefficients and range from about -1.0 to about $+1.0$, can be tested for significant departure from zero to determine whether *predicted* causal links are empirically supported. For example, we could propose a model in which vocabulary size is predicted by the number of pages an individual reads daily, which is in turn predicted by the average number of pages the individual's parents read to him or her daily during preschool childhood. If the beta of preschool pages predicting pages read is positive and significant, and beta of pages read predicting vocabulary size is significant, then the claim of causality in two links of a proposed causal chain is supported.

Cross-lagged panel analysis compares the correlations between two measures taken at two points in time. For example, the correlation of number of pages read daily at Time 1 and vocabulary at Time 2 would be compared with that of number of pages at Time 2 and vocabulary Time 1. If the correlation with vocabulary lagged is greater than that with pages lagged, then we make the inference that vocabulary is increased by reading. We know of no research in special education that uses this simple, powerful logic to test causal hypotheses in *ex post facto* research.

Linear structured equations (Joreskog & Sorbom, 1979) are conceptually similar to path analysis, except that it is possible to combine several measures of a construct into a single composite score, which is then used to evaluate predicted causal chains. Another virtue is that LISREL models can accommodate correlations between individuals' predicted scores and their deviations from predicted scores—"errors of measurement"— whereas regression analyses cannot.

Causal analytic techniques can be useful in shedding light on the question of whether or not the causal model of relationships postulated by the researcher is consistent with empirical data. Of course, utmost caution is necessary in interpreting such methods of analysis because correlation is no proof of causation. Such techniques have been very rarely used in special education research (Swanson & Alford, 1987). Examples of published studies include the work of Mink and her colleagues (Mink, Meyers, & Nihira, 1984; Mink & Nihira, 1987; Mink, Nihira, & Meyers, 1983), who used multivariate techniques to study the effect of different patterns or types of family environments on the home and school behavior of slow-learning and moderately mentally retarded children. Whitman, Borkowski, Schellenbach, and Nath (1987) have recently proposed to test a model of teenage parenting and child development using structural equation modeling techniques (Joreskog & Sorbom, 1984). While care must be taken in using these techniques correctly and conservatively to guard against spurious associations, causal modeling promises to help investigators greatly as they study more complex relationships among variables in exceptional populations and construct and test more sophisticated theories.

External Validity

Social science traditions pay much lip service to external validity, but the threats to its being achieved remain. Social scientists must always be aware of the limits on their sampling of individuals, settings, and assessments. Most importantly, external validity is much more of a reader's problem than a writer's problem. Important research can be done on the most unusual populations and in the most specialized laboratories. The reader must decide whether the findings of a particular investigation apply to his or her situation. One can hardly blame an investigator when principles established in research using gifted subjects are applied by research consumers to subjects with mental retardation. Nevertheless, research in applied social science should always strive to have the greatest possible relevance, which implies that it should sample from a broad population and ecology spectrum. But the dilemma for the social scientist in special education is that individual differences tend to be very great, and it is usually misleading to merge large numbers of very heterogeneous individuals into a "population" whose members have nothing in common except the label created by the investigator. This dilemma can be only partially resolved by the careful documentation of the characteristics of the subjects studied in any investigation.

Reliability and Validity of Measurement

The conventions for assessing measurement reliability and validity are very primitive in special education research. The nature of their research often forces investigators to prepare their own instruments, and it is rare that they thoroughly assess the reliability or validity of these instruments. Furthermore, indexes of internal consistency, inter-observer agreement, and test-retest reliability have not been standardized, although it is clear that different indices are preferable for these three different cases. Heal (1985) argued that Cronbach's alpha (Cronbach, 1951) is the index of choice for internal consistency because it considers the intercorrelations among all the items on an instrument. He proposed that Kappa (Cohen, 1968; Johnson & Heal, 1987) be used to index inter-rater agreement, since it is unaffected by high or low rates of occurrence of the observed behavior, a property that contaminates other percent agreement indices. Pearson's product moment (r) was recommended as the index of test-retest reliability because it indexes consistency of performance over time despite any general change, due to maturation or learning, in subjects on whom the correlation is based. These recommendations are discussed at greater length by Heal (1985).

These conventional ideas of reliability have recently been integrated by a new development, *generalizability theory* (Berk, 1979; Crocker & Algina, 1986; Cronbach, Gleser, Nanda, & Rajaratnam, 1972; Suen & Ary, 1989). This approach sees reliability sources as factors in an analysis-of-variance design, and through the analysis of variance in scores it provides estimates of the true variance and error variance attributable to various reliability sources. For example, a reliability design might include two or more occasions of measurement, two or more observers, two or more respondents, and two or more forms of the assessment instrument. An analysis of variance could partition the total variability among scores into components attributable to each of these sources. Furthermore, simple generalizability calculation formulas provide separate, independent reliability indices for time (cf. test-retest reliability), for observers (cf. inter-rater or inter-scorer reliability), for respondents, or for forms (cf. alternate form reliability). Suen and Ary (1989) provide an excellent introduction to generalizability theory, including its application to intra-individual variability (time series designs).

One virtue of generalizability theory is that it is useful both for classical norm-referenced tests, consisting of items drawn from homogeneous domains, and also for criterion-referenced tests, consisting of items of heterogeneous difficulty that are carefully sequenced so that each item is demonstrably more difficult than the one preceding it. Crocker and Algina (1986) present readable, detailed instructions for the application of generalizability theory to criterion-referenced tests. Their analysis includes instructions for making "mastery" classifications, since the usual purpose for criterion-referenced tests is to determine whether or not the examinee has mastered the skill being assessed.

Social Validity

The determination of whether our research has relevance to important social problems has been greatly neglected by social science tradition. Nevertheless, it is logically irrefutable in *applied* social science that this relevance be established: If science is to be applied, there must be documentation that it can be. Since research in special education is invariably applied research, it behooves every social scientist in this field to consider both (a) empirical comparisons of handicapped populations to populations they would emulate and (b) subjective evaluation by handicapped individuals and those who have a vested interest in the welfare of handicapped individuals. These concepts are easy to grasp conceptually, and their implementation depends only on the commitment of the investigator. There can be no excuse for neglecting the documentation of the social validity of one's applied research.

CONCLUSIONS

We have reviewed a variety of experiments in special education in order to examine their validity in terms of current social science validity standards. These standards included internal validity, external validity, measurement validity, and social validity.

The research reviewed above employed experimental or quasi-experimental designs. Many research problems in special education do not lend themselves easily to experimental inquiry using true experimentation involving randomization methods. In spite of its many weaknesses, much *ex post facto* research may need to be done. The development of new research techniques to study causal relationships in *ex post facto* research will invigorate the use of that research method in special education. Causal analytic research techniques, such as path analysis (Pedhazur, 1982), cross-lagged panel correlation (Kenny, 1979), and structural equation modeling (Joreskog & Sorbom, 1984), hold much promise in non-experimental research procedures to test causal models of hypotheses and linkages among variables based on empirical knowledge, theoretical for-mulations, and logical analyses.

Another area of recent but neglected advance is that of generalizability theory (e.g., Crocker & Algina, 1986), which indexes reliability using analysis-of-variance techniques to calculate the proportion of variance that can be attributed to each source of measurement "error" (e.g., time, rater, settings, etc.). This approach has tremendous potential for revolu-tionizing special education practices for evaluating the reliability of assess-ment devices. The methods of generalizability theory are useful not only for classical norm-referenced tests, consisting of items drawn from homo-geneous domains, but also for criterion-referenced tests, consisting of items of heterogeneous difficulty that have been carefully sequenced so that each item is demonstrably more difficult than the one preceding it, and for other measures derived from observations of the performance of behavioral operants.

Special education has an enormous challenge to face in providing em-pirical evidence to justify its claim to extraordinary resources. Everyone doing research in special education is obligated to conduct research that meets the highest standards of internal, external, measurement, and social validity.

But the obligation does not rest solely with investigators. Society must recognize the importance of valid methodology. Individuals and their guardians must be made to understand the importance of their complete participation if they are selected for a research project, as support for its external validity. They must realize the importance of random assignment and double or triple blinding to establish internal validity. They must tol-erate the inconvenience of standardized treatment and measurement pro-cedures in order to support internal, external, and measurement validity. And they must guide the scientist to socially relevant questions.

Nearly all the great civilizations have crumbled from within from an inadequate understanding of their social pathologies. For the first time in history, we have the research tools to understand and remediate our social degeneration. If our civilization is to thrive, social science will likely pro-vide the necessary knowledge, but only if social scientists accept the obli-gations inherent in their professional status to conduct research that is maximally valid and to persuade the public to support it.

REFERENCES

Ames, R. E., & Ames, C. (Eds.). (1984). *Research on motivation in education,* Vol. 1. New York: Academic Press.

Ames, C., & Ames, R. E. (Eds.). (1986). *Research on motivation in education,* Vol. 2. New York: Academic Press.

Asher, H. B. (1983). *Causal modeling* (2nd ed.; Sage Quantitative Applications in the Social Sciences, No. 3). Beverly Hills, CA: Sage.

Bandura, A. (1969). *Principles of behavior modification.* New York: Holt, Rinehart & Winston.

Bandura, A. (1978). The self-system in reciprocal determinism. *American Psychologist, 33,* 344–358.

Bandura, A., & Perloff, B. (1967). Relative efficacy of self-monitored and externally imposed reinforcement systems. *Journal of Personality and Social Psychology, 7,* 111–116.

Berk, R. A. (1979). Generalizability of behavioral observations: A clarification of inter-observer agreement and inter-observer reliability. *American Journal of Mental Deficiency, 83,* 460–472.

Berry, W. D. (1984). *Nonrecursive causal modeling* (Sage Quantitative Applications in the Social Sciences, No. 37). Beverly Hills, CA: Sage.

Borg, W. R., & Gall, M. D. (1983). *Educational research: An introduction* (4th ed.). New York: Longman.

Borkowski, J. G., & Kurtz, B. E. (1987). Metacognition and executive control. In J. G. Borkowski & J. D. Day (Eds.), *Cognition in special children* (pp. 123–152). Norwood, NJ: Ablex.

Bracht, G. H., & Glass, G. V. (1968). The external validity of experiments. *American Educational Research Journal, 5,* 437–474.

Brennan, R. L. (1983). *Elements of generalizability theory.* Iowa City, IA: American College Testing Program.

Bridgeman, P. W. (1927). *The logic of modern physics.* New York: Macmillan.

Briefs of the American Association of Colleges for Teacher Education. (1987). *8*(5), entire issue.

Brophy, J. (1983). Conceptualizing student motivation. *Educational Psychologist, 18*(3), 200–215.

Bruner, J. S. (1962). *On knowing: Essays for the left hand.* Cambridge, MA: Harvard University Press.

Call, R. J. (1968). *Motivation-hygiene orientation as a function of socioeconomic status, grade, race and sex.* Unpublished master's thesis, Tennessee State University, Nashville.

Campbell, D. T., & Fiske, D. W. (1959). Convergent and discriminant validation by the multitrait-multimethod matrix. *Psychological Bulletin, 56,* 81–105.

Campbell, D. T., & Stanley, J. C. (1966). *Experimental and quasi-experimental designs for research.* Chicago: Rand McNally.

Chamberlin, T. (1965). The method of multiple working hypotheses. *Science, 147,* 754–759.

Cohen, J. (1968). Weighted Kappa: Nominal scale agreement with provision for scaled disagreement or partial credit. *Psychological Bulletin, 70,* 213–220.

Connell, J. P., & Ryan, R. M. (1984). A developmental theory of motivation in the classroom. *Teacher Education Quarterly, 11*(4), 64–67.

Cook, T. D., & Campbell, D. T. (1979). *Quasi-experimental design and analysis issues for field settings.* Boston: Houghton-Mifflin.

Corno, L., & Mandinach, E. B. (1983). The role of cognitive engagement in classroom learning and motivation. *Educational Psychologist, 18*(2), 88–108.

Covington, M. V. (1987). Achievement motivation, self-attributions and exceptionality. In J. D. Day & J. G. Borkowski (Eds.), *Intelligence and exceptionality* (pp. 173–213). Norwood, NJ: Ablex.

Crocker, L., & Algina, J. (1986). *Introduction to classical & modern test theory.* New York: Holt, Rinehart & Winston.

Cronbach, L. J. (1951). Coefficient alpha and the internal structure of tests. *Psychometrika, 16,* 297–334.

Cronbach, L. J., Gleser, G. C., Nanda, H., & Rajaratnam, N. (1972). *The dependability of behavioral measurements: Theory of generalizability of scores and profiles.* New York: Wiley.

Cronbach, L. L., & Meehl, P. E. (1955). Construct validity in psychological tests. *Psychological Bulletin, 52,* 281–302.

deCharms, R. (1976). *Enhancing motivation: Change in the classroom.* New York: Irvington.

Deci, E. L., & Chandler, C. L. (1986). The importance of motivation for the future of the LD field. *Journal of Learning Disabilities, 19,* 587–594.

Edgerton, R. B., Bollinger, M., & Herr, B. (1984). The cloak of competence: After two decades. *American Journal of Mental Deficiency, 88,* 345–351.

Educating students with learning problems: A shared responsibility (1987). Clearinghouse on the Handicapped. Washington, DC: U.S. Government Printing Office.

Gage, N. L., & Berliner, D. C. (1984). *Educational psychology* (3rd. ed.). Dallas, TX: Houghton-Mifflin.

Gambro, J. S., & Switzky, H. N. (1988). Motivational orientation and self-regulation in young children. *Reflections of Learning Research, 3*(1), 6–17.

Ghiselli, E. E., Campbell, J. P., & Zedeck, S. (1981). *Measurement theory for the behavioral sciences.* San Francisco: W. H. Freeman.

Goldberger, A. S., & Duncan, O. D. (Eds.). (1973). *Structural equation models in the social sciences.* New York: Seminar Press.

Gottfried, A. E. (1982). Relationship between academic intrinsic motivation and anxiety in children and young adolescents. *Journal of School Psychology, 20,* 205–215.

Hartmann, D. P. (1977). Considerations in the choice of interobserver reliability estimates. *Journal of Applied Behavior Analysis, 10,* 103–116.

Haywood, H. C. (1964, May). *A psychodynamic model with relevance to mental retardation.* Paper presented at the annual meeting of the American Association on Mental Deficiency, Kansas City, KS.

Haywood, H. C. (1966). *Report of the Fourth OAMR Visiting Professor in Mental Retardation.* Toronto: Ontario Association for the Mentally Retarded.

Haywood, H. C. (1968a). Motivational orientation of overachieving and underachieving elementary school children. *American Journal of Mental Deficiency, 72,* 662–667.

Haywood, H. C. (1968b). Psychometric motivation and the efficiency of learning and performance in the mentally retarded. In B. W. Richards (Ed.), *Proceedings of the First Congress of the International Association for the Scientific Study of Mental Deficiency* (pp. 276–283). Reigate, England: Michael Jackson.

Haywood, H. C. (1971). Individual differences in motivational orientation: A trait approach. In H. I. Day, D. E. Berlyne, & D. E. Hunt (Eds.), *Intrinsic motivation: A new direction in education* (pp. 113–127). Toronto: Holt, Rinehart & Winston.

Haywood, H. C., & Burke, W. P. (1977). Development of individual differences in intrinsic motivation. In I. C. Uzgiris & F. Weizmann (Eds.), *The structuring of experience* (pp. 230–263). New York: Plenum.

Haywood, H. C., Meyers, C. E., & Switzky, H. N. (1982). Mental retardation. *Annual Review of Psychology, 33,* 309–342.

Haywood, H. C., & Switzky, H. N. (1975). Use of contingent social reinforcement to change the verbal expression of motivation by children of differing motivational orientation. *Perceptual and Motor Skills, 40,* 547–561.

Haywood, H. C., & Switzky, H. N. (1985). Work response of mildly mentally retarded adults to self versus external regulation as a function of motivational orientation. *American Journal of Mental Deficiency, 90,* 151–159.

Haywood, H. C., & Switzky, H. N. (1986). Intrinsic motivation and behavior effectiveness in retarded persons. In N. R. Ellis & N. W. Bray (Eds.), *International review of research in mental retardation* (Vol. 14, pp. 1–46). New York: Academic Press.

Haywood, H. C., & Switzky, H. N. (in press).'Ability and modifiability: How, and how much, can ability be changed? In E. Zuniga (Ed.), *The development of intellective processes in the child: School context.* Washington, DC: Department of Educational Studies of the Organization of the American States.

Haywood, H. C., & Weaver, S. J. (1967). Differential effects of motivational orientation and incentive conditions on motor performance in institutionalized retardates. *American Journal of Mental Deficiency, 72,* 459–467.

Heal, L. W. (1985). Methodology for community integration research. In R. H. Bruininks (Ed.), *Deinstitutionalization and education of handicapped children and youth* (pp. 199–224). Baltimore: Paul H. Brookes.

Heal, L. W., Colson, L. S., & Gross, J. C. (1984). A true experiment in evaluating adult skill training for severely mentally retarded secondary students. *American Journal of Mental Deficiency, 89*(2), 146–155.

Heal, L. W., & Fujiura, G. T. (1984). Toward a valid methodology for research on residential alternatives for developmentally disabled citizens. In N. R. Ellis & N. W. Bray (Eds.), *International review of research in mental retardation* (Vol. 12, pp. 205–244). New York: Academic Press.

Herzberg, F., & Hamlin, R. M. (1961). A motivation-hygiene concept of mental health. *Mental Hygiene, 45,* 394–401.

Herzberg, F., & Hamlin, R. M. (1963). The motivation-hygiene concept and psychotherapy. *Mental Hygiene, 47,* 384–397.

Hunt, J. McV. (1963). Motivation inherent in information processing and action. In O. J. Harvey (Eds.), *Motivation and social interaction: Cognitive determinants* (pp. 35–94). New York: Ronald.

Jackson, D. L., & Borgata, E. F. (1981). *Factor analysis and measurement in sociologi-*

cal research (Sage Studies in International Sociology, No. 21). Beverly Hills, CA: Sage.

Johnson, L. J., & Heal, L. W. (1987). Inter-observer agreement: How large should kappa be? *Capstone Journal of Education, 7*(3), 51–63.

Joreskog, K. G., & Sorbom, D. (1979). *Advances in factor analysis and structural equation models.* Cambridge, MA: Abt Books.

Joreskog, K. G., & Sorbom, D. (1984). *LISREL VI: Analysis of linear structural relationships by maximum likelihood, instrumental variables, and least squares methods.* Uppsala, Sweden: University of Uppsala Press.

Kahoe, R. D. (1966a). *Development of an objective factorial motivation-hygiene inventory.* Unpublished doctoral dissertation, George Peabody College, Nashville, TN.

Kahoe, R. D. (1966b). A factor-analytic study of motivation-hygiene variables. *Peabody Papers in Human Development, 4* (Whole No. 4).

Kane, M. T. (1982). A sampling model for validity. *Applied Psychological Measurement, 6,* 125–160.

Kazdin, A. E. (1982). *Single case research designs: Methods for clinical and applied settings.* New York: Oxford University Press.

Kenny, D. A. (1979). *Correlation and causality.* New York: Wiley.

Kenny, D. A., & Campbell, D. T. (1984). Methodological considerations in the analysis of temporal data. In H. J. Gergen & M. M. Gergen (Eds.), *Historical social psychology* (pp. 125–138). New York: Erlbaum.

Kerlinger, F. N. (1973). *Foundations of behavioral research* (2nd. ed.). New York: Holt, Rinehart & Winston.

Klein, S. P., & Kosecoff, J. P. (1975). *Determining how well a test measures your objectives* (CSE Report No. 94). Los Angeles: Center for the Study of Evaluation, University of California.

Kohl, F. L., Karlan, G. R., & Heal, L. W. (1979). Effects of pairing manual signs with verbal cues upon the acquisition of instruction-following behaviors and the generalization to expressive language with severely handicapped students. *AAESPH Review, 4,* 291–300.

Kratochwill, T. R. (1978). *Single subject research: Search for evaluating change.* New York: Academic Press.

Kunca, D. F., & Haywood, N. P. (1969). The measurement of motivational orientation in low mental age subjects. *Peabody Papers in Human Development, 7*(Whole No. 2).

Lord, F. M., & Novick, M. R. (1968). *Statistical theories of mental test scores.* Reading, MA: Addison-Wesley.

McCombs, B. L. (1983). Process and skills underlying continuing intrinsic motivation to learn: Toward a definition of motivational skills training intervention. *Educational Psychologist, 19*(4), 199–218.

McKinney, J. D., & Hocutt, A. M. (1988). The need for policy analysis in evaluating the regular education initiative. *Journal of Learning Disabilities, 21*(1), 12–18.

Merton, R. (1949). *Social theory and social structure.* New York: Free Press.

Miller, M. B., Haywood, H. C., & Gimon, A. T. (1975). Motivational orientation of

Puerto Rican children in Puerto Rico and the U.S. mainland. In G. Marin (Ed.), *Proceedings of the 15th Interamerican Congress of Psychology.* Bogata, Colombia: Sociedad Interamericana de Psicologia.

Mink, I. T., Meyers, C. E., & Nihira, K. (1984). Taxonomy of family life styles: II. Homes with slow-learning children. *American Journal of Mental Deficiency, 89,* 111–123.

Mink, I. T., & Nihira, K. (1987). Direction of effects: Family life-styles and behavior of TMR children. *American Journal of Mental Deficiency, 92,* 57–64.

Mink, I. T., Nihira, K., & Meyers, C. E. (1983). Taxonomy of family life styles: I. Homes with TMR children. *American Journal of Mental Deficiency, 87,* 484–497.

Nie, N. H., Hull, C. H., Jenkins, J. G., Steinbrenner, K., & Bent, D. H. (1975). *Statistical package for the social sciences* (2nd ed.). New York: McGraw-Hill.

Nunnally, J. (1978). *Psychometric theory.* New York: McGraw-Hill.

Orelove, F. P. (1979). *The effects of task components and vicarious reinforcement on attending and incidental learning in severely handicapped adults.* Unpublished doctoral dissertation, University of Illinois, Urbana.

Orelove, F. P. (1982). Acquisition of incidental learning in moderately and severely handicapped adults. *Education and Training of the Mentally Retarded, 17,* 131–136.

OSERS News in Print. (1987). *1* (3).

Paris, S. G., Jacobs, J. E., & Cross, D. R. (1987). Toward an individualistic psychology of exceptional children. In J. D. Day & J. G. Borkowski (Eds.), *Intelligence and exceptionality* (pp. 215–248). Norwood, NJ: Ablex.

Paris, S. G., & Oka, E. R. (1986). Self-regulated learning among exceptional children. *Exceptional Children, 55*(2), 103–108.

Paris, S. G., Olson, G. M., & Stevenson, H. W. (1983). (Eds.). *Learning and motivation in the classroom.* Hillsdale, NJ: Erlbaum.

Pedhazur, E. J. (1982). *Multiple regression in behavioral research* (2nd. ed.). New York: Holt, Rinehart & Winston.

Platt, J. (1964). Strong inference. *Science, 146,* 347–353.

Reynolds, M. C., Wang, M. C., & Walberg, H. J. (1987). The necessary restructuring of special and regular education. *Exceptional Children, 53*(5), 391–398.

Robinson, W. S. (1957). The statistical measurement of agreement. *American Sociological Review, 22,* 17–25.

Rovinelli, R. J., & Hambleton, R. K. (1977). On the use of content specialists in the assessment of criterion-referenced test item validity. *Dutch Journal of Educational Research, 2,* 49–60.

Rusch, F. R., Schutz, R. P., & Heal, L. W. (1983). The validity of sheltered and non-sheltered work behavior research: A review and discussion. In J. L. Matson & J. A. Mulick (Eds.), *Comprehensive handbook on mental retardation* (pp. 455–466). New York: Pergamon Press.

Sidman, M. (1969). *Tactics in scientific research.* New York: Basic Books.

Silon, E. F., & Harter, S. (1985). Assessment of perceived competence, motivational orientation, and anxiety in segregated and mainstreamed educable mentally retarded children. *Journal of Educational Psychology, 77,* 217–230.

Snow, R. E. (1974). Representative and quasi-representative designs for research on teaching. *American Educational Research Journal, 44,* 265–291, 217–230.

Suen, H. K., & Ary, D. (1989). *Analyzing qualitative behavioral observation data.* Hillsdale, NJ: Erlbaum.

Swanson, H. L., & Alford, L. (1987). An analysis of the current status of special education research and journal outlets. *Remedial and Special Education, 8*(6), 8–18.

Switzky, H. N. (1985). Self-reinforcement schedules in young children: A preliminary investigation of the effects of motivational orientation and instructional demands. *Reflections of Learning Research, 1,* 3–18.

Switzky, H. N. (1987). *School and home cooperation and linkages concerning the motivational and social development of elementary aged mildly handicapped students: Effects of motivational orientation, home and family psychosocial environments, and classroom demand characteristics, on academic and social competence.* Unpublished manuscript. Northern Illinois University, Dekalb.

Switzky, H. N. (1988). *Psychometric properties of the Picture Motivation Scale.* Unpublished manuscript. Northern Illinois University, Dekalb.

Switzky, H. N., & Haywood, H. C. (1974). Motivational orientation and the relative efficacy of self-monitored and externally imposed reinforcement schedules. *Journal of Personality and Social Psychology, 30,* 360–366.

Switzky, H. N., & Haywood, H. C. (1984). A biosocial ecological perspective on mental retardation. In N. S. Endler & J. McV. Hunt (Eds.), *Personality and the behavior disorders* (2nd ed., Vol. 2, pp. 851–896). New York: Wiley.

Switzky, H. N., & Haywood, H. C. (1985a, March). *Self-reinforcement schedules in the mildly mentally retarded: Effects of motivational orientation and instructional demands.* Paper presented at the 18th annual Gatlinburg Conference on Research and Theory in Mental Retardation and Developmental Disabilities.

Switzky, H. N., & Haywood, H. C. (1985b). *Self-reinforcement schedules in young children: Effects of motivational orientation and instructional demands.* Unpublished manuscript, Northern Illinois University, Dekalb.

Switzky, H. N., & Haywood, H. C. (1985c). Perspectives on methodological and research issues concerning severely retarded persons. In D. Bricker & J. Filler (Eds.), *Severe mental retardation* (pp. 264–284). Reston, VA: Council for Exceptional Children.

Switzky, H. N., Haywood, H. C., & Rotatori, A. (1982). Who are the severely and profoundly mentally retarded? *Education and Training of the Mentally Retarded, 17*(4), 268–272.

Switzky, H. N., & Schultz, G. F. (1988). Intrinsic motivation and learning performance: Implications for individual educational programming for learners with mild handicaps. *Remedial and Special Education, 9*(4), 7–14.

Wang, M. C., Reynolds, M. C., & Walberg, H. J. (1986). Rethinking special education. *Educational Leadership, 44*(1), 26–31.

Wehman, P., Renzaglia, A., & Bates, P. (1985). *Functional living skills for moderately and severely handicapped individuals.* Austin, TX: PRO-ED.

Whitman, T. L., Borkowski, J. G., Schellenbach, C. J., & Nath, P. S. (1987). Predicting and understanding developmental delay of children of adolescent mothers: A multidimensional approach. *American Journal of Mental Deficiency,* *92,* 40–56.

Wolf, M. M. (1978). Social validity: The case for subjective measurement, or how applied behavior analysis is finding its heart. *Journal of Applied Behavior Analysis, 11,* 203–214.

TABLE 1.2. The Search for Construct Validity: Individual Differences in Motivation and Personality in Special Populations

Type of Validity	Description	Control Strategy
I. INTERNAL VALIDITY		
A. Selection Bias	More promising cases are selected for the experimental group than for the control group.	*Randomly* assign subjects to experimental and control conditions; assess extent of equivalence of intact groups; match groups.
B. History	Unpredictable events occur coincidentally with the intervention.	Disentangle events and time.
1. Collateral Events Extrinsic to Research Design	Collateral events are external to the intervention.	Include a "proximal" control group in design; this control group must experience the same history as the experimental group.
2. Collateral Events Intrinsic to Research Design	Collateral events occur inadvertently with the intervention; "Multiple treatment interference."	Define treatment carefully. Partition treatment into setting and intervention components; use blinded intervenors with no vested interest in outcome of experiment.
3. Attrition	Loss of subjects that is systematically related to intervention effects due to mortality, upward mobility, or downward mobility.	Include various attrition results as score points on dependent variable; replace lost subjects by preselected, matched substitutes; compare attrited and surviving groups on pretest(s) to assess similarity.

64

Haywood (1968a)	Haywood (1968b)	Haywood & Switzky (1985)	Switzky & Haywood (1985a)
Questions of selection bias only partially resolved in this *ex post facto* study. Sex, school, teachers not controlled. Only 150 subjects of under- and overachieving students in 3 IQ ranges defined. A random subsample from the larger sample was obtained and carefully defined.	Questions of selection bias only partially resolved in this *ex post facto* study cross-validating Haywood (1968a). Random sample of 400 subjects from each IQ range chosen from larger sample of 5,000. Age and sex were matched over groups; school and teacher effects uncontrolled.	Subjects were randomly assigned to conditions and matched individually as to age, sex, and motivational orientation in all conditions in this *true* experiment. Subjects in the externally imposed reinforcement group were yoked individually to subjects in the self-regulated reinforcement group in terms of schedule of reinforcement.	Subjects were randomly assigned to conditions in this *true* experiment; thus selection factors were randomized.

| External historical events uncontrolled and a potential threat to validity. | External historical events uncontrolled and a serious threat to validity since study involves trends in achievement test scores over time. | *Both studies:* External historical events controlled. All experimental conditions occurred over similar time spans. | |

Both studies: Internal historical events uncontrolled and a potential threat to validity. Multiple treatment interference a potential threat.

Both studies: Internal historical events controlled. Experimenter blind to motivation orientation of subjects. All multiple treatment interference affected all conditions equally.

Both studies: No attrition in the sense that all subjects were tested. Attrition issues related to the differential loss of subjects in the larger sample of 5,000 subjects are a potential threat to validity.

Both studies: No attrition in the sense that no subjects were lost. Attrition partially threatened because only cooperative subjects were used in both experimental tasks and the determination of MO by the use of the Picture Motivation Scale.

TABLE 1.2. *Continued*

Type of Validity	Description	Control Strategy
C. Maturation	Growth, degeneration, warm-up, and/or fatigue effects that systematically impact on the dependent variable(s) regardless of any intervention.	Include a *randomly* constituted control group whose extra-experimental experiences are comparable to those of the experimental group.
D. Measurement	Measurement of the dependent variable(s) creates the illusion of a treatment effect where none exists in reality.	
1. Reaction to Assessment	Responsiveness to the intervention is catalyzed and systematically sensitized by testing or observation.	Omit pretests for all or a random half of all study groups; use unobtrusive measures, especially before and during intervention; repeatedly assess to desensitize subjects.
2. Biased Testers or Observers	Examiners who have a vested interest and whose scores are based on information other than that provided by the subject.	Employ "blinded" subjects and observers, who know only what they are measuring, not what scores are expected.
3. Floor or Ceiling Effects	The range of a measure is constrained so that performance of a high-scoring subject is underestimated or that of a low scoring subject is overestimated.	Employ measures whose ranges extend well above and below the levels that occur in the subjects of study.
E. Regression to True Scores	The statistical tendency for individuals with extreme scores on one occasion to achieve more nearly average scores on subsequent occasions.	Assign subjects *randomly* to groups. Never select subjects on the basis of scores higher or lower than those expected in a random sample from the population.

Haywood (1968a)	Haywood (1968b)	Haywood & Switzky (1985)	Switzky & Haywood (1985a)
Both studies: Maturation validity is confounded with subject groups; biological maturational issues may be related to effects involving comparisons of EMR, average, and superior IQ samples.		Effects of maturation controlled. Groups matched with regard to sex and age, controlled for IQ.	Effects of maturation controlled. Groups were randomly assigned to experimental conditions. Mean age and IQ of groups not significantly different.
Validity threatened. Groups defined as over- and under-achievers in the three IQ ranges may have reacted differentially to assessment.	Validity threatened. EMR, average, and superior IQ samples at different ages may have reacted differentially to assessment.	Reaction to assessment controlled by matching paradigm for all groups.	Reaction to assessment controlled by randomization of groups to conditions.
Both studies: Not reported; implication is that Choice Motivator scores were obtained by persons who had no knowledge of the research issues.		No threat. Individual who determined MO scores not the same one who ran experimental work tasks. Experimenter blind to purpose.	Slight threat. Experimenter knew purpose of the experiment but not MO of the subjects assigned to groups.
Both studies: Potential threat to validity on the scores on the Choice Motivator Scale; difference scores varied from +1 to -8.		*Both studies:* No ceiling effects on experimental work tasks. Previous studies with the Picture Motivation Scale showed that it had enough range.	
Validity questioned Defining under- and overachievement in terms of extreme z-score measures on the MAT may lead to regression effects.	Validity questioned Only extreme groups (high IM and high EM) used; regression effects may exist.	Validity questioned Only subjects in the top and bottom quartiles of the frequency distribution of MO responses (i.e., extreme groups) used; regression effects may exist.	Slight threat to validity. All subjects used divided up into top and bottom halves of the distribution.

TABLE 1.2. *Continued*

Type of Validity	Description	Control Strategy
II. EXTERNAL VALIDITY		
A. Population Validity	The experimental subjects are typical members of the population of subjects to which the research is claimed to apply; i.e., the results can reasonably be generalized to the population from which the subjects were drawn.	Population must be very carefully defined; all population members must be located and randomly sampled in a representative fashion to avoid biases.
B. Ecological Validity	The experimental setting is typical of all settings in which the experimental procedures might be applied; i.e., the results can reasonably be generalized to a broad array of settings differing along physical, temporal, and social dimensions.	Perform the experiment in the settings where findings are expected to be applied. This might require that a population of settings be defined and experimental settings randomly selected from it.
C. Referent Generality	The assessments of the experimental outcome are sufficiently diverse to assure that the measured attribute is indexed and measured by an adequate, accurate, and valid array of assessment measures.	Use several assessment techniques based on sound theoretical, pragmatic, reliable, and valid approaches so that dependent variables (e.g., behavior changes) are sampled from a meaningful population of possible outcomes.
III. MEASUREMENT VALIDITY		
A. Reliability	The consistency or stability of measuring the same variable(s) on 2 or more occasions.	
1. Internal Consistency	High correlations among test items indicate that measurement is of a single attribute. Errors due to variations in sampling of items from content domain may confound experimental outcomes.	Use item analysis procedures to eliminate any items that correlate negatively or negligibly with the others. Index with Cronbach's alpha.

STUDIES SELECTED FOR REVIEW			
Haywood (1968a)	*Haywood (1968b)*	*Haywood & Switzky (1985)*	*Switzky & Haywood (1985a)*

Validity threatened. Subpopulations of over- and under-achievers carefully selected in three IQ ranges, but data may hold only for Toronto schools in the 1960s.

Validity threatened. Subpopulations of high IM and high EM students carefully selected in three IQ ranges, but data may hold only for Toronto schools in the 1960s.

Validity threatened. Subjects residents in medium-size ICF in Illinois. Only extreme groups on the Picture Motivation Test used.

Validity threatened. Subjects residents in medium-size ICF in Illinois. Only extreme groups on the Picture Motivation Test used.

Validity threatened. Research findings may hold only for Toronto schools in the 1960s.

Validity threatened. Research findings may hold only for Toronto schools in the 1960s.

Ecological validity was attempted by making the experimental work task similar to activities carried out in sheltered workshops for MR adults. No test made to see if subjects' work behavior was similar to work in real sheltered workshops.

Validity threatened. Research findings may hold only for laboratory study and not apply to any other situations.

Both studies: Supported: Theory of intrinsic and extrinsic motivation carefully constructed and operationalized; instrument developed (Choice Motivator Scale) whose items were specific, concrete manifestations of the construct of motivational orientation.

Both studies: Supported: Theory of intrinsic and extrinsic motivation carefully constructed and operationalized; instrument developed (Picture Motivation Scale) whose items were specific, concrete manifestations of the construct of motivational orientation.

Both studies: Item analysis procedures used to determine internal consistency coefficients, which were in the .80's for the Choice Motivator Scale.

Both studies: Item analysis procedures used to determine test characteristics for the Picture Motivation Scale. Item cluster analyses using chi-square used in determining which items were most effective in differentiating IM and EM persons.

TABLE 1.2. *Continued*

Type of Validity	Description	Control Strategy
2. Interrater Agreement	Agreement among raters, judges, or observers concerning the correct score to assign the subject for each performance. Errors due to individual differences in raters' perceptions may confound experimental outcomes.	Have a "blinded" (i.e., uninformed) observer complete assessments and compare them with those of the experimenter. Index with Cohen's kappa, Robinson's *a*, or Generalizability Theory.
3. Test-retest Reliability	Stability of subjects' scores over time. Errors due to time-related changes in subjects' scores may confound experimental outcomes.	Retest subjects, using same procedures that were used in their first test, after a period of time that is sufficient for them to forget particular responses but too short for them to change extensively regarding the measured attribute. Index with Pearson's *r* as a coefficient of stability.
B. Face Validity	Investigators and readers find the measures used to be credible operationalizations of the attribute being measured.	Have subject populations and consumers of research examine, evaluate, and modify measures.
C. Content Validity	The selected items are a representative sample from the universe that comprises the attribute or construct being measured.	Identify systematically all the properties included in and excluded from the performance domain of the attribute; select a panel of qualified experts in the content domain; provide a structured framework for the process of matching a selected representative sample of items which have those properties tapped by the performance domain; collect and summarize the data from the matching process.

STUDIES SELECTED FOR REVIEW			
Haywood (1968a)	*Haywood (1968b)*	*Haywood & Switzky (1985)*	*Switzky & Haywood (1985a)*
Interrater agreement on objective form of the Choice Motivator Scale is 100%.	Interrater agreement on objective form of the Choice Motivator Scale is 100%.	Interrater agreement on objective form of the Picture Motivation Scale is 100%.	Interrater agreement on objective form of the Picture Motivation Scale is 100%.

Both studies: Test-retest reliability using Pearson's *r* ranged from .79 to .85 over a two-week period.

Both studies: Test-retest reliability using Pearson's *r* for both long and short intervals was generally in the range of .80 to .85.

Both studies: Considerable effort made to determine if the items on the Choice Motivator Scale had face validity.

Both studies: Considerable effort made to determine if the items on the Picture Motivation Scale had face validity.

Both studies: Considerable effort made to determine if the items on the Choice Motivator Scale had content validity using classical item analysis procedures.

Both studies: Considerable effort made to determine if the items on the Picture Motivation Scale had content validity using classical item analysis procedures.

TABLE 1.2. *Continued*

Type of Validity	Description	Control Strategy
D. Empirical Validity	Correlation of the measure with an established index of the attribute being measured. The measure is of interest only insofar as it is related to the criteria. If it were possible to obtain criterion scores, there would be no need for the predictor measure or for criterion-related empirical validity.	Identify a suitable criterion behavior, a method of measuring it, and an appropriate sample of subjects who are presumed to differ on the measured attribute. Administer the measure to the subjects and keep a record of their performance on the criterion behavior. Determine the strength of the relationship between the measure and the criterion performance by correlating the measure with the criterion index; see if it discriminates between groups who are presumed to differ on the measured attribute.

Haywood (1968a)	Haywood (1968b)	Haywood & Switzky (1985)	Switzky & Haywood (1985a)
Considerable empirical validity demonstrated. Overachievers were found to be relatively more IM than underachievers in all three academic areas (reading, spelling, and arithmetic). The differences in MO between over- and underachievers were largest in the EMR group and smallest in the superior range of IQ. Overachievers tended to be motivated to a greater extent by factors inherent in the performance tasks (IM factors), while underachievers tended to be motivated by factors extrinsic to the task (EM factors).	Considerable empirical validity demonstrated. MO made a sizable difference in achievement scores on the MAT for the EMR and average-IQ groups. In all three areas IM children achieved at a significantly higher level than EM children with age, sex, and IQ held constant. On average, IM children in the average-IQ and EMR groups had achievement test scores about one full school year higher than those of EM children in the same IQ group. The achievement of IM/EMR children was not different from that of the EM/average-IQ group. Thus there was evidence that (a) IMness is associated with higher school achievement independent of the effects of IQ, and (b) the effects of individual differences in MO appear to be greater as IQ is less.	Considerable empirical validity demonstrated. In both the self-regulation and control conditions, IM subjects filled more compartments than did EM subjects, while IM and EM subjects did not differ under the external-reinforcement condition. IM subjects also filled more of the compartments under the self-regulation condition than they did under the external-reinforcement condition. A higher level of intrinsic motivation is associated with more self-regulatory behavior than is a lower level of intrinsic motivation.	Considerable empirical validity demonstrated. Both external-environmental task demand conditions and internal-self characteristics had significant effects on performance. Subjects in the stringent demand condition and IM subjects, respectively, worked harder, set higher goals, and arranged leaner schedules of reinforcement than did those in the lenient demand condition or than EM subjects in all demand conditions. IM subjects chose a higher goal than had been demonstrated to them (lenient demand condition) and arranged a leaner schedule of self-reinforcement than had been demonstrated to them in all demand conditions; EM subjects copied the schedule set by the experimenter or set richer ones. Differences between IM and EM subjects were sharpest in situations with less external support and guidance.

TABLE 1.2. *Continued*

Type of Validity	Description	Control Strategy
E. Construct Validity	The primary objective of construct validation (Cronbach & Meehl, 1955) is to develop a measure of an individual difference characteristic for its own sake. The principal focus is not on the prediction of a criterion or on the one-to-one correspondence between the content of the test and a specific domain of behavior but on the ability of the test itself to measure the hypothesized individual trait or characteristic of interest. A measure has construct validity if its items are representative of the content domain being sampled (referent validity) and if it consistently predicts behaviors that are associated with the hypothetical construct according to some theoretical position (empirical validity).	Procedures for determining construct validity are the following (Cronbach & Algina, 1986): (a) correlations between a measure of the construct and designed criterion variables; (b) differentiation between groups differing on the measured attribute; (c) factor analysis to determine whether item responses "cluster" together in patterns predictable or reasonable in light of the theoretical structure of the construct of interest; (d) multitrait multimethod (Campbell & Fiske, 1959); (e) applications of generalizability theory (Kane, 1982) can determine whether observations for an individual are invariant over different methods of measurement through analysis components.

Haywood (1968a)	Haywood (1968b)	Haywood & Switzky (1985)	Switzky & Haywood (1985a)
Some construct validity for the MO concept emerges: (a) The Choice Motivator Scale appears to satisfy preliminary referent validity of the motivational orientation concept in terms of its theoretical structure based on factor analysis and item analysis techniques. Hence we make the claim that the MO concept has been operationalized in terms of scores on this instrument. (b) A priori theoretical expectations regarding interactions among ranges of intelligence, over- and underachievement, and scholastic achievement tests were empirically supported. Alternative theories and hypotheses were considered and partially eliminated.	This cross-validating of Haywood (1968a) further strengthens the construct validity of the MO concept: (a) The Choice Motivator Scale remains the operational measure of MO. (b) A priori theoretical expectations regarding the interactions among ranges of intelligence, school achievement, and motivation are supported empirically in a different subset of the larger population of subjects used in Haywood (1968a). Alternative theories and hypotheses were considered and partially eliminated.	More construct validity for the MO concept emerges: (a) The Picture Motivation Scale appears to satisfy preliminary referent validity of the MO concept in terms of preliminary item analysis and test-retest reliability measurements. Thus we have a measure that has been used to operationalize MO for both low MA and child populations. (b) The theoretical model of MO has been expanded from its earlier (Haywood, 1964) basis in motivation-hygiene theory (Herzberg & Hamlin, 1961, 1963) and Hunt's (1963) concepts of intrinsic motivation to Bandura's (1969, 1978) theory of internal self-system influences interacting with external demand characteristics of the environment, and to theories of self-regulation. (c) A priori theoretical expectations regarding MO, external and internal reinforcement oper-	This study provides additional strong evidence concerning construct validity for the MO concept and self-regulation of behavior in mentally retarded samples: (a) The Picture Motivation Scale remains the operational MO measure. (b) A priori theoretical expectations among motivational orientation, demand characteristics of the environment, and dependent measures (total work behavior, average performance standard chosen, % of modeled standard, schedule of reinforcement, and % of modeled schedule of reinforcement) are supported empirically. (c) Alternative theories and hypotheses were considered and eliminated.

TABLE 1.2. *Continued*

Type of Validity	Description	Control Strategy

IV. SOCIAL VALIDITY

A. Empirical Comparison — The goals, procedures, and outcomes for the experimental population are consonant with those practiced in the standard population, i.e., the one into which the experimental group aspires to be integrated. — Observe the practices of the standard population and select outcome goals, intervention procedures, and standards of performance for the experimental population that are consonant with standard practices.

Haywood (1968a)	Haywood (1968b)	Haywood & Switzky (1985)	Switzky & Haywood (1985a)
		tions, and performance maintenance (task persistence) were mostly empirically supported. Alternative theories and hypotheses were considered and partially eliminated. (d) Study provides cross-validation of Switzky and Haywood (1974) research done on ordinary elementary school children to adult MR samples, illustrating the generalizability of the MO concept and its theoretical prediction over different tasks and experimental populations.	
Comparative populations were included in the experimental design.	Comparative populations were included in the experimental design.	Comparative populations were included in the experimental design.	Comparative populations were included in the experimental design.

TABLE 1.2. *Continued*

Type of Validity	Description	Control Strategy
1. Goals		
2. Procedures		

Haywood (1968a)	Haywood (1968b)	Haywood & Switzky (1985)	Switzky & Haywood (1985a)
Ultimate goal of research is to identify crucial individual difference characteristics such as motivational orientation that may influence learning so that optimal instructional strategies, which facilitate performance in special education populations, may be implemented	Ultimate goal of research is to identify crucial individual difference characteristics such as motivational orientation that may influence learning so that optimal instructional strategies, which facilitate performance in special education populations, may be implemented	Ultimate goal of research is to identify crucial individual difference characteristics such as MO that may influence independent learning, performance, and self-regulation in the community and in the classroom and determine strategies that may facilitate independent functioning in MR adults. The proximal goal of the research was to replicate the Switzky & Haywood (1974) study concerning self-monitored and externally imposed reinforcement in ordinary school children and see if similar processes and effects existed in MR samples.	Ultimate goal of research is to identify crucial individual difference characteristics such as MO that may influence independent learning, performance, and self-regulation in the community and in the classroom and determine strategies that may facilitate independent functioning in MR adults. The proximal goal of the research was to demonstrate that self-system characteristics interact with external demand characteristics to determine patterns of self-regulatory behavior.
Standard research procedures were used for retarded, average, and gifted school children.	Standard research procedures were used for retarded, average, and gifted school children.	Study the relationship of MO, IQ, and incentive operations of the self-monitored and externally imposed reinforcement on the work performance of MR adults.	Study internal self-system characteristics interacting with external demand characteristics of the environment to see if individual differences in patterns of self-reward behavior exist in MR adult samples.

TABLE 1.2. *Continued*

Type of Validity	Description	Control Strategy
3. Outcomes		
B. Subjective Evaluation	The goals, procedures and outcomes for the experimental population are appropriate in the eyes of those who have a vested interest in their well-being.	Question individuals in the experimental population or their advocates to determine that the goals, procedures, and outcomes are appropriate.
1. Goals		
2. Procedures		
3. Outcomes		

Haywood (1968a)	Haywood (1968b)	Haywood & Switzky (1985)	Switzky & Haywood (1985a)
Outcomes were useful for understanding the academic motivation for retarded, average, and gifted school children.	Outcomes were useful for understanding the academic motivation for retarded, average, and gifted school children.	Ultimate outcome is to find evidence for construct validity of MO concept in MR and non-MR samples. More limited goal is to demonstrate empirical validity among our measures of MO, IQ, reinforcement operations, and indices of work behavior and schedules of reinforcement.	Ultimate outcome is to find evidence for construct validity of MO concept and to test and verify its relationships to theories of self-regulation in classrooms, workshops, and community-based settings for MR samples, and to design optimal environments that encourage independence.
Not addressed.	Not addressed.	Not addressed.	Not addressed.
Not addressed.	Not addressed.	Not addressed.	Not addressed.
Not addressed.	Not addressed.	Not addressed.	Not addressed.

CHAPTER 2

Early Intervention for Disabled Infants, Toddlers, and Preschool Age Children

JOHN FILLER
JENNIFER OLSON

It is an exciting time to be writing a chapter focused on the issues and research relevant to the education of very young disabled children. Questions basic to the nature of what we have come to accept as essential components of early intervention programs are being asked and answers are being proposed with ever-increasing frequency. Perhaps this new spirit of inquiry is a by-product of the focused attention that has accompanied the long process of passage of the landmark legislation represented in Public Law 99-457 (1986). Or, perhaps, we are only witnessing the current thrust of a steadily growing body of literature that has reflected concern for the same issues for the past 20 years. Regardless of the reason, there is currently much discussion in the professional literature centered upon components of models which stress the importance of an understanding of family-systems theory. We have moved from a uni-dimensional view of the parent as trainer to one which emphasizes the family as both the target of and the vehicle for intervention. Additionally, in the last few years an increasing number of authors have questioned the soundness of widely held assumptions regarding the effectiveness of early intervention programs for young children with physical and/or intellectual disabilities. Some have argued that past claims for the positive impact of early intervention upon the child are not so well supported by research as is widely thought. We have chosen to examine family-systems approaches to intervention and efficacy debates not only because of current relevancy to the

Preparation of this paper was supported, in part, by U.S. Department of Education Grant No. G008630003 and Grant No. G008730189 to the University of Idaho. No official endorsement should be inferred.

literature, but because of the implications that discussion of each has to an understanding of the major requirements of Public Law 99-457 (1986).

There are many reasons for current controversies over questions of efficacy, parental involvement, and the implementation dilemmas posed by Public Law 99-457. While we believe that it is important in any field of endeavor to examine carefully the reasons for current concerns, that is not our focus here. Rather, we shall present in the pages that follow some brief discussion of what concerns exist today relevant to those areas mentioned above.

EFFICACY OF EARLY INTERVENTION

Many would argue that a discussion of the efficacy of early intervention is unnecessary. For a variety of social and political reasons, early intervention is here to stay. It would be well, then, as Dunst and Snyder (1986) have argued, for us to conduct our review of research with the purpose of delineating the conditions of intervention most likely to result in positive effects. As professionals (and parents) we share the widely held belief that early, continuing, and intensive intervention that is heavily family focused will significantly benefit even the most severely disabled child. Extensive previous reviews of research indicate sufficient empirical evidence to support such a view (e.g., Bailey & Wolery, 1984; Bricker, 1986; Bronfenbrenner, 1975; Hanson, 1984). Nevertheless, it is important, in fact critical, for us to reexamine periodically the foundations upon which such views are based.

Meisels (1985) has pointed out that the question, Is early intervention effective? is not new. In fact, that exact question was addressed by Bronfenbrenner (1975) and had been around in one form or another for decades before then. Meisels offers the suggestion that the question continues to nag us because there is confusion from the failure to take into account four assumptions of the intervention program: its theoretical base, the specific intervention strategies employed, the method of measuring change, and the criteria used for selecting participants. In other words, the answer to the question Is early intervention effective? depends upon the goals of a given intervention program, the specific intervention strategies it employs, and the measures of efficacy. We add another factor to Meisels' list; the method used to answer the question. That is, if one employs a weak research design and/or inappropriate method of analysis, the likelihood of achieving a valid result is greatly lessened. Before we discuss some recent research that has stimulated debate, it is necessary to describe in more detail each of these assumptions.

Theoretical/Conceptual Base

Previous research (Filler, 1983) has shown that early intervention begins with both a theory of child development and a theory of intervention. Assumptions about the way in which children acquire successively more complex forms of behavior should direct our interventions. Without a well-defined conceptual framework, treatment is not likely to produce a significant effect or at the very least what effects are detected will not be adequately explained by reference to procedure. There are discussions in the literature of programs based in developmental quantitative theory (e.g., Gentry & Adams, 1978; Shearer & Shearer, 1976), developmental qualitative approaches (e.g., Dunst, 1981), and eco-behavioral approaches (Vincent, Salisbury, Walter, Brown, Gruenewald, & Powers, 1980). There are also numerous early intervention programs with no coherent theoretical or conceptual base at all (Dunst, 1986).

From the perspective of efficacy research it is the set (or sets) of intervention strategies employed that constitute the independent variables. In order to provide a valid test of any theory that predicts positive benefits to disabled children, the operations that constitute the interventions must be clearly specified and must follow directly from the theory. In other words, the value of the findings is largely dependent upon the validity of the intervention methods used in the study. Consider, for example, the Piper and Pless (1980) investigation which, when published, stimulated widespread discussion. These investigators reported findings that appeared to contradict those of several earlier and very well known studies (e.g., Clunies-Ross, 1979; Hanson, 1977). In the Piper and Pless (1980) study, 37 Down syndrome infants (CA<24 mos.) were assigned to one of two groups, an intervention group and a nonintervention control group. The 21 infants assigned to the intervention group received center-based, twice-weekly one-hour therapy for six months. Stimulation activities were also demonstrated to their parents. At the end of a six-month period, pre-post change scores on the Griffith Scale and on the Caldwell (1978) Home Observation for Measurement of the Environment Inventory for the two groups were compared. Change scores for the group of intervention infants did not differ significantly from those of the control infants.

Piper and Pless (1980) were the first to acknowledge that such a brief and limited intervention may not have constituted an adequate treatment. Others (e.g., Bricker, 1986; Bricker, Carlson & Schwartz, 1981; Meisels, 1985) were quick to agree. As Bricker (1986) has stated, "In the Clunies-Ross (1979) and Hanson (1977) investigations, the length of intervention was considerably longer, the content more comprehensive and the measurement instruments (dependent variable measures) more relevant to the focus of training" (p. 70). Virtually every theory of child development, whether quantitative or qualitative, would require a longer and more intensive period of intervention before any positive effects could be expected in the treatment group. Indeed, had the Piper and Pless (1980) study reported a significant difference between the groups at posttest, one which was not present at pretest and which favored the treatment group, their findings could more appropriately be interpreted as evidence for divine intervention than for early intervention.

Measures of Change

Much of the recent controversy regarding the efficacy of early intervention for disabled children can be traced to the fact that there is disagreement as to what dependent variable measure (or set of measures) should be used. Since the choice of efficacy measure is, in turn, determined largely by one's view of what the goal of early intervention should be, these disagreements can be said to occur as the inevitable result of different conceptual orientations. The interventionist who holds strongly to a Piagetian view will likely insist that an evaluation of effects include pre–post comparison of participants' scores on scales designed to assess sensorimotor performance. On the other hand, those who embrace an eco-behavioral approach will view such changes (or lack of change) as being largely meaningless and insist instead that the focus be upon those skills that are the specific targets of instruction with an accompanying assessment of both maintenance and setting generalization.

A series of articles in the *Archives of Neurology* illustrate this point quite well. In a section of the March 1986 issue entitled *Controversies in Neurology*, Ferry (1986) has stated:

> I submit that most of us who deal with handicapped children are victims of our own good intentions. We engage in neurologic wishful thinking by trying to deny and reverse the permanent, nonfixable nature of most pediatric brain damage. (p. 281)

Later, in a different article in the same series, Russman (1986) cited Piper and Pless (1980) in refutation of "several early studies" that "suggested that cognitive and motor deficits could be enhanced with infant stimulation programs," and concluded that "there are no data that stimulation programs for the infant who either is at risk for, or has a biologically caused disability, can enhance the development of that infant compared with (normal) rearing practices" (p. 283). Hachinski (1986) concluded the series of articles with a brief three-paragraph note wherein he stated, "scant data sustain the objective value of these programs" (p. 283). Clearly these authors have the biologically impaired child in mind, and it would not be fair to extend their criticisms to programs for nonbiologically handicapped children. Nevertheless, either they are ignorant of a significant amount of research recently reviewed by Bricker (1986) and Hanson (1984), or they are focusing upon the failure of most efficacy studies to report data relevant to basic brain physiology. We believe that the latter is the case.

If one begins with a conceptual orientation to treatment that emphasizes the primary importance of specific structures of the brain, then it is only reasonable to insist that evidence of effectiveness include demonstrations of change in brain structure and function. On the other hand, if one begins with a conceptual orientation that assumes a less-than-perfect relationship between brain and behavior (that is, that the developmentally relevant behaviors typically included in the communication, motor, cognition, and social skills areas may change without detectable corresponding alteration in brain physiology), then there is not much reason to include measures other than behavioral. There is a paucity of evidence to suggest that early intervention results in positive alterations in brain physiology; as a result, we agree wholeheartedly with Ferry (1986) who has stated:

> What we as neurologists can do is to redirect the focus of these programs towards the aspects that are helpful, i.e., strengthening the parent-child relationship, improving the communication skills, feeding, posture, ambulation and positioning of these children; and curtailing the development of future behavioral problems. (p. 282)

Such a statement suggests that there is broad-based support for the effectiveness of early intervention and that there is more room for agreement as to what may reasonably be the intervention goals than is often assumed.

Strategies for Summarizing Efficacy Research

As we lack the ability to perform a single critical experiment that could provide an unequivocal answer to the question, Is early intervention effective?, the only way we can approach the issue is by drawing conclusions from previously conducted studies. As White (1986) has put it, "What can be concluded from existing research about the efficacy of early intervention?" (p. 401). White certainly is not the first (nor will he be the last) to examine the literature in an attempt to provide an answer. Numerous other reviews have been published (e.g., Bronfenbrenner, 1975; Filler, Robinson, Vincent-Smith, Bricker, & Bricker, 1975; Hayden & McGinnis,

1977). What is unique about the White (1986) review is the manner in which he and his colleagues at the Utah State University Early Intervention Research Institute have summarized results of their reviews and drawn conclusions.

Typically, reviewers have relied upon some variant of what Light and Smith (1971) have referred to as the *vote-counting* technique. In essence the reviewer tabulates the number of studies that fall into one of three categories; those that demonstrate a significant difference between the intervention group and the comparison group(s) in the predicted direction, those that demonstrate a significant difference between the intervention and the comparison group(s) in the nonpredicted direction, and finally, those studies that fail to detect any significant differences among groups. Typically, conclusions drawn are based upon the simple frequency of studies that fall into each of the three groups with no statistical analysis to determine if, for example, the distribution of frequencies exceeds by a significant degree an assumed distribution of one-third for each category. However, since one would have to assume a degree of homogeneity that rarely exists among studies on a number of dimensions (e.g., sample size), application of such procedures is largely meaningless and could well result in underestimates of overall intervention effectiveness (Hedges & Olkin, 1985).

The Utah State group (Casto & Mastropieri, 1986; White, 1986; White & Casto, 1985) have criticized the conclusions drawn from previous counting reviews and have advocated the use of meta-analysis as a more appropriate technique. Central to the application of meta-analysis is the computation of effect size (ES). More specifically, standardized effect is $(X_E - X_C / SD)$ for each dependent variable experimental and control group comparison for each study included in the review. ES provides a common metric enabling the reviewer to treat each group comparison as if it were a single subject in one of the more traditional group designs. It is then possible to calculate the probability that a mean ES, taken across replicated studies, could have arisen by chance. An application for example, could determine whether or not the mean ES for studies that have intensive parent involvement is significantly greater than the average ES for studies with less intensive emphasis upon parent involvement (e.g., Casto & Mastropieri, 1986).

Utilizing meta-analysis Casto and Mastropieri (1986) computed 215 effect sizes from 74 studies and concluded that

1. Early intervention programs do result in immediate benefits for the handicapped participants.

2. Intervention programs that utilize parents are not more effective than those that do not.
3. The notion that "the earlier the intervention begins the better" cannot be supported.
4. The degree of program structure does not appear to be a strong factor related to outcome measures.

These findings contradict a number of widely held assumptions and run directly counter to the conclusions drawn by other reviewers (e.g., Bricker, 1986; Bronfenbrenner, 1975). It is, therefore, not surprising that they have stimulated considerable interest among early intervention researchers. With this interest has come criticism of the manner in which the Utah State group have applied meta-analysis. Dunst and Snyder (1986), for example, have argued that much of this work is fraught with both conceptual and methodological errors and that, as a result, conclusions such as those drawn by Casto and Mastropieri (1986) are completely unwarranted.

Of course it is only reasonable to expect that findings which run counter to current thought will meet strong criticism, but, in our view, much of the criticism leveled at the Utah State meta-analytic studies (e.g., Casto & Lewis, 1984; Casto & Mastropieri, 1986; White, 1986) is well deserved. Before one can meaningfully apply meta-analysis, one must first formulate a reasonable argument for treating the different independent variable manipulations of different studies as replicates of one another (Dunst & Snyder, 1986). Similarly, it is necessary to identify the logical basis upon which one assumes that the different dependent variable measures of numerous different studies included in the review constitute unrelated measures of a single construct or group of constructs. Failure to meet these assumptions reasonably will greatly increase the likelihood of a Type II error; concluding that there is no effect of a particular treatment when, in fact, there is. Given that the Utah studies typically do not include a convincing explanation concerning the rationale for pooling studies with quite different treatments and dependent variable measures and given that the conclusions drawn often run counter to those of earlier reviews, one must seriously question the validity of their findings. Further, their failure to allow for the possibility of interaction effects (e.g., between severity of disability and outcome measures) as well as their tendency to include studies in the analysis without critical evaluation of the appropriateness of the methodology provide additional bases for questioning their conclusions.

We find less bothersome the criticism that Dunst and Snyder (1986) have leveled at the assumption inherent in most of the meta-analytic reviews, namely that the effects of early intervention should be maintained over long periods of time. They have argued that it is not reasonable to expect that a review yield evidence that the effects of early intervention, once discontinued, be maintained. Others, however (Guess, Horner, Utley, Holvoet, Maxon, Tucker, & Warren, 1978; Sailor & Guess, 1983), have pointed out that the degree to which one can expect a skill to be maintained over time will depend in large part upon the degree to which it is required by daily activities and produces an immediate and motivating effect. If the array of post-intervention environments demands the performance of a previously learned behavior and provides for intrinsic reward, then maintenance should be evident. In other words, whether or not it is reasonable to expect that the effects of early intervention be maintained over time after cessation of programming is largely dependent upon the nature of the intervention target.

Is Early Intervention Effective?

There have been demonstrations that interventions which follow directly from a well-defined theory of child development, are carefully and consistently applied, and which involve parents and primary caregivers, can lead to significant positive changes in a wide range of developmental skills (e.g., Connolly & Russell, 1976; Filler & Kasari, 1981). Positive effects of early intervention have been shown with Down Syndrome children (Clunies-Ross, 1979; Hanson & Schwarz, 1978), children disabled because of genetic anomalies (e.g., Bricker & Dow, 1980), children with cerebral palsy (e.g., Scherzer, Mike, & Illson, 1976), and children with severe multiple handicaps (e.g., Bricker, 1981; Bricker & Dow, 1980; Shearer & Shearer, 1976). With such evidence it would seem at first that there would be little basis for questioning the efficacy of early intervention. Why, then, does this question continue to nag us? We believe that there are several reasons.

First, not all studies of efficacy have found significant differences between groups of disabled children who have participated in early intervention programs and comparison groups of similarly disabled children who have not participated in early intervention programs (e.g., Piper & Pless, 1980). Second, there are studies which report mixed results, that is, that early intervention may result in positive changes in some areas of development but not in others (e.g., Bidder, Bryant, & Gray, 1975; Rynders & Horrobin, 1975). Third, recent reviewers (e.g., Casto & Mastropieri, 1986; White, 1986; White & Casto, 1985) who have utilized meta-analysis as a technique to summarize the results of numerous previous efficacy studies have concluded that the case for early intervention is not nearly so strong as other very well known reviewers (e.g., Bronfenbrenner, 1975) would have us believe.

These results would appear to present considerable confusion. In reality, however, there is not so much room for disagreement as may first appear. If we reject the initial question, Is early intervention effective?, realizing that, as posed, it is no more answerable than is a question like, Is medicine effective? and instead ask, *Can* early intervention be effective? we would find that there is almost no room for disagreement. Early intervention efforts that consist of a well-specified set of operations clearly related to a guiding theory of child development and consistently applied over an appropriate period of time can result in lasting positive changes in those areas of behavior development targeted for change. The validity of the theory, the specificity of the operations, and the nature of the goals all act to determine the degree of effectiveness of any given early intervention program.

One final caution is needed before we conclude our discussion of efficacy. It is important to realize that questions concerning the value of early intervention programs for very young disabled children are rarely asked by the participant parents and professionals, for it is they more than anyone else who witness daily the positive benefits to both children and families. Questions of efficacy often occur in the context of educational policy. They are posed by the policy developers (school boards, state legislatures, and the U.S. Congress) who, as Noel, Burke, and Valdivieso (1985) have pointed out, are largely responsible for defining the parameters of what we know as public education. At the heart of this process is the determination of funding levels. Funds are not likely to be forthcoming unless a convincing argument can be made that the programs they support will result in significant benefits to the participants. Those who live in the political climate of competing interests tend not to be very tolerant of overly complex and qualified answers. Parents and professionals alike are thus faced with the need to simplify. In our attempt to eliminate the gray areas we must be even more cautious than the researcher in guarding against a Type II error. To say that there is only questionable evidence to support the case for early intervention, when in fact, early intervention programs may result in lasting positive benefits runs the risk of eliminating the option for thousands of young children and their families. On the other hand, overly optimistic claims for what can be accomplished (Type I error) could result in the establishment of many early intervention programs that are only minimally effective. In public policy, as in applied research, where the consequences of a conclusion will have significant impact on access to treatment, we must be particularly careful to guard against a Type II error. We believe that it is better to provide the resources to ensure program access for all handicapped children and families, knowing that not all programs will be effective, than it is to risk denying access to children in need of such services.

PUBLIC LAW 99-457

In October 1986, President Ronald Reagan signed into law one of the most far-reaching and significant sets of provisions ever to affect services to young disabled children, the Education of the Handicapped Act Amendments of 1986 (Public Law 99-457, 1986). This legislation authorizes, for the first time, federal assistance to states for the development and delivery of educational and related services, to all handicapped children from birth to age 6 years. It is interesting to note that, while much of the discussion that accompanied its passage through the House and Senate was focused upon specific provisions, there was an almost total absence of any criticism regarding the effectiveness of early intervention. Members of Congress, parents, and expert witnesses testifying before various committees all agreed that a major federal investment in early intervention was both needed and warranted by the available efficacy literature. As stated in the report (U.S. House of Representatives, 1986) to accompany H.R. 5520 (which ultimately became Public Law 99-457):

> More specifically, testimony and research indicate that early intervention and preschool services accomplish the following:
> 1) help enhance intelligence in some children;
> 2) produce substantial gains in physical development, cognitive development, language and speech development, psychosocial development and self-help skills;
> 3) help prevent the development of secondary handicapping conditions;
> 4) reduce family stress;
> 5) reduce societal dependency and institutionalization;
> 6) reduce the need for special class placement in special education programs once children reach school age; and
> 7) save substantial costs to society and our nation's schools. (p. 5)

Nevertheless, since the passage of the law several important issues surrounding implementation have arisen. To understand the nature of these issues it becomes necessary to examine first some of the major provisions of the law. Since the rules and regulations that will govern the administration of Public Law 99-457 have, as yet, not been published we are unclear as to what clarifying effect they may have.

Part H Provisions

Public Law 99-457 provides a new Part H for Public Law 94-142. These amendments describe the development and establishment of a statewide system of identification of and service delivery to handicapped infants and toddlers (birth to 3 years of age). The definition of the eligible population is deliberately broad and stipulates only that children in the birth to 3 years age range who are "developmentally delayed" or have conditions that typically result in delay, or who are "at risk" of substantial delay, shall be included. By September 1, 1991, all states participating must make available appropriate early intervention services to all handicapped infants and toddlers residing within the state. Appropriate early intervention services are defined minimally to include special education, speech and language development and audiology, occupational therapy, physical therapy, psychological services, parent and family training and counseling services, transition services, and medical services both for diagnostic purposes and, when necessary, for enabling the child to benefit from other early intervention services. All services must be provided at no cost to the parents except where state law provides for a system of payments, including provision for sliding fee schedule. Funds to support Part H activities are allocated to states based upon census estimates of the number of children birth to 3 years of age. Fifty million dollars was allocated by Congress for fiscal year 1987 and $70 million for fiscal year 1988 to support Part H programs.

Several problem areas inherent in the Part H provisions are apparent. First, because Congress has decided to allow each individual state to develop its own definition of "developmental delay" and to establish its own list of criteria for "at risk," it is quite possible that considerable variation will exist from state to state. Should the possibility of definitional variation become a reality, then a family of a child who is eligible for services in one state may find that their child is ineligible for services in another state, necessitating that they examine very carefully the impact of, for example, a job-related relocation. The dilemmas posed by the prospect of developing eligibility standards will be most evident in the 44 states that do not already have a special education mandate to serve children from birth.

A second problem area is focused upon the latitude which states are allowed in determination of the lead agency and the designation of individual service providers. A recent survey (March 1987) of the State Directors of Special Education and the National Association of State Directors of Special Education (NASDSE) found that 26 states that responded had already designated a lead agency. Fewer than half (11) indicated that the lead agency would be the Department of Public Instruction (public schools). Fifteen states had already decided that the lead agency would be either Public Health, Mental Health, or Developmental Disabilities.

Most often such decisions are based solely upon already defined areas of responsibility. In our state (Idaho), for example, the agency responsible for coordinating services to disabled children birth to five years of age is the Department of Health and Welfare. It is not surprising then that the Department of Health and Welfare has been designated to be the lead agency for Part H programs, particularly since public schools have neither been mandated to provide nor have they chosen to initiate discretionary programs for handicapped children below the age of five years. The problem arises when one considers the number of probable program transitions a family may experience over a five-year period.

The first transition is likely to occur when the child moves from a primarily home-based program to either a part- or full-time center-based program. For many children this transition will certainly occur during the first three years and could well entail the transfer of program responsibility from one service provider to another. A second transition is likely to occur when the child reaches age 3 and the lead agency responsibility shifts to the Department of Public Instruction as required by Section 619 of the law. While it is possible that the needs of the child will dictate continuation of the existing program, it is more likely that services will be provided by a different service provider (perhaps the local public schools) since at this age all of the requirements of Public Law 94-142 (1975) apply, including the least restrictive environment provision. Yet a third transition may occur for those children not previously served in public school programs once they reach the state-mandated age for public school inclusion. Given the possibility of at least two and as many as four program transitions, the Part H provision that there be a carefully developed and well-coordinated Individualized Family Service Plan with clearly delineated procedures for transition assumes extreme importance.

A third area of the Part H provisions that will be the focus of much discussion and debate is centered upon the necessity of qualified personnel. Part H requires that each state participating maintain a comprehensive system of personnel development and appropriate standards for qualified personnel who will provide services for birth to 3-year-old handicapped children. While most states currently have standards for personnel who work with disabled infants and toddlers, these standards are often minimal when compared to the standards required of personnel who serve children included in the Public Law 94-142 (1975) mandate. The development of both inservice and university-based preservice plans for personnel development will be one of the first tasks facing participating states. It will be complicated by the fact that there is already a nationwide shortage of qualified special education teachers and resources for program expansion at the university level are extremely scarce.

New 619 Provisions

Title II of Public Law 99-457 provides an amended Section 619 for Public Law 94-142 that, in effect, extends all of the rights and provisions of Public Law 94-142 (EHA) to handicapped children ages three through five years in school year 1990–91. To assist in the accomplishment of this goal additional federal funds have been authorized to be distributed to states that have submitted approved plans according to two formulas. For children 3 through 5 years of age who have not previously been served, a maximum of $3,800 per child has been authorized for each child for the first year of service. These funds are intended to be available to each newly served child for one year for a four-year period beginning in school year 1987–88. For each child served during the previous school year, $300 was authorized for fiscal year 1987, which increases to an amount equal to $1000 per year per child by fiscal year 1990. This program must be administered by the state education agency in consort with local education agencies. However, contracts that provide for a broad range of services are allowed with other agencies and service providers.

Whereas compliance with the provisions of Part H is totally voluntary, there are specific sanctions that will be applied to those states which have not complied with the new 619 provisions by school year 1990–91. No state not in compliance by school year 1990–91 may receive: (a) funds authorized under the preschool grant program, (b) funds generated under Part B of the Public Law 94-142 (1975) formula for children three to six years of age, and (c) grants and contracts related to preschool special education authorized in Parts C through G of Public Law 94-142. Should actual appropriations of funds fail to meet the authorized level of 656 million dollars by fiscal year 1990, the full service mandate is extended until school year 1991–92.

There will be many issues that arise as states attempt to implement the provisions of the new Section 619. One of the most important that has already emerged involves the least restrictive environment mandate contained in Public Law 94-142. States which serve 3- through 5-year-old children will have to ensure that these children are afforded the same range of least restrictive placement options as are afforded to handicapped children above the age of 6 years. This requirement presents a considerable challenge to the more than 30 states that do not already provide mandated services to handicapped children by age 3. The lack of public school classrooms for nonhandicapped children will mean that private daycare centers and preschools, as well as existing Head Start programs may provide the only options for integration. In developing state plans, great care will have to be taken to include as wide a range of placement options as possible, while at the same time assuring that program quality (including personnel qualifications) is not compromised. This can be a difficult task, particularly when one considers that, as Osowski (1987) has pointed out, many such programs do not meet state educational standards. In addition, private programs as well as such public programs as Head Start may well perceive the prospect of an additional infusion of handicapped children to constitute a threat to the integrity of the existing focus of the program. While some (e.g., Garwood, 1987) argue that the least restrictive environment mandate "was not the driving issue" in the passage of Public Law 99-457, it is, nevertheless, one that will perplex parents and professionals alike for a long time to come.

The Challenge of Public Law 99-457

It should be apparent that the provisions of PL 99-457 present a considerable challenge to parents and service providers alike. Congress has created a very significant piece of enabling legislation that will require the best efforts of all concerned if it is to translate into wider program access for families and children. Since funding for both Part H and Section 619 are tied directly to child count, it will be necessary to project figures as accurately as possible. Balance must be reached between those forces which urge a conservative approach for fear of overestimating (for example, the number of children currently unserved but to be served in the next school year) and those forces that urge liberal counts to insure maximal funding. In areas of the country where the law has allowed for charges to families for services to 3- to 6-year-old disabled children, the transition to free appropriate public education will be painful, particularly if the promised funding levels are not realized. In addition, the temptation to designate a single agency as either the primary or sole service provider will have to be resisted as will the simplistic adoption of a limited range of service options. For example, in some rural states like Idaho there has already been a tendency to conceive of the service to newborn to 3-year-old children as primarily home based and the service to 3- to 6-year-old children as primarily center based. Such decisions should be made only after there has been a careful inventory of all of the resources and options available in each community. This information must then be evaluated in light of the needs of families and children. To do less would be to deny the intent of the law.

PARENT/FAMILY ROLE IN EARLY INTERVENTION

Public Law 99-457 acknowledges and ensures that parent involvement is a necessary component of early intervention programs. Historically, parent involvement has been defined as participation in group meetings, direct instruction of children, and attendance at Individualized

Education Program planning meetings. There are research findings that support the value of parental participation in the maintenance and generalization of programming objectives to the home and other settings (Bronfenbrenner, 1975; Filler & Kasari, 1981; Shearer & Shearer, 1976). It is evident that whenever parents elect to involve themselves in teaching and maintaining objectives, the outcome is reflected in child progress. However, the key phrase is "when parents elect to become involved." Not all parents choose to act as teachers of their handicapped children or to attend parent meetings. Some parents now question the rationale which seems to imply that those who do not commit to active involvement in teaching their children are somehow responsible for diminishing their child's opportunity for growth towards his or her full potential (Turnbull & Turnbull, 1982). Other concerned parents write of the burden placed upon them by the educational community and have pointed to the needs of other children in their family, burn-out, and guilt caused by failure to meet expectations for teaching their child (Featherstone, 1981).

Simultaneously, early interventionists and teachers often express their frustration and concern over a lack of parent involvement. Teachers complain of declining interest in skill building, poor attendance at meetings, and failure of parents to continue ongoing intervention programs at home. By these standards, parent involvement seems to be limited to those parents who have the time, energy, and inclination towards the particular options that a program offers. As Dunst (1985) has pointed out, parents often have been subtly viewed as doing less than their duty. The need for a change in strategies for involving parents is evident.

The effectiveness of parental involvement will depend upon many of the same factors discussed in this chapter in relation to efficacy. Often there is a tendency to embrace the constructs of an approach (e.g., family systems) without understanding of or adherence to its theoretical premises. Little effort is made to obtain evidence of the relationship between various approaches and child change data. Those favoring a family approach to early intervention are proclaiming the need to broaden our focus to include the entire family unit as the target of intervention (e.g., Dunst, 1985). As this broadening occurs, care must be taken to examine the application of various conceptual orientations or theories to early intervention with disabled children.

There are several conceptual orientations that are especially applicable to families with young handicapped children. These include the systems approaches (Bowen, 1978; Haley, 1973, 1976; Minuchin, 1974), family-stress theories (Burr, 1973; Hill, 1949; McCubbin et al., 1980), and stress-adaptation orientations (Farran, Metzger, & Sparling, 1986). Each approach discusses areas relevant to the circumstances facing the family with a young disabled child.

Family-Systems Theory

Most systems approaches are predicated on the assumption that the family is a unit in which all the various subparts are interconnected. Intervention with one part of that system affects all other parts as well as their interaction. In order to produce change, interventionists who hold to a systems-theory approach attempt to identify patterns of interaction and suggest new patterns to the family when a problem is identified.

Foster, Berger, and McLean (1981) were among the first to move towards a systemic approach to services for handicapped infants and young children. They suggested that due to the interrelatedness of family members, an intervention with a child or a parent is an intervention into the entire family system. Consequently, it becomes important for early interventionists to understand and build upon the existing strengths within the family. Further, professionals should work through the existing power structure in the family, making sure not to displace the parents' position as authorities and thereby enhancing the likelihood of cooperation in home programs.

Turnbull, Brotherson, and Summers (1986) isolate the components of a family system and their application to programs for families with handicapped members. They describe the family function, structure, interaction, life cycle, and the importance of each when planning for family goals. Particular emphasis is placed upon the family's movement through the life cycle.

A concern with the use of any systems approach, without careful analysis of the implications of its application to families with handicapped children, is that the methods associated with the theory have a family therapy orientation. A family who seeks therapy does so because of a problem and is requesting suggestions for change. The family with a handicapped child oftentimes is not seeking therapy, and therefore many of the therapeutic techniques integral to family therapy may not work when applied to these families. Their need for professional expertise stems primarily from the fact that a family member has been newly diagnosed as handicapped or disabled. Thus, while systems theory is useful when conceptualizing families undergoing a crisis (which demands that the system adapt), some of the strategies or therapeutic methods used in the systems approach may not translate to general use with families of handicapped children.

The recognition of the family as an interactive unit is particularly appealing given that intervention goals often include infant-caregiver interaction, or strategies for enhancing the living environment of the home. Early interventionists often ask the family to begin not only the process of assimilation and adaptation to a disabled member but also encourage the assumption of new routines and responsibilities associated with that person's needs. This new demand can place additional strain on other areas and requires adaptation within the system. Being able to identify these changes and discuss their impact upon previous patterns and responses of the system may assist a service provider in helping the family move through the process of adaptation. Further, service providers can be more circumspect when they suggest change to a family that is already struggling to accommodate and adapt.

Identifying family characteristics has been the substance of much of the work done by Olson and McCubbin and their colleagues (Olson et al., 1985). A series of assessment tools have been developed to evaluate family adaptation/cohesion, coping, and stress. These assessments are beginning to be utilized in early intervention programs for disabled children. However, care must be taken to avoid the supposition that the purpose of family assessment is to identify deficits in the family and thereby select areas which need to be "fixed." Olson et al. (1985) have normed their instruments on non-maladaptive populations. They have designed their assessments to assist in the development of a family portrait or profile, which the interventionist uses first to clarify a family's unique characteristics and subsequently to build on the strengths and resources identified during the assessment process. Family-focused programs can be as individualized as the instructional programming provided in the classroom for the child. Assessment of family resources and needs can be conducted and family goals established based on particular characteristics of that family unit. Several model demonstration programs throughout the nation have incorporated family-systems theory into the family goal-setting process (e.g., Bailey et al., 1986; Dunst, 1985; Gentry & Olson, 1986). The materials generated by these projects may provide a good framework for the development of the Individualized Family Service Plan described in PL 99-457.

Family-Stress Theory

Family-stress theory shows great promise in its applicability to families with handicapped members. Stress theory has much of its foundation in Hill's (1949) classic research on war-induced separation and reunion in families. In his A,B,C,X formulation, Hill outlined several major variables and discussed their interrelationship. From this perspective:

> A (the event and related hardships) interact with B (the family's crisis meeting resources) interacting with C (the definition the family makes of the event), which produces X (the crisis and associated stress). (Hill, 1958, p. 141)

McCubbin and Patterson (1982) extend the original theory to include the phenomenon of "pile-up" of stressors, which can result in an additional need for adjustment or adaptation within the system. From their observations and data collected in a longitudinal study of families facing Vietnam-war separation, they concluded that the coping efforts of families can produce additional stress. Families, attempting to manage a crisis, experience a "pile-up" of stressors over time as a result of (a) the hardships inherent in the original stressful event, (b) normal change and development of family members over time, and (c) the trial-and-error methods to manage the situation. The effect of a singular event such as the birth of a handicapped child is affected by the resources the family has available and their perception of the fact that their child is diagnosed as disabled or handicapped, which in turn produces a crisis. (Crisis here is defined as a circumstance to which the family system must adjust or adapt.) In addition, as the family uses coping strategies to successfully negotiate adjustment, there is a "pile-up" of other stressors that occurs, thereby creating the potential for additional stress.

The existence of "pile-up" stressors may influence a family's willingness to participate in programs critical to their infant's development. If early interventionists are merely the fourth phone call of the day from professionals seeking to offer service, a family is more likely to be nonresponsive, thereby protecting themselves from yet another issue to which they must adapt. Accordingly, interventionists must be sensitive to the possibility of "pile-up" and work to improve interdisciplinary cooperation among the numerous agencies and professions involved with the young handicapped child.

McCubbin et al. (1980) suggest that the purpose of adjustment after crisis is to reduce or eliminate the disruptiveness in the family system. Family adaptation can be achieved when the discrepancy between demands on the family unit and its resources are reconciled or reduced to a minimum (Melson, 1980). The family of the handicapped infant or young child must undergo many periods of adjustment in response to the infant's development and diagnosis, the family's resources, and the normal transitions over the life cycle of all families. It becomes the task of the interventionist to assist with the process of reducing the discrepancy between resources and demand in order that successful adaptation can occur. Early intervention programs can either provide or assist the family in acquiring the resources necessary to meet crises or to reduce demands until adjustment can occur or additional resources can be located.

The parent-professional partnership is one of ongoing interaction that should be responsive to the current demands upon the system. In some cases the expectations of the professional may require revision in order to

maintain parental willingness to participate. This flexibility and responsiveness to changes in the system will minimize the occurrence in which
the interventionist adds to the "pile-up" of stressors already being juggled
by the family.

Two research studies have focused on the area of stress of the family
of a handicapped child. Wikler (1986) categorizes the major research studies of the last 20 years according to Hill's (1949) *ABCX* model. She reviews
the research effects in each of the *ABCX* components, concluding that the
field has barely begun to examine the factors that influence a family's
adaptive process. Peterson and Lippa (1978) operationalized each of the
ABCX components and then studied the interaction between *A, B, C,* and
X factors. They found the stressor *A,* when interacting with *B* and *C* factors,
is positively correlated with the outcome *X* ($r = .37\ p < .01$). However,
when *B* (family resources) and *C* (family perception) were removed from
the analysis, the relationship between the stressor *A* and outcome *X*
dropped from +.37 to −.02. Wikler (1986), researching the impact of
stress on families at different points of transition throughout the life cycle,
found that the normal transitions that occur in a family due to the progression through the events associated with the life cycle are stressful periods in which the effect of a handicapped child upon the family can be
compounded.

These two studies point the way for more research but the need for
commitment to research from a common theoretical basis is required if an
in-depth understanding of family adaptation is to occur.

Stress-adaptation Theory

The stress-adaptation model (Farran, Metzger, & Sparling, 1986)
compliments the multiple *ABCX* Stress Model discussed above, by emphasizing the process in which families engage as they cope with the stress of
a disruptive event. This model has also been applied to families of handicapped persons. Farran et al. (1986) indicate that "if service providers and
policy makers understand the way an event exerts its influence, they can
intervene earlier in the process of adaptation" (p. 151). They claim that
there are at least two foci for intervention: (1) to reduce the number of
changes a family must undergo, and (2) to assist the parents to adapt
through such efforts as parent groups and individual counseling.

In our view, Farran's insistence that interventionists understand the
actions associated with adaptation within a family system is commenda-
ble. However, suggestions that the family participate in support groups
and/or counseling is limiting the family to only one strategy associated
with crisis adaptation. There is the possibility that the family will be more

successful in dealing with stress and determining a method for adaptation from an internal rather than external perspective. A family may already have some reservoir of resources (Hill's variable B) that they have used to cope with and adapt to previous stress producing events. In such situations intervention must start with what is already in existence and involve the determination of need for additional resources. Efforts to categorize the process families follow while adapting to stressors associated with the presence of a handicapped member could lead to the same difficulties surrounding traditional parent-involvement techniques where well-intentioned professionals identify a series of general strategies for helping parents, rather than individualize helping strategies based upon the unique characteristics of each family.

From the perspective of adaptation theory, the role of the interventionist must emphasize facilitation. This process should include:

1. An evaluation and enumeration of existing family resources (Hill's B variable).
2. An accounting and documentation of the family's perception of the impact of the handicapping condition (Hill's C variable) through self-report and assessment.
3. A delineation of family needs for accommodating the handicapped member and adapting to the ongoing demands that will be placed upon the system over time.
4. An agreed-upon strategy for evaluating progress in the adaptive process.

In order to achieve these steps, reliable measures must be developed. Although there are numerous quality efforts underway to assess family resources and perceptions (e.g., Dunst, 1985; McCubbin et al., 1980; Peterson & Lippa, 1978; Wikler, 1986), there is no convenient way of comparing results among the various studies. Efforts must be undertaken to operationalize family resources in a manner that will allow for cross-study comparison (Wikler, 1986). Equally important is the need to examine the relationship between measures of family adaptation and measures of child change.

The following case study illustrates the use of these theoretical approaches when working with families of handicapped children.

The Scott family is a young couple living in a rural community. They have been married ten years and have a 10-month-old boy. They have extended family members living in the same vicinity. Both pairs of grandparents and several siblings of each live within a radius of ten miles. The father is employed as a cook at a local restaurant and the mother works as a nurse's aide at the local hospital from 3:00 to 11:00 p.m. Because of their work schedules the father takes a very active role in child care and home activities. The couple is hopeful that the father will be able to quit his job soon and start a computer consulting business. The mother will need to stay employed to assist him in this venture.

The Scott family has been told by their physician that their child is developing at a slower rate than normal and the physical characteristics suggest the possibility of a genetic disability. A neurological evaluation is recommended but the family must wait until they are eligible for financial assistance through Medicaid before they can afford the evaluation. In addition, the physician is suggesting that many of the physical health problems experienced by the infant may be due to allergies. She suggests the family use a milk substitute, position the baby differently before and after feeding, and provide smaller, more frequent meals. Finally she refers the family to an early intervention program for a full developmental assessment.

The assessment reveals a delay of 6 months in the fine-motor, communication, and cognitive domains. During the assessment both parents express their feelings regarding their son's prognosis. Father believes the "problem" to be related to potential allergies, and he has already "noticed improvement since the change in diet and feeding activities." Mother feels less certain and is worried about the fact that their baby "looks different." She believes they should have the genetic evaluation. She indicates that her parents support her in this position.

The early interventionist who does not consider the needs of the entire system and those of its members would be more inclined to suggest the immediate beginning of fine motor, social, and communication programs in the home. These efforts would frequently be supported by a couple of the Scotts' description since they are eager to assume any activities or responsibilities that might help their child. Their eagerness is even more pronounced because they must wait for a neurological evaluation until financial assistance is forthcoming.

First, it is critical to assess the current tasks in which the family is engaged prior to assigning more responsibilities to the family. The family is already engaged in changing the baby's feeding schedule and diet, which may mean a major adjustment. The added task of intervention may be too time-consuming for the family. Instead, suggestions that integrate intervention into existing family routine for a short period each day might lessen the burden on the family and prevent the cycle of guilt and failures parents can experience when they fail to follow a professional's recommendations (Foster et al., 1981).

Another factor to consider when introducing intervention strategies into the home is the level of stress already present and the level of acceptance demonstrated by the parent. In the Scott case the father is placing great emphasis upon the relationship between allergies and the developing delay. His energy is directed towards changing and evaluating food intake and feeding procedures. Formal intervention programs may be interpreted to mean that he must agree to the possibility of problems other than those that are diet related. Another factor to consider is that the possible dissent between the mother's and the father's opinion regarding the potential handicap may be exaggerated by a forced-choice circumstance in which the mother decides to do formal intervention and the father is opposed.

Finally, the couple may be experiencing tension owing to the potential delay or altering of their plans for employment and financial stability. The mother may not be able to work full time and meet her child's needs in a manner satisfactory to her. The father may be reluctant to give up financial security when medical bills are looming. This may result in a major disappointment that will influence their relationship to each other and to the infant and their overall self-esteem.

It is desirable to assess the resources of the family, and examine the possible interpretations being placed upon the stressful event (*ABCX* Model approach, Hill, 1949). From a resource standpoint the family has time and energy to commit to the baby, but some is currently directed towards feeding and diet, not including the normal caregiving activities associated with a 10-month-old. Their financial resources are, however, a limiting factor, prolonging the period of indecision prior to further testing and possible diagnosis.

The interpretation the parents place upon the event is mixed: the father feels it is health/diet related; the mother is able to admit that developmental delay and possible genetic disability may be present. Because of the lack of agreement in interpretation, the couple will need time to resolve their individual feelings and differences.

In terms of pile-up of stressors (Double *ABCX* Model, McCubbin & Patterson, 1982), there are two sets of factors to consider. The family is moving into the child-rearing stage from the couple phase. This constitutes a major transition and is stress-producing. Family routines, styles of interaction, family norms or rules, and time commitments must all be renegotiated. A second major pile-up stressor is the financial pressure and the delay of self-employment status.

The interventionist must seek to maintain services to the child without further disruption to the system. At some point the interventionist becomes an additional pile-up stressor. There is little that can be done to avoid this intrusion, but the stress can be minimized by careful planning of intervention strategies and sensitivity to the current state of the family.

In summary, the conceptual approaches described above appear to constitute a very real and important addition to traditional efforts directed toward family involvement. Early intervention programs will be improved through adherence to a position that (1) acknowledges the interrelatedness of family members, (2) recognizes the need to minimize actions that contribute to the pile-up of family stressors associated with assimilating a new member, and (3) identifies family adaptation as a desired outcome of intervention. However, as these approaches to family involvement are developed and applied, it is critical to validate their effectiveness with research. Such research should first be focused upon a determination of the degree to which successful application of procedures derived from various theoretical approaches are related to measure of child change; only then should a determination be made of the degree to which family involvement can be demonstrated to cause change in measures of child progress.

SUMMARY AND CONCLUSIONS

Undoubtedly questions concerning the efficacy of intervention will continue to be raised for a long time to come. Such will be the inevitable outcome of both consumer and professional efforts to extend downward to birth the protections of Public Law 94-142 (1975). Educational programs for very young handicapped children cannot hope to escape the close scrutiny that is being cast upon all of American education, nor should they hope to. There is clearly an abundance of evidence to indicate that early intervention *can* be effective. That is enough reason to ensure program access for all children in need. Certainly there is the necessity to respond to those who raise such questions, but in the future, it should be the task of parents and practitioners to do so. Those engaged in research to extend our knowledge should, as Dunst and Snyder (1986) have argued, remain focused upon discoveries which will allow for a determination of those aspects of early intervention programs that are most effective. We believe that it is important that such research reflect an awareness of the necessity to include measures of child change in the list of dependent variables. To find a measure, or set of measures, sensitive to the gradual changes that one can realistically expect may well be the first task. Most available norm-referenced scales of development are inappropriate for a variety of reasons.

The awareness that early intervention programs can result in significant lasting positive benefits to young disabled children is central to Public Law 99-457 (1986). While this law holds considerable promise for literally thousands of families, it also presents a number of implementation dilemmas. States will have to resist the temptation to use new funds simply to underwrite already existing services or to adopt simplistic single models for service delivery. It is no more justifiable to serve all 3- to 6-year-old disabled children in segregated centers than it is to serve all 10- to 21-year-old students in segregated schools. Similarly, to rely only upon existing models of service delivery is to deny the fact that in many areas of this country there are no out-of-home child care services for young children at all.

Available efficacy research as well as the requirements of Public Law 99-457 point to the central role of the family in early intervention programs for young disabled children. Not long ago interventionists viewed the family and its role in the intervention process in a narrowly circumscribed manner. Involvement meant training and that training most often focused upon the mother or primary caregiver who was expected to act like a teacher at home. There are now a number of alternative models for family involvement which emphasize that a family is a dynamic system consisting of numerous members. It is a system that must adapt to a range of events, the existence of a handicapped or disabled child being only one. It is important that the interventionist perceive his or her role as one that has impact on the entire system. To the degree that the effect is to reduce stress and encourage adaptation, it is reasonable to expect that the direct benefits to the disabled child will be enhanced. However, it is important that we recognize that there is currently a paucity of research to indicate that family-systems approaches are any more beneficial to the long-term development of the child than were the parent-training approaches of years past. About all that can safely be concluded at this point is that they seem to offer considerable promise.

REFERENCES

Bailey, D., Simeonsson, R., Winton, P., Huntington, G., Comfort, M., Isbell, P., O'Donnell, K., & Helm, J. (1986). Family focused intervention: A functional model for planning, implementing and evaluating individualized family services in early intervention. *Journal of the Division of Early Childhood, 10* (2), 156–171.

Bailey, D. D., & Wolery, M. (1984). *Teaching infants and preschoolers with handicaps.* Columbus, OH: Merrill.

Bidder, R. T., Bryant, G., & Gray, O. P. (1975). Benefits to Down's syndrome children through training their mothers. *Archives of Disease in Childhood, 50,* 383–386.

Bowen, M. (1978). *Family therapy and clinical practice: The collected papers of Murray Bowen, M.D.* New York: Jason Aronson.

Bricker, D. (1981). *A handicapped children's early education program: Rationale, program description, and impact* (Final report). Division of Innovation and Development, Office of Special Education, Eugene, OR.

Bricker, D. (1986). *Early education of at-risk and handicapped infants, toddlers and preschool children.* Glenville, IL: Scott, Foresman.

Bricker, D., Carlson, L., & Schwarz, R. (1981). A discussion of early intervention for infants with Down's syndrome. *Pediatrics, 67,* 45–46.

Bricker, D., & Dow, M. (1980). Early intervention with the young severely handicapped child. *Journal of the Association for the Severely Handicapped, 5,* 130–142.

Bronfenbrenner, U. (1975). Is early intervention effective? In B. Friedlander, G. Sterritt, & G. Kirks (Eds.), *Exceptional infant: Assessment and intervention* (Vol. 3, pp. 449–475). New York: Brunner/Mazel.

Burr, W. F. (1973). *Theory construction and the sociology of the family.* New York: Wiley.

Caldwell, B. (1978). *Home observation for measurement of the environment.* Syracuse, NY: Syracuse University Press.

Casto, G., & Lewis, A. (1984). Parent involvement in infant and preschool programs. *Journal of the Division for Early Childhood, 9,* 49–56.

Casto, G., & Mastropieri, M. (1986). The efficacy of early intervention: A meta-analysis. *Exceptional Children, 52*(5), 417–424.

Clunies-Ross, G. (1979). Accelerating the development of Down's syndrome infants and young children. *Journal of Special Education, 13,* 169–177.

Connolly, B., & Russell, F. (1976). Interdisciplinary early intervention program. *Physical Therapy, 56*(2), 155–158.

Dunst, C. J. (1981). *Infant learning: A cognitive-linguistic intervention strategy.* Hingham, MA: Teaching Resources.

Dunst, C. J. (1985). Rethinking early intervention. *Analysis and Intervention in Developmental Disabilities, 5,* 165–201.

Dunst, C. J. (1986). Overview of the efficacy of early intervention programs: Methodological and conceptual considerations. In L. Bickman & D. Weatherford (Eds.), *Evaluating early intervention programs for severely handicapped children and their families* (pp. 165–201). Austin, TX: PRO-ED.

Dunst, C. J., & Snyder, S. (1986). A critique of the Utah State University early intervention meta-analysis research. *Exceptional Children, 53,* 269–279.

Farran, D. C., Metzger, J., & Sparling, J. (1986). Immediate and continuing adaptations in parents of handicapped children. In J. Gallagher & P. Vietze (Eds.), *Families of handicapped persons* (pp. 143–163). Baltimore, MD: Paul H. Brooks.

Featherstone, H. (1981). *A difference in the family: Living with a disabled child.* New York: Penguin Books.

Ferry, D. C. (1986). Infant stimulation programs: A neurological shell game? *Archives of Neurology, 43*(3), 281–282.

Filler, J. (1983). Service models for handicapped infants. In G. Garwood, and R. Fewell (Eds.), *Educating handicapped infants* (pp. 369–387). Rockville, MD: Aspen.

Filler, J., & Kasari, C. (1981). Acquisition, maintenance and generalization of parent taught skills with two severely handicapped infants. *Journal of the Association for the Severely Handicapped, 6*, 30–38.

Filler, J., Robinson, C., Vincent-Smith, L., Bricker, D., & Bricker, W. (1975). Mental retardation. In N. Hobbs (Ed.), *Issues in the classification of children* (Vol. 1, pp. 194–239). San Francisco, CA: Jossey-Bass.

Foster, M., Berger, M., and McLean, M. (1981). Rethinking a good idea: A reassessment of parent involvement. *Topics in Early Childhood Special Education, 1*(3), 55–65.

Garwood, G. (1987). Quoted from *The Biweekly Newsletter on Programs for Early Childhood Development, 19*(4). Alexandria, VA: Capitol Publications.

Gentry, D., & Adams, G. (1978). A curriculum-based direct intervention approach to the education of handicapped infants. In N. Haring & D. Bricker (Eds.), *Teaching the severely handicapped* (Vol. 3, pp. 89–102). Columbus, OH: Special Press.

Gentry, D., and Olson, J. (1986). *The parent family support network series, monographs, I, II, III, and IV.* Moscow, ID: University of Idaho.

Guess, D., Horner, D., Utley, B., Holvoet, J., Maxon, D., Tucker, D., & Warren, S. (1978). A functional curriculum sequencing model for teaching the severely handicapped. *AAESPH Review, 3*, 202–215.

Hachinski, V. (1986). Infant stimulation programs. *Archives of Neurology, 43*(3), 283.

Haley, J. (1973). *Uncommon therapy.* New York: W. W. Norton.

Haley, J. (1976). *Problem-solving therapy.* San Francisco: Jossey-Bass.

Hanson, M. (1977). *Teaching your Down's syndrome infant: A guide for parents.* Baltimore, MD: University Park Press.

Hanson, M. (1984). Effects of early intervention. In M. Hanson (Ed.), *Atypical infant development* (pp. 385–407). Baltimore, MD: University Park Press.

Hanson, M., & Schwarz, R. (1978). Results of a longitudinal intervention program for Down's syndrome infants and their families. *Education and Training of the Mentally Retarded, 13*(4), 403–407.

Hayden, A., & McGinnis, G. (1977). Basis for early intervention. In E. Sontag, J. Smith, & N. Certo (Eds.), *Educational programming for the severely and profoundly handicapped* (pp. 153–166). Reston, VA: Council for Exceptional Children.

Hedges, L. V., & Olkin, I. (1985). *Statistical methods for meta analysis.* Orlando, FL: Academic Press.

Hill, R. (1949). *Families under stress.* New York: Harper & Row.

Hill, R. (1958). Generic features of families under stress. *Social Casework, 39*, 139–150.

Light, R. J., & Smith, P. V. (1971). Accumulative evidence: Procedures for resolving contradictions among different research studies. *Harvard Educational Review,* *41,* 429–471.

McCubbin, H., Joy, C., Cauble, E., Comeau, J., Patterson, J., & Needle, R. (1980). Family stress and coping: A decade review. *Journal of Marriage and the Family,* *42*(4), 855–872.

McCubbin, H., & Patterson, J. (1982). Family adaptation to crises. In H. McCubbin, E. Cauble, & J. Patterson (Eds.), *Family stress, coping, and social support* (pp. 29–43). Springfield, IL: Charles C. Thomas.

Meisels, S. (1985). The efficacy of early intervention: Why are we still asking these questions? *Topics in Early Childhood Special Education, 5*(2), 1–12.

Melson, G. F. (1980). *Family and environment: An ecosystems approach.* Minneapolis, MN: Burgess.

Minuchin, S. (1974). *Families and family therapy.* Cambridge, MA: Harvard University Press.

Montalvo, B., & Haley, J. (1973). In defense of child therapy. *Family Process, 12,* 227–244.

Noel, M. M., Burke, P. J., & Valdivieso, C. (1985). Educational policy and severe mental retardation. In D. Bricker & J. Filler (Eds.), *Severe mental retardation: From theory to practice* (pp. 12–36). Reston, VA: Council for Exceptional Children.

Olson, D., McCubbin, H., Barnes, H., Larsen, A., Maxen, M., & Wilson, M. (1985). *Families: What makes them work.* Beverly Hills: Sage.

Osowski, J. (1987). Quoted from the *Biweekly Newsletter on Programs for Early Childhood Development, 19*(4). Alexandria, VA: Capitol Publications.

Peterson, H., & Lippa, S. (1978). *Life cycle encountered by families of developmentally disabled children: Implications and recommendations for practice.* Paper presented at the annual meeting of the American Association on Mental Deficiency, Denver, Colorado.

Piper, M., & Pless, I. (1980). Early intervention for infants with Down's syndrome: A controlled trial. *Pediatrics, 65,* 463–468.

Public Law 94-142: The education of all handicapped children act of 1975. (1975). Washington, DC: U.S. Government Printing Office.

Public Law 99-457: Education of the handicapped act amendments of 1986. (1986). Washington, DC: U.S. Government Printing Office.

Russman, B. (1986). Are infant stimulation programs useful? *Archives of Neurology, 43*(3), 282–283.

Rynders, J. E., & Horrobin, J. M. (1975). Project EDGE: The University of Minnesota's communication stimulation program for Down's syndrome infants. In B. Friedlander, G. Sterritt, & G. Kirk (Eds.), *Exceptional infant: Assessment and intervention,* (Vol. 3, pp. 173–193). New York: Brunner/Mazel.

Sailor, W., & Guess, D. (1983). *Severely handicapped students: An instructional design.* Boston, MA: Houghton Mifflin.

Scherzer, A. L., Mike, V., & Illson, J. (1976). Physical therapy as a determinant of change in the cerebral palsied infant. *Pediatrics, 58*(1), 47–52.

Selye, H. (1956). *The stress of life.* New York: McGraw-Hill.

Shearer, M., & Shearer, M. (1976). The Portage project: A model for early childhood intervention. In T. Tjossem (Ed.), *Intervention strategies for high risk infants and young children* (pp. 335–351). Baltimore, MD: University Park Press.

Turnbull, A. P., Brotherson, M. J., & Summers, J. A. (1986). Family life cycle: theoretical and empirical implications and future directions for families with mentally retarded members. In J. Gallagher & P. Vietze (Eds.), *Families of handicapped persons* (pp. 45–65). Baltimore, MD: Paul H. Brooks.

Turnbull, H. R., & Turnbull, A. P. (1982). Parent involvement in the education of handicapped children: A critique. *Mental Retardation, 20*(3), 115–122.

U.S. House of Representatives (1986). *Education of the Handicapped Act Amendments of 1986.* (Report 99-860). Washington, DC: U.S. Government Printing Office.

Vincent, L., Salisbury, C., Walter, G., Brown, P., Gruenewald, L., & Powers, M. (1980). Program evaluation and curriculum development in early childhood/ special education: Criteria of the next environment. In W. Sailor, B. Wilcox, & L. Brown (Eds.), *Methods of instruction for severely handicapped students* (pp. 129–159). Baltimore, MD: Paul H. Brooks.

White, K. (1986). Efficacy of early intervention. *Journal of Special Education, 19*(4), 401–416.

White, K. R., & Casto, G. (1985). An integrative review of early intervention efficacy studies with at-risk children: Implications for the handicapped. *Analysis and Intervention in Developmental Disabilities, 5*, 7–31.

Wikler, L. (1986). Family stress theory and research on families of children with mental retardation. In J. Gallagher & P. Vietze (Eds.), *Families of handicapped persons* (pp. 167–195). Baltimore, MD: Paul H. Brooks.

CHAPTER 3

Integration of Students with Severe and Profound Disabilities: A Review of Research

ANN T. HALVORSEN
WAYNE SAILOR

From where she was to where she is now is phenomenal. When she started into the educational system she was extremely spastic, she made no meaningful movements. She was tube-fed, she was deep-suctioned. . . . She gave no indication of being aware of her environment. Her expression, her demeanor, everything was the same no matter what she was doing. She actually seemed even semicomatose . . . a perfect candidate to overprotect. Also a perfect candidate to set artificial barriers for—mental barriers that we set for these kids: "She doesn't even know where she is; how can we improve her quality of life when she doesn't show any indication that she knows where she is?" When we place these artificial barriers there we make them self-fulfilling prophecies. They said, "Let her die" after her accident; "She'll be a vegetable; she'll never know the difference; why ruin three lives for the benefit of one who's never going to do anything anyway?" Then they said to put her in the state hospital. . . . When we brought her home from the hospital the back of her head was touching her buttocks; that's how she was neurologically postured. . . . Our barriers were identified for us: "She won't go any further so what are you worrying about? Get on with your lives and forget about it." But early on we learned that we don't decide what she'll accomplish or what she won't accomplish. We have to provide

This research was supported in part by U.S. Department of Education Contract No. 300-82-0365. No official endorsement should be inferred.

her with every opportunity to show *us* what she can accomplish. . . .
If they're not on an integrated school site, you're taking away those
opportunities to break down those barriers. . . . Now, she moves,
she's totally flexible, she gets herself sitting up; she's starting to pull
herself in a kind of a crawl; she can stand up, she sits in a wheelchair. She gets herself moving around in a wheelchair; she feeds herself with a spoon, she says a few words, she smiles when she's
happy, she's aware, she has a personality. I mean, we've gone so far
beyond the *optimum* quality of life that was identified for her to us
that you can't even talk about it. Integrated opportunities have been
a major part of that ongoing growth. When they're educated in their
own communities they are a part of their community—when they're
educated outside of that community, they become invisible members
of the community.
            —Excerpts from a talk by Don Vesey, parent (1986)

Burton Blatt (1985) asserts that to continue to ask whether integration is a good idea is to ask the wrong question; rather, that the question
to be investigated when examining integrated environments for students
with disabilities is: How do we make integration work? Baer (1986), in
his review of a contemporary volume on exemplary service strategies for
severely disabled students, cautions us to give serious empirical attention
to our definitions of "what works well," that is, to both the outcomes of
these interventions and to the social validity of the interventions themselves. Social validity in this sense refers to whether these outcomes are
considered valuable and meaningful by the affected consumers: students,
parents, and community members such as potential employers (cf. Voeltz,
Wuerch, & Bockout, 1982).

In this chapter we shall focus on existing research and on various
published positions that form the background for integration for students
with severe and profound disabilities, including investigations of factors
that predict access to integrated opportunities; outcomes associated with
integration; and validated, "best practice" strategies to facilitate these outcomes.

WHO ARE STUDENTS WITH SEVERE AND PROFOUND DISABILITIES?

In a book of this nature, which deals with research relating to the full
spectrum of students participating in special education programs, it is important to define the particular population of interest here, even though as
Pumpian, West, and Shephard (1988) have noted, such definitions can be

dangerous. Labels are dangerous when they lead to overgeneralization about a group of individuals when, in fact, these individuals are extremely diverse in their needs and strengths. Students who experience severe and profound disabilities have been variously described as "severely handicapped," "severely/profoundly handicapped," "severely intellectually impaired," and "multiply handicapped." In the past, homogeneous models of classification led to further labeling of separate groupings within the service categories such as "students with autism," "trainable mentally retarded students," "deaf-blind students," etc. The field is progressing towards heterogeneous or less categorical groupings of all special education students; here, when we speak of severely and profoundly disabled individuals, we are referring to people who experience the most significant developmental delays. These individuals may have one or more additional disabilities (sensory, physical, or emotional) besides severe functional retardation. At the same time, there is a broad range and diversity within the population. No student would be considered so disabled as not to be included in the population, regardless of medical fragility, minimal communication skills, or lack of consistent motor responses (Sailor, Goetz, Anderson, Hunt, & Gee, 1988). However, some students might acquire a sufficient repertoire of expressive and academic skills to "graduate out" of the population of interest here.

Finally, Sailor, Gee, Goetz, and Graham (1988), in reviewing research literature on the most severely disabled students, argued for a return to the inclusion of the term "profound" when addressing issues or conducting research inclusive of that particular subgroup of the population of students with severe disabilities. Most of the available research literature on best practices appears not to have addressed the most severely disabled population. In this chapter, where there are indications that the research literature on integration pertains to the most disabled students (including "medically fragile," "multiply handicapped," "deaf-blind with profound retardation," etc.) as well as the larger population that has historically been addressed as "severely handicapped," then the term "profound" will be used to indicate that evidence in the review and discussion.

WHAT IS INTEGRATION?

Educational integration of severely disabled students with their nondisabled age peers is a complex, dynamic phenomenon, not a unitary concept, involving far more than the mere placement of students in regular education settings (cf. Wilcox, 1986). Sailor, Anderson, Halvorsen, Filler, and Goetz (1989) have conceptualized it as having each student participate as a valued member of a *sustained social network within his or her home community*. This process is accomplished through a range of interventions designed to promote functional competence within and across integrated contexts, characterized by successful ongoing interactions with nondisabled peers. Toward these ends, these authors have proposed the *comprehensive local school model* of integrated service delivery, which encompasses several critical integration markers:

1. All students are served in the *age-appropriate school* that they would attend if they were nondisabled. This means that if regular education, secondary-age students attend their neighborhood high school, then students with severe disabilities aged 15–18 should attend this same school. In many communities, because of racial desegregation programs or the rural nature of an area, regular education students may be bused out of their immediate neighborhood, or may travel to more centrally located schools. These exceptions to the neighborhood school would apply to the severely disabled student as well. The important feature of this marker is that—regardless of where the school is located—it serves both the disabled and nondisabled students who reside in a particular area, so that relationships that develop in school may be extended to nonschool, extracurricular environments and activities.

2. A specific *single-site administrator* or principal is responsible for all comprehensive local school services. He or she may receive technical assistance, inservice, or consultation from special education administrative personnel; however, the site administrator runs all programs on a day-to-day basis, including evaluation of special education staff. In other words, the same professional practices are utilized for the special education program as for the regular education program.

3. The severely and profoundly disabled students in integrated and/or mainstreamed programs at the school should represent the *natural proportion* (Brown et al., 1983) of severely disabled to nondisabled students in the population of the community at large, which is generally estimated to be 1% to a maximum of 5%.

4. *Related services* (e.g., occupational, physical and speech therapy, adaptive physical education and transportation) should be delivered in an integrated manner; that is, therapy services are provided in natural instructional environments in the school and community rather than in "pull-out" programs (Nietupski, Schutz, & Ockwood, 1980), and students travel to and from school utilizing the same methods of transit (school bus, public bus, walking) as their nondisabled peers. (Thus, regular school buses should become accessible to students who use wheelchairs.)

These four markers represent the minimum setting events for educational integration within the comprehensive local school. Before our analysis of the available research on integration outcomes and strategies, we shall examine some traditional educational service delivery models for severely disabled students, and some of the forces that combined to bring about the current strong trend toward less restrictive opportunities for this population.

HISTORICAL BACKGROUND

Brown et al. (1983) and more recently Meyer and Putnam (1987) have outlined several phases in the progression of service delivery for children and youth who experience severe disabilities. Reynolds and Birch (1982) have characterized this evolution of services as a trend toward "progressive inclusion." These overlapping stages include:

No Schools

The first period evidenced a lack of educational opportunities, when individuals were assumed to be "ineducable" or unable to benefit from education and thus not entitled to these services (Scheerenberger, 1983). Although this period is generally considered to have ended early in this century, it is important to note that the attitudinal legacy from this period, that is, the "educability" debate, has lingered into the 1980s among some professionals in the field (Burton & Hirshoren, 1979; Goldberg & Cruickshank, 1958; Tawney & Smith, 1981; see also Stainback & Stainback, 1983), despite an ever-expanding body of literature demonstrating student skill acquisition under educational programs for this population.

Residential Schools

These schools typified the second stage (early to mid-1800s) of service development, and were seen as part of a reform movement to bring education as well as training to persons of different disabilities, and thus to bring about more positive treatment of these individuals. However, by the late 1800s, these "schools" were evolving into massive public institutions, whose focus had changed from the original intent of "making deviant individuals undeviant" (Wolfensberger, 1975), to one of "protecting" persons with disabilities from the outside world (e.g., Kerlin, 1884, in Wolfensberger, 1975). This change appears to have occurred as a result of several interactive forces. Originally, when institutions were designed to fulfill an educational need, compulsory education did not exist, and free public education for nondisabled students was in its infancy. As the public educational system developed and began to take responsibility for "ungraded classes" for mildly disabled students in the early 1900s (Kanner, 1964; Wallin, 1955), the training function of residential schools diminished, hastening their movement toward custodial care. In turn, as the higher functioning student was provided for within the public schools, parents of these students saw less reason to place or institutionalize their children. Thus, the more severely disabled population became the more prevalent group within our nation's institutions. Instructional technology for this population was virtually nonexistent at this time, resulting in characterizations of these individuals as "unimprovables" (Kerlin, 1885, in Wolfensberger, 1975). State hospitals, in turn, shifted their focus further away from their educational goals. Wolfensberger has conceptualized the institutional trend in this period as one of "protecting nondeviant individuals from deviant people" (1975, p. 33). This segregationist period was stimulated by the development of the eugenics movement's belief in the heritability of retardation and the resultant social policy of isolating disabled persons, with the intention of preventing population growth (Fernald, 1915, in Wolfensberger).

Segregated Private and Public Schools

Significant change in the form of development of community services and initiation of public and private school programs for individuals with severe disabilities did not occur until the postwar period of the late 1940s and early 1950s. Wolfensberger (1975) hypothesized that two reasons for the perpetuation of the status quo were the Great Depression of the 1930s, which inhibited progress in all but the "essential" social services, and both world wars, only after which did we experience what Burello and Sage (1979) have characterized as a "liberalization of attitudes toward human variance" (p. 34). They point out that although the depression delayed societal focus on disabled persons, it had lasting effects on attitudes toward government intervention and support, coupled with new recognition of rights versus privileges. In addition, the return of permanently disabled servicemen from both World War II and the Korean War, and concurrent rehabilitation efforts on their behalf, facilitated positive attitude change toward disability in general.

Despite the growth of public and private special education classes in the 1940s and 1950s, these options were not generally extended to the more severely multiply disabled student until the 1960s. Much of the advocacy for and development of these programs was brought about by parent-founded organizations, such as the National Association for Retarded Citizens, United Cerebral Palsy, and others. The growth of these segregated placements continued after the passage of Public Law 94-142 (1975), which was unexpectedly interpreted by some as a mandate to "establish new and expand old segregated public schools" (Brown et al., 1983, p. 72).

However, it is fair to say that a great many parents, educators, and advocates disagreed with this interpretation on a number of bases and, using a variety of educational, legal, ethical, and political arguments, provided the impetus for the *integration movement,* i.e., the location of students in chronologically age-appropriate regular school programs.

Legal and Ethical Bases for Integration

The civil right of severely disabled individuals to a free, appropriate public education in integrated environments has been supported both by legislation and litigation. Turnbull (1986) has described the derivation of the principle of the *least restrictive environment* (LRE), one of the six major principles of PL 94-142 (1975), as stemming from the constitutionally based legal doctrine of the least restrictive alternative: that legitimate government activities (e.g., education) may not be pursued through means that stifle personal liberties when these purposes can be achieved by less restrictive means. Procedural due process, substantive due process, and equal protection are the three constitutional principles supporting the least restrictive alternative, and these constitutional protections have been applied by the judicial system in numerous cases bearing upon an individual's right to education with his or her nondisabled peers. (See Laski, 1985; Martin, 1986, for reviews.) The finding of the Supreme Court on racial segregation in *Brown v. Board of Education* (1954), that the doctrine of "separate but equal" has no place in public education, has been applied to individuals with severe disabilities in landmark cases, such as *Pennsylvania Association for Retarded Citizens (PARC) v. Commonwealth of Pennsylvania* (1971), where the court found that "placement in a regular public school class is preferable to placement in a special public school class, and placement in a separate public school class is preferable to placement in any other type of program of education and training" (344 F. Supp. 1257). In 1982, the court further stated that programs for severely disabled students must be provided "in age-appropriate schools attended also by nonhandicapped students in natural proportions" (*PARC v. Pennsylvania*, Consent Decree, 1982, p. 2).

Educational Bases

The finding of preference for regular education environments also characterizes the viewpoint of many educators and families in the late 1960s and early 1970s, when the effectiveness of special education in general came under fire (cf. Christopolos & Reny, 1969; Dunn, 1968; Lilly, 1970), particularly in terms of programs for mildly disabled students. This criticism of special education's minimal accountability in terms of meaningful student outcomes led to concomitant growth of mainstreamed and integrated opportunities for mildly disabled students (e.g., Heller, 1972; Reger, 1972), but little initial change for the severely disabled student population, 70% of whom were being served in segregated special education centers in 1978 (Kenowitz, Zweibel, & Edgar, 1978).

In the mid-1970s, concurrent with the passage of PL 94-142 (1975), educational arguments for the integration of severely disabled students began to appear in the literature and in presentations at national professional conferences (Brown et al., 1979; Brown, Nietupski, & Hamre-Nietupski, 1976; Brown et al., 1977; Martin, 1976). Central to this body of literature are both the principles of normalization (Wolfensberger, 1972) and the criterion of ultimate functioning (Brown et al., 1976). This latter criterion established the curricular imperative for integrated programs which focus on skills that will facilitate the individual's functioning "in complex, heterogeneous postschool environments" (Brown et al., 1977, p. 201). The criterion of ultimate functioning embodies the normalization principle, which prescribes that the quality and conditions of the disabled person's life should mirror as closely as possible the norms and cultural patterns of the larger society (Wolfensberger, 1972). Therefore, to attend the same school as one's nondisabled peers was argued to be both culturally normative and facilitative of future functioning in a diverse society.

The political-social climate reflected in public opinion and general social trends strengthened the integration position of educators and parents. Few who viewed Geraldo Rivera's 1972 national television exposé of the conditions in a major New York institution can forget the images of neglect and abuse depicted there. These images had already reached a smaller audience of practitioners and parents with the publication of a series of photographic volumes by Burton Blatt (1966, 1970), but the national media attention stimulated by the 1972 and subsequent broadcasts opened many more eyes to the need for community services, for programs that would be visible in the community and therefore accountable both to the individuals and to their communities.

BARRIERS TO INTEGRATED OPPORTUNITIES

We have discussed the historical development of integration and the possible influences on the trend toward including severely disabled students in our schools and communities. However, the proposed comprehensive local school model of integration remains, in fact, but a model. Movement toward full integration has been sporadic and uneven in most areas of the nation; for example, in 1987 more than 21,000 severely disabled students in California were attending segregated special centers, approximately 55% of the total student population (reported in California as "severely handicapped"), despite the integration efforts of such metropolitan areas as San Francisco, Whittier, and Santa Monica (Farron-Davis & Halvorsen, 1987). Meyer and Putnam (1987) estimate that 10% to 55% of severely disabled students nationally are segregated, figures that are substantiated by the U.S. Department of Education's 1986 Eighth Report to Congress (*Newsletter*, April 1987) in which states report that up to 43% of their students classified as mentally retarded are served in segregated educational settings. In Massachusetts, for example, a recent study by Landau (1987) reported that between 1974 and 1985 a 243% increase occurred in the number of children served in segregated classrooms and separate schools, while at the same time, a 61% decrease occurred in the number of students placed in integrated settings. Landau indicates that if current placement trends continue, by the early 2000s the number of disabled (not just severely disabled) students placed in segregated settings will exceed the number served in integrated programs.

Given these trends and legal mandates, we must now examine why integration is not yet an option in many areas throughout the United States and why it appears to be decreasing in others. Why are families often required to take an adversarial stance with their districts to bring about integrated education for their sons and daughters? From its work with school districts throughout California and the nation over a 5-year period, the California Research Institute on the Integration of Students with Severe Disabilities (CRI) has developed an analysis of barriers to integration which is presented in its present (draft) form in Table 3.1. Each of these identified "barriers" is listed as a function of its systemic nature (cf., philosophical/attitudinal; systemic/administrative/fiscal; pedagogical/ curricular; and legal/ethical). Attempted and suggested solutions to each identified barrier are listed and the source of the information is credited.

The most interesting finding from an analysis of identified barriers to integration is the extent to which there are readily identifiable solutions to each problem, solutions effectively implementing integration in large urban as well as suburban and rural areas, including San Francisco; Madison, Wisconsin; Tacoma, Washington; Montgomery County, Maryland; Philadelphia; DeKalb County, Illinois; and numerous other locations, including statewide implementation in some cases such as Vermont and Hawaii (Meyer & Putnam, 1987). In light of these strategies which appear to have applicability across settings, what are the factors which have influenced the adoption of integrated practices in some areas, and the continuing segregation in others?

PREDICTORS OF INTEGRATED PLACEMENT

Much of the extant knowledge base regarding the placement of severely disabled students in regular schools is most properly in the realm of theory, although a number of factors have been identified that appear to facilitate or inhibit LRE placements. There are, to date, only a handful of studies that have attempted to delineate causative factors in LRE placement (cf. Brinker & Torpe, 1984a, 1985; Filler, Goetz, & Sailor, 1986). Table 3.2 identifies 20 student, family, instructional, administrative, and logistical factors (and the supporting literature) that appear to be predictive of student placement. Student-related issues, such as perceived extent of disability, and family-related issues, such as extent of involvement and advocacy for integration, have been demonstrated to be significant predictors of placement in a large sample study conducted by Filler et al. (1986). This study utilized multiple regression techniques to investigate factors related to teacher estimates of daily contact between students with severe disabilities and their nondisabled peers. In the first set of analyses, 11 factors were used to predict opportunities for interaction for 104 students, 70 of whom attended classes located at regular age-appropriate schools (integrated) with the remainder attending special, disabled-only centers (segregated) in seven California school districts. The results indicated that students who attended integrated schools spent proportionally more time in contact with nondisabled peers than did their segregated counterparts, an important finding, since it contradicts the argument that center-based programs that engage in community vocational programming and the like lead to equivalent interactions with nondisabled peers.

Another finding of the study was that students with severe *multiple* disabilities were significantly more likely to attend an integrated school than were their peers with a single severe disability. However, once on

Text continues on p. 123.

TABLE 3.1. Analysis of "Barriers" to Integration

BARRIER	SOLUTIONS

Philosophical/Attitudinal

1. "Societal discrimination against minority group members" (Biklen, 1985, p. 112)	1. Increased preservice and in-service personnel training for administrators, regular and special educators in rationale for/outcomes of integration (Albright, Brown, Van Deventer, & Jorgenson, 1987; W. Stainback & Stainback, 1984a)
2. Traditional approaches have been protective, segregationist	2. Advocacy and provision of information by parent, professional, and legal groups (Meyer & Kishi, 1985; Piuma et al., 1983; Stetson, 1984)
3. Intolerance/negative attitudes toward difference/ "deviance" (see Ashmore, 1975; Donaldson, 1980)	3. (a) LRE state and local policy development to encourage attitude change (Brinker & Thorpe, 1985; Halvorsen, 1986; McGregor et al., 1986)
	(b) Development of pilot model integrated sites for visitation by personnel and parents (Piuma et al., 1983)

Administrative/Systematic

1. Governance structure encourages segregation (e.g., county model: Advisory Commission, 1986)	1. County/LEA agreements to share resources; incentives to LEAs to serve students in home districts (Advisory Commission, 1986)
2. Funding formulas reinforce restrictive placements (Advisory Comm., 1986) and centralized services	2. Financial incentives to serve in home LEA/ integrated setting (AB 4074); fiscal data indicating integration less expensive (Campbell, personal communication, 1986; Copeland & Iverson, 1985; Piuma et al., 1985)
3. Space limitations in regular schools (Halvorsen, 1984)	3, 4. Conversion of special centers to regular schools; funding for additions to regular schools given integration plan (Greene Funds, California; Orelove & Hanley, 1979)
4. Existence of multiple special center facilities (Farron-Davis & Halvorsen, 1987)	
5. Inaccessibility of regular schools/architectural barriers	5. See 3 above. Also, not all students require barrier-free environment; survey schools and utilize site selection criteria (e.g., Halvorsen, 1986); modify as needed (Orelove & Hanley, 1979)
6. Difficulty of arranging services in sparsely populated areas	6. Cooperative arrangements between LEAs (Vogelsberg, Williams, & Friedl, 1980); heterogeneous groupings, regional specialists
7. Multifaceted nature of systems change process: redefinition of roles/responsibilities, coordination & communication breakdowns, problems in decentralizing related services	7. LRE systems change planning process to address all aspects; utilize support teams with all constituencies represented, specific objectives and timelines, interagency agreements (e.g., Halvorsen, 1986; Haring & Billingsley, 1984; McGregor et al., 1986; Meyer & Kishi, 1985; Piuma et al., 1983)

120

TABLE 3.1. *Continued*

BARRIER	SOLUTIONS
8. Parallel regular/special education administrative responsibility and structure	8. Merging of responsibility (W. Stainback & Stainback, 1984b); site-specific administration and supervision (Biklen & Taylor, 1985; Bogdan & Biklen, 1985; Knapczyk & Dever, 1979; Raske, 1979; Stetson, 1984)

Pedagogical/Curricular

1. Categorical teacher licensing reinforces separate services	1. Movement to less and noncategorical models (e.g., Massachussetts) and/or to more heterogeneous models (Pumpian, pers. comm., 1985)
2. Specialized services needed for medically fragile students; students with severe behavior problems	2. Services can be designed and provided more efficiently (Piuma, 1985) and effectively in regular public school settings (e.g., LaVigna & Donnellan, 1987); transdisciplinary team model and integrated therapy (see Campbell, 1987; Frassinelli et al., 1983; McCormick & Goldman, 1979)
3. Educational and performance demands are easier for students to meet in special center settings	3. Segregated centers are commonly overadapted, prohibiting skill generalization to other environments (see Voeltz, 1984); natural contexts necessary for development of generalized skills and behaviors (see Brown, Nisbet, et al., 1983)
4. Shortage of trained personnel (Biklen, 1985)	4. Incentives to reduce turnover (Biklen, 1985), retraining of existing staff

Legal/Ethical

1. Parents may not be aware of rights to LRE or due processes for advocating for children's rights	1. (a) Rights materials, assistance, and training through state education agency (SEA) DOE Personnel Development network (e.g., California Special Education Resource Network), advocacy groups (e.g., Protection & Advocacy), university projects (Halvorsen, 1983a; Meyer & Kishi, 1985)
	(b) Establishment of parent support and trainer-of-trainer networks (Halvorsen, 1983a); recruitment of surrogate parents (Biklen, 1985) to advocate
	(c) Recognition of parents as equal-status partners in educational process and decision making (see Vincent, Laten, Salisbury, Brown, & Baumgart, 1980)
2. Past mandates lacking provision of services to preschool students	2. Cooperative interagency programs to provide infant and preschool service models (e.g., LEAs and Divisions Developmental Services), implementation of new legislative mandates (e.g., PL 99-457, 1986)

TABLE 3.2. **Independent Variables**

FACTORS AFFECTING PLACEMENT	APPLICABLE RESEARCH	OTHER LITERATURE
Student Issues		
1. Age	Filler, Goetz, & Sailor, 1986	
2. Perceived extent of severity of disability	Filler et al., 1986	
3. Number and type of services needed (on IEP)	Filler et al., 1986; Piuma, 1985	
Family Issues		
4. Family socioeconomic status	Filler et al., 1986	
5. Perceived family involvement and advocacy for integration	Filler et al., 1986; Laski, 1985; Stetson, 1984	Halvorsen, 1983; Meyer & Kishi, 1985
Instructional Issues		
6. Teacher recency of training (date of graduation & no. of yrs. teaching this population)		
7. Amount of teacher in-service on integration	Brinker & Thorpe, 1984a, 1985	Murray & Beckstead, 1983
8. Teacher advocacy for integration	Filler et al., 1986; Stetson, 1984	
9. Individual Education Plan (IEP) process/document effect on placement		
10. State and/or local policy interpretation	Brinker & Thorpe, 1985; McGregor, Janssen, Larsen, & Tillery, 1986; Stetson, 1984	Halvorsen, 1986
11. Amount of administrator in-service		Piuma et al., 1983
12. Administrator advocacy for integration	Bogdan & Biklen, 1985; Stetson, 1984; Taylor, 1982	Piuma et al., 1983
13. Perception of regular school site administrator attitude	Pelligrini, 1986; Raske, 1979	Halvorsen, 1984; Meyer & Kishi, 1985
14. Perception of space/transportation availability	Kenowitz, Zweibel, & Edgar, 1978; Orelove & Hanley, 1979	Halvorsen, 1984
15. Perception of ancillary services		
16. Perception of cost feasibility	Piuma, 1985; Stetson, Elting, & Raimondi, 1982	
Logistical Issues		
17. Governance or educational responsibility		Advisory Commission, 1986
18. Type of community		
19. Perception of IHE involvement in integration	Haring & Billingsley, 1984	Freagon et al., 1983; Piuma et al., 1983
20. Perception of the status of existing special school faciltities	Kenowitz et al., 1978	Finch & Landriau, 1987

a perception stemming from the belief that fewer personnel and resources are required. However, in their work with over 50 public school systems, these authors found that administrators of integrated programs noted cost savings in transportation and administrative overhead. The authors thus hypothesize that while perceived cost increases appear to inhibit integration, information regarding decreases in costs will facilitate integrated placements. Further systematic investigation of this variable and its impact on placement is needed.

A related question is Which program type delivered more to the consumer per dollar spent: the segregated model or the integrated one? It has been assumed by many that the location of all services on a single site for severely disabled students would tend to hold costs down. A recent review of the literature and pilot study by Piuma (1985), however, cast doubt on even this assumption. Piuma compared costs of four classes of matched groups ($N = 28$) of severely disabled students operated by a county office of education (COE) in California, two on a special school (segregated) site and two on a regular school site. With all service factors held constant, the average cost per student for the segregated classes was $13,329, while for the integrated classes, the costs were $12,209, or a difference of 8.4%. The results, of course, are extremely limited in inference due to the small sample size and the case study approach. The data, however, receive some cross-validation from a second informal study conducted in a southern California county by Campbell (personal communication, 1986). Campbell compared severely disabled classes operated by a COE in segregated facilities with comparable costs of operating classes for similar severely disabled students by the local educational agencies on regular school grounds, and found the average cost per year for the student in the segregated program to be $18,500, whereas the average cost for students in the integrated programs was found to be $9,300, almost a 50% saving. Transportation costs were not factored into these computations, but other services to the students were informally calculated to be equal. Again, this study was conducted informally with only limited survey data in the absence of experimental controls, so inferences are limited.

The administrative perception of space availability has also been hypothesized to contribute to placement decisions for or against integration. Both declining enrollments and school closings as well as increasing enrollments and limited space are cited as reasons for maintaining or adding to segregated special centers in many areas, rather than providing for severely disabled students' education in the least restrictive environment. An early study by Kenowitz et al. (1978) examined future integration opportunities nationally for severely disabled students across 81 LEAs, and found that 20% of the administrators polled had plans to build additional segregated centers while 88% reported that their facilities had been built within the preceding five years. This may be explained by the growth of segregated centers, which peaked after the passage of PL 94-142 (1975), as discussed earlier.

Logistical factors such as the governance structure or educational responsibility for students are hypothesized to have a direct impact on placement. This hypothesis is supported by the *California Sunset Review of Special Education* (Advisory Commission on Special Education, 1986), which noted the tendency of the county office of education (or intermediate agency) model to promote segregated options for severely disabled students.

An additional potential predictor of integrated placement in the logistical category is university involvement in the integration process. A variety of districts throughout the United States have collaborated with institutions of higher education (IHE), special education departments, and projects such as CRI in systems change efforts for integration (e.g., San Francisco; Hawaii; Syracuse, New York; Albuquerque, New Mexico; Montgomery County, Maryland; Seattle, Washington; Madison, Wisconsin), while other systems have been directly affected through advocacy efforts and litigation in which IHE personnel participated (Laski, 1985). Further investigation of the contribution of this variable and the range of additional student, family, instructional, and administrative factors listed in Table 3.2 is needed to determine their generalizability as causative agents in placement decisions.

INTEGRATED BEST PRACTICES

There is a considerably larger research basis for the efficacy of integrated placements (cf. Brinker & Thorpe, 1984a; Falvey, 1980; Meyer, Eichinger, & Park-Lee, 1987; Pumpian, 1981; Sailor et al., 1989; Sailor et al., 1986; Voeltz, 1980, 1982), particularly in terms of various "best practices" that become possible when students with severe disabilities are educated alongside their nondisabled, same-age peers. Table 3.3 delineates those best practices, or "integration markers" (Meyer & Kishi, 1985), which have been investigated and described by numerous researchers working to facilitate maximal integration in regular school settings. The major sources of these quality indicators include Meyer, Eichinger, and Park-Lee (1987), California Research Institute literature reviews Years 1–5 (Sailor, 1987), the Brinker (1985) and Brinker and Thorpe studies (1984a, b; 1985; 1986), and a series of nearly two dozen investigations carried out by the California Research Institute on Integration (Sailor & Halvorsen,

1986). Papers by Brown, Helmstetter and Guess (1986) and by Sailor, Gee, Goetz, and Graham (1988) concluded that best practices may well be a function of the degree of severity of the disability of the particular student, with profoundly disabled students receiving much less of "best practices" instruction than severely disabled students.

We have identified nine major best practice variables that facilitate maximal integration and positive outcomes for severely disabled students across age groups, with two additional variables for students in the upper age group (12–22). A comprehensive list of indicators of these variables is contained in Table 3.4. We acknowledge a particular debt to Dr. Luanna Meyer from whose recent paper on program quality indicators (Meyer, 1985; Meyer, Eichinger, & Park-Lee, 1987) we borrowed heavily to compile this list. Specific studies related to each variable merit discussion.

Degree of Physical Integration

In the investigation by Filler and associates (1986) discussed earlier, involving more than 100 students across seven school districts, the amount of physical integration of students was found to be predictive of a second integration marker: opportunities for interaction between these students and their peers in regular education. A small sample study by Anderson and Goetz (1983) demonstrated that horizontal (peer-peer) interactions between severely disabled students and their nondisabled peers comprised 89% of the interactions in an integrated setting, while vertical (adult-child) interactions comprised 100% of these in a situation that was not physically integrated. Brinker (1985) also found that, despite inherent biological and behavioral limitations, students in integrated groups engaged in more than twice as much social behavior as did their peers in segregated groups and the proportion of positive interactions was significantly greater for integrated groups.

Extent of Contact with Same-age Nondisabled Peers.

This quality indicator has been highly associated with positive outcomes in numerous investigations. Brinker and Thorpe (1986) found that the best predictor of integration, defined again as social bids from severely disabled to nondisabled students, was the interactive environment, or the social output of the nondisabled students to their severely disabled (SD) peers. Specifically, in this investigation of 245 students, 60% of whom had no verbal communication, 83% of whom were dependent on others for some aspects of functional self-care activities, and 32% of whom had no

Text continues on p. 134.

TABLE 3.3. Best Practices Facilitating Maximal Integration

PREDICTOR VARIABLES	SELECTED APPLICABLE RESEARCH	OTHER LITERATURE
Groups 1 and 2 (Students aged 3-11 and 12-22)		
1. Degree of physical integration	Anderson & Goetz, 1983; Brinker, 1985; Filler et al., 1986; Meyer, Eichinger, & Park-Lee, 1987; Murray, 1986	Brown et al., 1979, 1983; Brown, Nietupski, & Hamre-Nietupski, 1976; Piuma et al., 1983
2. Extent of contact with same-age nondisabled peers	Anderson & Goetz, 1983; Brady et al., 1980; Brinker & Thorpe, 1984, 1986; Filler et al., 1986; Haring et al., 1987; Johnson & Meyer, 1985; Kohl, Moses & Stettner-Eaton, 1983; McHale & Simeonsson, 1980; Meyer, Eichinger, et al., 1987; Murray, 1986; Rynders et al., 1980; Schleien, 1984; Voeltz, 1982	Hamre-Nietupski et al., 1978; Murray & Beckstead, 1983; W. Stainback & Stainback, 1982; Voeltz, 1980, 1984; Williams et al., 1982
3. Extent of normalized professional practices	Brinker & Thorpe, 1986; Cole, 1986; Halvorsen & Anderson, 1986; Knapczyk & Dever, 1979; Meyer, Eichinger, et al., 1987; Meyer, Fox, et al., 1987; Pellegrini, 1986; W. Stainback, Stainback, Courtnage, & Jaben, 1985; Stetson, 1984	Halvorsen, 1983b, 1984; Hamre-Nietupski & Nietupski, 1981; Meyer & Kishi, 1985; Murray & Beckstead, 1983; Sailor et al., 1986; Searl, Ferguson, & Biklen, 1985; S. Stainback & Stainback, 1985a
4. Extent of parent (or surrogate) involvement in program	Biklen, 1985; Blacher & Turnbull, 1983; Cone, Delawyer, & Wolfe, 1985; Meyer, Eichinger, et al., 1987; Snell & Beckman-Brindley, 1984; Voeltz, Wuerch, & Bockhaut, 1982	Allen, 1981; Blacher-Dixon, Leonard, & Turnbull, 1981; Doering & Hunt, 1983; Halvorsen, 1983a, 1984; Lipton, 1983; Meyer & Kishi, 1985; S. Stainback & Stainback, 1985a; Strully & Strully, 1985; Vincent et al., 1980
5. Extent and degree of personnel training	Brinker & Thorpe, 1985b; Doering, 1985; Fredericks, Anderson, & Baldwin, 1979; Ganschow et al., 1984; Meyer, Eichinger, et al., 1987; S. Stainback, Stainback, Strathe, & Dedrick, 1983; W. Stainback & Stainback, 1982; Wang et al., 1985	Anderson, 1986; Anderson & Doering, 1985; Bogdan & Biklen, 1985; Filler & Halvorsen, 1986; Filler, Halvorsen, & Rosenberg, 1984; Iacino & Bricker, 1978; W. Stainback & Stainback, 1984a
6. Extent to which instruction is data-based	Brinker & Thorpe, 1984b; Fredericks et al., 1979; Holvoet et al., 1983; Meyer, Eichinger, et al., 1987; Searl et al., 1985; Snell & Browder, 1986	Favell, 1977; Sailor & Guess, 1983; Sailor & Haring, 1977

TABLE 3.3. *Continued*

PREDICTOR VARIABLES	SELECTED APPLICABLE RESEARCH	OTHER LITERATURE
7. Extent to which instruction is geared to functional, generalized skills	Billingsley, 1984; Holvoet et al., 1980; Horner, Bellamy, & Colvin, 1984; Hunt et al., 1986; Kayser, Billingsley, & Neel, 1986; Liberty, 1985; McDonnell & Horner, 1985; Meyer, Eichinger, et al., 1987; Sailor, Goetz, et al., 1988; Searl et al., 1985	Brown et al., 1983; Horner, Sprague, & Wilcox, 1982; Hunt, 1985; Stokes & Baer, 1977
8. Extent to which educational program is transdisciplinary	Gee & Goetz, 1985, 1986; Gee, Harrell, & Rosenberg, 1987; Giangreco, 1986; Goetz & Gee, 1987; Hunt, Alwell, & Goetz, 1988	Campbell, 1987; Frassinelli et al., 1983; Iacino & Bricker, 1978; Lyon & Lyon, 1980; McCormick & Goldman, 1979; Nietupski et al., 1980; Orelove & Sobsey, 1987; Sailor & Guess, 1983; Sailor, Goetz, et al., 1988; Sternat et al., 1977
9. Extent of involvement in regular education program	Brinker & Thorpe, 1984b, 1985, 1986; Meyer, Eichinger, et al., 1987; Murray, 1986; Voeltz, 1984; Wang & Birch, 1984	Biklen, 1985; Grenot-Scheyer & Falvey, 1986; Halvorsen, 1983b, 1984, 1986; Knoll & Meyer, 1987; Meyer & Kishi, 1985; Piuma et al., 1983; S. Stainback & Stainback, 1985b; W. Stainback & Stainback, 1982, 1983, 1984a, 1984b; Stetson, 1984; Taylor, 1982; Voeltz, 1984; Will, 1986; Winston, 1985

Group 2 Supplemental Predictor Variables (Students aged 12-22)

PREDICTOR VARIABLES	SELECTED APPLICABLE RESEARCH	OTHER LITERATURE
10. Extent of community-intensive instruction	Biklen & Foster, 1985; Gaylord-Ross, Forte, Storey, Gaylord-Ross, & Jameson, 1987; Gee et al., 1986; Sailor, Goetz, et al., 1988; Searl et al., 1985; Snell & Browder, 1986; White, Leber, & Phifer, 1985	Anderson, 1984; Bellamy & Wilcox, 1982; Bellamy, Wilcox, Rose, & McDonnell, 1986; Brown, Helmstetter, & Guess, 1986; Freagon et al., 1985; Hamre-Nietupski, Nietupski, Bates, & Maurer, 1982; Horner, Sprague, & Wilcox, 1982; Kregel, 1985; Nietupski, Hamre-Nietupski, Clancy, & Veerhusen, 1986; Sailor et al., 1986; Sailor & Guess, 1983
11. Extent of coordinated transitional planning	McDonnell, Wilcox, Boles, & Bellamy, 1985; McDonnell, Wilcox, & Boles, 1986; Schalock, 1986; Vogelsberg, Williams, & Friedl, 1980	Brown et al., 1981, 1984; Freagon et al., 1985; Graff & Sailor, 1986; McDonnell & Hardman, 1986; Wehman, Kregel, Barcus, & Schalock, 1986; Will, 1985

TABLE 3.4 Best Practice Indicators for Students Aged 3-22

1. Extent of Physical Integration

Special education classroom is centrally located in the age-appropriate comprehensive local school,or students are dispersed across regular classrooms throughout the school day

The ratio of disabled students attending the school represents the natural proportion of disabled to nondisabled students in the community

Special education classrooms are dispersed (if more than one)

Students travel to and from school using the general education transportation system*

Students use school enrichment areas (e.g., library) on a regularly scheduled basis*

All programs (regular and special) share the same school calendar and hours

Instructional arrangements, materials, and activities are age-appropriate

All special education and related personnel (including therapists) participate in generic professional and extracurricular school activities along with regular education staff*

The program philosophy emphasizes the goal of maximum participation in integrated community environments*

Each student participates in heterogeneously grouped instruction (including students with different levels of disability and nondisabled peers) at least 3 times weekly*

Instruction to teach new skills takes place in actual community environments*

Adapted playground equipment on the playground is also used by nondisabled peers*

The program philosophy emphasizes integrated therapy rather than a pull-out direct service model*

All school facilities, programs, and activities are accessible to students with disabilities

Students aged 12-22

Regular education students accompany the student off campus for portions of the community-based instruction

Community intensive instruction occurs in natural proportions with nondisabled persons in vocational, leisure, and domestic settings

Students pass in halls, use lockers between classes on the same schedule as their regular education peers

General school classrooms (such as shop, computer area, home economics rooms, etc.) are accessible and/or adapted for use by students with multiple disabilities*

2. Extent of Contact with Same-Age, Nondisabled Peers

Student participates in daily social and leisure activity interactions with same-age non-disabled peers (recess, sports, etc.)*

Program includes planned daily interactions with same-age nondisabled peers for at least a third of the school day

Student participates in extracurricular activities typical for his/her age range along with nondisabled students*

Students disperse and eat lunch in the cafeteria with same-age nondisabled peers

Each IEP includes at least one measurable behavior objective in each domain involving interactions with a peer or peers who are not disabled*

Nondisabled peers spontaneously interact with students when passing them in the hall or meeting them in central areas such as the lunchroom or playground*

Students aged 12-22

Natural proportions are observed in the use of general school facilities

Students attend dances, parties, games, rallies, and other integrated extracurricular events at least twice a month

---

*Items marked with an asterisk are reprinted with permission from Meyer, Eichinger, & Park-Lee (1987), *Program Quality Indicators* (PQI)

TABLE 3.4 *Continued*

3. *Extent of Normalized Professional Practices*

School site administrator is responsible for both special and regular education program supervision and administration

The setting is normalized for students' chronological ages (e.g., decor/decorations, furniture, wall displays)*

Professional staff talk with (and about) students in a manner that communicates respect (i.e., do not yell at, make fun of, or talk about students as if they were not present)*

All equipment and individual prosthetic devices are kept in good working order*

Changes in activity and position are explained to students (rather than just pushing a wheelchair to another location, etc.)*

Student is physically positioned according to individual needs throughout the day and various instructional programs*

Alternative communication modes and adaptive equipment devices are used as needed for the student across all program areas*

The student has adaptive equipment*

Medical records are up-to-date, including information on medications and monitoring of any effects of medication for students*

Staff systematically fade out teacher intervention from nondisabled-disabled student interaction

Instructional strategies are individualized*

Team collaboration is involved in both planning and delivery of instruction*

The schedule reflects a variety of situations for the student, including independent work, small group, large group, one-to-one instruction, socialization, and free time*

Caregiving interactions and natural routines (eating, going to the bathroom, etc.) are utilized as opportunities for instruction*

Pupil-teacher staffing ratios are adequate and appropriate to meet the students' needs*

The student is given opportunities to make choices, provide input, and so forth (e.g., asking a student where he or she would like to sit)*

Behavior problems are viewed as instructional needs, indicating areas where skills for more appropriate behaviors must be acquired and practiced*

The program reflects a balance between safety concerns and normalized risk-taking based upon the student's age*

The student's transitions are facilitated by regular contact between "feeder" and "next" programs/schools (including community college and/or rehabilitation agency for secondary age)

An educative approach and "least intrusive means" (nonaversive) guidelines are followed to intervene with behavior problems*

Program philosophy emphasizes continuous updating of services by actively seeking information on new curricular developments*

Students aged 12-22

Each IEP includes personal management objectives reflecting a concern for teaching decision-making, choice-making, and autonomy*

The program philosophy emphasizes the development of both autonomy and individual responsibility by the student*

4. *Extent of Parent (or Surrogate) Involvement in Program*

Teachers communicate regularly with parents (e.g., log books back and forth, phone calls)

Student records are shared with the family while maintaining confidentiality*

Parent training is available and parents might be asked for assistance in working on skills with their child at home*

TABLE 3.4 *Continued*

Parents are invited to participate in staff development and site preparation (disability awareness) programs

There is active family involvement in assessing the students' needs, designing instructional priorities, and designing the IEP

Parents are encouraged to help identify individually effective instructional strategies (e.g., effective reinforcers)*

There is an "open door" policy regarding visits by parents and other relevant persons*

Parents receive a formal report on their child's progress on a quarterly basis*

General school parent groups (e.g., PTA) are open to and involve participation of parents of severely disabled students

The program philosophy emphasizes an individualized approach and responsiveness to families, with support to meet family needs

The state has joint state certification practices for special and regular educators (e.g., regular educators have special education course requirements and vice versa)

Supervised preservice fieldwork for teaching credentials occurs in model integrated school sites

Instructional staff have attended a regional or national professional conference within the past year*

The program maintains a collaborative research, development, and/or training relationship with a college or university*

The building principal or program supervisor observes personnel during instruction at least quarterly and provides staff with written feedback on performance at least annually*

Instructional staff maintain collegial interactions with at least one colleague in another school whose students have similar needs*

The program philosophy emphasizes the continuous updating of services by actively seeking collegial interactions with experts in the field*

Al least once each year, the program utilizes an outside consultant with recognized expertise to provide technical assistance and/or training*

The program philosophy emphasizes sharing its own innovative and effective efforts with other services in the region*

The program philosophy supports the need for staff in-service training on a regular basis through provision of released time, etc.

The school principal has received training directly relevant to disability areas served in the school*

All processional personnel are certified by the state in the disability areas served*

Staff meet formally and consult with one another at least once a month regarding specific educational issues*

Teachers schedule time for training paraprofessionals with students on an ongoing basis and monitor paraprofessional program implementation in nonclassroom environments

6. *Extent to Which Instruction Is Data-Based*

Data on the student's performance are collected at least once weekly for each IEP objective, and those data are used to make program changes as needed*

The student spends most of his/her time engaged in active learning activities, with "down time" comprising on more than a few minutes at a time between activities*

Individualized task analyses and discrepancy analyses are done on the basis of individual instructional programs*

The IEP specifies present levels of performance referenced to environmental activities rather than IQ scores, mental age, or norm-referenced achievement test scores*

The IEP specifies measurable criteria for mastery of objectives*

TABLE 3.4 *Continued*

Teaching staff alternate observing one another during instruction to both monitor programs and solve problems, when needed*

7. *Extent to Which Instruction Is Geared to Functional, Generalized Skills*

Instructional programs specify procedures for fading teacher assistance, including instructional cues, corrections, and consequences*

Instructional cues are designed to be closely related to natural cues available in criterion environments*

Longitudinal planning occurs to prepare students for the demands of subsequent environments

Ecological inventories are used to provide input into the design of individualized programs (i.e., assessing environmental domains)*

The IEP specifies mastery as performance in criterion situations in actual environments without teacher assistance*

Instructional trials are presented throughout the day, in addition to scheduled program sessions, whenever natural opportunities occur*

The IEP specifies measurable criteria for mastery of objectives*

Objectives in the IEP focus on functional skills and critical activities that are immediately useful in community settings (e.g., at home, in a store, etc.)*

The IEP requires performance in the presence of nondisabled persons in actual situations in the community to indicate mastery of objectives*

All IEPs state objectives to describe what the student will do, not what he or she will stop doing or what staff will do*

New skills are taught in the context of naturally occurring activities and daily routines*

8. *Extent to Which Educational Program Is Transdisciplinary*

The program philosophy emphasizes integrated therapy (across schedule and environments) rather than a pull-out direct service model

Related services personnel (OT/PT/ST/VH) conduct functional assessments in natural environments and develop objectives with IEP/ITP team

Therapy occurs across natural environments and is integrated into functional activities where skills will be utilized

Therapists engage in consultative as well as direct services to ensure incorporation across the school day

Students aged 12-22

Relevant community agency personnel (e.g., current/future residential care provider, case manager, Habilitation or Rehabilitation Services representative, vendor(s) of adult services) participate with parents and school personnel in Individualized Transition Plan (ITP) development beginning at age 15

9. *Extent of Involvement of the Regular Education Program*

Special education staff attend general faculty meetings and regularly interact with all school staff*

Special and regular education teachers share responsibilities (e.g., yard and lunch duty, chaperoning extracurricular events, etc.)

Students participate in a range of regular education classes and activities on an ongoing individualized basis (e.g., music, art, home economics, physical education, etc.)

Students' yearbook pictures are dispersed throughout as with regular education students

Students participate in regular graduation ceremonies from high school

Teachers take breaks/preparation periods with regular education faculty

Teachers assist regular education staff with specific program planning for nondisabled students who experience behavior and learning difficulties

TABLE 3.4 *Continued*

Parents participate in regular school parent/family activities (e.g., PTA, "room parents," chaperoning, career days, etc.)

Supplemental Best Practice Indicators for Students Aged 12-22

10. Extent of Community Intensive Instruction

Each student receives instruction in the community (outside the school setting) at least once a week (ages 3-8), twice weekly (ages 9-11), or four times a week (ages 12-18), spending 80-100% of the day off campus by age 19-22

11. Extent of Coordinated Transitional Planing

The program philosophy reflects the expectation that the student will be a member of a sustained social network in his/her community

The program philosophy emphasizes the goals of competitive and/or supported employment in integrated, community work environments*

The program philosophy emphasizes preparation for living in the least restrictive adult environment*

Nonschool, community-based instruction is provided at least four times a week and increases with student age

The students have regular, consistent access to community training environments across vocational, domestic, leisure, and general community domains

The IEP for any student 12 and older includes vocational training objectives for specific job sampling

Each secondary age student participates in a competitive job or job training for part of the school day*

Each IEP includes objectives to develop social skills, including interaction with others in nonschool environments*

Objectives to develop leisure and vocational activity skills reflect attention to the student's personal preferences*

Parents, districts, and relevant agency personnel participate in a coordinated transition planning process for each student beginning several years prior to graduation

---

independent mobility skills, the authors found that the interactive behavior of nondisabled students accounted for five times the variance in the disabled student's social bids (40.9%) as did the second best integration predictor. The second best integration predictor, the average number of nondisabled students in the integrated environment, accounted for 8.4% of the variance. In a related study, Brinker and Thorpe (1984b) found that the rate of social interaction with nondisabled peers accounted for a statistically significant proportion of objectives met on the Individualized Education Program (IEPs) of SD students ($p < .025$), or 2.1% of the variance in the proportion of IEP objectives achieved.

A qualitative investigation by Murray (1986), which utilized participant observation strategies to examine the social relationships of high-school-age SD students and their nondisabled peers, suggests that high degrees of contact (on average, 33%–38% of instructional time) contributed to the development of reciprocal friendships between SD students and the peer tutors working with them. Haring, Breen, Pitts-Conway, Lee, and Gaylord-Ross (1987) also found that contact between nondisabled (ND) students and their SD peers through tutoring and friends programs resulted in significant increases in the amount and type of interaction during noninstructional periods, and that nondisabled high school students stated more positive reasons for their participation in these programs following contact.

Normalized Professional Practices

This variable has been cited by increasing numbers of researchers and practitioners in integrated settings, and has been further broken down by Meyer (1985) and Meyer and Kishi (1985), among others (see Table 3.4). Pellegrini (1986) found that "ownership" by elementary school site principals, measured by the extent to which they engaged in the same (normalized) supervisory practices with teachers of SD students as with regular education teachers at their site, was significantly related to the amount of integration reported by these principals. Specific research that separates normalized professional practices from other best practice variables is lacking; however, numerous reports from teachers (Halvorsen, 1983b, 1984) and data collected in a small group study on best practices utilized by teachers of Bay Area integrated classes (Halvorsen & Anderson, 1986) provide support for the importance of normalized practices such as talking about and with students in a manner that communicates respect (see also Meyer, 1987), and emphasize student similarities and strengths, thus modeling positive, age-appropriate, or normalized ways of interacting. Brinker and Thorpe (1986) demonstrate that several indicators of normalized professional practice are associated with rates of interaction. Four of their 19 ratings of resources and staff support, including support from the building principal and regular education teachers, accounted for 15% of the variance in the rate of social bids to regular education students from their SD peers. Individualized educational planning accounted for 7.2% of the variance, and three aspects of physical environment organization—age appropriateness of materials, clearly defined materials grouping, and separation of groups of materials—accounted for 5% of the variance in the rate of social bids. All of these variables characterize aspects of normalized professional practices.

Recent work by Cole (1986); Cole, Meyer, Vandercook, and McQuarter (1986); and Meyer, Fox, et al. (1987) suggests that another indicator of normalized professional practices is the systematic fading of teacher intervention in interactions between disabled and nondisabled peers. These studies, which compared the effects of high teacher-intrusive and low teacher-intrusive conditions, suggest that while high rates of intervention by teachers may be important in the initial stages of interaction, these levels should be diminished as students' familiarity with each other and the activity increases. Generally, more positive social interactions were observed in the low intrusive conditions as the interventions continued. An unnecessary adult presence may actually interfere with the development of the students' relationships. It can also be hypothesized that, by fading teacher intervention, a positive message is provided regarding the disabled student's competence, as opposed to the implication inherent when a teacher "hovers over" his or her pupils. It is not unreasonable to expect that this message, coupled with normalized practices that demonstrate respect for the student, may have an impact on the nondisabled students' attitudes as well.

Finally, these studies tend to lend support to the *contextual relevance* model suggested by Sailor, Goetz, et al. (1988), in which instructional tactics are recommended that are embedded in the context of the functional response to the environment required of the severely disabled student. These tactics differ from the more familiar (and more intrusive) tactics of verbal and physical prompting from instructional staff.

Extent of Parent Involvement

Biklen (1985), Halvorsen (1983a), and Meyer and Kishi (1985) discussed parent concerns that must be addressed prior to and during integration transitions, and suggested some strategies that promote parent/guardian participation in the integrated program. Further experimental research is needed to examine the impact of different levels and types of parent/family involvement in the integrated educational program; the majority of studies to date have focused solely on the function of parents as teachers of their disabled child (cf. Baker, Heifetz, & Murphy, 1980; Karnes & Teska, 1980). The current perspectives voiced by parents indicate the need for attention to a range of individual preferences on the nature and degree of their involvement (see Turnbull, Brotherson, & Summers, 1985). Position statements by Lipton (1983) and Strully and Strully (1985), which reflect their personal experiences with integration, emphasize the need for recognition of parents as equal-status partners in the integrated educational process. This recognition is critical to establishing the social validity of best practice outcomes, as Voeltz, Wuerch, and Bockhaut (1982) demonstrated in soliciting parental opinions of the outcomes of a leisure-training program.

A promising practice described by numerous authors (e.g., Doering & Hunt, 1983; California State Department of Education Individualized Critical Skills Model (ICSM), 1985; Vincent et al., 1980) is the use of parent interview strategies to obtain information about priorities for both the current and future environments and activities within which instruction will occur. Parents and/or care providers are asked about the family and student's weekday and weekend schedule and activities outside of school hours, and about their son's or daughter's performance in each of these settings. Information is obtained as to whether this activity (e.g., making breakfast) is a high priority for the family, and this information, combined with ecological/functional assessment data from other members of the team, is utilized to develop specific objectives in each curricular domain. Parents are also asked about their preferences for their child's future activities in vocational, leisure, domestic, and community domains. As a part of the overall process, the teacher also conducts inventories of neighborhood environments in order to assure that instruction will occur in these settings or ones that will closely match those utilized by the family.

As with the best practice exemplars discussed earlier, the involvement of families in the integrated educational process is closely tied to the comprehensive local school model of service delivery. Again, although specific research is not available, it appears that parents will be more likely to become involved in regular school activities (e.g., PTAs, advisory groups, chaperoning events, serving as "room parent" in elementary sites) if their child is attending his or her local neighborhood school. This type of involvement can facilitate the development of friendships with other parents and their children and, in turn, has been reported to facilitate the carryover of student relationships outside of school hours (Oshima, 1986).

Extent and Degree of Personnel Training

In two investigations, Stainback and Stainback (1982) and Stainback, Stainback, Strathe, and Dedrick (1983) have demonstrated the positive impact of inservice training on the attitudes of regular educators toward SD students. These teachers serve as models for their students, and collaboration of regular and special educators is critical to maximize integrated opportunities throughout the school day. As previously mentioned, Brinker and Thorpe (1985b), in their investigation of state policy predictors, found that joint teacher certification requirements for special and regular educators were predictive of integration. Bogdan and Biklen (1985) discuss the principal's role in mainstreaming and provide support for normalized professional practice and for principal self-education about special education, as well as for principal leadership in staff development programs on integration for the entire faculty.

Numerous authors have reported the need for revisions in preservice training programs for special education that should reflect the changing roles and new competencies required by teachers in integrated settings (cf. Anderson & Doering, 1985; Filler, Halvorsen, & Rosenberg, 1984). Some of the competencies are addressed by joint certification requirements, such as those in California, where teachers are required to obtain a regular education credential and therefore have had some experience with "real schools" when they begin their special education training program. In addition, preservice special education fieldwork experiences that utilize model integrated school sites as a part of the training process are key to preparing teachers for these roles, as has been demonstrated by follow-up data collected on graduates of two Bay Area universities (Anderson, 1986; Filler & Halvorsen, 1986). A separate evaluation study of the state-sponsored inservice training program in California (Doering, 1985) demonstrated that teachers who had received training in integrated, community-intensive programming for their severely disabled students were more effective in utilizing a variety of integrated nonclassroom and community environments for instruction than were the control group who had not yet participated in inservice, as demonstrated by higher quality IEPs, documented instruction and data collection on specified objectives.

Extent of Data-Based Instruction

For over a decade the literature has reflected the belief that data-based decisions made by teachers about student skill acquisition are less prone to error than are subjective judgments (cf., Favell, 1977; Sailor & Guess, 1983; Sailor & Haring, 1977). Holvoet, O'Neill, Chazdon, Carr, and Warner (1983) demonstrated that comparative judgments and decision-making about student performance were more accurate in the presence of systematic data collection. As reflected in Table 3.4, the components of this quality indicator signify more than simply the collection of periodic performance data. Student time engaged in learning activities with minimal "downtime" in transition periods, the existence of individualized task-analytic instructional programs based on discrepancy analysis procedures, and the presence of IEP objectives that exhibit meaningful performance statements, conditions, and measurable mastery criteria are essential best practices. Fredericks, Anderson, and Baldwin's (1979) investigation of competence needed by teachers of this population yielded two primary indicators: engaged instructional time and proportion of task-analyzed programs. In addition, as Brinker and Thorpe (1984b) have noted, although functioning level and rates of interaction with nondisabled students accounted for a statistically significant 15% of the variance in proportion of IEP objectives achieved; it is most likely that specialized educational techniques accounted for much of the remaining 85% of unexplained variance.

Extent of Functional, Generalized Skill Instruction

This quality indicator is at the core of best practices for the population of students with severe disabilities. The rationale for this is articulated succinctly by Brown et al. (1983) in a discussion of the learning and performance characteristics of persons with severe disabilities, and has been well documented elsewhere in the literature (e.g., Billingsley, 1984; Holvoet, Guess, Mulligan, & Brown, 1980; Horner, Sprague, & Wilcox, 1982; Liberty, 1985; Stokes & Baer, 1977). The reader is also referred to Sailor et al. (1986) and Sailor, Goetz, et al. (1988) for a detailed synthesis of the literature in terms of both functional, generalized skills and instruction within the community-intensive model; and to Snell and Browder (1986) for an overall evaluation of research focusing on community-intensive instructional practices, in terms of both effectiveness and social validity.

It is instructive to note that when Billingsley (1984) conducted his evaluation of nearly 500 objectives on IEPs for a sample of 22 students in two school districts, all of whom were attending segregated school programs, he found that the number of objectives in which a generalized outcome was specified was negligible, at most 7%. Further analysis to determine whether objective clusters that indicated or implied the need for a generalized outcome existed, turned up only one objective cluster (two objectives) for one student. We can speculate about the reasons for this, but the fact remains that, as Billingsley emphasizes, generalization is not a "frill"; regardless of how many potentially functional skills are taught in simulated settings, the value of these skills is minimal unless students have been trained to use them and can apply them within natural environments that are utilized on a regular basis (p. 191).

An experimental investigation by Hunt, Goetz, and Anderson (1986) compared the IEPs written by teachers on integrated school sites with those from segregated teachers of severely disabled students with control for type and recency of teacher training. Three categories of quality indicators were utilized to evaluate objectives on IEPs, one of which was generalizability. IEPs of integrated teachers contained more objectives that specified instruction across settings and materials, as well as more objectives to be taught in the natural setting; the data analysis demonstrated significantly higher quality overall for the IEPs of integrated students. While this study properly belongs in the examination of integrated outcomes, it is useful here in a discussion of best practices because of its implication that integrated settings are inherently more conducive to generalized instruction.

Extent to Which Program is Transdisciplinary

Several recent investigations support the importance of a *transdisciplinary model,* which results in the provision of integrated therapy across natural environments. For example, Gee and Goetz (1985) and Goetz and Gee (1987) taught effective use of residual vision in conjunction with fine motor skills within the ongoing activity routines of play, household chores, and self-care tasks, where completion of the task within the activity routine was made contingent upon the use of vision. Instruction occurred only at the natural points in the activity where visual skills were necessary to activity continuation. Gee and Goetz (1986) taught basic orientation and mobility skills to four profoundly disabled students within the context of travel routes that the students needed to learn, in order to gain access to specific activities and environments. In spite of the fact that these students lacked traditional prerequisites (concept discrimination items of the Peabody Mobility Scale) for this type of instruction, they all succeeded in generalizing their motor skills to new, unfamiliar routes, and also demonstrated a high level of incidental learning of landmarks or other natural cues and memory tasks specific to each route. The authors speculate that generalized learning in each of these situations was enhanced by the provision of instruction within the context of actual routes, or the integration of vision and orientation/mobility services throughout natural contexts. This research and additional work in the area of communicative conversational skills (Hunt, Alwell, & Goetz, 1988) provide support for both the teaching of functional, generalized skills, and for the transdisciplinary model of assessment and instruction of basic communicative, motor, visual, and mobility skills within the context of naturally occurring critical activities (Lyon and Lyon, 1980; Nietupski, Schutz, and Ockwood, 1980; Sailor, Goetz, et al., 1988; Sailor & Guess, 1983).

Extent of Involvement in the Regular Education Program

This is clearly a critical integration marker, particularly for elementary-age students. The positive outcomes associated with close cooperation and sharing of special and regular education responsibilities have been documented by numerous authors, including many of the researchers cited previously (e.g., Biklen, 1985; Brinker & Thorpe, 1984a, b, 1985, 1986; Meyer, Eichinger, & Park-Lee, 1987; Murray, 1986; Pellegrini, 1986; W. Stainback & Stainback, 1982, 1983, 1984a, b). Taylor (1982) found that staff must be integrated in order for severely disabled students to experience effective interaction.

In her qualitative ethnographic study at a Bay Area high school, Murray (1986) found that one of the constraints to maximal integration was the existence of a separate department and chairperson of special education, in contrast to regular education departments organized by subject/content areas. Knoll and Meyer (1987), Sailor, Goetz, et al. (1988), Stainback and Stainback (1984b), Voeltz (1984), and Will (1986), among others, have advocated for a merger of special and regular education administrative structures as necessary to facilitate quality integration, where students with severe disabilities will be regarded as having equal status with their nondisabled peers. Voeltz (1984) and Stainback, Stainback, Courtnage, and Jaben (1985) have described modifications that can be made in regular education curricula and classroom arrangements in order to assure the ongoing awareness and acceptance of disabled students as a part of the overall school community. Teachers and administrators from effectively integrated programs (cf. Halvorsen, 1983b, 1984; Meyer and Kishi, 1985) have reported the importance of consistent and regular interaction with regular education faculty, including participation in faculty meetings, committees, social events, extracurricular clubs, and student organizations. Biklen (1985), Piuma et al. (1983), Stetson (1984), Taylor (1982), and numerous others who have worked with integrated programs support the notion of integrated regular and special education services through the designation of single administrative responsibility (e.g., site principal) for all services and programs in a given school. As Biklen (1985) states, "When we no longer need the term *special,* we will have achieved equality" (p. 176). Thus, the extent of our involvement in the regular education program, and the diminishing of the lines between these two parallel structures, is expected to result in the full instantiation of integration as a part of everyday life.

Extent of Community Intensive Instruction

Two additional markers for students twelve years of age and older must be considered in a review of best practices for quality integrated education. The first of these is the extent of community intensive instruction, which increases in importance as students progress in age. As Sailor, Goetz, Anderson, Hunt, and Gee (1988) note, evidence that directly compares the outcomes of integrated, community-intensive instruction with outcomes of segregated, classroom intervention is minimal. The need for efficacy research, particularly with the most severely, multiply disabled (or "profoundly disabled") students has been discussed by Brown, Helmstetter, and Guess (1986), who note that much of the outcome data that does exist has focused on the less disabled students within the severely handicapped range. One initial validation study that utilized a multiple baseline design to examine the efficacy of this model for young profoundly, multiply disabled students was conducted by Gee, Goetz, Graham, and Lee (1986). Four students classified as deaf-blind with accompanying profound retardation and motor disabilities, participated in multiple nonclassroom and community contexts for the instruction of basic motor and sensory skills. Contextual functional assessment procedures were followed by instruction of targeted skills such as orienting to sound, increasing range of motion in a specific limb, grasping, and visual fixation within leisure, vocational, and community purchasing activities. Successful acquisition of skills was demonstrated. The theory of contextual relevance and related research that supports community intensive instruction on this basis have been discussed elsewhere (Sailor, Goetz, et al., 1988) as have the design and implementation of the model (Anderson, 1984; Sailor et al., 1986; Sailor, Goetz, et al., 1988). Here we shall note only that nonclassroom instruction in other school environments is seen as critical to the integration of young (3–6-year-old) students, comprising approximately 25% of instructional time, with nonschool or community intensive instruction increasing from 10% at this age to 90–100% for students aged 19–22.

Extent of Coordinated, Transitional Planning

The need for continual expansion of instruction in relevant community environments for students approaching graduation age underlies this final best practice indicator of integration. This type of planning is necessary to ensure postschool integrated living and meaningful work placements. A national survey conducted by McDonnell, Wilcox, and Boles (1986) concluded that individualized interagency planning must occur to increase students' access to community services. Evidence exists that specific transition-planning strategies combined with an integrated program that reflects all of the best practices variables discussed above will result in increases in nonsheltered, integrated placements of program graduates (Graff, 1987; Brown et al., 1985, 1987). In San Francisco, for example, although an integrated community-intensive model had been implemented generally for high-school-age severely disabled students since 1983, it was not until comprehensive individualized transition planning and supported employment programming were initiated for 1987 graduates that the majority of these graduates obtained integrated, nonsheltered, meaningful, postschool work placements (Gaylord-Ross et al., 1987; Graff, 1987).

OUTCOMES OF INTEGRATED PROGRAMMING

As we noted at the beginning of this chapter, until this decade, the principal question for programmatic research was, should students with severe disabilities be moved to less restrictive educational placements? The answer is a clear yes: Virtually all available research reviews indicate better educational outcomes associated with integrated placements as compared to their segregated counterparts (Sailor, Goetz, et al., 1988). Both the California Research Institute (CRI) and the Minnesota Consortium on the Education of Students with Severe Disabilities (USDOE/SEP Contract No. 300-82-0363) have delineated multiple positive outcomes of integration for SD students, which in the interest of space limitations are listed with the supporting research in Table 3.5.

Degree of Integration in the Next Educational Environment

This integration outcome refers to the increased likelihood that, for example, severely disabled preschoolers who are currently integrated will be more likely to experience future elementary and secondary education in settings with their nondisabled peers, and that students graduating from integrated programs will have greater access to nonsheltered postschool environments, as discussed above (cf. Brown et al., 1985, 1987). The ongoing growth of integrated school placements in areas such as Hawaii (Voeltz, 1984) and the San Francisco Bay Area (Sailor and Halvorsen, 1986) further substantiates this outcome.

Social Development

This outcome of integrated best practices has been described by multiple investigators, including Gaylord-Ross and Pitts-Conway (1984) in a high school program for students with autism; Schactili (1987), who found decreased rates of inappropriate behavior and increased social initiations in elementary-age students as a function of peer interaction in a game setting; and Falvey (1980), who demonstrated changes in the social competence of kindergarten-age integrated students. Anecdotal reports of improved appearance (e.g., Kahan, 1984) of integrated students are fre-

Text continues on p. 146.

Table 3.5. Outcomes of Integration for Students Aged 3-22

Dependent Variable	Applicable Research	Other Literature
1. Degree of integration in next educational environment	Brown et al., 1985, 1987; Crapps, Langone, & Swain, 1985; Hasazi et al., 1985	Graff, 1987; Sailor & Halvorsen, 1986; Voeltz, 1984
2. Social development (including appearance); less excess behavior	Brinker, 1985; Borthwick, Meyers, & Eymann, 1981; Chin-Perez et al., 1986; Donnellan, LaVigna, Zambito, & Thvedt, 1985; Falvey, 1980; Gaylord-Ross & Pitts-Conway, 1984; Hanline, 1985; Hunt et al., 1988; Jenkins, Speltz, & Odom, 1985; Schactili, 1987; Selby, 1984	Giannini (pers. comm.), 1987; Kahan, 1984; Meyer & Evans, 1986
3. Affective development	Park & Goetz, 1985	
4. Interactive social development	Anderson, 1984; Anderson & Goetz, 1983; Baldwin, 1979; Brady et al., 1984; Breen et al., 1985; Brinker & Thorpe, 1984a, 1985a; Cole, 1986; Cole et al., 1986; Goldstein & Wickstrom, 1986; Guralnick, 1976; Haring et al., 1987; Hendrickson et al., 1982; Hunt et al., 1988; James & Egel, 1986; Kohler & Fowler, 1985; Lord & Hopkins, 1986; Meyer, Fox, et al., 1987; Meyers-Winton, 1980; Murata, 1984; Odom et al., 1985; Odom & Strain, 1984; Powell et al., 1983; Smith, 1984; Strain et al., 1977; Strain & Odom, 1986; Voeltz, 1982; Voeltz & Brennan, 1982	Brown et al., 1983; Guralnick, 1976, 1984; Hamre-Nietupski, Nietupski, Stainback, & Stainback, 1984; Johnson & Johnson, 1983, 1986; Sailor et al., 1986
5. Skill generalization in multiple environments	Gee & Goetz, 1985, 1986; Goetz & Gee, 1987; Goldstein & Wickstrom, 1986; Keyser et al., 1986; Lord & Hopkins, 1986; Murata, 1984; Sailor, Goetz, et al., 1988; Selby, 1984; White et al., 1985	
6. Parent expectations for child's future	Anderson & Farron-Davis, 1987; Freagon et al., 1983; Hanline & Halvorsen, 1989; Disability Rights, 1985	Giannini (pers. comm.), 1987; Lipton, 1983; Strully & Strully, 1985; Turnbull & Turnbull, 1985; Vesey, 1986

Table 3.5. *Continued*

DEPENDENT VARIABLE	APPLICABLE RESEARCH	OTHER LITERATURE
7. Health and increased independence	Anderson & Farron-Davis, 1987; Turnbull & Turnbull, 1985	Forest, 1984, 1986; Vesey, 1986
8. Proportion of IEP objectives obtained	Almond, Rodgers, & Krug, 1979; Brinker & Thorpe, 1984a; Wang & Baker, 1986	Hunt, Goetz, & Anderson, 1986
9. Attitudes of nondisabled students at school	Bricker & Bricker, 1977; Brinker & Thorpe, 1984a; Donaldson, 1980; Fenrick & Petersen, 1984; Haring et al., 1987; McHale & Simeonsson, 1980; Odom et al., 1984; Peck et al., 1978; Ray, 1985; Sasso, Simpson, & Novak, 1985; Siperstein & Bak, 1985; Voeltz, 1980, 1982	Johnson & Meyer, 1985; Murray, 1986; Murray & Beckstead, 1983
10. Postschool or school-related integrated work placement	Brown et al., 1985, 1987; Crapps et al., 1985; Gaylord-Ross et al., 1987; Gersten, Crowell, & Bellamy, 1986; Pumpian et al., 1980; Pumpian, Shephard, & West, 1986; Schalock, 1982; Wehman et al., 1982; Wehman, Hill, et al., 1985; Wehman, Kregel, & Seyfarth, 1985	Bellamy et al., 1986; Graff, 1987
11. Postschool or school-related job earnings	Gaylord-Ross et al., 1987; Hasazi et al., 1985; Hill & Wehman, 1983; Wehman et al., 1982	
12. Attitudes of persons in the community	Bates, Morrow, Pancsofar, & Sedlak, 1984; Hurd, Costello, Pajor, & Freagon, 1981; Pumpian, 1981; Pumpian et al., 1986	Halvorsen, 1983a; Nietupski et al., 1980
13. Normal living circumstances	Close, 1977; Conroy et al., 1982; Gage et al., 1987; Hasazi et al., 1985; Hill, Lakin, & Bruininks, 1984; Lakin & Bruininks, 1985; Sokol-Kessler, Conroy, Feinstein, Lemanowicz, & McGurrun, 1983; Walbridge & Conroy, 1981; Walbridge, Whaley, & Conroy, 1981; Wyngaarden, Freedman, & Gollav, 1976	Singer, Close, Irvin, Gersten, & Sailor, 1984

quently provided by teachers and parents of previously segregated students as well (Giannini, personal communication, January 1987).

Affective Development

Closely tied to social development outcomes is evidence that integrated settings result in significantly more positive affect for persons with severe disabilities than do segregated settings (Park & Goetz, 1985). These investigators compared the affect of young adults with severe, multiple disabilities who were attending a program based at a community college (integrated) with a matched group of adults attending a sheltered day activity center (segregated), utilizing a scale adapted from one previously validated by Dunlap and Koegel (1980). Analysis using nonparametric statistics indicated significant differences between the groups in the direction of more positive affect for the community college group across two settings.

Interactive Development and Skill Generalization

Empirical support for increases in severely disabled students' interactive behavior as a function of structured intervention in integrated settings is perhaps the most prevalent finding reported in the integration literature (e.g., Anderson, 1984; Anderson & Goetz, 1983; Baldwin, 1979; Brady et al., 1984; Breen, Haring, Pitts-Conway, & Gaylord-Ross, 1985; Brinker & Thorpe, 1984a, 1985; Cole, 1986; Cole et al., 1986; Haring et al., 1987; Kohler & Fowler, 1985; Meyer, Fox, et al., 1987; Meyers-Winton, 1980; Murata, 1984; Smith, 1984; Strain & Odom, 1986; Voeltz, 1982; Voeltz & Brennan, 1982; etc.).

The hypothesis of enhanced motivation accruing to situations involving reciprocal horizontal (child to child) interactions is an outgrowth of some anecdotal observations of dramatic changes that have seemed to occur when formerly segregated students with severe disabilities were brought into a social context of involvement with same-age, nondisabled peers. Much of the early enthusiasm shown by special educators in response to the push for integration from Lou Brown (Brown et al., 1983) and others stemmed from these observations. There seemed to be something "magic" about regular and sustained contact with nondisabled age mates that produced increased responsiveness and indications of positive affect, even in students who had been very largely unresponsive in the absence of these contacts. The focus of research under this hypothesis has thus been to discover elements of the child-child interactive process that might explain increased responsiveness, and to validate the assumption that this increase would be reflected in more efficient instruction in new skill acquisition and generalization.

Much of the available research on horizontal interaction has been discussed elsewhere (Sailor, Halvorsen, Anderson, Goetz, Gee, Doering, & Hunt, 1986; Sailor, Anderson, Halvorsen, Filler, & Goetz, 1989); however, a number of studies merit comment. As we discussed briefly before, Anderson and Goetz (1983) conducted a comparative study of the nature of social interaction available in segregated versus integrated sites. Interactions were measured using the Educational Assessment of Social Interaction (EASI) checklist developed in conjunction with California Research Institute (Goetz, Haring, & Anderson, 1983). The results indicated that there were significantly more opportunities for interaction between severely disabled children and nondisabled children in the integrated setting. More important, these researchers found that 100% of the interactions sampled in the segregated settings were vertical (from a nondisabled adult caregiver to a severely disabled child). In the integrated settings 89% of the total interactions were horizontal (child to child), and only 11% were vertical caregiver interactions. These data indicate that not only are there more opportunities for interaction in integrated environments, but that students take advantage of these opportunities, as demonstrated by the fact that the overwhelming majority occur between ND and SD peers.

In addition, research is beginning to show that these reciprocal horizontal (peer-peer) interactions available in integrated settings enhance *skill acquisition and generalization* (Sailor et al., 1989). For example, studies have shown that communication skills (Goldstein & Wickstrom, 1986; Hunt, Alwell, & Goetz, 1988), play skills (Murata, 1984; Selby, 1984), and social skills (Lord & Hopkins, 1986) can be generalized and maintained when taught within the framework of horizontal relationships.

Goldstein and Wickstrom (1986) taught nondisabled children specific strategies to promote communicative interactions on the part of their preschool disabled classmates. The intervention resulted in increased rates of communicative interactions as well as generalizations, particularly in the incidence of "on-topic" responding to initiations from the nondisabled children. The authors expressed the conclusion that "peers who act as intervention agents in one setting or activity will also share in many other activities with the handicapped child, and can thus serve as common stimuli for interactive behavior in untrained settings" (p. 214).

Murata (1984) conducted a study to evaluate a role-playing procedure for training nondisabled peers to play age-appropriate games with severely disabled students. Her dependent variable was changes in the severely disabled students' social interaction behaviors. Her multiple baseline design revealed significant positive changes across three students as an outcome of the peer-training procedure.

Lord and Hopkins (1986) reported a study in which they examined the social behavior of children with autism in interactive dyads with both same-age (10–12 years) and younger (5–6 years) nondisabled peers. In this study, the nondisabled children were not specifically trained in ways to interact with the autistic children, yet when opportunities to interact spontaneously in dyads were presented, the autistic children not only spontaneously interacted, as measured by several indices, but generalized interactive skills to still other nondisabled peers, an effect also found by Smith (1984) in a similar study. The effects were stronger with the same-age peer dyads.

Other studies that have demonstrated positive peer-mediated social interaction effects in severely disabled children include those of Guralnick (1976); Hendrickson, Strain, Tremblay, and Shores (1982); Odom, Hoysun, Jamieson, and Strain (1985); Odom and Strain (1984); Strain (1977); and Strain, Shores, and Timm (1977). Many earlier studies were reviewed by Strain, Kerr, and Raglund (1981).

Finally, several recent studies have examined benefits to disabled children from structured efforts to improve interactions with their nondisabled siblings. Powell, Salzberg, Rule, Levy, and Itzkowitz (1983) trained parents to engage in particular strategies to promote more functional and effective interactions between their disabled children and those children's nondisabled siblings. Sustained, generalized improvements in interactions were associated with parents' acquisition of the trained skills.

James and Egel (1986) evaluated a direct prompt–training strategy to increase reciprocal interactions between and, by generalization, among siblings. Using a multiple baseline design across three pairs of siblings, the authors' training procedures, which consisted of direct prompting and modeling techniques, resulted in increased reciprocal interactions, including increased levels of imitations by the disabled preschool-age children, and generalization of improved interaction skills to other play groups. The changes in interactive behavior were further shown to maintain themselves at least six months after intervention.

Brinker's (1985) large sample studies on integration provided still further support for the importance of horizontal interactions. The degree of integration measured in this study was the rate per minute of social bids that severely disabled students directed toward nondisabled students in the environment. In this sample, 245 students with severe disabilities of all school ages were observed over eight 10-minute observation periods scheduled throughout the school year. The most significant proportion of the total variance in this multiple regression study that predicted the degree of integration was the amount of social behavior directed toward the students with severe disabilities. The authors concluded that nondisabled, same-age peers are the key to successful integration efforts.

What can be attributed to the outcomes of the research to date on the nature and efficacy of horizontal social interactions? There is a growing body of evidence that students with severe disabilities are indeed motivated to interact with their nondisabled age mates and that these interactions are facilitative of acquisition and generalization of a range of contextually relevant skills. The evidence also suggests that horizontal relationships can and should be directly facilitated by teaching staff, if not specifically trained.

Much research remains to be done to shed light on the elements of horizontal relationships that most directly benefit instructional goals and objects. Further research is clearly needed on the differential nature of various styles of horizontal interactions, such as peer tutorials, compared to spontaneous, nontutorial friendship relationships (cf. Haring et al., 1987; Murata, 1984; Selby, 1984; Smith, 1984; and Voeltz, 1980; 1982).

The point of this hypothesis is that a part of context relevance (in this case the relevance of the *social* context) that enhances instruction in natural community environments accrues to the presence of reciprocal interactive relationships among students with severe disabilities and their nondisabled age mates. The question for the future is how to apply this knowledge to increase the motivation of these students to acquire socially beneficial skills.

Improved Parental Expectations for Their Child's Future

Anderson and Farron-Davis (1987), and Freagon et al. (1983) have documented these outcomes, which have been reported by numerous parents (e.g., Vesey, 1986) as well. Parental reports have also included statements attributing the *increased health and independence* of their sons and daughters (Turnbull & Turnbull, 1985; Vesey, 1986) to the integrated environment, and this outcome has also been anecdotally reported in the literature (Forest, 1984; 1986).

The longitudinal study conducted by Anderson and Farron-Davis (1987) utilized a structured parent interview format within integrated and segregated groups to obtain information about (a) in what types of environments across the categories of home, respite, eating, personal fitness/ health, religious, vacation, cultural, sports, recreation, occupation, education and transportation did the family participate, and in what proportion (with what frequency) did the disabled child participate with the family; (b) what level of assistance was required by the student in these environments; and (c) the parents' expectations for the student's future level of independence in the settings. Two groups of parents of five integrated and five segregated matched students participated in the study over a four-year period, and results indicated an appreciably higher level of assistance across the range of activities was perceived as needed by the parents of students in the segregated group. This perceived level of assistance increased over time, but was not statistically significant. Similarly, the perceived level of assistance needed by integrated students decreased over the four-year period. Initial data from a descriptive parent interview study by Hanline and Halvorsen (1989) indicated that movement of the child to an integrated setting significantly increased family expectations for their son's or daughter's future functioning.

A recent study by the Disability Rights Education and Defense Fund (DREDF, 1985) examined educational equity and disabled high-school-age students, in order to ascertain factors that influenced the future plans of disabled students, their families and teachers, in two northern California school districts. Results from questionnaires/interviews with 130 parents demonstrated strong correlations between parental expectations for post-school living and working opportunities, and the extent to which their children were integrated, both at school and in social situations outside of school. For example, only 17% of the parents of disabled high school students attending fully segregated school settings expected their children to live independently, as opposed to 95% of parents of integrated students. Similarly, only 20% of parents of the fully segregated group expected full employment for their children, while approximately 90% of parents of integrated students expected full employment. Approximately 27% of the total sample were parents of students with severe disabilities; however, analyses indicated that for all skill levels, school segregation had a strong, negative relationship to parent expectations.

Increases in the Proportion of IEP Objectives Obtained

This outcome has been demonstrated in studies by Brinker and Thorpe (1984b), which we discussed earlier, and by Wang and Baker (1986). Wang and Baker utilized meta-analysis techniques to select and examine eleven empirical studies from a total pool of 264 studies of mainstreaming effects over a ten-year period. Results showed that mainstreamed special education students consistently outperformed their segregated peers from comparable disability classification groups. In addition, as was discussed in the previous best practices section, the quality of IEPs of integrated students has been demonstrated to be significantly better overall than that of segregated students' IEPs (Hunt et al., 1986).

Improved Attitudes Toward Severely Disabled Peers

McHale and Simeonsson (1980) and Voeltz (1980, 1982) were among the first to demonstrate the impact of interaction on peer attitudes, illustrating that when students receive accurate information about each other and are provided with opportunities to use that information on an ongoing basis, social acceptance occurs (cf. Donaldson, 1980; Johnson & Meyer, 1985; Siperstein & Bak, 1985). Voeltz (1982), Murray and Beckstead (1983), and Murray (1986) argued further that these longitudinal interactions lead to children having increased tolerance for diversity and difference in general. Additional research has demonstrated that nondisabled students continue to experience expected developmental gains when integrated with their severely disabled peers (Bricker & Bricker, 1977; Odom, DeKlyen, & Jenkins, 1984; Peck, Apolloni, Cooke, & Raver, 1978).

Community Employer Attitudes and Future Work Earnings and Placement

Pumpian, Shephard, and West (1986) have demonstrated the benefit associated with integrated, community-intensive vocational instruction for students with severe disabilities in terms of community and employer attitudes (see also Bates, Morrow, Pancsofar, & Sedlak, 1984; Hurd, Costello, Pajor, & Freagon, 1981; Pumpian, 1981), and in terms of future integrated work placements. Research conducted by, for example, Gaylord-Ross et al. (1987) has demonstrated that best practices within this model result in student advancement to more traditional work experience programs during school years, where they are employed at minimum wage and are supervised increasingly by employers. Graff's data on graduates from San Francisco integrated programs (1987) and data from Madison, Wisconsin (Brown et al., 1985, 1987), coupled with studies by Wehman et al. (1982); Wehman, Hill, et al. (1985), and Wehman, Kregel, and Seyfarth (1985) provide further evidence of positive postschool employment outcomes in terms of placement and wages.

Normalized Living Arrangement

A final outcome related to the quality of life for students with severe disabilities is a full range of individualized living options, particularly for individuals approaching adulthood. It can be hypothesized that this outcome is related not only to best practices, but also to other predicted integration outcomes, such as heightened community awareness, increased parental expectations, and the improved health, independence, and social skills of severely disabled persons. Walbridge and Conroy (1981) found that neighbors of a community group home experienced a positive shift in attitudes over time, further support for the thesis that contact and interaction result in acceptance of severely disabled persons. Additional study of the characteristics of neighbors with positive attitudes toward community living arrangements indicated that approximately 20% of the variance in this variable was accounted for by individuals' knowledge of mental retardation. Singer, Close, Irvin, Gersten, and Sailor (1984) have demonstrated that individuals can live successfully in the community regardless of their skill level, behavior problems, or the geographic nature of their receiving region. These authors evaluated a rural deinstitutionalization project for young, very severely disabled adults who also exhibited severe aberrant behaviors and were considered a "threat to the community" at the outset of the project. This study extended earlier findings by Close (1977); Conroy, Efthimiou, and Lemanowicz (1982); and Gage, Fredericks, Baldwin, Moore, and Grove (1987) in demonstrating that institutional residents not considered good candidates for community placement can nevertheless adapt to and thrive in community settings when there are highly structured but nonaversive behavior management programs and where there is close coordination among various service agency personnel, including integrated school programs where applicable (as in the Singer et al., 1984 study).

Hill, Lakin, and Bruininks (1984) conducted a nationwide survey of state-licensed and operated facilities and found both a decrease in the numbers of out-of-home placements for children, and an increase in the proportion of severely handicapped persons being served in the community. Sokol-Kessler, Conroy, Feinstein, Lemanowicz, and McGurrin (1983) contrasted behavioral data on matched groups of institutionalized and community-based residents, and found no developmental growth in the former group, but significant positive changes, including reductions in maladaptive behavior, in residents living in the community. This type of evidence coupled with improved attitudes, expectations, and skills, as well as a broader range of community service delivery models provides support for the prediction of increases in normalized living environments for integrated students approaching adulthood.

FUTURE DIRECTIONS

The overwhelming majority of research studies conducted over the past ten years provides clear support for integrated, less restrictive environments. By comparison, only a handful of studies and position papers have surfaced arguing against less restrictive placements (Cruickshank, 1977; Haywood, 1981; and Gottlieb, 1981; see also research reported by Biklen, 1979.)

Further research on the efficacy of integrated instruction, for all age groups, in comparison to segregated service models, is probably not needed. The case has been made. What is needed now is a body of research that relates best practice instructional procedures in specified integrated settings to reliable and socially valid outcomes. Questions requiring investigation include, for example, up to what ages should severely and profoundly disabled students have a mainstream regular class as their primary placement in order to maximize sustained horizontal interactions, leading to a more functional repertoire of age-appropriate skills? When and under what conditions should students begin to receive more community intensive instruction, with less concentration on peer-contact time in the school setting?

Related to these questions is the need for research on more effective, community-based teaching technologies. Sailor, Gee, et al. (1988) have argued that profoundly disabled students have been largely neglected in the recent advances in "best practices." Increased attention, for example, is needed on the development of microswitch systems and individualized adaptations that will facilitate the inclusion of this subgroup in the least restrictive environment. Concurrent investigations on the efficacy of heterogeneous groupings and the outcomes of these arrangements for both severely and profoundly disabled students should also be a focus of future research.

In addition, research is needed on nonaversive tactics with which to manage difficult behavior in community settings. Without this technology, recidivism and backlash are predictable concomitants to further integration efforts. Increased longitudinal and ethnographic investigations of integration's impact on students' quality of life outside of school, would also strengthen the existing data base and provide more information regarding the social validity of integrated "best practices."

Finally, the development of techniques to reduce prompt dependency and to facilitate the acquisition of generalized skills in natural settings offers a "new frontier" of research in applied teaching technology that is likely to sustain and enhance the movement toward the education of all students with disabilities in fully integrated and nonsheltered environments.

REFERENCES

Advisory Commission on Special Education (1986). *Sunset review report on special education programs: A report to the California legislature.* Sacramento, CA: Author.

Albright, K. Z., Brown, L., VanDeventer, P., & Jorgensen, J. (1987). *What regular educators should know about students with severe intellectual disabilities.* Unpublished manuscript, University of Wisconsin—Madison and Madison Metropolitan School District.

Allen, K. (1981). Curriculum models for successful mainstreaming. *Topics in Early Childhood Special Education, 1,* 45–55.

Almond, P., Rodgers, S., & Krug, D. (1979, Summer). Mainstreaming: A model for including elementary students in the severely handicapped classroom. *Teaching Exceptional Children,* pp. 135–139.

Anderson, J. (1984). *San Francisco school district evaluation report: Jose Ortega School study (1982–83).* Unpublished manuscript, San Francisco State University, California Research Institute.

Anderson, J. L. (1986). *Nonschool personnel preparation project: Final report.* San Francisco, CA: San Francisco State University.

Anderson, J., & Doering, K. (1985). *The changing role of teachers and administrators.* San Francisco State University, Nonschool Personnel Preparation Grant.

Anderson, J., & Farron-Davis, F. (1987). *A longitudinal comparison of parental expectations for their severely disabled sons and daughters attending integrated and segregated programs.* Manuscript in preparation, San Francisco State University, Department of Special Education, California Research Institute.

Anderson, J., & Goetz, L. (1983, November). *Opportunities for social interaction between severely disabled and nondisabled students in segregated and integrated educational settings.* Paper presented at the 10th Annual Conference of the Association for Persons with Severe Handicaps, San Francisco, CA.

Ashmore, R. D. (1975). Background considerations in developing strategies for changing attitudes and behavior toward the mentally retarded. In M. T. Begaba & S. A. Richardson (Eds.), *The mentally retarded and society: A social science perspective* (pp. 227–241). Baltimore, MD: University Park Press.

Baer, D. (1986). "Exemplary service to what outcome?" Review of *Education of learners with severe handicaps: Exemplary service strategies. Journal of the Association for Persons with Severe Handicaps, 11*(2), 145–147.

Baker, B. L., Heifetz, L. J., & Murphy, D. (1980). Behavioral training for parents of retarded children: One-year follow-up. *American Journal of Mental Deficiency, 85,* 31–38.

Baldwin, M. (1979, November). *The role of early peer interactions in the development of later cooperative play in the severely handicapped.* Unpublished manuscript, University of California, Berkeley, and San Francisco State University Joint Doctoral Program.

Bates, P., Morrow, S. A., Pancsofar, E., & Sedlak, R. (1984). The effective functional vs. nonfunctional activities on attitudes/expectations of nonhandicapped college students: What they see is what we get. *Journal of the Association for Persons with Severe Handicaps, 9*(2), 73–78.

Bellamy, G. T., & Wilcox, B. (1982). Secondary education for severely handicapped students: Guidelines for quality services. In K. Lynch, W. Kiernan, & J. Stark (Eds.), *Prevocational and vocational education for special needs youth: A blueprint for the 1980s* (pp. 84–92). Baltimore, MD: Paul H. Brookes.

Bellamy, G. T., Wilcox, B., Rose, H., & McDonnell, J. (1986). Education and career preparation for youth with disabilities. *Journal of Adolescent Health Care, 6,* 125–135.

Biklen, D. (1979). The community imperative. *Institutions, 2*(8), 31–38.

Biklen, D. (1985). *Achieving the complete school: Strategies for effective mainstreaming.* New York: Teachers College Press.

Biklen, D., & Foster, S. (1985). Principles for integrated community programming. In M. Brady & P. Gunter (Eds.), *Integrating moderately and severely handicapped learners* (pp. 16–46). Springfield, IL: Charles C. Thomas.

Biklen, D., & Taylor, S. (1985). School district administrators: Leadership strategies. In D. Biklen (Ed.), *Achieving the complete school: Strategies for effective mainstreaming* (pp. 104–149). New York: Teachers College Press.

Billingsley, F. F. (1984). Where are the generalized outcomes? An examination of instructional objectives. *Journal of the Association for Persons with Severe Handicaps, 9*(3), 186–192.

Binkard, B. (1985). A successful handicap awareness program—run by special parents. *Teaching Exceptional Children, 18*(1), 12–16.

Blacher, J., & Turnbull, A. P. (1983) Are parents mainstreamed? A survey of parent interactions in the mainstreamed preschool. *Education and Training of the Mentally Retarded, 18*(1), 10–16.

Blacher-Dixon, J., Leonard, J., & Turnbull, A. P. (1981). Mainstreaming at the early childhood level: Current and future perspectives. *Mental Retardation, 19*(5), 235–241.

Blatt, B. (1966). *Christmas in Purgatory.* Boston, MA: Allyn & Bacon.

Blatt, B. (1970). *Exodus from pandemonium.* Boston, MA: Allyn & Bacon.

Blatt, B. (1985). Foreword. In D. Biklen, *Achieving the complete school: Strategies for effective mainstreaming.* New York: Teachers College Press.

Bogdan, R., & Biklen, D. (1985). The principal's role in mainstreaming. In D. Biklen (Ed.), *Achieving the complete school: Strategies for effective mainstreaming* (pp. 30–51). New York: Teachers College Press.

Borthwick, S. A., Meyers, C. E., & Eymann, R. K. (1981). Comparative adaptive and maladaptive behavior of mentally retarded clients of five residential settings in three western states. In R. H. Bruininks, C. E. Meyers, B. B. Sigford, & K. C. Lakin (Eds.), *Deinstitutionalization and community adjustment of mentally retarded people* (pp. 351–359). Washington, DC: American Association on Mental Deficiency.

Brady, M. P., Shores, R. E., Gunter, P., McEvoy, M. A., Fox, J. J., & White, C. (1984). Generalization of an adolescent's social interaction behavior via multiple peers in a classroom setting. *Journal of the Association for Persons with Severe Handicaps (JASH), 9*(4), 278–288.

Breen, C., Haring, T., Pitts-Conway, V., & Gaylord-Ross, R. (1985). The training and generalization of social interaction during breaktime at two job sites in the natural environment. *Journal of the Association for Persons with Severe Handicaps (JASH), 10*(1), 41–50.

Bricker, D., & Bricker, W. (1977). A developmentally integrated approach to early intervention. *Education and Training of the Mentally Retarded, 12*(2), 100–107.

Brinker, R. P. (1985). Interactions between severely mentally retarded students and other students in integrated and segregated public school settings. *American Journal of Mental Deficiency, 89*(6), 587–594.

Brinker, R. P. (in press). *The rate and quality of social behavior of severely handicapped students in integrated and nonintegrated settings.* Princeton, NJ: Educational Testing Service.

Brinker, R., & Thorpe, M. (1984a). *Evaluation of the integration of severely handicapped students in regular education and community settings* (Final report). Princeton, NJ: Educational Testing Service, Division of Education Policy Research and Services.

Brinker, R. P., & Thorpe, M. E. (1984b). Integration of severely handicapped students and the proportion of IEP objectives achieved. *Exceptional Children, 51*(2), 168–175.

Brinker, R. P., & Thorpe, M. E. (1985). Some empirically derived hypotheses about the influence of state policy on degree of integration of severely handicapped students. *RASE, 6*(3), 18–26.

Brinker, R., & Thorpe, M. (1986). Features of integrated educational ecologies that predict social behavior among severely mentally retarded and nonretarded students. *American Journal of Mental Deficiency, 91*(2), 150–159.

Brown v. Board of Education, 347 U.S. 483 (1954).

Brown, F., Helmstetter, E., & Guess, D. (1986). *Current best practices with students with profound disabilities: Are there any?* University of Kansas, manuscript in preparation.

Brown, L., Branston, M. B., Hamre-Nietupski, S., Johnson, F., Wilcox, B., & Gruenewald, L. (1979). A rationale for comprehensive longitudinal interactions between severely handicapped students and nonhandicapped students and other citizens. *AAESPH Review, 4*(1), 3–14.

Brown, L., Nisbet, J., Ford, A., Sweet, M., Shiraga, B., York, J., & Loomis, R. (1983). The critical need for nonschool instruction in educational programs for severely handicapped students. *Journal of the Association for Persons with Severe Handicaps, 8,* 71–77.

Brown, L., Nietupski, J., & Hamre-Nietupski, S. (1976). The criterion of ultimate functioning and public school services for severely handicapped students. In M. A. Thomas (Ed.), *Hey, don't forget about me: Education's investment in the severely, profoundly, and multiply handicapped* (pp. 197–209). Reston, VA: Council for Exceptional Children.

Brown, L., Pumpian, I., Baumgart, D., VanDeventer, P., Ford, A., Nisbet, J., Schroeder, J., & Gruenewald, L. (1981). Longitudinal transition plans in programs for severely handicapped students. *Exceptional Children, 47*(8), 624–630.

Brown, L., Rogan, P., Shiraga, B., Zanella Albright, K., Kessler, K., Bryson, F., VanDeventer, P., & Loomis, R. (1987). *A vocational follow up evaluation of the 1984–1986 Madison Metropolitan School District graduates with severe intellectual disabilities.* Madison, WI: University of Wisconsin and Madison Metropolitan School District.

Brown, L., Shiraga, B., York, J., Kessler, K., Strohm, B., Rogan, P., Sweet, M., Zanella, K., VanDeventer, P., & Loomis, R. (1984). Integrated work opportunities for adults with severe handicaps: The extended training option. *Journal of the Association for Persons with Severe Handicaps* (JASH), 9(4), 262–269.

Brown, L., Shiraga, B., York, J., Solner, A. U., Albright, K. Z., Rogan, P., McCarthy, E., & Loomis, R. (1985). On integrated work. In L. Brown, B. Shiraga, J. York,

A. U. Solner, K. Z. Albright, P. Rogan, E. McCarthy, & R. Loomis. (Eds.), *Educational programs for students with severe intellectual disabilities* (Vol. 15, pp. 1–16). Madison: University of Wisconsin—Madison and Madison Metropolitan School District.

Brown, L., Wilcox, B., Sontag, E., Vincent, B., Dodd, N., & Gruenewald, L. (1977). Toward the realization of the least restrictive educational environments for severely handicapped students. *AAESPH Review, 4*, 3–14.

Burello, L., & Sage, D. D. (1979). *Leadership and change in special education.* Englewood Cliffs, NJ: Prentice-Hall.

Burton, T. A., & Hirschoren, A. (1979). Some further thoughts and clarification on the education of severely and profoundly retarded children. *Exceptional Children, 45,* 618–625.

California State Department of Education. (1985). *Individualized critical skills model significant other interview* (rev. ed.). Sacramento, CA: Special Education Resource Network.

Campbell, P. H. (1987). Integrated programming for students with multiple handicaps. In L. Goetz, D. Guess, & K. Stremel-Campbell (Eds.), *Innovative program design for individuals with dual sensory impairments* (pp. 159–190). Baltimore, MD: Paul H. Brookes.

Chin-Perez, G., Hartman, D., Sook Park, H., Sacks, S., Wershing, A., & Gaylord-Ross, R. (1986). Maximizing social contact for secondary students with severe handicaps. *Journal of the Association for Persons with Severe Handicaps, 22*(2), 118–124.

Christopolos, G., & Reny, P. A. (1969). Critical examination of special programs. *Journal of Special Education, 3,* 371–379.

Close, D. (1977). Community living for severely and profoundly retarded adults: A group home study. *American Journal of Mental Deficiency, 86*(6), 581–587.

Cole, D. A. (1986). Facilitating play children's peer relationships: Are we having fun yet? *American Education Research Journal, 23*(2), 201–215.

Cole, D. A., Meyer, L. M., Vandercook, T., & McQuarter, R. J. (1986). Interactions between peers with and without severe handicaps: The dynamics of teacher intervention. *American Journal of Mental Deficiency, 91*(2), 160–169.

Cone, J. D., Delawyer, D. D., & Wolfe, V. V. (1985). Assessing parent participation: The parent/family involvement index. *Exceptional Children, 51*(5), 417–424.

Conroy, J., Efthimiou, J., & Lemanowicz, J. (1982). A matched comparison of the developmental growth of institutionalized and deinstitutionalized mentally retarded clients. *American Journal of Mental Deficiency, 86*(6), 581–587.

Copeland, W., & Iverson, I. (1985). Developing financial incentives for placement in the least restrictive alternative. In C. Lakin & R. Bruininks (Eds.), *Strategies for achieving community integration of developmentally disabled citizens* (pp. 291–312). Baltimore: Paul H. Brookes.

Crapps, J., Langone, J., & Swaim, S. (1985). Quantity and quality of participation in community environments by mentally retarded adults. *Education and training of the Mentally Retarded, 20*(2), 124–129.

Cruickshank, W. M. (1977). Least restrictive placement: Administrative wishful thinking. *Journal of Learning Disabilities, 10,* 193–194.

Disability Rights Education and Defense Fund. (1985). *Educational equity and high school aged disabled students.* Unpublished manuscript, DREDF, Berkeley, CA.

Doering, K. (1985). *The effects of inservice training on documented instruction and quality of IEP objectives with students with severe disabilities.* Unpublished master's thesis, San Francisco State University, San Francisco, CA.

Doering, K., & Hunt, P. (1983). *Inventory processes for social interaction (IPSI).* San Francisco, CA: San Francisco State University, Project REACH. (ERIC Document Reproduction Service No. ED 242 181)

Donaldson, J. (1980). Changing attitudes toward handicapped persons: A review and analysis of research. *Exceptional Children, 46*(7), 504–514.

Donnellan, A., LaVigna, G., Zambito, J., & Thvedt, J. (1985). A time-limited intensive intervention program model to support community placement for persons with severe handicaps. *Journal of the Association for Persons with Severe Handicaps, 10*(3), 123–131.

Dunlap, G., & Koegel, R. (1980). Motivating autistic children through stimulus-change. *Journal of Applied Behavior Analysis, 13,* 619–628.

Dunn, L. M. (1968). Special education for the mildly retarded: Is much of it justifiable? *Exceptional Children, 35,* 5–22.

Falvey, M. (1980). *Changes in academic and social competence of kindergarten aged handicapped children as a result of an integrated classroom.* Unpublished doctoral dissertation, University of Wisconsin—Madison.

Farron-Davis, F., & Halvorsen, A. (1987). *Survey of California's special centers for severely disabled students.* San Francisco, CA: San Francisco State University, California Research Institute on Integration.

Favell, J. E. (1977). *The power of positive reinforcement: A handbook of behavior modification.* Springfield, IL: Charles C. Thomas.

Fenrick, N. H., & Petersen, T. K. (1984). Developing positive changes in attitudes towards moderately/severely handicapped students through a peer tutoring program. *Education and Training of the Mentally Retarded, 19*(2), 83–90.

Fernald, W. E. (1915). Cited in Wolfensberger, W. (1975). *The origin and nature of our institutional models.* Syracuse, NY: Human Policy Press.

Filler, J., Goetz, L., & Sailor, W. (1986). *Factors which predict opportunities for interaction between students with severe disabilities and their nondisabled peers.* Manuscript submitted for publication.

Filler, J., & Halvorsen, A. (1986). [Follow-up data on program graduates]. Unpublished raw data, California State University, Hayward, Special Education Option, Educational Psychology Department.

Filler, J., Halvorsen, A., & Rosenberg, W. (1984). *Teacher Facilitators of Integration Personnel Preparation Project* (Contract #Goo-840-1336). California State University, Hayward.

Finch, L., & Landriau, D. (1987). *Creating integrated options for pupils with severe disabilities in Alameda County: Exploratory five-year plan.* Alameda, CA: County Office of Education.

Forest, M. (1984). *Education/integration: A collection of readings on the integration of children with mental handicaps into regular school systems.* Downsview, Ontario, Canada: National Institute on Mental Retardation.

Forest, M. (1986). *Making a difference: What communities can do to prevent mental handicap and promote lives of quality:* Vol. 3. *Helping children live, learn and grow in their communities.* Downsview, Ontario, Canada: National Institute on Mental Retardation.

Frassinelli, L., Superior, K., & Meyers, J. (1983). A consultation model for speech and language intervention. *ASHA Newsletter,* November 25–30.

Freagon, S., Wheeler, J., Brankin, G., McDannel, K., Costello, D., & Peters, W. (1983). *Curricular processes for the school and community: Integration of severely handicapped students aged 6–21* (Project replication guide). DeKalb, IL: Northern Illinois University.

Freagon, S., Wheeler, J., Brankin, G., McDannel, K., Stern, L., Usilton, R., & Keiser, N. (1985). Increasing personal competence in the community. In M. Brady & P. Gunter (Eds.), *Integrating moderately and severely handicapped learners* (pp. 238–263). Springfield, IL: Charles C. Thomas.

Fredericks, H. D., Anderson, R., & Baldwin, V. (1979). The identification of competency indicators of teachers of the severely handicapped. *AAESPH Review, 4,* 81–95.

Gage, M., Fredericks, H., Baldwin, V., Moore, W., & Grove, D. (1987). Group homes for handicapped children. In N. Haring & D. Bricker (Eds.), *Teaching the severely handicapped* (Vol. 3, pp. 263–281). Columbus, OH: Special Press.

Ganschow, L., Weber, D., & Davis, M. (1984). Preservice teacher preparation for mainstreaming. *Exceptional Children, 52,* 74–76.

Gaylord-Ross, R., Forte, J., Storey, K., Gaylord-Ross, C., & Jameson, D. (1987). Community-referenced instruction in technological work-settings. *Exceptional Children, 54*(2), 112–120.

Gaylord-Ross, R., Haring, T., Breen, C., & Pitts-Conway, V. (1984). The training and generalization of social interaction skills with autistic youth. *Journal of Applied Behavior Analysis, 17,* 229–247.

Gaylord-Ross, R. J., & Pitts-Conway, V. (1984). Social behavior development in integrated secondary autistic programs. In N. Certo, N. Haring, & R. York (Eds.), *Public school integration of the severely handicapped: Rational issues and progressive alternatives* (pp. 197–220). Baltimore: Paul H. Brookes.

Gee, K., & Goetz, L. (1985). *Outcomes of instructing orientation and mobility skills across purposeful travel in natural environments.* Manuscript in preparation.

Gee, K., & Goetz, L. (1986). *Establishing generalized use of residual vision through instruction in natural contexts.* Unpublished manuscript, San Francisco State University, Department of Special Education.

Gee, K., Goetz, L., Graham, N., & Lee, M. (1986, November). *Community intensive education for students with sensory impairments: A curriculum model integrating basic skill needs into community contexts.* Presentation at 13th annual conference, The Association for Persons with Severe Handicaps (TASH), San Francisco, CA.

Gee, K., Harrell, R., & Rosenberg, R. (1987). A model for teaching orientation and mobility skills within and across functional travel routes. In L. Goetz, D. Guess, & K. Stremel-Campbell (Eds.), *Innovative program design for individuals with dual sensory impairments* (pp. 127–158). Baltimore, MD: Paul H. Brookes.

Gersten, R., Crowell, F., & Bellamy, T. (1986). Spillover effects: Impact of vocational training on the lives of severely mentally retarded clients. *American Journal of Mental Deficiency, 90*(5), 501–506.

Giangreco, M. (1986). Effects of integrated therapy: A pilot study. *Journal of the Association for the Severely Handicapped, 11,* 205–208.

Goetz, L., & Gee, K. (1987). Functional vision programming: A model for teaching visual behaviors in natural contexts. In L. Goetz, D. Guess, & K. Stremel-Campbell (Eds.), *Innovative program design for individuals with dual sensory impairments* (pp. 77–99). Baltimore, MD: Paul H. Brookes.

Goetz, L., Gee, K., & Sailor, W. (1985). Using a behavior chain interruption strategy to teach communication skills to students with severe disabilities. *Journal of the Association for Persons with Severe Handicaps, 10*(1), 21–30.

Goetz, L., Haring, T., & Anderson, J. (1983). *Educational assessment of social interaction (EASI).* San Francisco: San Francisco State University and Project REACH. (ERIC Document Reproduction Service No. ED 242 184)

Goldberg, I. I., & Cruickshank, W. (1958). The trainable but noneducable: Whose responsibility. *National Education Association Journal, 47,* 622–623.

Goldstein, H., & Wickstrom, S. (1986). Peer intervention effects on communicative interaction among handicapped and nonhandicapped preschoolers. *Journal of Applied Behavior Analysis, 19,* 209–214.

Gottlieb, J. (1981). Mainstreaming: Fulfilling the promise? *American Journal of Mental Deficiency, 86,* 115–126.

Graff, S. (1987). [Comparison of student placement in postschool environments from the 1986–87 school year.] Unpublished raw data. San Francisco, CA: San Francisco State University, Department of Special Education, Community Transitional Services Project.

Graff, S., & Sailor, W. (1986). Individual transition plan. San Francisco, CA: San Francisco State University, Department of Special Education, Community Transitional Services Project.

Grenot-Scheyer, M., & Falvey, M. (1986). Integration issues and strategies. In M. Falvey, *Community based curriculum* (pp. 217–233). Baltimore, MD: Paul H. Brookes.

Guralnick, M. (1976). The value of integrating handicapped and non-handicapped preschool children. *American Journal of Orthopsychiatry, 46,* 236–245.

Guralnick, M. (1984). The peer interactions of young developmentally delayed children in specialized and integrated settings. In T. Field, J. Roopnarine, & M. Segal (Eds.), *Friendships in normal and handicapped children* (pp. 139–152). Norwood, NJ: Ablex.

Halvorsen, A. (1983a). *Parents and community together (PACT).* San Francisco: San Francisco State University; San Francisco Unified School District. (ERIC Document Reproduction Service No. ED 242 183)

Halvorsen, A. (Ed.). (1983b). *Proceedings of the Bay Area Conference on the Integration of Students with Severe Disabilities* (LRE Module I). San Francisco: San Francisco State University, California Research Institute.

Halvorsen, A. T. (Ed.). (1984). *Proceedings of the Conference on the Transition of Stu-*

dents with Severe Disabilities into Integrated School Environments (LRE Module II). San Jose: San Francisco State University and San Jose State University, California Research Institute.

Halvorsen, A. (1986). *LEA needs assessment and planning process for integration*. San Francisco, CA: San Francisco State University, Department of Special Education, California Research Institute.

Halvorsen, A., & Anderson, J. (1986). *Teacher survey of integration best practices*. San Francisco: San Francisco State University, Department of Special Education, California Research Institute.

Hamre-Nietupski, S., Branston, M., Ford, A., Stoll, A., Sweet, M., Gruenewald, L., & Brown, L. (1978). Curricular strategies for developing longitudinal interactions between severely handicapped and nonhandicapped individuals in school and nonschool environments. In L. Brown, S. Hamre-Nietupski, S. Lyon, M. Branston, M. Flavey, & L. Gruenewald (Eds.), *Curricular strategies for developing longitudinal interactions between severely handicapped students and others and curricular strategies for teaching severely handicapped students to acquire and perform skills in response to naturally occurring cues and correction procedures* (Vol. 8, Part 1). Madison, WI: Madison Metropolitan School District.

Hamre-Nietupski, S., & Nietupski, J. (1981). Integral involvement of severely handicapped students within regular public schools. *TASH Journal, 6*, 30–39.

Hamre-Nietupski, S., Nietupski, J., Bates, P., & Maurer, S. (1982, Winter). Implementing a community-based educational model for moderately/severely handicapped students: Common problems and suggested solutions. *TASH Journal, 7*(2), 38–43.

Hamre-Nietupski, S., Nietupski, J., Stainback, W., & Stainback, S. (1984). Preparing school systems for longitudinal integration efforts. In N. Certo, N. Haring, & R. York (Eds.), *Public school integration of severely handicapped students: Rational issues and progressive alternatives* (pp. 107–141). Baltimore, MD: Paul H. Brookes.

Hanline, M. (1985). *Integrated versus nonintegrated play: Effects on social play, cognitive play, and communicative responses of disabled toddlers*. Unpublished doctoral dissertation, University of California, Berkeley.

Hanline, M., & Halvorsen, A. (1989). Parental perception of the integration transition process. *Exceptional Children, 55*(6), 487–492.

Haring, N., & Billingsley, F. (1984). Systems-change strategies to ensure the future of integration. In N. Certo, N. Haring, & R. York (Eds.), *Public school integration of severely handicapped students* (pp. 83–106). Baltimore, MD: Paul H. Brookes.

Haring, T., Breen, C., Pitts-Conway, V., Lee, M., & Gaylord-Ross, R. (1987). Adolescent peer tutoring and special friend experiences. *Journal of the Association for Persons with Severe Handicaps, 12*(4), 280–286.

Hasazi, S., Gordon, L., Roe, C., Finck, K., Hull, M., & Salembier, G. (1985). A statewide follow-up on post high school employment and residential status of students labeled "mentally retarded." *Education and Training of the Mentally Retarded, 20*(4), 222–234.

Haywood, H. (1981). Reducing social vulnerability is the challenge of the eighties (AAMD presidential address). *Mental Retardation, 19*(4), 190–195.

Heller, H. (1972). The resource room: A mere change or a real opportunity for the handicapped? *Journal of Special Education, 6,* 369–376.

Hendrickson, J., Strain, P., Tremblay, A., & Shores, R. (1982). Relationship between toy and material use and the occurrence of social interactive behaviors by normally developing preschool children. *Psychology in the Schools, 19,* 212–220.

Hill, B., Lakin, C., & Bruininks, R. (1984). Trends in residential services for people who are mentally retarded: 1977–1982. *Journal of the Association for Persons with Severe Handicaps, 9*(4), 243–250.

Hill, M., & Wehman, P. (1983). Cost benefit analysis of placing moderately and severely handicapped individuals into competitive employment. *Journal of the Association for Persons with Severe Handicaps, 8,* 30–38.

Holvoet, J., Guess, D., Mulligan, M., & Brown, F. (1980). The individualized curriculum sequencing model: A teaching strategy for severely handicapped students. *Journal of the Association for Persons with Severe Handicaps, 5*(4), 337–351.

Holvoet, J., O'Neill, C., Chazdon, L., Carr, D., & Warner, J. (1983). Hey, do we really have to take data? *Journal of the Association for Persons with Severe Handicaps, 8*(3), 56–69.

Horner, R., Bellamy, T., & Colvin, G. (1984). Responding in the presence of non-trained stimuli: Implications of generalization error pattern. *Journal of the Association for Persons with Severe Handicaps, 9,* 287–295.

Horner, R., Sprague, J., & Wilcox, B. (1982). General case programming for community activities. In B. Wilcox & G. Bellamy (Eds.), *Design of high school programs for severely handicapped students* (pp. 61–98). Baltimore, MD: Paul H. Brookes.

Hunt, P. (1985). *The acquisition and generalization of communication and language skills by severely handicapped students in integrated vs. segregated educational environments.* Unpublished manuscript, San Francisco State University, Department of Special Education.

Hunt, P., Alwell, M., & Goetz, L. (1988). Acquisition of conversation skills and the reduction of inappropriate social interaction behaviors. *Journal of the Association for Persons with Severe Handicaps, 13*(1), 20–27.

Hunt, P., Goetz, L., & Anderson, J. (1986). The quality of IEP objectives associated with placement on integrated versus segregated school sites. *Journal of the Association for Persons with Severe Handicaps, 11*(2), 125–130.

Hurd, D., Costello, D., Pajor, M., & Freagon, S. (1981). Administrative considerations in changing from a school-contained to a community-based program for severely handicapped students. In S. Freagon, M. Pajor, G. Brankin, A. Galloway, D. Rich, P. Karel, M. Wilson, D. Costello, W. Peters, & D. Hurd (eds.), *Teaching severely handicapped students in the community* (pp. 29–38). DeKalb, IL: Northern Illinois University.

Iacino, R., & Bricker, D. (1978). The generative teacher: A model for preparing personnel to work with the severely/profoundly handicapped. In N. Haring &

D. Bricker (Eds.), *Teaching the severely handicapped* (Vol. 3, pp. 131–150). Seattle, WA: American Association for the Education of the Severely/Profoundly Handicapped.

James, S. D., & Egel, A. L. (1986). A direct prompting strategy for increasing reciprocal interactions between handicapped and nonhandicapped siblings. *Journal of Applied Behavior Analysis, 19*(2), 173–186.

James, L., Mulaik, S., & Brett, J. (1982). *Causal analysis: Assumptions, models and data*. Beverly Hills: Sage Publication.

Jenkins, J., Speltz, M., & Odom, S. (1985). Integrating normal and handicapped preschoolers: Effects on child development and social interaction. *Exceptional Children, 52*(1), 7–17.

Johnson, D., & Johnson, R. (1986). Mainstreaming and cooperative learning strategies. *Exceptional Children, 52*(6), 553–561.

Johnson, R., & Johnson, D. (1983). Effects of cooperative, competitive, and individualistic learning experiences on social development. *Exceptional Children, 49*, 323–330.

Johnson, R., & Meyer, L. (1985). Program design and research to normalize peer interactions. In M. Brady & P. Gunter (Eds.), *Integrating moderately and severely handicapped learners: Strategies that work* (pp. 79–101). Springfield, IL: Charles C. Thomas.

Kahan, E. (1984, August). Social skills and the disabled child: A guide to appearance. *The Exceptional Parent*, pp. 47–48.

Kanner, L. (1964). *History and care of the mentally retarded*. Springfield, IL: Charles C. Thomas.

Karnes, M. B., & Teska, J. A. (1980). Toward successful parent involvement in programs for handicapped children. In J. J. Gallegher (Ed.), *New directions for exceptional children: Parents and families of handicapped children* (Vol. 4, pp. 85–109). San Francisco, CA: Jossey-Bass.

Kenowitz, L., Zweibel, S., & Edgar, E. (1978). Determining the least restrictive opportunity for the severely and profoundly handicapped. In N. Haring & D. Bricker (Eds.), *Teaching the severely handicapped* (Vol. 3, pp. 150–169). Columbus, OH: Special Press.

Keyser, J., Billingsley, F., & Neel, R. (1986). A comparison of in-context and traditional instructional approaches: Total task, single trial versus backward chaining, multiple trials. *Journal of the Association for Persons with Severe Handicaps, 11*(1), 28–38.

Knapczyk, D. R., & Dever, R. B. (1979). The role of supervisory personnel in programs for the severely handicapped. *AAESPH Review, 4*(4), 346–353.

Knoll, J., & Meyer, L. (1987). *Principles and practices for school integration of students with severe disabilities: An overview of the literature*. Syracuse, NY: Syracuse University Community Integration Project, Center on Human Policy.

Kohl, F. L., Moses, L. G., & Stettner-Eaton, B. A. (1983). The results of teaching fifth and sixth graders to be instructional trainers with students who are severely handicapped. *Journal of the Association for Persons with Severe Handicaps, 8*(4), 32–40.

Kohler, F., & Fowler, S. (1985). Training prosocial behaviors to young children: An analysis of reciprocity with untrained peers. *Journal of Applied Behavior Analysis, 3,* 187–200.

Kregel, J. (1985). Training for community integration. *The Exceptional Parent, 15*(9), 39–44.

Landau, J. (1987). *Out of the mainstream: Education of disabled youth in Massachusetts* (Report). Boston, MA: Massachusetts Advocacy Center.

Lakin, K. C., & Bruininks, R. (1985). Contemporary services for handicapped children and youth. In R. Bruininks & K. C. Lakin (Eds.), *Living and learning in the least restrictive environment* (pp. 3–22). Baltimore, MD: Paul H. Brookes.

Laski, F. (1985). Right to habilitation and right to education: The legal foundation. In R. Bruininks & K. C. Lakin (Eds.), *Living and learning in the least restrictive environment* (pp. 67–79). Baltimore, MD: Paul H. Brookes.

LaVigna, G. W., & Donnellan, A. M. (1987). *Alternatives to punishment: Solving behavior problems with nonaversive strategies.* New York: Irvington.

Liberty, K. (1985). Enhancing instruction for maintenance, generalization, and adaptation. In K. Lakin & R. Bruininks (Eds.), *Strategies for achieving community integration of developmentally disabled citizens* (pp. 3–25). Baltimore, MD: Paul H. Brookes.

Lilly, S. M. (1970). Special education: A teapot in a tempest. *Exceptional Children, 37,* 43–49.

Lipton, D. (1983). A parent's perspective on integration. In A. Halvorsen (Ed.), *Proceedings of the Bay Area Conference on the Integration of Students with Severe Disabilities* (LRE Module I, pp. 25–30). San Francisco: San Francisco State University, California Research Institute.

Lord, C., & Hopkins, J. (1986). The social behavior of autistic children with younger and same-age nonhandicapped peers. *Journal of Autism and Developmental Disorders, 16*(3), 249–262.

Lyon, S., & Lyon, G. (1980). Team functioning and staff development: A role release approach to providing integrated educational services for severely handicapped students. *Journal of the Association for Persons with Severe Handicaps, 5*(3), 250–263.

Martin, E. (1976). Address to the 1976 American Association for the Education of Severely/Profoundly Handicapped (AAESPH) Conference. Reported in N. Certo, W. Haring, & R. York (Eds.), *Public school integration of severely handicapped students* (p. 3). Baltimore, MD: Paul H. Brookes.

Martin, R. (1986). *Ending segregation of handicapped students: Taking steps toward the least restrictive environment.* Austin, TX: Advocacy.

McCormick, L., & Goldman, R. (1979). The transdisciplinary model: Implications for service delivery and personnel preparation for the severely and profoundly handicapped. *AAESPH Review, 4*(2), 152–161.

McDonnell, J., & Hardman, M. (1986). Planning the transition of young adults with severe handicaps from school to community services. *Education and Training of the Mentally Retarded, 20*(4), 275–286.

McDonnell, J., & Horner, R. (1985). Effects of in vivo versus simulation-plus-in vivo training on the acquisition and generalization of grocery item selection by high school students with severe handicaps. *Analysis and Intervention in Developmental Disabilities, 5,* 323–343.

McDonnell, J., Wilcox, B., & Boles, S. (1986). Do we know enough to plan for transition? *Journal of the Association for Persons with Severe Handicaps, 11*(1), 53–60.

McDonnell, J., Wilcox, B., Boles, S., & Bellamy, G. T. (1985). Transition issues facing youth with severe disabilities: Parents' perspective. *Journal of the Association for Persons with Severe Disabilities, 10*(1), 61–65.

McGregor, G., Janssen, C., Larsen, L., & Tillery, W. (1986). Philadelphia's urban model project: A system-wide effort to integrate students with severe handicaps. *Journal of the Association for Persons with Severe Handicaps, 11*(1), 61–67.

McHale, S. M., & Simeonsson, R. J. (1980). Effects of interaction on nonhandicapped children's attitudes toward autistic children. *American Journal of Mental Deficiency, 85*(1), 18–24.

Meyer, L. H. (1985). *Program quality indicators: A checklist of most promising practices in educational programs for students with severe disabilities.* Syracuse, NY: Syracuse University, Division of Special Education and Rehabilitation.

Meyer, L. H., Eichinger, J., & Park-Lee, S. (1987). A validation of program quality indicators in educational services for students with severe disabilities. *Journal of the Association for Persons with Severe Handicaps, 12*(4), 251–263.

Meyer, L. H., & Evans, I. M. (1986). Modification of excess behavior: An adaptive and functional approach for educational and community contexts. In R. Horner, L. H. Meyer, & H. D. Fredericks (Eds.), *Education of learners with severe handicaps: Exemplary service strategies* (pp. 315–350). Baltimore, MD: Paul H. Brookes.

Meyer, L. H., Fox, A., Schermer, A., Ketetson, D., Montan, N., Maley, K., & Cole, D. (1987). The effects of teacher intrusion on social play interactions between children with autism and their nonhandicapped peers. *Journal of Autism and Developmental Disorders, 17*(3), 315–332.

Meyer, L., & Kishi, G. S. (1985). School integration strategies. In K. Lakin, & R. Bruininks (Eds.), *Strategies for achieving community integration of developmentally disabled citizens* (pp. 231–252). Baltimore, MD: Paul H. Brookes.

Meyer, L., & Putnam, J. (1987). Social integration. In V. B. Van Hasselt, P. Strain, & M. Hersen (Eds.), *Handbook of developmental and physical disabilities* (pp. 107–133). New York: Pergamon.

Meyers-Winton, S. (1980). *The comparative effects of peers and adults instructing severely handicapped students on the generalization of social skills.* University of California—Berkeley/San Francisco State University Joint Doctoral Program.

Murata, C. (1984). The effects of an indirect training procedure for nonhandicapped peers on interaction response class behaviors of autistic children. In R. Gaylord-Ross, T. Haring, C. Breen, M. Lee, V. Pitts-Conway, & B. Roger (Eds.), *The social development of handicapped students.* San Francisco, CA: San Francisco State University.

Murray, C. (1983). Social interaction, disability education, and attitude change: Integrated schooling for students with severe/multiple disabilities. In E. Chigier (Ed.), *Special education and social handicap* (pp. 109–119). London: Freund.

Murray, C. (1986). *Integration in high school: A qualitative study of social relationships between nondisabled students and students with severe handicaps.* Doctoral dissertation, San Francisco State University/University of California, Berkeley, Joint Doctoral Program, Department of Special Education.

Murray, C., & Beckstead, S. P. (1983). *Awareness and inservice manual (AIM).* San Francisco: San Francisco State University, San Francisco Unified School District. (Eric Document Reproduction Service No. ED 242 182)

Newsletter of the Association for Persons with Severe Handicaps. (1987). *13*(4), 7.

Nietupski, J., Hamre-Nietupski, S., Clancy, P., & Veerhusen, K. (1986). Guidelines for making simulation an effective adjunct to in vivo community instruction. *Journal of the Association for Persons with Severe Handicaps, 11*(1), 12–18.

Nietupski, J., Schutz, G., & Ockwood, L. (1980). The delivery of communication services to severely handicapped students: A plan for change. *Journal of the Association for the Severely Handicapped, 5*(1), 13–24.

Odom, S., DeKlyen, M., & Jenkins, J. (1984). Integrating handicapped and non-handicapped preschoolers: Developmental impact on nonhandicapped children. *Exceptional Children, 51*(1), 41–48.

Odom, S., Hoysun, M., Jamieson, B., & Strain, P. (1985). Increasing handicapped preschoolers peer social interactions: Cross-setting and component analysis. *Journal of Applied Behavior Analysis, 18*, 3–16.

Odom, S., & Strain, P. (1984). Peer-mediated approaches to promoting children's social interaction: A review. *American Journal of Orthopsychiatry, 54*, 544–557.

Orelove, F. P., & Hanley, C. D. (1979). Modifying school buildings for the severely handicapped. A school accessibility survey. *AAESPH Review, 4*(3), 219–236.

Orelove, F., & Sobsey, D. (1987). *Educating children with multiple disabilities.* Baltimore, MD: Paul H. Brookes.

Oshima, G. (1986, November). *Effective integration of severely multiply disabled students.* Paper presented at the Association for the Severely Handicapped Conference, San Francisco, CA.

Park, H., & Goetz, L. (1985). *Affect differences between students with severe disabilities in differing educational programs.* Unpublished manuscript.

Peck, C., Apolloni, T., Cooke, T., & Raver, S. (1978). Teaching retarded preschoolers to imitate the free play behavior of nonretarded classmates: Trained and generalized effects. *Journal of Special Education, 12*(2), 195–207.

Pellegrini, S. (1986). *Principals' ownership of programs for students with severe disabilities and associated factors on integrated sites.* Unpublished manuscript, San Jose State University/San Francisco State University, California Research Institute.

Pennsylvania Association for Retarded Citizens v. Commonwealth of Pennsylvania, 334 F. Supp. 1257 (1971).

Pennsylvania Association for Retarded Citizens (PARC) v. Commonwealth of Pennsylvania, 343 F. Supp. 278 (E.D. Pa. 1972).

Pennsylvania Association for Retarded Citizens (PARC) v. Commonwealth of Pennsylvania, Consent Decree on Enforcement Petition in *Fialkowski et al.* v. *School District of Philadelphia et al.*, entered June 1982.

Pindyck, R., & Rubinfeld, D. (1981). *Econometric models and economic forecasts.* New York: McGraw-Hill.

Piuma, C. (1985). *A case study: Cost analysis study of selected integrated and segregated classrooms serving severely disabled students in San Mateo County.* Unpublished manuscript, San Francisco State University, California Research Institute.

Piuma, C., Halvorsen, A., Murray, C., Beckstead, S., & Sailor, W. (1983). *Project REACH administrator's manual (PRAM).* San Francisco State University; San Francisco Unified School District. (Eric Reproduction Service Document No. ED 242 185).

Powell, T., Salzberg, C., Rule, S., Levy, S., & Itzkowitz, J. (1983). Teaching mentally retarded children to play with their siblings using parents as trainers. *Education and Treatment of Children, 6*(4), 343–362.

Public Law 94-142: The Education of all Handicapped Children Act of 1975. (1975). Washington, DC: U.S. Government Printing Office.

Pumpian, I. R. (1981). *Variables affecting attitudes toward the employability of severely handicapped adults.* Unpublished doctoral dissertation, University of Wisconsin—Madison.

Pumpian, I., Baumgart, D., Shiraga, B., Ford, A., Nesbit, J., Loomis, R., & Brown, L. (1980). Vocational training programs for severely handicapped student in Madison Metropolitan School District. In L. Brown, M. Falvey, I. Pumpian, D. Baumgart, J. Nisbet, A. Ford, J. Schroeder, & R. Loomis (Eds.), *Curricular strategies for teaching severely handicapped students functional skills in school and nonschool environments* (Vol. 10, pp. 273–310). Madison, WI: Madison Metropolitan School District.

Pumpian, I., Shephard, H., & West, E. (1986). *Negotiating job training stations with employers.* In P. Wehman & M. Sherrill Moon (Eds.), *Vocational rehabilitation and supported employment* (pp. 177–192). Baltimore, MD: Paul H. Brookes.

Pumpian, I., West, E., & Shephard, H. (1988). The training and employment of persons with severe handicaps. In R. Gaylord-Ross (Ed.), *Vocational education for persons with handicaps* (pp. 335–386). Palo Alto, CA: Mayfield.

Raske, D. E. (1979). The role of general school administrators responsible for special education programs. *Exceptional Children, 5,* 645–646.

Ray, B. (1985). Measuring the social position of the mainstreamed handicapped child. *Exceptional Children, 52*(1), 57–62.

Reger, R. (1972). Resource rooms: Change agents or guardians of the status quo? *Journal of Special Education, 6,* 355–360.

Reynolds, M. C., & Birch, J. (1982). *Teaching exceptional children in all America's schools* (rev. ed.). Reston, VA: Council for Exceptional Children.

Rynders, J., Johnson, R., Johnson, D., & Schmidt, B. (1980). Effects of cooperative goal structuring in producing positive interaction between Down syndrome and nonhandicapped teenagers: Implications for mainstreaming. *American Journal of Mental Deficiency, 85,* 268–273.

Sailor, W. S. (1987). *Review of literature Years 1–5: Integration of students with severe disabilities.* San Francisco, CA: San Francisco State University, California Research Institute on Integration.

Sailor, W., Anderson, J., Halvorsen, A., Filler, J., & Goetz, L. (1989). *The compre-*

hensive local school: Regular education for all students with disabilities. Baltimore, MD: Paul H. Brookes.

Sailor, W., Gee, K., Goetz, L., & Graham, N. (1988). Progress in educating students with the most severe disabilities: Is there any? *Journal of the Association for Persons with Severe Handicaps, 13,* 87–99.

Sailor, W., Goetz, L., Anderson, J., Hunt, P., & Gee, K. (1988). Research on community intensive instruction as a model for building functional, generalized skills. In R. Horner, G. Dunlap, & R. Koegel (Eds.), *Generalization and maintenance: Lifestyle changes in applied settings* (pp. 67–98). Baltimore, MD: Paul H. Brookes.

Sailor, W., & Guess, D. (1983). *Severely handicapped students: An instructional design.* Boston: Houghton Mifflin.

Sailor, W., & Halvorsen, A. (1986). *California Research Institute Annual Report, Year 4.* San Francisco: San Francisco State University, Department of Special Education, CRI.

Sailor, W., Halvorsen, A., Anderson, J., Goetz, L., Gee, K., Doering, K., & Hunt, P. (1986). Community intensive instruction. In R. Horner, L. Meyer, & B. Fredericks (Eds.), *Education of learners with severe handicaps: Exemplary service strategies* (pp. 251–288). Baltimore, MD: Paul H. Brookes.

Sailor, W., & Haring, N. G. (1977). Some current directions in education of the severely/multiply handicapped. *AAESPH Review, 2*(2), 67–87.

Sasso, G., Simpson, R., & Novak, C. (1985). Procedures for facilitating integration of autistic children in public school settings. *Analysis and Intervention in Developmental Disabilities, 5,* 233–246.

Schactili, L. (1987). *The effects of trained and untrained peer tutors on social behavior of severely disabled students.* Unpublished master's thesis, California State University, Hayward, Department of Special Education, California Research Institute.

Schalock, R. (1986). Employment outcomes from secondary school programs. *RASE, 7*(6), 37–39.

Scheerenberger, R. C. (1983). *A history of mental retardation.* Baltimore, MD: Paul H. Brookes.

Schleien, S. (1984). The development of cooperative play skills in children with severe learning disabilities: A school-based leisure education program. *Journal of Leisurability, 11*(3), 29–34.

Searl, S., Ferguson, D., & Biklen, D. (1985). The front line . . . teachers. In D. Biklen (Ed.), *Achieving the complete school: Strategies for effective mainstreaming* (pp. 52–103). New York: Teachers College Press.

Selby, P. (1984). *A comparison of learning acquisition by teacher instruction and handicapped peer tutor instruction on leisure and gross motor skills of three mentally retarded children.* Unpublished master's thesis, San Francisco State University, San Francisco, CA.

Singer, G., Close, D., Irvin, L., Gersten, R., & Sailor, W. (1984). An alternative to the institution for young people with severely handicapping conditions in a rural community. *Journal of the Association for Persons with Severe Handicaps, 9*(4), 251–261.

Siperstein, G., & Bak, J. (1985). Effects of social behaviors on children's attitudes toward their mildly and moderately mentally retarded peers. *American Journal of Mental Deficiency, 90*(3), 319–327.

Smith, B. (1984). *Generalization of social interactions between two autistic children and their nonhandicapped age peers.* Unpublished master's thesis, California State University, Hayward.

Snell, M. E., & Beckman-Brindley, S. (1984). Family involvement in intervention with children having severe handicaps. *Journal of the Association for Persons with Severe Handicaps, 9*(3), 213–230.

Snell, M., & Browder, D. (1986). Community-referenced instructions: Research and issues. *Journal of the Association for Persons with Severe Handicaps, 11*(1), 1–11.

Sokol-Kessler, L., Conroy, J., Feinstein, C., Lemanowicz, J., & McGurrin, M. (1983). Developmental progress in institutional and community settings. *Journal of the Association for Persons with Severe Handicaps, 8*, 43–48.

Stainback, S., & Stainback, W. (1985a). *Integration of students with severe handicaps into regular schools.* Reston, VA: Council for Exceptional Children.

Stainback, S., & Stainback, W. (1985b). The merger of special and regular education: Can it be done? A response to Lieberman and Mesinger. *Exceptional Children, 51*(6), 517–521.

Stainback, S., Stainback, W., Strathe, M., & Dedrick, C. (1983). Preparing regular classroom teachers for the integration of severely handicapped students: An experimental study. *Education and Training of the Mentally Retarded, 18*(3), 204–209.

Stainback, W., & Stainback, S. (1982). Preparing regular class teachers for the integration of severely retarded students. *Education and Training of the Mentally Retarded, 17*(4), 273–277.

Stainback, W., & Stainback, S. (1983). A review of research on the educability of profoundly retarded persons. *Education & Training on the Mentally Retarded, 18*(2), 90–100.

Stainback, W., & Stainback, S. (1984a). Facilitating integration through personnel preparation. In N. Certo, N. Haring, & R. York (Eds.), *Public school integration of severely handicapped students* (pp. 143–154). Baltimore, MD: Paul H. Brookes.

Stainback, W., & Stainback, S. (1984b). A rationale for the merger of special and regular education. *Exceptional Children, 51*(2), 102–111.

Stainback, W., Stainback, S., Courtnage, L., & Jaben, T. (1985). Facilitating mainstreaming by modifying the mainstream. *Exceptional Children, 52*, 144–152.

Sternat, J., Messina, R., Nietupski, J., Lyon, S. & Brown, L. (1977). Occupational and physical therapy services for severely handicapped students: Toward a naturalized public school service delivery model. In E. Sontag (Ed.), *Educational programming for the severely/profoundly handicapped* (pp. 112–119). Reston, VA: Council for Exceptional Children.

Stetson, F. (1984). Critical factors that facilitate integration: A theory of administrative responsibility. In N. Certo, N. Haring, & R. York (Eds.), *Public school integration of severely handicapped students* (pp. 65–81). Baltimore, MD: Paul H. Brookes.

Stetson, F., Elting, S., & Raimondi, S. (1982). *Report on project impact with regard to cost effectiveness of service delivery to handicapped students in the least restrictive environment.* Annandale, VA: JWK International Corporation.

Stokes, T., & Baer, D. (1977). An implicit technology of generalization. *Journal of Applied Behavior Analysis, 10,* 349–367.

Strain, P. (1977). Effects of peer social initiations on withdrawn preschool children. *Journal of Abnormal Child Psychology, 5,* 445–455.

Strain, P., Kerr, M., & Raglund, E. (1981). The use of peer social initiations in the treatment of social withdrawal. In P. Strain (Ed.), *The utilization of classroom peers as behavior change agents* (pp. 101–128). New York: Plenum.

Strain, P., & Odom, S. (1986). Peer social initiations: Effective intervention for social skills development of exceptional children. *Exceptional Children, 52*(6), 543–551.

Strain, P., Shores, R., & Timm, M. (1977). Effects of peers social initiation on the behavior of withdrawn preschool children. *Journal of Applied Behavior Analysis, 10,* 289–298.

Strully, J., & Strully, C. (1985). Teach your children. *Canadian Journal of Mental Retardation, 35*(4), 3–11.

Tawney, J. W., & Smith, J. (1981). An analysis of the forum: Issues in education of severely and profoundly retarded. *Exceptional Children, 48,* 5–18.

Taylor, S. (1982). From segregation to integration: Strategies for integrating severely handicapped students in normal school and community settings. *Journal of the Association for Persons with Severe Handicaps, 7*(3), 42–49.

Turnbull, A. P., Brotherson, M. J., & Summers, J. A. (1985). The impact of deinstitutionalization on families: A family systems approach. In R. H. Bruininks (Ed.), *Living and learning in the least restrictive environment* (pp. 115–152). Baltimore, MD: Paul H. Brookes.

Turnbull, A., & Turnbull, R. (1985). Developing independence. *Journal of Adolescent Health Care, 6,* 108–119.

Turnbull, R. (1986). *Free appropriate public education: The law and children with disabilities.* Denver, CO: Love Publishing.

Vesey, D. (1986, November). *The perspective of a parent and special education commissioner on the benefits of integration and plans for statewide implementation.* Paper presented at 13th annual conference, Association for Persons with Severe Handicaps (TASH), San Francisco, CA.

Vincent, L., Laten, S., Salisbury, C., Brown, P., & Baumgart, D. (1980). Family involvement in the educational processes of severely handicapped students. In B. Wilcox & R. York (Eds.), *Quality education for the severely handicapped: The federal investment* (pp. 180–191). Washington, DC: U.S. department of Education, Office of Special Education.

Voeltz, L. M. (1980). Children's attitudes toward handicapped peers. *American Journal of Mental Deficiency, 84*(3), 455–464.

Voeltz, L. M. (1982). Effects of structured interactions with severely handicapped peers on children's attitudes. *American Journal of Mental Deficiency, 86*(4), 380–390.

Voeltz, L. M. (1984). Program and curriculum innovations to prepare children for integration. In N. Certo, N. Haring, & R. York (Eds.), *Public school integration of severely handicapped students: Rational issues and progressive alternatives* (pp. 155–184). Baltimore, MD: Paul H. Brookes.

Voeltz, L. M., & Brennan, J. (1982, August). *Analysis of interactions between nonhandicapped and severely handicapped peers using multiple measures.* Paper presented at the 6th International Congress of the International Association for the Scientific Study of Mental Deficiency (IASSMD), Toronto, Canada.

Voeltz, L. M., Wuerch, B. B., & Bockout, C. H. (1982). Social validation of leisure activities training with severely handicapped youth. *Journal of the Association for Persons with Severe Handicaps, 7*(4), 3–13.

Vogelsberg, R., Williams, T., & Friedl, M. (1980). Facilitating systems change for the severely handicapped: Secondary and adult services. *Journal of the Association for Persons with Severe Handicaps, 5*(1), 73–85.

Walbridge, R., & Conroy, J. (1981). *Changes in community attitudes.* Philadelphia, PA: Temple University.

Walbridge, R., Whaley, A., & Conroy, J. (1981). *Models of change in community attitudes.* Philadelphia, PA: Temple University.

Wallin, J. E. (1955). *Education of mentally handicapped children.* New York: Harper Bros.

Wang, M., & Baker, E. (1986). Mainstreaming programs: Design features and effects. *Journal of Special Education, 19*(4), 503–521.

Wang, M. C., & Birch, J. W. (1984). Comparison of a full-time mainstreaming program and a resource room approach. *Exceptional Children, 50,* 391–398.

Wang, M. C., Vaughan, E. D., & Dytman, J. (1985). Staff development: A key ingredient of effective mainstreaming. *Teaching Exceptional Children, 17,* 112–121.

Wehman, P., Hill, M., Goodall, P., Cleveland, P., Brooke, V., & Pentecost, J. (1982). Job placement and follow-up of moderately and severely handicapped individuals after three years. *Journal of the Association for Persons with Severe Handicaps, 7*(1), 5–16.

Wehman, P., Hill, M., Hill, J., Brooke, V., Pendleton, P., & Britt, C. (1985). Competitive employment for persons with mental retardation: A follow-up six years later. *Mental Retardation, 23*(6), 274–281.

Wehman, P., Kregel, J., Barcus, J., & Schalock, R. (1986). Vocational transition for students with developmental disabilities. In W. Kiernan & J. Stark (Eds.), *Pathways to employment for adults with developmental disabilities* (pp. 113–127). Baltimore, MD: Paul H. Brookes.

Wehman, P., Kregel, J., & Seyfarth, J. (1985). Transition from school to work for individuals with severe handicaps: A follow-up study. *Journal of the Association for Persons with Severe Handicaps, 10*(3), 132–136.

White, O., Leber, B., & Phifer, C. (1985). Training in the natural environment and skill generalization: It doesn't always come naturally. In N. Haring (Prin. Ed.), *Investigating the problem of skill generalization* (3rd ed., pp. 63–79). Seattle, WA: University of Washington Research Organization.

Wilcox, B. (1986). Review of *Integrating moderately and severely handicapped learners: Strategies that work,* and *Integration of students with severe handicaps into regular schools. Journal of the Association for Persons with Severe Handicaps, 11*(1), 74–75.

Wilcox, B., & Sailor, W. (1980). Service delivery issues: Integrated educational systems. In B. Wilcox & B. York (Eds.), *Quality education for the severely handicapped: The federal investment* (pp. 277–304). Washington, DC: U.S. Department of Education.

Will, M. (1985). OSERS programming for the transition of youth with disabilities: Bridges from school to working life. *Rehabilitation WORLD, 42,* pp. 4–7.

Will, M. (1986). Educating children with learning problems: A shared responsibility. *Exceptional Children, 52*(5), 411–415.

Williams, W., Iverson, G., Schutz, R., Duncan, D., & Holbrook, L. (1982). *Burlington's making special friends project: Model overview: Vol. 2.* Burlington, VT: University of Vermont, Center for Developmental Disabilities.

Winston, S. (1985, January). Providing special education services without a special education department. *Thrust,* pp. 44–46.

Wolfensberger, W. (1972). *The principle of normalization in human services.* Toronto: National Institute on Mental Retardation.

Wolfensberger, W. (1975). *The origin and nature of our institutional models.* Syracuse, NY: Human Policy Press.

Wolfensberger, W., & Glenn, L. (1975). *PASS 3: Program analysis of service systems handbook.* Toronto, Canada: National Institute on Mental Retardation.

Wyngaarden, J., Freedman, R., & Gollav, E. (1976). *Descriptive data on the community experiences of deinstitutionalized mentally retarded persons. A study of the community adjustment of deinstitutionalized mentally retarded persons: Vol. 4* (U.S. Office of Education, Contract No. OEC-0-74-9183). Cambridge, MA: Abt Associates.

CHAPTER 4

Research in Vocational Special Education

SHEPHERD SIEGEL
HYUN-SOOK PARK
TOM GUMPEL

JERRY FORD
PHYLLIS TAPPE
ROBERT GAYLORD-ROSS

The field of vocational special education addresses the need to prepare students with disabilities for the world of work. Recent surveys have found that only 20% to 70% (median 30%) of disabled adults are gainfully employed. A national "transition" movement has begun that attempts to move disabled students leaving school to successful employment. Such transitional programs include

1. Career counseling
2. Occupational training
3. On-site work experience
4. Vocational assessment
5. Interagency collaboration between school and adult service agencies
6. Job development and placement
7. Supported employment and follow-up services

It is hoped that such comprehensive and longitudinal programs will reverse the exceedingly high rate of unemployment.

The purpose of this chapter is to review the most important research topics in vocational special education. The question of program efficacy is critical: Do the components of special education programs lead to substantive gains in student learning and performance?

We have identified five topics that currently share preeminence in the vocational special education field. The first, actuarial type of research deals with follow-up studies of disabled individuals. If vocational training programs are efficacious, then a significant proportion of their graduates should be successfully employed. In this sense, follow-up employment data is the bottom-line, primary indicator of program effectiveness. As our review indicates, though, there are other important measures, such as quality of life and social support, that ought to be included in the evaluation of program effectiveness. Thus, our second topic addresses social support systems in the workplace.

Vocational special education is primarily concerned with the efficient learning of a large number of job-related skills. The major challenge is to make sure that skills learned in a training setting will transfer to a real work setting, as well as be maintained after the student has graduated. Our third topical review examines techniques to promote skill generalization in vocational contexts.

Social skills may be the most important vocationally related skill to learn. Job retention research has pointed to the fact that interpersonal problems on the job are as important as other reasons for job termination. Social skill training at work sites is just beginning to emerge as a full-fledged research endeavor, and is the fourth topic under review here. It is possible that such training procedures may enhance job retention and satisfaction, engendering a higher rate and quality of social interactions, as well as building a network of friends and social support.

Finally, the cognitive behavioral notion of self-management offers promise for solving many problems in vocational special education. Self-management has individuals self-monitor and self-evaluate their performance. It is a technique that can induce generalization in responding across settings and people. It may also be included in "process" approaches to social-skills training, which have the person interpret the meaning of a social context. Above all, self-management enables the person to function more independently in vocational and other settings and is the fifth topic in our review.

Thus, this chapter attempts to make a comprehensive review of the most critical issues in vocational special education. A number of syntheses of the current status of our data bases on the five topics are made. Training methods supported by data are highlighted. The needs and directions for future research are signaled. We hope to provide the reader with an understanding of the many exciting developments in vocational special education.

FOLLOW-UP RESEARCH

At first glance, the reporting of employment outcomes would seem to be a fairly straightforward endeavor. The investigator simply identifies the population to be studied and then makes the necessary arrangements and calculations that will produce an employment rate. However, a review of the literature documenting such attempts reveals diverse methodologies and findings that are very often misleading or tenuous. Furthermore, some disability groups have been the subject of voluminous study, while others have been neglected. The journalist's six stock questions—who, what, where, when, why, and how—provide a constructive approach to an examination of the motives, methods, and results of follow-up studies.

Why does an investigator engage in such a study? Most studies share similar concerns, but the motivation to get people off welfare rolls and save taxpayers money, for example, can be in conflict with the more altruistic desire to give handicapped people a happier life. What are the criteria of a successful outcome? Community adjustment is a generally agreed-upon goal, but it has been viewed as anything from sheltered employment at subminimum wage to gainful employment above the poverty level, from successful marriage to social and interpersonal satisfaction. Who exactly is the population of interest? Populations and participants can be identified by diagnosis as well as by the receipt of services. For example, there is still controversy over the populations inferred by labels such as Educable Mentally Handicapped, and by services such as Resource Specialist Programs. Where does the study take place? The variations between urban and rural, prosperous and impoverished environments, need to be controlled if any comparability of the findings is to be considered. When does the study take place? It may be over a period of years or a single probe. It may be done during a time of recession, war, low overall employment rates, high immigration rates, low public concern for persons with handicaps, or other events likely to have an impact on the targeted group's outcome. Finally, a review must consider methodology: how the population was chosen, and how the investigation was conducted. One must critically analyze how the investigator decided upon and measured the factors considered to be of most importance. Was numerical measurement emphasized, or did the study take a more ethnographic approach? Only then can the results of the study be correctly understood. This review will highlight those aspects of studies that exemplify the above dimensions.

Table 4.1 provides a guide for the investigator who wishes to obtain a general sense of the state of follow-up studies. The information presented reflects some of the emerging concerns of intervention and follow-up. Studies are presented in alphabetical order. Sample size and the disability group involved are then listed. Following that, the nonsheltered employment rate is presented. If no distinction was made in the study, that fact is noted as well. Whenever possible, the type of region is listed: metropolitan, urban, suburban, and rural (see Hasazi, Gordon, & Roe, 1985, for definitions). Finally, the main concerns of the study are summarized in the

Text continues on p. 180.

TABLE 4.1. Summary of Follow-up Studies of Handicapped Students and Adults

Study	N	Disability Group	Nonsheltered Employment Rate	Type of Region	Main Concerns
Ballantyne, McGee, Patton, & Cohen (1984)	2,000	All special education	85%	All (Oklahoma)	Program evaluation; project dissemination
Baller, (1936)	173	Moderately retarded	19% (including homemaking)	Urban & rural (Nebraska)	Improve sampling procedures; investigate successes
Bolton, Rowland, Brookings, Cook, Taperek, & Short (1980)	225	All handicaps & disadvantaged	56%	All (Hot Springs Rehabilitation Center)	Overall adjustment of former clients; program evaluation
Brickey & Campbell (1981)	17	Moderately & mildly retarded; sensory impaired	76%	Urban (Columbus, OH)	Program evaluation; job retention
Clemmons & Dodrill (1983)	42	Epileptic	43% (including post-secondary education)	All	Correlation to WAIS and neuropsychological tests; vocational outcomes
Dalton & Latz (1978)	1,395	Mentally retarded, seriously emotionally disturbed, & orthopedically handicapped	75%	All (Pennsylvania)	Development of information systems for rehabilitation agencies
Delp & Lorenz (1953)	41	Moderately retarded	12%	Metropolitan (St. Paul, MN)	Outcomes of public school training programs
Dinger (1961)	333	Educable retarded	83.2% (including homemaking)	Urban (Altoona. PA)	Improving school curriculum
Edgar (1987)	39	Mildly mentally retarded	13% (including sheltered)	All (Washington)	Improving school curriculum; interagency cooperation
Edgar (1987)	12	Sensory impaired	17% (including sheltered)	All (Washington)	Improving school curriculum; interagency cooperation
Edgar (1987)	115	LD/behavior disordered (dropouts)	30%	All (Washington)	Improving school curriculum; interagency cooperation

Study	N	Population	%	Location	Focus
Edgar (1987)	160	LD/behavior disordered (graduates & ageouts)	61%	All (Washington)	Improving school curriculum; interagency cooperation
Fardig et al. (1985)	113	LD, mildly retarded, seriously emotionally disturbed	50%	Rural (Florida)	Employment outcomes in rural areas
Fernald (1919)	325	Institutionalized "subnormals"	14% (including homemaking)	All (Massachusetts)	Investigating link between retardation and crime
Gill (1984)	194	All special education	50%	Urban, suburban, rural (Pierce Co., WA)	Employment and postsecondary educational outcomes
Goros & Kowalski-Glickman (1983)	60	Deaf-blind	47-48%	Suburban	Program evaluation
Hardy (1968)	40	Reading handicapped	100%	Urban (Toronto, Ont)	Social adjustment
Hasazi, Gordon, & Roe (1985)	459	All special education	54%	All (Vermont)	Development and evaluation of programs
Hasazi et al.(1985)	242	Educable & trainable mentally retarded	43%	All (Vermont)	Development and evaluation of programs
Kernan & Koegel (1984)	48	Mildly retarded	23% (including homemaking)	Metropolitan (Los Angeles)	Longitudinal tracking of employment status
Kernan & Koegel (1984) (2½ years later)	48	Mildly retarded	46% (including homemaking)	Metropolitan (Los Angeles)	Longitudinal tracking of employment status
Lehtinen-Rogan & Hartman (1976)	91	Learning disabled	73% (including postsecondary school)	Suburban (USA)	Overall adjustment; students from a private school compared to general figures
Linden & Forness (1986)	40	Mildly mentally retarded with psychiatric disorders	62%	Metropolitan (Los Angeles)	Overall adjustment
Lurie, Schlan, & Freiberg (1932)	55	"Feebleminded"	70%	All (Los Angeles)	Overall adjustment

TABLE 4.1. Continued

Study	N	Disability Group	Nonsheltered Employment Rate	Type of Region	Main Concerns
Mathews (1922)	100	Institutionalized "subnormals"	78% (under supervision)	All (Massachusetts)	Program evaluation
McCormick & Clarke (1986)	142	All special education	48%	All (California)	Program evaluation
Mithaug, Horiuchi, & Fanning (1985)	234	All special education	69%	All (Colorado)	Overall adjustment; earnings; statewide sampling
Peterson & Smith (1960)	45	Educable mentally retarded	51-53%	Urban (Cedar Rapids, IA)	Comparison to nonhandicapped adults of low SES
Richardson & Hill (1980)	38	Mildly mentally retarded, seriously emotionally disturbed, orthopedic handicaps	82%	Urban	Program evaluation
Richardson & Krieger (1976)	92	Mild & moderate mental retardation, seriously emotionally disturbed, orthopedic handicaps, and other health impairments	63%	Urban	Rehabilitation center evaluation
Richardson & Krieger (1976) (2 years later)	92	Mild & moderate mental retardation, seriously emotionally disturbed, orthopedic handicaps, and other health impairments	43%	Urban	Rehabilitation center evaluation
Saenger (1957)	520	Trainable mentally retarded	23%	All (New York)	Overall adjustment
Semmel, Cosden, & Konopak (1985)	48	All special education	83% (including sheltered)	Metropolitan & urban (Southern CA)	Program evaluation

Study	n	Population	%	Location	Focus
Stanfield (1973)	120	Trainable mentally retarded	5%	Metropolitan (Southern CA)	Overall adjustment; mobility and independent living skills
Thomson & Lucas (1981)	71	Deaf	77% (including post-secondary)	All (Illinois)	Outcomes of deaf college students
Tisdall (1958)	128	Trainable mentally retarded	2%	All (Illinois)	Outcomes of public school training programs
Wehman, Hill, Goodall, Cleveland, Brooke, & Pentecost (1982)	63	Moderately to severely handicapped	67%	Urban (Richmond, VA)	Retention; earnings; Program evaluation
Wehman, Kregel, & Seyfarth (1985)	125	Mildly to profoundly mentally retarded	26%	Urban, suburban, & rural (Virginia)	Comprehensive regional sampling; evaluation of services
Wehman, Seyfarth, & Kregel (1985)	117	Moderately to profoundly mentally retarded	67%	Urban, suburban, & rural (Virginia)	Comprehensive regional sampling; earnings
Zigmond & Thornton (1985)	27	Learning handicapped (graduates)	74%	Urban (Northeastern U.S.)	Employment outcomes of LD graduates
Zigmond & Thornton (1985)	33	Learning handicapped (dropouts)	44%	Urban (Northeastern U.S.)	Employment outcomes of LD dropouts

last column. Sources for each study can be located in the references. These, then, constitute the majority of studies conducted that measure the employment experiences of handicapped individuals in the United States.

Community Adjustment

Whether they are clearly articulated or merely implied, the factors identified in any follow-up study are an interpretation of values assumed or considered to be important to society. An apt description of this imbedded search for meaningfulness is given by Michael Rose (1985)

> The full range of a society's values relating to work . . . are projected in social institutions, structures, and practices; in organisational rules and operating procedures; in laws and legal decisions; and in social and economic policies. What occupations exist? Who enters them? What training do entrants get? What are their rewards—including their non-money rewards like prestige? How long is the working day, week, or year? What do laws about health, safety and fair treatment say and how vigilantly are they enforced?
>
> We habitually regard many such questions as purely technical or administrative. Yet their answers imply social values; and these latent values give the tissue of work culture as a whole its great intricacy. (pp. 127–128)

Thus, past studies should be read with regard for the value constraints of the time, and the theoretical commitments of the investigators. Even the most common global variable, *adjustment*, is value laden, implying a static norm that might be attained through some social service. Edgerton (1984) prefers the term *adaptation*, which he describes as "far less a measurable dependent variable than a multiplex process marked by change and contradiction" (p. 2). He makes a case for ethnographies that detail handicapped persons' actions and their perceptions of the society to which they are adapting. Adjustment, then, is a dependent variable whose parameters cannot be cursorily presumed.

As an example, Baller's (1936) follow-up study of mentally retarded adults was made in response to research practices that only identified those who were institutionalized and then proceeded to make generalizations about all retarded individuals. The doctrines of the time also unfairly linked retardation to criminal activity; this was a variable of concern to investigators as late as 1960 (Peterson & Smith, 1960). Baller himself chose to define adjustment as including those individuals who were wholly self-supporting and had no records of arrest.

Marriage by a retarded woman to a man of higher economic status signified community adjustment as well. "Better personal appearance and superior training in domestic responsibility" (p. 229) played a significant role in the upwardly mobile, "well-adjusted" marriages made by 21 women in the group. Such marital standards of adjustment were also common in other studies (Dinger, 1961; Fernald, 1919).

Yet when Hasazi, Gordon, Roe, Hull et al. (1985) showed that in Vermont, retarded female graduates worked only 23% of the time, while retarded males had an employment rate of 56%, they found these statistics to be troubling. Marriage was no longer acceptable as a successful outcome for a woman, and the figures for the nonhandicapped Vermont women supported this change. In 1984, 86%–88% of Vermont women aged 16 to 24 were employed. In fact, one other study recommended that "work placement programs . . . should also educate special education girls against the social tide that motivates them to limit their post-high school experiences" (Semmel, Cosden, & Konopak, 1985, p. 46). This major shift in values since Baller's time may only slightly affect the measurement of outcome studies. Marriage *per se* no longer qualifies as an indicator of adjustment, but homemaking is considered as a valid employment status (Dinger, 1961; Kernan & Koegel, 1984).

The above findings should be surprising to no one, yet should alert investigators to bias. For example, the goals of vocational training for persons with handicaps have been part of an overall movement toward mainstreaming, "normalization," and independent living. The position inferred by Stanfield's (1973) follow-up study is that vocational success for retarded adults often depends upon independence from the home, and that both of these ends are good and should be pursued. Yet, in a family whose culture has not affirmed independent living as a valued and desired outcome, fewer children—nonhandicapped and handicapped alike—move away from their parents. The most socially valid standard of "adjustment" might not be a generic criterion, but instead the status of a nonhandicapped sibling, or of a culturally similar peer. Special education and rehabilitative services must therefore face the difficult task of defining adjustment (or adaptation) fairly, and offering services that will facilitate it in such a way that respects diverse lifestyles and cultures.

Studies in the late 1950s and early 1960s measured community adjustment by asking participants, among other things, what television programs they watched and magazines they read, the number of times they violated the law, and whether they had or used credit (Dinger, 1961; Peterson & Smith, 1960). A study in the early seventies (Stanfield, 1973) emphasized questions concerning the amount of mobility that retarded individuals had in the community, and their ability to live independently of their family. More recent studies focused on the overall adjustment—occupational, social, and interpersonal—of diagnostically more specific populations: mentally retarded adults with a history of psychiatric disorders (Linden & Forness, 1986), deaf-blind individuals (Goros & Kowalski-Glickman, 1983), persons with epilepsy (Clemmons & Dodrill, 1983), deaf persons (Thomson & Lucas, 1981), or a group of mentally retarded adults stratified by IQ scores (Hill, Wehman, Hill & Goodall, 1985).

One investigation (Kaufman, 1984) posed a strong challenge to the working assumption of so many other studies that having x number of friends and visits with them is sufficient and necessary evidence of social adjustment (Linden & Forness, 1986; Mithaug, Horiuchi, & Fanning, 1985; Stanfield, 1973). Kaufman (1984) reported that having nonretarded friends was a "pressing need" according to the *parents* of retarded individuals. Yet her study presented evidence that experiences of contentment and loneliness were not correlated with whether individuals were solitary or had a wide circle of friends, or whether they had preferences for retarded or nonretarded people as friends. Though this study is not directly related to employment, it is an excellent example of some of the assumptions that often lie behind empirically stated standards of social behavior.

In actuality, many investigators consistently choose similar variables to measure: school completion and history, diagnosis of disability, employment retention and history, job profiles, job satisfaction, fringe benefits, earnings and economic self-sufficiency, marital status, and postsecondary training (Baller, 1936; Dinger, 1961; Edgar, 1987; Edgerton, 1984; Harnisch, Chaplin, Fisher, & Tu, 1986; Hasazi, Gordon, & Roe, 1985; Hasazi et al., 1985; Linden & Forness, 1986; Stanfield, 1973). In the conclusion to their review of the literature on the placement of retarded individuals in the community, McCarver and Craig (1974) note that post-institutional follow-up may become obsolete since the vast proportion of developmentally disabled persons are now living in the community. In fact, over 85,000 residents were released from public institutions for retarded persons between 1963 and 1970, at which point the focus of research was shifting to evaluation of programs in the community. Until that time, the criteria of successful adjustment were usually based only on whether or not the individual returned to an institutional setting (Madison, 1964). Using this criterion, McCarver and Craig (1974) found a median success rate of 74% when they considered the findings of 44 studies done between 1918 and 1970.

The literature since then reflects a research and advocacy shift that no longer accepts living in the community as sufficient. More recent studies oriented towards special education and rehabilitative services have emphasized the ability to survive without Social Security and Social Security Income (SSI) payments, and to contribute to the tax base (Brickey & Campbell, 1981; Wehman et al., 1982; Wehman, Seyfarth & Kregel, 1985).

Focus on such "bottom line" indictors is complemented by the Office of Special Education and Rehabilitation Services' (OSERS) policy statements of Will (1984) that emphasize employment. Halpern's (1985) call for community adjustment to include also residential environments and social and interpersonal networks necessitates studies that probe the interrelationships of employment and social life as perceived by the handicapped individual (Edgerton, 1967, 1984; Linden & Forness, 1986; Mithaug, Horiuchi, & Fanning, 1985).

Any study is limited by time and resources. Only so much data can be collected, and targeted populations will tolerate only so much inquiry. But if a study's purpose is clear, it can bring its efforts to bear on relevant questions. For example, there is the occasional study whose purpose is solely to describe (rather than predict) the lives of its participants. Robert Edgerton's *Cloak of Competence* (1967) is a classic of this genre (see also Edgerton, 1984; Jones, 1983). Studies of this type are critical because they provide investigators with a personal orientation to the population of interest, and may be an excellent resource for correlates and predictors.

In the late 1980s, parallel movements can be detected in follow-up studies. On the one hand are studies that focus on the training and cost-effectiveness of vocational services. The central question of these studies is whether handicapped youth are growing up to be taxpayers. Studies that concentrate their efforts on earnings, deductions, taxes paid, taxes spent on special services, worker's compensation, benefits, etc., will ultimately provide answers, predictions, and replicable results (McCormick & Clarke, 1986; Peterson & Smith, 1960; Wehman et al., 1982; Wehman, Kregel, & Seyfarth, 1985; Wehman, Seyfarth, & Kregel, 1985; Wehman & Hill, 1985).

Consumer satisfaction and the social validity of programs have been the concerns of other studies. In these cases, social validity requires investigation of the degree of socially significant goals, socially appropriate procedures, and socially important effects (Kazdin, 1977; Wolf, 1978). Such studies tend to see vocational outcomes as one important component of overall adjustment—the socially important effect—that is the central variable of interest (Lehtinen-Rogan & Hartman, 1976; Linden and Forness, 1986; Lurie, Schlan, & Freiberg, 1932; Mithaug et al., 1985; Saenger, 1957; Stanfield, 1973). Budgetary constraints of time and resources for research usually prevent one study from effectively addressing both social adjustment variables (consumer satisfaction or social validity) and employment outcomes. But to the extent that American culture identifies success and adjustment with income level, the outcomes of social and employment investigations will be complementary. A society such as Sweden's offers a contrast, where poverty and its concomitant lacks have been virtually eliminated. Here, employment may cease to be a reliable correlate of adjustment.

Finally, there is the majority of studies that focus more narrowly on vocational outcomes and efficacy of services, be they at the national, state, regional, local, institutional, or program level. They frequently do not investigate the cost of services and consumer satisfaction. In their review of follow-up studies, Harnisch et al. (1986) stated that "research needs to be conducted on specific programs and teaching strategies which lead to employment and advancement within the job setting for handicapped youth" (p. 50.). The public policy inferred by research that proceeds from this position is that (1) if a particular vocational service is associated with vocational success, it is worth the cost, and (2) if the targeted population is experiencing vocational success, that population is happy to be employed, or at least no more unhappy than the population at large. Though it will not be taken up here, valid arguments can be made for both assumptions.

The problem of many of these studies, as discussed by McCarver and Craig (1974), is the lack of an appropriate control group. Even if the target population does not achieve employment on par with the general population (the eventual control group), there is still a need to find out if particular intervention is at least better than none at all. Despite the ethical problems of withholding services, many public school districts are so poor in resources that it may actually be feasible to identify a matched sample to or construct control and experimental groups through random assignment. In the case of residential institutions, barriers to control group research on their released population persist; it is unclear who should compose an appropriate control group. Baller (1936), for example, compared 173 retarded individuals with IQ scores under 70 to a control group whose IQ scores ranged from 100 to 120. He did not control for socioeconomic status. Goldstein (1964) recommends matching to a "common and contemporary socio-physical milieu" (p. 243), and some studies have used this procedure (Peterson & Smith, 1960; Ross, Begab, Dondis, Giampiccolo, & Meyers, 1985).

Participants

In a comprehensive review of research conducted since 1975, Harnisch et al. (1986) cited studies in the 10 areas of handicap (defined by Public Law 94-142, 1975) and on disadvantaged youth. Of the 149 cited studies, 37% were done with retarded populations, 42% persons with sensory and orthopedic handicapping conditions combined, and 21% with learning disabled, severely emotionally disturbed, and disadvantaged combined. In reviews by McCarver and Craig (1974), Harnisch et al. (1986), and this chapter, no fewer than 236 follow-up studies of mentally retarded people are mentioned. Clearly, the most frequently observed population for transitional outcomes has been the mentally retarded adult. Mental retardation does represent the most prevalent handicap whose diagnosis is the least controversial. Learning disability is a more elusive and controversial construct (Sleeter, 1986; Ysseldyke, Algozzine, Shinn, & McGue, 1982), and people with learning disabilities were not recognized as a group in the United States until 1963. Thus, the high incidence rate of retardation, funding priorities, and the accessibility of mentally retarded populations to researchers may explain the preponderance of research on that population.

Few studies have investigated the socioeconomic status of the families of handicapped youth. One study from the early 1970s (Stanfield, 1973) noted that in a sample of 120 trainable mentally retarded youth, 42% of the graduates came from families whose average yearly incomes were less than $5,000, and the majority of these families were of ethnic minorities.

The study of mildly handicapped populations, who comprise over 80 percent of the special education population (Edgar & Hayden, 1985) has engendered research problems of its own. A search of ERIC and ECER/ Exceptional Children data bases using descriptors such as "job placement," "career education," "vocational adjustment," "learning disabilities," and "emotional disturbance," produced only six citations of follow up studies or reports with follow-up statistics, but turned up 31 citations of program descriptions and reports with no follow-up statistics.

Horn, O'Donnell, and Vitulano (1983) reviewed 24 follow-up studies of learning disabled students, but differences in the professional perception of the handicap greatly affected the focus of the studies. For example, the major concerns of learning disability research are the duration of the disorder, basic skills achievement, and behavioral/emotional functioning. Since there is some speculation that learning disabilities are school based, and that people with learning disabilities "get better," there is less attention to their vocational outcomes. That is, if they get better, it is assumed that they have normal outcomes. However, most studies have reported that learning disabilities endure. Of the 24 studies reviewed, 10 did include measures of educational and vocational attainment, and 8 of those 10 reported average or better attainment levels for the majority of the learning disabled participants when compared to the general population. The review failed to find any correlations between "catching up" academically and vocational success, and the authors hypothesize that valid measures of self-concept and attributional styles may have better correlations with positive vocational outcomes.

The findings of this review must be considered in light of the serious problem of attrition among persons with mild handicaps. In his statewide follow-up of special education students from 11 Washington school districts, Edgar (1987) reported that 29% of all students who begin the ninth grade drop out. But among the students with learning disabilities and behavior disorders, the dropout rate is 42%. (Among special education students, excluding learning disabled and behavior disordered, the dropout rate is only 16%.) In their cross-categorical follow-up study, Mithaug et al. (1985) attribute the underrepresentation of the emotionally and behaviorally disturbed to the dropout phenomenon. Similarly, the Horn et al. (1983) review may have found equivalent levels of postsecondary vocational and educational attainment for learning disabled adults because the samples did not include dropouts from high school.

Zigmond and Thornton (1985) conducted a study that compared the outcomes of a learning disabled group ($n = 60$) with a control group ($n = 61$) of regular education students. An earlier study (Levin, Zigmond, & Birch, 1985) had shown learning disabled students ($N = 52$) dropping out at a higher rate (47%) than the school district average of 36%. Zigmond and Thornton (1985) showed an even greater disparity: dropout rates of 54% for the learning disabled group and 33% for the control group. The employment rate for learning disabled graduates was 74% and for the control group, 88% (not a statistically significant difference). The learning disabled and control group dropouts were also equally successful in finding employment (44% and 50% respectively), and significantly less so than those completing school. The study makes the very dramatic point that in this large, northeastern, urban school district, school completion was clearly a better predictor of employment than placement in a learning disability program. Furthermore, the authors point out that transition programs for special needs students cannot help students who are no longer in the educational system. For this population at least dropping out is the most disabling feature, and a learning disabled student is more likely to leave school before graduating. The study did not investigate the commonalities between the two groups of dropouts, or between the two groups of graduates.

Edgar (1987) intends to rectify this methodological effect—skewing of the sample due to attrition—by tracking students from seventh grade and thereby researching the moment of dropout. His study will spend more energy maintaining contact, and making more vigorous efforts to contact dropouts who are potential participants. But the task will not be easy. The conscientious attempts of his staff have succeeded in contacting 51% of the graduates, but only 20% of the dropouts.

There are certain implications from these data that need to be considered. The studies that follow up students with mild handicaps are based on those school leavers that the investigators are able to contact, and there is little doubt that a significant proportion of the mildly handicapped population is "missing." Edgar (1987) hypothesizes that "most dropouts come from multiproblem families that are more transient than the general population" (p. 557), and his assertions are supported elsewhere (Semmel et al., 1985). Horn et al. (1983) proposed subgroups of learning disabled students based on IQ, hyperactivity, and etiology, but investigation of the school-leaving process is clearly a variable most critical to follow-up studies at this time.

Geography and Era

The time and place in which studies are undertaken can provide a critical context for analysis, yet this consideration is infrequently considered in follow-up studies. For example, there are no records that report the treatment of retarded citizens before 1850. Goodfellow (1947) speculates that they were sent to jails and almshouses if they presented problems. The late-nineteenth-century institutions that set out to rehabilitate retarded individuals failed, creating a backlash to custodial care. Fernald's (1919) classic study revived the concept of adjustment, but the eugenics movement, which recommended sterilization of "defectives" and went counter to the idea, was also popular in the 1920s.

Baller's study (1936) recorded instances when participants from his sample applied for relief during the Great Depression. Learning disabilities, which were not discovered until the 1940s, and not represented by a professional organization until 1963, probably did not interfere so greatly with adjustment in the simpler, pre-World War II American society.

McCarver and Craig (1974) divided 44 representative studies of outcomes for retarded individuals into four chronological eras. They achieved a rough estimate of possible fluctuations in outcomes, with the highest success rate being during the period of 1936–1953. This may be explained by the demand for workers created by World War II, and by the waning popularity of eugenics. The lowest success rate was for the most recent period, 1960 to 1970; probably because the trend to institutionalize only those with the very lowest IQ's came into conflict with the increased complexity of society (Skaarbrevik, 1971). Deinstitutionalization has placed more people of lower functioning abilities in situations where it is more difficult to adapt. Most recently, the passage of laws mandating increased participation of handicapped individuals in the work culture has not yet stimulated significant increases in employment (Habeck, Galvid, Frey, Chadderden, & Tate, 1985).

In earlier times, retarded men were able to find work on farms or in manufacturing, and retarded women more frequently found domestic work (McCarver & Craig, 1974). As late as the 1950s, retarded individuals were likely to drop out of school by age 16 (Peterson & Smith, 1960), probably to assume such employment. Today, such individuals tend to stay in school until their 22nd birthday (Edgar, 1987).

Until recently, little thought was given to the types of jobs held by handicapped individuals. Baller (1936) noted that the industries of a particular region will influence employment. Another study (Wilson & Rasch, 1982) observed that of 53 psychiatrically handicapped individuals, the longest placements were of those who had a things-related (as opposed to people-, data-, or ideas-related) occupation. Hasazi, Gordon, Roe, Hull, Finck, and Salembier (1985) noted the effect of region when they reported that 18% of their sample from metropolitan areas held clerical jobs, while none of their rural participants did. Conversely, 38% of the rural participants worked in structural occupations, but none of those from the metropolitan areas did.

Semmel et al. (1985), in their evaluation of a statewide program to increase the employment of handicapped youths, chose their sample from four southern California areas. Initially it appeared from the summary statistics that program participants fared better in the job market than the comparison group; but the superior outcome was actually confined to only one of the four areas. When that area was removed from the sample, the program differences disappeared. It is not clear whether region, program implementation, or some other variable determined the difference.

Wehman, Seyfarth, and Kregel (1985) and Hasazi, Gordon, Roe, Hull, et al. (1985) chose samples that were spread out among metropolitan, urban, suburban, and rural environments, in an effort to make their research sensitive to different environments, and also to derive outcomes with implications for an entire state (Virginia and Vermont, respectively). The possibility of creating an analysis that employs a sophisticated interface between regionally specific economic conditions and the employment of handicapped persons has not yet been explored.

A variable specific to the individual—length of time in the community (deinstitutionalized)—is one that follow-up studies are beginning to measure (McCarver & Craig, 1974), in order to evaluate the effectiveness of institutionalization. Finally, Kernan and Koegel (1984), through their ethnography that probes the same population over time, offer us a methodology that allows sensitivity to external factors and to the individuals' development. This approach is taken up in the next section.

Methodological Considerations

One begins to appreciate the flaws of much of the cited research after reading Kernan and Koegel's (1984) fascinating and careful research on the employment experiences of mildly retarded adults in the Los Angeles area. Discrepant employment rates (cited in Table 4.1) and the paucity of conclusive findings on predictors begin to make sense when the actual employment experience is observed close up. As Cobb (1972) stated, there is no simple formula for the prediction of employment outcomes. While the commonly measured variables have some effect, their interaction is extremely complex, and make simple percentages seem crude and inadequate.

Kernan and Koegel (1984) examined a group of 48 individuals, aged 19 to 49, and identified as having the most to gain from services and the best prognosis for adjustment. They were studied over a period of 30 months, using a participant-observation methodology. The study tracked the job-seeking, getting, and retaining activities of the sample population. Kernan and Koegel (1984) derived seven categories or steps to describe employment status: competitive full-time employment, competitive part-time employment, housewife, workshop, actively seeking, sporadically seeking, and not seeking employment. Combining qualitative methodology with their data-gathering, they visited each of the 48 individuals in the study twice a month and tracked their movements from one category to another.

Seven individuals moved backwards an average of 2.78 steps over the course of the study, but 14 moved up an average of 3.0 steps, lending moderate support to the findings of increased capability and stability as the retarded person's time in the community increases (Cobb, 1972; McCarver & Craig, 1974). To present a complete picture, however, the investigators also report that 10 of the "no movement" group ($n = 27$) actually did move up and down the employment "ladder," but happened to be on the same step at the conclusion of the two-and-a-half-year study. Thus, over a 30-month period, their statistics do not reflect a single reading, but the fluctuations over time in employment status, as well as variations in each individual's situation (family support, program involvement, negative influences inhibiting employment, etc.). On a given date, the employment rate of the sample could range anywhere from 23% to 46%.

Outcome studies that furnish a single figure for a particular population, bound together only by a common label and placement, pale in comparison to this more intensive approach. For example, a workshop-to-competitive-employment program for health-impaired and multihandicapped individuals reported a very high placement rate (76%) of a sample ($n = 25$) who completed the program (Radar, Shapiro, & Rodin, 1978). However, the job retention rate was much lower, with further descriptive characteristics of the placements not reported in any detail. Many major adjustments take place when adults who have been served in a sheltered setting for a considerable duration first move to nonsheltered employment contexts. Transition and placement research needs to document these changes.

The Radar et al. (1978) study also illustrates the problems of participant selection. If all of the 34 persons who were contacted for participation were to be considered, the placement rate of 76% would be reduced to 56%. If all of the individuals initially referred and judged by the vocational service to be suitable for employment were to constitute the sample ($n = 44$), the rate of placement would be further reduced to 43%. Finally, of the 58 clients discussed by the project's staff, only 35% were employed at the time of the study. Thus, the issue remains as to what is the most appropriate criterion for job placement or retention. Kirchner and Peterson (1979), for example, reviewed national statistics of the employment outcomes of adults with visual impairments. The two sources for their brief, the Bureau of the Census and the National Center for Health Statistics, differed in their definitions of the population. But the most drastic impact of the statistics reported was made by the definition of whether or not a person was considered to be in the labor force. Job status as well as labor-force participation were determined by the self-perception of the interviewee. When considering those in the labor force, the employment rate of working-age persons with visual loss was 83% to 91%, at a time when the employment rate of the U.S. population was 93% (Kirchner & Peterson, 1979). This rate appears to be quite healthy until one considers that only 32% of all working-age persons with visual loss were in the labor force by the survey's definition: "All persons who had jobs or were looking for work" (p. 240). The criterion of labor-force participation is one that changes with every advance in the vocational education and rehabilitation field. Any professional's authority on such matters can be easily challenged (M. Dick, personal communication, August 1987). The question of to what degree the judgment of employability resides in the community, in the social service agencies, or in the individual still awaits a satisfactory answer.

Thus, quantitative studies may be useful to the extent that the reported indicators can identify a significant trend over time or validate a particular intervention. Otherwise, program development will benefit more from studies that give fuller portraits of the lives of unemployed and underemployed persons with handicaps. Such studies might not only indicate which interventions have an impact on employment status, but also identify the decisive issues for the population of concern. Problems in participant selection, for example Edgar's (1987) difficulties in contacting high school dropouts with mild handicaps, might be solved by qualitative studies that suggest more productive procedures for data-based follow-up studies. A coordinated effort that combines qualitative and quantitative research is clearly called for.

Absenteeism and social skills are also factors related to job retention for handicapped individuals and in need of ethnographic research (Edgar, 1987; Forte, Storey, & Gaylord-Ross, 1985; Mithaug et al., 1985; Wehman et al., 1982; Wehman, Kregel, & Seyfarth, 1985). The problem of widespread illiteracy (e.g., in California, 57% of the state's welfare recipients lack the basic skills to find and keep a job) ("Workfare Tests," 1987) presents the ultimate life-span task of educating hard-to-teach people.

A unique opportunity is afforded by efforts to evaluate Project WorkAbility, a statewide program designed to enhance the employability of special education students in California. Two different teams of investigators (McCormick & Clarke, 1986; Semmel et al., 1985) conducted studies and though they both employed a control-group approach, a comparison of their results points to some of the differential effects of methodology. Sample size and selection differed. Semmel et al.'s (1985) sample ($N = 109$) was rigorously matched to its comparison group, but lacked participation by minority individuals and overrepresented women (compared to the overall special education populations). McCormick and Clarke's (1986) sample was much larger ($N = 296$) and had about 40% minority individuals, but contained significantly more severely handicapped youths in the WorkAbility group than were present statewide. Semmel et al.'s (1985) study focused on gender and class-placement differences, while McCormick and Clarke (1986) found earnings and weeks employed to be the most significant factors. The statistical tests employed differed as Semmel et al.'s study conducted a series of chi-square and other single factor comparisons, while McCormick and Clarke employed a multiple regression analysis to identify factors that correlated most highly with the number of weeks employed.

There was corroboration on many findings: WorkAbility participants were identified as less dependent, and more likely to use placement agencies than handicapped peers (It is interesting that these same findings came from two different sources, teacher prediction [Semmel et al., 1985] and actual use of agencies [McCormick & Clarke, 1986]). Furthermore, both studies found that handicapped students most often worked in low-paying service occupations, and most frequently used the self-family-friend network to find jobs.

The studies' differences, however, indicate serious methodological issues. First, Semmel et al. (1985) reported an employment rate of 83% and McCormick and Clarke (1986) only 48%. Semmel et al.'s gender comparisons between a WorkAbility group and a non-WorkAbility group of special education students (matched on sex, special education placement, IQ, reading achievement, and primary language) showed a poorer outlook for young graduating women. McCormick and Clarke, however, adjusted the *expected* employment outcome, based upon how a nonhandicapped group of the same age, socioeconomic status, and race as the WorkAbility group could expect to fare in the job market, and presented a more optimistic prognosis for the women in their sample. The implications for service design thus differ significantly: Is the program intended to erase the effects of handicap only, or rather to serve the identified persons so that they might even exceed the expectations for their age, race, gender, and socioeconomic status? Which is the more appropriate evaluation criterion?

Finally, the studies differ in their assertions that WorkAbility participants are chosen for either lack (McCormick & Clarke, 1986) or likelihood (Semmel et al., 1985) of employability; this premise affects the bias of the evaluation, and the calculations of expected outcomes. Our point here is that most studies, if done within the bounds of conventional rigor, are rarely challenged to justify the appropriateness of their methods, or to describe the original condition precisely. This controversy is brought into clear relief by the differences between these two studies.

McCarver & Craig (1974) feel that the methodological problem in this research area lies in the fact that most follow-up studies are conducted post hoc, rather than being true experiments. Only one study since their review (Mertens & Seitz, 1982) made a direct comparison to a nonhandicapped cohort that was matched to a group of special education students. A more urgent need is the adoption of a standardized protocol for follow-up studies that would generate meta-analyses and more generalized conclusions. Procedures might include

1. Functional classifications of handicap sample (i.e., Edgar, 1987)
2. Definitions of stages of employment and success in the community: multiple probes (e.g., Kernan & Koegel, 1984)
3. Benefit-cost analysis (e.g., Hill, Hill, Wehman & Banks, 1985)
4. The effects of interagency agreements (e.g., Hasazi et al., 1985)
5. Measures of participant satisfaction and social validity (e.g., Edgerton, 1967, 1984; Edgerton & Langness, 1978; Forte, Storey, & Gaylord-Ross, 1985; Hobbs, 1983)
6. Earnings (e.g., Wehmen, Seyfarth & Kregel, 1985)
7. Adequate controls for economic factors.

The replication of such standardized studies would begin to provide the empirical base necessary to advocate for improvements in service delivery, and justification for a more proportionately diverse labor force. McCarver and Craig (1974) comment on the sad lack of standardized procedures, noting that between 1968 and 1973, over 39,000 retarded residents were released from institutions, but only 26% of the 34 states that responded to a survey had available data on the discharged clients' adjustment in the community

Critical Findings

This section will first review one influential study and then examine some of the more frequently substantiated findings in the follow-up literature of handicapped youth and adults.

A follow-up study conducted in Vermont in 1984 (Hasazi, Gordon, & Roe, 1985) provides a focus for identifying factors associated with employment status, and has implications for vocational programming. The study examined the employment status of 459 handicapped youths exiting nine Vermont public school districts between 1979 and 1983, and analyzed the relationships between their employment status and their manner of exit, gender, style of job search, location, school experiences, wages, and job histories. Of the sample, 59% graduated, 13% were over 18 when they left, and 28% dropped out of school before age 18; 66% were from resource rooms, 29% from special classes, and 6% from other programs.

The overall employment rate of the youths was 54%. The employment rate for students who had graduated was 60%, for those leaving after age 18, it was 51%, and for those dropping out, it was 30%. The highest employment rates were associated with youths who had kept part-time jobs during their high school years (70% employed of 114 youths), and those who had an unsubsidized summer job during high school (69% of 157 youths). The lowest employment rates were associated with those who left school after age 18 without graduating (30% of 33 youths) and those who had neither a subsidized nor an unsubsidized summer job during high school (37% of 114 youths). Of those students who could be clearly identified as mildly handicapped (Resource room students, $n = 187$), 62% were employed at the time of the study. Finally, of the 301 youths for whom employment data were obtained, only 166 or 55% were paid employees. Of this employed group, 84% found work, through the self-family-friend network; the remainder used more institutional means such as job-related service agencies, the military, or school personnel.

The authors comment that Vermont's vocational education programs are fully integrated. Handicapped students learn side by side with non-handicapped peers. Participation in mainstreamed vocational education has a positive correlation with employment status (61% employed vs. 45%). These findings are in contrast to those of the National Longitudinal Survey, which found that vocational education is not correlated with higher employment rates in the general population (Borus, 1984). This suggests that special education students actually profit more than regular education students by having access to regular vocational education.

On the other hand, the majority of Vermont's "work experience" programs specifically designed for handicapped students are segregated, exploratory, subsidized (or volunteer), short in duration, and unrepresentative of real work settings. Perhaps these classes are composed of students who are lower functioning as well. The findings were that students who participated in work experience programs associated with special class programs were no more likely to be employed than those who did not participate.

By now, there is little debate over the fact that almost all handicapped youth, even when they are employed, earn well below the average income for their region and era. Peterson and Smith (1960) reported that 45 educable mentally retarded individuals earned only 61% of what a group of nonhandicapped adults of low socioeconomic status did. Mithaug et al. (1985) conducted a statewide follow-up of all special education students and found that 43% earned less than $3.00 per hour and 13% of them earned less than $4.00 per hour. Over 86% of 117 retarded individuals observed by Wehman, Seyfarth, & Kregel (1985) had earned less than $1,000 in the one to four years since they left secondary school. But when a group of 63 individuals who had had the benefits of an ongoing supported work program was probed (Wehman et al., 1982), the average client earned $4,464 per year (compared to the $414 per-year average for a workshop client). These figures seem impressive and do indicate progress, but Edgar (1987) states that any salary under $7,000 per year does not enable a person to live independently; thus the employment of special education youths at these levels is not significant.

Harnisch et al. (1986) reviewed numerous studies and noted that handicapped youths, besides earning at a marginal level, received fewer (if any) raises than nonhandicapped peers, and fewer if any fringe benefits (i.e., sick leave, vacation, insurance, profit sharing). In a study that showed almost three-fourths of 125 retarded adults to be earning less than $500 per month, the only salient fringe benefit observed by Wehman et al. (1985) was free meals. Other investigations have found the same low wages for handicapped individuals (Hasazi, Gordon, Roe, Hull, et al., 1985; McCormick & Clarke, 1986; Ross, Begab, Dondis, Giampiccolo, & Meyers, 1985; Wolfe, 1979).

Besides earning low wages, handicapped persons frequently find themselves in service-related and unskilled labor occupations (Dinger, 1961; Harnisch et al., 1986; Hasazi, Gordon, Roe, Hull, et al., 1985; McCormick & Clarke, 1986; Wehman, Kregel, & Seyfarth, 1985; Wehman,

Seyfarth, & Kregel, 1985; Wolfe, 1979). Although Kirchner and Peterson (1979) reported that less than one-third of working-age, visually disabled persons were in the labor force, this is the one disability group that has been able to gain access to managerial, professional, technical, or official employment fields (Cook, 1976; Harnisch et al., 1986).

The next most common finding, and a more recent one, is that families and friends play a critical role in job development and placement. They have been the source of employment or an employment lead more often than placement agencies (Peterson & Smith, 1960; Wehman, Kregel, & Seyfarth, 1985). This kind of support includes the family that persists in organizing and supporting a job search, as well as the benefactor type of relationship where a friend gives ongoing, and perhaps on-the-job direction to a handicapped individual (Kernan & Koegel, 1984). Hasazi, Gordon, Roe, Hull, et al. (1985) found that as the environment became more rural, reliance on the self-family-friend network for a job increased. Figures on the use of the self-family-friend network for job development range from 59% (Dinger, 1961) to 68% (Richarson & Hill, 1980) to 84% (Hasazi, Gordon, Roe, Hull, et al., 1985) of those employed. One interesting and contrary finding by Mithaug et al. (1985) was that, in their state-wide sample, the handicapped person himself—but definitely *not* the family—was responsible for finding employment. In fact, they concluded that the parents were the people *least* involved in the job search effort. Whether this difference is based on region, economy, or research methods is unknown at this time, and needs investigation.

Overall, these findings imply that the socioeconomic status of the handicapped individual's family is perhaps the best predictor of where and how successfully a youth will be placed in the work world. If the network is one of nonworking people, for example, it cannot be expected to supply a job for that individual. To take these implications a step further, services whose mission is better accomplished by the family and friends might shift their emphasis to improve the employment status of the network rather than the handicapped individual.

Two findings with more direct implications for educational services are that part-time, real jobs and summer jobs correlate with higher earnings and positive post-school employment outcomes (Hasazi, Gordon, Roe, Hull, et al., 1985; Semmel et al., 1985), and that vocational education classes are associated with employment success (Halpern, 1978; Hasazi, Gordon, Roe, Hull, et al., 1985; Mertens & Seitz, 1982; Rosenberg, 1978; Semmel et al., 1985). Further substantiation is especially critical in light of the fact that national surveys of vocational education's effectiveness have not found it to be correlated with higher than average employment when the general population is considered (Borus, 1984; Catterall & Stern,

1986; Flynn, 1982; Rumberger & Daymont, 1984). As mentioned before, if a truly valuable service is being performed by vocational education, namely, that it is making handicapped youth more employable, the significant aspects of that service need to be identified and retained. The aforementioned studies also show that vocational education is effective in reducing the number of dropouts in the general school population. Some would argue, however, that youths get access to vocational education only after the high-risk dropout ages (freshman and sophomore years in high school) have passed (N. Zigmond, personal communication, November 10, 1988).

　　Job status changes and reasons for job separation also require investigation; the findings could indicate the skills handicapped individuals need to retain jobs and thus redefine the training priorities of the service delivery system. Mithaug et al. (1985) found that their statewide sample ($N = 234$) had held an average of 3.1 jobs in the first three to four years after leaving school. One study of retarded adults reported an increase in job changes over time (Clark, Kivitz, & Rosen, 1968), while another found the opposite to be true (Kraus, 1972). Though employment for handicapped females is consistently reported to be more difficult than for males, Peterson and Smith (1960) observed retarded females holding onto their jobs for 33 to 38 months, while retarded males averaged only 18 months.

　　Wehman, Kregel, and Seyfarth (1985) present a number of reasons for job separations in their sample ($N = 125$) of retarded adults, ranging from problems with co-workers (8%) to disliking the work (7%) to transportation problems (4%) to loss of SSI payments (less than 1%). Another study (Wehman et al., 1982) found that only 11% of their sample of 63 retarded individuals resigned or were terminated due to an inability to perform job tasks at an acceptable rate. In a related study designed specifically to study this topic, Hill, Wehman, Hill, and Goodall (1985) investigated over 107 job terminations. They developed seven categories covering client-related and environmental causes for separations and analyzed them in terms of the IQ levels of the retarded participants. The findings revealed that the more severely retarded individuals tended to lose jobs due to environmental causes (layoffs, family decisions, coworker discomfort), whereas the mildly retarded workers would more often be the "actors" in their terminations (attitude problems and skill deficits). Other data have been presented that support the hypotheses that retarded adults who are male (Tarjan, Dingman, Eyman, & Brown, 1960), or who have higher IQ scores (Baller, 1936; Hill, Hill, Wehman, Banks, Pendleton, & Britt, 1985) were more difficult to retain in employment. A larger economic factor may be involved here. The service-oriented jobs where retarded individuals usually work are appropriate for a more retarded person, but efforts to match higher functioning abilities to more challenging tasks have not been made available in the economy. The emphasis of the supported employment movement has not been to train more mildly handicapped persons for more complex jobs. Rather, its intent has been to prove the employability of even the most profoundly handicapped person.

Discussion

The issues raised by this body of literature intimate the near-impossible task of integrating the findings. It is far easier to identify the deficits of the literature than to condense and summarize the contributions. The varying methodologies, reflecting the varying purposes of investigators, create a temptation to discard all of the findings, or at least resist comparison. Single-figure statistics begin to look less and less useful when ethnographic studies and personal experience bring the true complexity of causes to mind. When none of the studies show employed handicapped people even approaching the poverty level, let alone exceeding it, the importance of the forty-odd studies enumerated in Table 4.1 seems negligible. Edgar (1987) reinforces this notion by commenting that nothing productive is being accomplished when only 18% of the special education students in this study ($N = 360$) earned more than the minimum wage, and only 5% when the learning disabled and behavior disordered persons were removed from the sample.

Yet something tugs at the mind as study after study is read and reviewed. Something is missing from the equation. That something is attention to those aspects of the economic structure that promote the underemployment of handicapped people. The role of special educators and rehabilitation professionals has been to make the handicapped student more employable. This task is obviously not yet completed, and it makes a certain sense that the literature focus on it. But underlying the rationale of most studies seems to be a naive belief, not articulated, but implied, that educational interventions and analyses of youths will perfect ways to employ handicapped persons, that through the manipulation of educational factors such as follow-up, vocational education, work experience, and so forth, low employment rates and low wages will disappear because we have developed good interventions. This notion is limited. The employment of handicapped youth commensurate with the rest of the population requires better training and placement services, to be sure, but the other half of the equation is the commitment of employers to create jobs that pay higher wages and offer better benefits.

This commitment is more the domain of public policy, but it affects the results of every study cited in this review. For example, suppose a program evaluation is being conducted, and the school or agency has made an informal agreement with a local company that the company will hire many of the youths exiting the program. If the management is compelled to adopt cost-cutting measures, and decides not only to terminate the agreement, but to lay off a number of the handicapped individuals, what might have been touted as an exemplary program would be quickly transformed into a failed effort. Thus, the actual processes and behaviors of the targeted employers must be fed into the equation of follow-up studies as well. Wehman, Seyfarth, and Kregel (1985) at least begin to address this issue by commenting on the economic health of Virginia at the time of their follow-up study. Brickey and Campbell (1981) discuss their program in terms of the economic needs of the time. But in the same way that Kernan and Koegel (1984) closely follow the lives of retarded adults, authentic explanations of employer behavior are the missing pieces of indepth data that will bring significant change to the employment status of handicapped persons.

Nonetheless, findings up to this time are still significant. Adjustment, for example, has been reinterpreted to mean more than deinstitutionalization; competitive, nonsheltered employment is now considered essential. If the small gains made so far strengthen the arguments for enlarging opportunities and increasing wages, they have not been in vain. For this reason, Table 4.1 reflects an effort to include only studies for which a nonsheltered employment rate can be found. Thus, this present review presents data representative of a time when sheltered employment is not considered significant. Yet it is also a time when there is little to report in the way of earnings above the poverty level.

A review of the outcomes for the two most frequently studied populations reveals great disparity. For retarded individuals, nonsheltered employment rates of 2% (Tisdall, 1958), 12% (Delp & Lorenz, 1953), 19% (Baller, 1936), 43% (Hasazi, Gordon, Roe, Hull, et al., 1985), and 76% (Brickey & Campbell, 1981) can all be found in the literature. For mildly handicapped populations, the range extends from rates of 40% (Lehtinen & Tuomisto, 1978), 45% (Cordero, 1975), and 50% (Blalock, 1981) to 62% (Hasazi, Gordon, & Roe, 1985), 77% (White, Schumaker, Warner, Alley & Deshler, 1980), and 100% (Hardy, 1968). Surely, generalizations are difficult to make with any degree of certainty. These populations present special problems due to their numbers and the unique challenges of their disabilities.

The subject of disability category raises further issues in methodology: Should persons with mental retardation, for example, be investigated using the same methods as for those with mild handicaps? Edgar (1987) indicates that even the mechanics of contacting these two populations must differ if they are to succeed. Hasazi et al. (1985) and Zigmond and Thornton (1985) concur on the hypothesis that visible handicaps preclude the importance of a diploma, while for the mildly, "invisibly" handicapped (who are more likely to drop out), high school graduation is given an exaggerated importance that works against their success in the job market. In another vein, the family situations that generally occur, the employment possibilities, and the interaction with different sets of factors (justice system, workshops, ethnic identity, learned helplessness, etc.), create social systems that may suit different research approaches. Finally, the close overlap between mildly handicapped youth and populations identified as poor, delinquent, and disadvantaged, calls for sharing of research literatures that has up to now only infrequently occurred (Phelps, 1986).

The final question posed by this review is the same as the first one considered: What is community adjustment? Wolfensberger (1972) makes the case for entitling retarded adults to full participation in community life. Defining that transition, be it in terms of income, personal satisfaction, or social integration, is no easy task. What are the levels of participation that can be measured as "full"? Who constitutes the norm for such standards? For example, a number of studies report on the fact that handicapped women are employed much less frequently and earn less than handicapped men (Dinger, 1961; Harnisch et al., 1986; Hasazi, Gordon, Roe, Hull, et al., 1985; Semmel et al., 1985), despite the fact that they show greater ability to hold on to a job (Peterson & Smith, 1960). Even allowing for parents' overprotectiveness of their daughters, the phenomenon tapped by these studies clearly extends beyond the handicapped community. The question becomes whether services should attain a status for handicapped persons beyond or merely on par with whatever other disadvantaged group to which they belong. This is the crux of one of the methodological differences between McCormick and Clarke's (1986) and Semmel et al.'s (1985) studies. Shall the progress of one group set the standards, or be allowed to impinge on the advancement of another? Ironically, it is the large-scale entry of women into the labor market (Rose, 1985; Habeck, Galvid, Frey, Chadderden, & Tate, 1985) that has possibly had the greatest negative impact on employment of handicapped persons over the last 14 years.

The goals of the rehabilitation movement, by defining adjustment in social, psychological, and vocational terms, are to effect that elusive "full participation." In other words, the ultimate refinement of services to handicapped persons may enable them to live *better* than their nonhandicapped peers! The one conclusive finding of the data—handicapped persons tend to be underemployed and poor—shows how far away this possibility is from reality. Yet if the dedication to service improvement defines a powerful enough movement in the coming decades, such an outcome would not be inconceivable. In fact, it is not untenable to propose a social system where the community adjustment of handicapped persons constitutes its basic premise, and the standard to which nonhandicapped individuals may strive.

SOCIAL SUPPORT IN THE WORK PLACE

The successful adjustment and integration of handicapped people in competitive settings depends on more than their job or social skills. Social support, in the form of relationships, contributes to employer acceptance and employee adjustment in times of a transition to a new job setting. In this respect social support is an important adjunct to the training of social skills. Studies indicate that social relationships contribute to the successful adjustment of handicapped individuals in both community and work settings (Close & Keating, 1988; Edgerton, 1967; Edgerton & Bercovici, 1976; Ross, Begab, Dondis, Giampiccolo, & Meyers, 1985).

Definitions

Social support may be defined as the formal and informal relationships that assist an individual in coping with stressful situations. This assistance can be both emotional and functional; often it is multifaceted, working towards increasing the fit between the individual and the ecological source of stress. This view reflects some of the salient points derived from definitions given by researchers in the field of mental health (Caplan & Killilea, 1976; Cobb, 1976; Gottlieb, 1983).

An epidemiologist, Cobb (1976) defines social support in terms of situational and environmental resources that provide a sharing of information. He states that informational aspects of social support fall into one or more of three areas, people's belief that they (1) are cared for, (2) are loved, esteemed and valued, and (3) belong to a network of communication and mutual obligation. Some of this information is obviously in the form of emotional support.

While Cobb (1976) stresses informational aspects of social support, Caplan (1976) stresses adaptive competence and cognitive aspects of stress mastery. From a social psychiatric perspective, Caplan defines social support as attachments among individuals or between individuals and groups that help to improve adaptive competence. This competence should apply to both short-term crises and life transitions, as well as with long-term challenges and stresses. Adaptive capabilities should arise from emotional mastery, guidance, and feedback gained from indigenous mutual-help groups and enhanced by helping professionals.

Gottlieb (1983) agrees with Caplan's (1976) definition and states that in addition to information, social support consists of tangible aid, or action offered by social intimates or inferred by their presence. Social support has beneficial emotional or behavioral effects on the recipient. Gottlieb also affirms Caplan's belief that professionals can play a leading role in mobilizing support from more informal, indigenous sources.

All three definitions share the common concept of enhanced mental well-being through social relationships that allow an individual to adapt to stressful situations and develop coping strategies. However, the definitions lead to different types of research. Research using Cobb's (1976) definition would stress proving information and encouragement within a given ecological setting. On the other hand, Caplan's (1976) and Gottlieb's (1983) definitions would also include active aid such as making phone calls, contacts, and monitoring to enhance adaptation to stressful settings.

Caplan's (1976) and Gottlieb's (1983) definitions amplify Cobb's (1976) definition by stressing different functional aspects of how social support works in the life of the recipient. They advocate using preexisting support groups, and stress ways that professionals can enhance and encourage indigenous aid to groups on behalf of people undergoing transitions and stresses.

In recent years social support has also emerged as an important concept that can contribute to the successful transitions of handicapped individuals in community and employment settings (Chadsey-Rusch & Rusch, 1988; Karan & Knight, 1986; O'Connor, 1983; Shafer, 1986). O'Connor (1983) defines social support for mentally retarded persons in a way consistent with mental health definitions. She states that support consists of "emotional, informational, and material support provided by friends, relatives, neighbors, service providers, and others with whom one has an ongoing relationship, and to whom one can turn in times of need or crisis" (p. 187). Interestingly, all of these definitions stress the promotion of well-being through relationships rather than developing new skills in order to adapt to a situation.

Since relationships depend on mutuality and working together, an ecologically realistic view of social support becomes important. Such a view is consistent with Cobb's (1976) definition and, in the case of vocational education for handicapped persons, can be enhanced by the action-oriented definitions of Caplan (1976) and Gottlieb (1983), because it is often professionals who take action to encourage a good ecological match for the client.

This ecological perspective has been advocated by a number of au-

GOVERNORS STATE UNIVERSITY
UNIVERSITY PARK
IL. 60466

thors in the mental health and vocational education fields (Hirsch, 1981; Chadsey-Rusch & Rusch, 1988). These authors stress that the success of social support or the retention of employees depends on a good match between individuals and their environment. Hirsch (1981) states that healthy ecological formulations consist of goodness of fit that permits individuals to participate actively in viable segments of society. Chadsey-Rusch and Rusch (1988) emphasize that the workplace should strive to maximize the physical, social, and organizational fit or congruence between persons with special needs and their workplaces.

If the issues of goodness of fit are ignored, then potentially adverse consequences may follow. Among the negative consequences for a mismatch between person and environment are a subversion of the regimen, and an undermining of a person's self-esteem. This undermining occurs if people believe that their status is that of an impaired person. They may consequently see themselves as a burden or become socially detached to avoid the stigma.

Conversely, Karan and Knight (1986) contend that employment retention occurs where matches have been reasonable to good, and where environments have provided sufficient support to help individuals meet the demands of the workplace. This combination of a match and support offers an effective model for transition, since success in the workplace depends on the mutual satisfaction of employers and the employees. Social support should arise from a good ecological match and emphasize action-oriented support in order to promote successful employment transitions.

Reviews of Current Studies

Numerous studies have examined social support in the mental health field in a wide variety of circumstances, such as community residents experiencing pregnancy, health problems, divorce, unemployment, and death in the family (Gottlieb, 1983). However, social support is a relatively new field for handicapped people with special needs. Romer and Heller (1983) examined social support for handicapped individuals in community settings, but few studies have examined the supportive relationships that handicapped individuals experience when making a transition to nonsheltered, competitive employment.

Much of the empirical research on social development for handicapped persons in the workplace has stressed social skills training. More currently, the building of social support networks in the workplace has been advocated by a number of authors, many of whom offer theories and strategies to best implement and utilize social support systems. Despite the

GOVERNORS STATE UNIVERSITY
UNIVERSITY PARK

expansion of theory beyond skills training to include a person-workplace fit, very little empirical research has been generated in this field (Karan & Knight, 1986; O'Connor, 1983; Shafer, 1986).

Analogous empirical work done in the mental health field examines the buffering effects of social support on work stress (House & Wells, 1978; LaRocco, House, & French, 1980; LaRocco & Jones, 1978). The study by LaRocco et al. (1980) will be examined here as an example of how mental health research has demonstrated that social support can have a positive impact on individuals experiencing occupational stress. There is obvious relevance to research and theory regarding employees with handicaps, and this research may be useful as a model for data collection. Results of other research that examines handicapped individuals in vocational settings will also be examined here, even when social support is reported as a secondary concern. This research indicates an emerging concern with social support as a preventive intervention to facilitate a successful transition in a vocational setting.

In a mental health article on social support, LaRocco et al. (1980) explore the impact of social support on occupational stress and its relation to job-related strain and health. This article does not address handicapped individuals, but it is a well-designed empirical study. It shows that social support acts as a buffer on the impact of job stress on several mental and physical health variables including anxiety, depression, irritation, and somatic symptoms. The article demonstrates a conceptual and empirical basis for examining the effects of social support relative to life stress and individual well-being.

LaRocco et al. (1980) use a statistical regression technique to analyze data from an occupationally stratified random sample of 636 men drawn from 23 different blue-collar and white-collar occupations. Measures included perceived job stress, person-environment fit, job-related strain, and general mental health. Social support measures examined perceived support from three sources: supervisors, co-workers, and family and friends.

LaRocco et al. (1980) examined the data in terms of both main effect (additive) and interactive effect (buffering) hypotheses. The interaction findings indicated no significant relation between social support and the impact of job stress on the subjects' general attitude and affect regarding work. Social support did not ameliorate feelings of job dissatisfaction, boredom, and workload dissatisfaction. However, it was found that social support had a significant impact on the relationship between job stress and health. Of four dependent health variables, three had significant effects: Depression, irritation, and somatic complaints had been buffered by social support, while the effects on anxiety were not significant. In sum, the results indicated that social support buffered the effects of job stress on overall mental health, but did not buffer the effects on the subject's attitudes toward work.

In a further examination of the data, the authors found that of the three sources of support, the co-workers produced about twice as many effects as supervisors or friends and family. The results also indicate that in many cases the effects of social support on mental health were more beneficial when stress or strain was high. At these high levels support made a difference of 1.5 to 2.5 standard deviations in the level of the mental health variable.

These findings verify the role of social support in the mitigation of the effects on job stress on various psychological factors. While this study does not address social support questions in relation to handicapped individuals in vocational settings, the study does demonstrate that social support has complex components, and does not offer all-encompassing answers to social problems. Whether social support has beneficial effects on mental health and coping for others besides those experiencing stress remains an unanswered question. The study also emphasizes the need to specify which stress/strain relationships are most susceptible to buffering effects, and which are relatively impervious to social support.

Findings on the social support of handicapped individuals in competitive employment settings are rare. A few studies of handicapped people employed in noncompetitive settings indicate that social support from their peers is important to their emotional well-being. The absence of peer support detracted from their feelings of self-satisfaction. Close and Keating (1988) stated that recent studies have shown that handicapped persons in competitive employment often felt less support than those in sheltered workshops. These individuals felt alone and detached from the social network provided by their agency supervisors and peers in the sheltered settings. Such studies raise an important question about the best method for assuring person-environment fit. These studies, however, should not be taken to mean that sheltered workshops are better. Rather, they should show the need to attend to creating better social support systems for individuals in competitive settings.

In another study Brickey, Browning, and Campbell (1982) examined the placement histories of 73 mentally retarded, sheltered workshop employees who made a transition to less restrictive positions with either Projects with Industry (PWI) or to competitive employment. Of the 73 placements, 27 were PWI positions, which included work at a book bindery, helping to make patio stones for a garden store, factory work, and janitorial work. Of these 27, 13 (48%) went on to competitive jobs, making a total of 58 placements, which included dishwashing, janitorial, food service, and factory jobs.

The authors were primarily interested in studying the work histories of these employees. However, their discussion on group placements prove to be interesting for several reasons. They state that the most successful (longest term) placements were with McDonald's outlets. In these positions the mean record was 17.5 months per employee, which compared favorably to a mean of 7.2 months per employee in other food-service positions. The authors believed the amount of support was substantially increased because training staff studied the jobs in more detail and were better able to prepare the groups. The authors also cite support from the regional and unit leadership of the outlets. The authors state that group placements may be more productive for retarded people than individual placements with a variety of employers. In this instance group placements appear to offer more support and have more success as measured by more stable job placements.

Two other studies on social skills training indicate a growing trend toward linking formal and informal support systems (Rusch & Menchetti, 1981; Shafer, Brooke, & Wehman, 1985). While both of these studies stress the development of specific social skills rather than continuing support, they offer examples of how professional trainers can utilize the support of co-workers as well. In this way the indigenous co-workers can offer social validation to professional programs so that performance within a client's repertoire can be brought into a better ecological match with situational demands.

In the study by Rusch and Menchetti (1981) the social skills training for a competitively employed, moderately retarded male, Jim, was effectively carried out by professional follow-up staff in conjunction with his supervisors and co-workers. The staff trained Jim to comply with his fellow workers and warned him that failure to comply would result in his being sent home. The staff relied on reports from Jim's fellow workers to chart Jim's progress, and it was a supervisor who sent Jim home for noncompliance. This latter action resulted in Jim's compliance with supervisors, cooks, and laborers for the remainder of the study.

In another study also cited above, Shafer et al. (1985) examined the effects of modeling, role-play, and response feedback in developing appropriate social interpersonal skills in a mentally retarded worker. An important aspect of the study was its stress on using the supervisor to socially validate the study and extend the support from the vocational trainer to on-site support people. The supervisor identified three areas for social improvement: the development of appropriate skills for accepting criticism, humor, and requests for assistance.

The study achieved its primary purpose of demonstrating that effective strategies can be applied in competitive work settings. However, the lowered effectiveness scores on the employer probes indicate that professionals need to incorporate others into treatment plans to help assure generalization and greater congruency with the employment setting. Both of the social skills training studies indicate that indigenous personnel can work effectively with vocational trainers to create more socially valid treatments. The treatments effectively taught social skills but did not specifically address the subjects' social link to others in the work environment. Social skills training does address the employee's needed skills for job retention. But if such training had been coupled more directly with social support by encouraging relationships in the work environment, perhaps even greater generalization would have ensued. Social skills training is probably an important first step for employee acceptance, but the mutuality offered through social support goes beyond skills.

Future Directions

Social support is a relatively new topic in the field of mental health, and is even newer to the field of special education. Except for some research dealing with the placement of persons with handicaps in community settings, theory has not advanced beyond confirmatory empirical research. Social support research as it applies to persons with handicaps is urgently needed if the field is to become a viable model for transition.

Future research needs to focus on the goodness-of-fit between people and their environments, and stress the interrelationships that occur therein. Skills training puts the onus of social acceptability on the handicapped person. On the other hand, social support stresses a receptive emotional environment where supervisors, co-workers, and new employees all strive to achieve a conducive work environment.

Further investigation might examine a number of related issues. Case studies, program evaluation research, and outcome studies could examine employment longevity and satisfaction. Issues related to longevity and satisfaction should include the composition of support networks, and look at whether naturally occurring support systems offer more emotional support for mental well-being than do those artificially created by a trainer or professional within a work environment. Methods for successfully linking professional and nonprofessional networks should also be examined. Other methods to be developed would be those that promote reciprocity in relationships as opposed to ones in which the clients feel that they have nothing to offer.

Another area for research would be to examine whether peers or professionals offer more socially valid support, and if the two groups can offer comprehensive services rather than fragmented services. Combined efforts offer the advantage of promoting a more efficient support, one which recognizes the whole person in an ecological context.

Social support is an important area for future research because it addresses the client's needs as well as the employment demands. However, without further empirical findings to support the current theories, the field will not grow. New research should provide a perspective and direction, developing a structure for providing mutual support and a stable environment for employers and employees adjusting to the stresses of new settings.

GENERALIZATION TRAINING

The growing emphasis on preparing students with skills to function as independently as possible across a wide variety of domestic, community, recreational/leisure, and vocational domains has heightened the need for students to learn these skills not only in specific teaching situations, but to be able to generalize them across appropriate non-trained environments, people, and activities as well. It is no longer sufficient that a student correctly perform learned skills only in the training environment. Several authors have suggested that the utility of most functional skills is determined by the successful performance of the skill across non-trained natural situations (Coon, Volgelsberg, & Williams, 1981; Falvey, Brown, Lyon, Baumbart, & Schroeder, 1980). As Baumeister (1969) stated: "It is one thing to show that well defined response sequences can be shaped in a highly structured, controlled, and atypical environment and quite another matter to demonstrate that conditioning can produce permanent adaptive changes in complex areas of adjustment over a wide variety of environmental circumstances" (p. 50). It is widely recognized that generalization of learned skills with severely disabled children does not occur automatically, but that it is necessary to build procedures directly into the instructional program in order to ensure its occurrence (Rusch & Schutz, 1981; Stokes & Baer, 1977).

Generalization has generally been viewed as a passive phenomena instead of a specific outcome of training. Stokes and Baer (1977), in their review of the literature, demonstrated the extent to which this passive perspective has carried over into teaching practices. The majority of the research reviewed used a "train and hope" method (i.e., a skill was trained and the occurrence of any generalized effect was assessed but not specifically programmed). Most studies employing this approach failed to achieve expected levels of generalization.

Stokes and Baer (1977) defined generalization as the "occurrence of relevant behavior under different, non-training conditions (i.e., across subjects, settings, people, behaviors, and/or time) without the scheduling of the same events in those conditions as had been scheduled in the training conditions" (p. 350). Advances in instructional technology have facilitated the teaching of responses that are performed in novel (non-trained) situations (Drabman, Hammer, & Rosenbaum, 1979; Saunders & James, 1983; Stokes & Baer, 1977). While a complete technology is not presently available, several generalization strategies are proving to be effective.

Training Functional Skills

The participation and integration of individuals with disabilities is dependent upon their competence in a variety of skill areas across a variety of present and probable future environments (Brown, Nietupski, & Hamre-Nietupski, 1976; Wilcox & Bellamy, 1982). Given the difficulty many individuals with severe disabilities encounter in learning new skills, efficient and effective use of instructional time is of critical concern. Thus, training time should not be squandered on nonfunctional or irrelevant tasks that do not generalize to targeted community settings. Instead, skills trained should be those that are valued and that produce naturally available reinforcers in the environment. In the context of generalization, training functional skills increases the likelihood that an individual will use these skills to gain access to naturally reinforcing contingencies that are routinely available in natural settings (Stokes & Baer, 1977). For example, teaching an individual to operate a vending machine at a job site is a functional skill since it allows the individual to have access to desirable items (e.g., soft drinks, food) in that environment. Further, by determining the demands of the targeted natural settings where an individual would be expected to perform, and then training the relevant skills, we would increase the probability of that individual receiving reinforcement (e.g., money, break-time, social praise), and thus refining and maintaining those skills without continued interventions.

Training in the Natural Environment

As the content of instruction becomes increasingly focused on teaching functional skills, the context of instruction is being given greater significance. One hypothesis offered for why generalization often fails to occur is that the training environment is unlike the environment in which generalized responding is expected (Stokes & Baer, 1977). Either it lacks the relevant stimulus variables to ensure generalized and adaptive responding, or it contains irrelevant stimuli that may come to be associated with responding. Thus, a number of authors have suggested that teaching that occurs exclusively in the classroom, or exclusively involves simulation activities, is inadequate for disabled individuals who are expected to ultimately function in a wide variety of community settings (Brown et al., 1976; Certo, Brown, Belmore & Crowner, 1977; Sailor & Guess, 1983).

Consequently, it has been advocated that there is a need to provide functional skills training in the natural environments where the skills are ultimately to be performed (Brown et al., 1976). However, others have suggested that training in natural environments may not be the most effective or efficient approach (Giangreco, 1983; Neef, Iwata, & Page, 1978; Nietupski, Welch, & Wacker, 1983; Page, Iwata, & Neef, 1976). In addition, teaching that combines simulation activities with regular training in natural contexts has also been recommended as an effective approach for developing generalized skills (Gaylord-Ross, Haring, Breen, & Pitts-Conway, 1984; McDonnell & Horner, 1985). Unfortunately, evidence is insufficient regarding the superiority of any of these instructional approaches or how experiences in one should relate to the other. In general, research suggests that both simulated and natural environments can be used effectively (Mithaug, 1981). However, until an individual can demonstrate correct performance in the targeted natural setting, training cannot be considered a success. What is needed now are specific guidelines to assist in determining which instructional approaches are the most effective and efficient for various populations and stimulus conditions.

Training the General Case

Two strategies suggested by Stokes and Baer (1977) closely correspond with general case programming (i.e., programming common stimuli and training a sufficient number of exemplars). General case programming emphasizes the role of stimulus control in designing and implementing instructional programs for teaching generalized responding. According to Becker and Engelmann (1978), a general case has been taught when, after teaching some members of a set of activities, a student will respond correctly to any member within that set. This method was originally developed to teach academic and social skills to mildly handicapped and culturally disadvantaged children (Becker, Engelmann, & Thomas, 1975), and later extended for use with severely handicapped students to teach vocational, community living, and self-help skills (Horner & McDonald, 1982; McDonnell, Horner, & Williams, 1984; Pancsofar & Bates, 1985; Sprague & Horner, 1984).

Horner, Sprague, and Wilcox (1982) characterize general case programming as "those behaviors performed by a teacher or trainer that increase the probability that skills learned in one training setting will be successfully performed with different target stimuli, and/or in different settings, from those used during training" (p. 63). The general case approach provides specific recommendations regarding the development of the precise generalized performance demands expected in natural settings. The procedures in this approach have been translated into six steps:

1. Define the instructional universe by identifying all stimulus conditions in which the student will be expected to perform
2. Define the range of relevant stimulus and response variations within the instructional universe
3. Select appropriate examples from the instructional universe to use for teaching and probe testing
4. Sequence the teaching examples
5. Teach the examples
6. Test with non-trained examples and/or settings

Recently Horner, Eberhard, and Sheehan (1986) utilized a general case approach to examine the effects of using positive and negative training examples to minimize inappropriate generalization. In this study, four students labelled as moderately and severely mentally retarded were taught to bus tables in different cafeteria settings. The primary dependent variable was percentage of tables bussed correctly across a set of 15 nontrained tables systematically selected to sample the range of different stimulus-and-response variations for table bussing in cafeteria settings. A multiple-baseline design was utilized in which each participant received baseline assessment, training, and general case instruction. During the training phase teaching examples were used that systematically sampled the types of stimulus conditions the students were expected to encounter after training. Both positive training examples (tables to be bussed) and negative training examples (tables not to be bussed) were presented within each training session. During the general case phase, daily training sessions continued to occur. During each phase, probe sessions were conducted on 15 different table situations. The results indicated that after receiving instruction that followed the general case guidelines, the students correctly bussed and correctly rejected nontrained probe tables. The results of this study suggest the value of selecting training examples that sample the range of variability within the response set and the inclusion of a dependent variable that assesses inappropriate generalization. It would appear that general case programming offers an approach to developing generalized skills that is effective, efficient and functional for individuals with severe disabilities.

Summary

The strategies presented above are meant to be representative of some of the options available when training for generalized responding. While these approaches can by no means be considered exhaustive, they do represent significant contributions toward the goal of generalized performance. The selection of a particular technique would be dependent upon several factors. These include the specific skills to be learned in the natural setting(s) and/or situations in which performance is expected, and the discrepancies between an individual's present level of functioning and the response demands required of any particular strategy. At present, an effective generalization technology is not available to assist in evaluating the effects of combining the various strategies. Rules are needed regarding optimal strategies and procedures for combining the various approaches for particular types of generalization.

SOCIAL SKILLS TRAINING

Recently, as many disabled persons obtain employment in competitive work environments, the issue of maintaining their employment over time has begun to receive attention. Studies have reported that mentally retarded workers are experiencing nonvocational problems in work settings that may lead to unsuccessful employment (Brickey, Browning, & Campbell, 1982; Cheney & Foss, 1984; Edgerton & Bercovici, 1976; Ford, Dineen, & Hall, 1984; Foss & Bostwick, 1981; Greenspan & Shoultz, 1981; Kochany & Keller, 1981; Wehman et al., 1982). Although both production skills performed at certain criteria levels and effective social skills appear to be necessary for employment maintenance, there is ample evidence that most job terminations are due to lack of appropriate social skills rather than to actual work performance (Chadsey-Rusch, 1986; Gold, 1975; Greenspan & Shoultz, 1981; Kochany & Keller, 1981; Schalock & Harper, 1978). Yet, despite its actual impact upon job maintenance, social skills training in work settings has failed to receive anything near sufficient attention.

Social skills training, as mentioned before, serves several purposes. To begin with, it helps disabled persons become better prepared for entry into nonsheltered work environments. It has been found that employers value appropriate social skills when hiring disabled employees. Rusch, Schutz, and Agran (1982) conducted a survey with 120 potential competitive employers and found that a considerable portion of the survival skills necessary for entry into competitive employment consisted of social survival skills (e.g., following directions). Also, certain jobs seem to require more and better social behaviors than others. Salzberg, Agran, and Lignugaris/ Kraft (1985) found that social behaviors were deemed more important for kitchen helpers and food service workers than for janitors, dishwashers, and maids for the reason that some jobs (e.g., kitchen helpers) take place in a social context where workers frequently interact with co-workers and customers. Here, persons with the appropriate social skills are more likely to be hired in competitive work environments than those with inappropriate social behaviors. Survey studies like these, which identify critical behaviors for employees, may be called *social competence investigations.*

Second, social skills training for disabled workers increases the probability of maintaining employment in competitive work settings. Even though no study has been conducted to find a specific correlation between the demonstration of appropriate social skills and job retention, the following studies have found the listed social behaviors to be related to job termination:

1. Greenspan & Shoultz (1981)—lack of social awareness, e.g., walking into a meeting
2. Kochany & Keller (1981)—complaining, destroying property, interacting inappropriately with supervisors
3. Wehman et al. (1982)—noncompliance with supervisors' directives, failure to notify an employer, and bizarre and/or aggressive behavior
4. Brickey et al. (1982)—poor relations with peers
5. Ford et al. (1984)—poor interactions with co-workers
6. Cheney and Foss (1984)—not accepting criticism, failure to request assistance, and failure to follow instructions

Third, social skills training helps disabled workers establish a positive social support network with co-workers and/or supervisors. When disabled workers establish positive social interpersonal relationships with co-workers and/or supervisors, they have a support group or an individual to whom they can turn in time of need. Co-workers and/or supervisors can serve as advocates for disabled workers, which in turn increases the probability of the maintenance of employment. In addition, the formation of a social network can contribute to the overall quality of life of the disabled individual (Edgerton, 1967; Edgerton & Bercovici, 1976; Landesman-Dwyer & Berkson, 1983; Weiss, 1974).

With the realization of the importance of social skills training, professionals have recently begun to concentrate on social skills intervention in work settings. Unfortunately, social competence studies, which had identified valued and unvalued social behaviors in work settings, were not utilized in selecting target behaviors for the social intervention studies. This points to the limited generalizability of the social competence studies; that is, the social competence studies failed to answer the key questions related to social skills training: *how* and *what* to assess and teach. This failure had several causes:

First, each study employed a different system for categorizing social behaviors, making it difficult to be conclusive about the social behaviors basic to various employment settings. Second, except for a 1987 study by Salzberg, McConaughy, Lignugaris/Kraft, Agran, and Stowitschek, none of the research identified specific social behaviors pertinent to certain types of jobs. This does not allow practitioners to prepare disabled individuals appropriately for entering specific jobs (e.g., better conversational skills are needed for kitchen helper). Third, the majority of the categories of social behaviors are so broadly stated as to be unusable for effective assessment and intervention. There is a great need for the development of a social skills model that can suggest a uniform way of defining, categorizing, and assessing social behaviors (Chadsey-Rusch, 1986). Without such uniformity, it becomes very difficult to synthesize, compare, or generalize in this area. McFall's (1982) framework for social competence is proposed as an initial solution by Chadsey-Rusch (1986).

Target behaviors for social intervention studies have not been validated by co-workers or supervisors in most studies. The following section reviews studies on social skills intervention in work settings with mentally retarded workers.

Intervention Strategies

Training packages. The majority of the studies in social skills training with mentally retarded persons have used all or part of social skills training packages. The packages have had the following components: rationale, modeling, behavior rehearsal or role-play, and feedback. Most studies implemented these packages in natural settings, although there is a line of research that used these packages in analogue settings.

Rusch and Menchetti (1981) utilized the portions of a social skills training package that involved instruction and practice in order to teach compliance behavior to one moderately mentally retarded male employed as a kitchen laborer in a university dormitory in Illinois. The employee was given instructions on how to follow requests by either supervisors or professional kitchen laborers. He was instructed to (1) immediately stop what he was doing when asked by a co-worker (supervisor or kitchen laborer) to perform a job, (2) say, "ok" or "yes" in a friendly voice, to acknowledge that he heard the request, (3) perform the task correctly, and finally (4) return to the original job when completed. He was also provided an opportunity to practice these responses verbally. In addition to the practice, warning was given to the employee that if he failed to comply with the supervisors or professional kitchen laborers, he would be sent home by the shift supervisors. A multiple-baseline design across persons (supervisors, kitchen laborers, cooks) was used to assess treatment effectiveness. Data on the participant's compliance behavior were collected by having supervisors, professional kitchen laborers, and cooks answer the appropriate questions regarding his compliance throughout the day: (1) Did the employee help? (2) Did the employee sigh, complain, or grimace? (3) Did the employee help or respond within five seconds? (4) Were you happy with the employee's answer? (5) Did the employee do the task correctly, independently, and return to the scheduled task? The study indicated that providing instructions, practice, and warning was effective in increasing compliant responding across supervisors and professional kitchen laborers. Of particular interest was the generalized treatment effect that occurred not only with supervisors and professional kitchen laborers but also with a third, nontreated group: cooks. That is, the participant became compliant to cooks, for whom treatment was never associated, as well as to supervisors and professional kitchen laborers for whom treatment was introduced. This study makes a significant contribution to vocational training literature by showing the effectiveness of including co-workers (e.g., professional kitchen workers and cooks) and supervisors in identifying the targeted behavior, delivering the consequences, and evaluating performance during the intervention period.

In a recent study, Chadsey-Rusch, Karlan, Riva, and Rusch (1984) used a social skills training package (consisting of rationale, modeling, role-playing, and practice) plus verbal prompts (A trainer said, "It's your turn to ask me a question.") to increase the frequency of question-asking appropriate to a conversational context. Three adult males who were moderately mentally retarded and competitively employed as kitchen laborers participated in this study. All the training was conducted in an analogue setting arranged in a university dormitory dining hall where all employees took their breaks. The data were collected via tape-recorded, structured conversations with the same female trainer across all participants. The results of the study indicated that the training procedure increased the conversational ability of the three retarded men when they interacted with a group of four community members (two lawyers, one plumber, and one laborer). However, generalization effects were not measured with co-workers in the natural setting.

Bates (1980) used a social skills training package consisting of verbal instruction, modeling, role-playing, feedback, contingent incentives, and homework in teaching four interpersonal skills (small talk, asking for help, differing with others, and handling criticism) to 16 mildly and moderately retarded adults. In his study, a typical behavior analytic method (based on the prior work of Goldfried and D'Zurilla, 1969) was used to generate role-play situations. These situations and responses were solicited from group home parents, retarded adults, vocational supervisors, and assertiveness training leaders. Performance measures on eight role-playing situations were taken once a week after the training; data on untrained role-playing situations were taken prior to and after the study. All training was conducted in analogue settings (residential settings). Role-play was done in an office, and generalization assessment was done at a local grocery store. The results from this study indicated that experimental groups (eight participants) provided with social skills training packages increased their mean scores on trained role-play scenes along with generalization to untrained role-play situations. Here again, however, no significant generalization effects were assessed in the natural setting.

A replication of the above study was done by Shafer, Brooke, and Wehman (1985) in an attempt to teach three different social tasks (handling criticism, taking a joke or sarcastic remark, and soliciting assistance) to a moderately retarded individual working as a custodian in a large shopping mall. All training and posttraining probes were conducted in an analogue setting isolated from the natural environment. The results of the study showed increased mean effectiveness scores on the role-plays along with generalization to untrained role-play scenes. In addition, generalization to the natural environment was probed by having the employee's supervisors "set up" situations that called for the use of the social behaviors being trained. Partial generalization to a natural environment was found to occur; that is, the participant showed improvement on the social tasks, but failed to meet the supervisor's minimal acceptance standard, a criterion in evaluating the social competence of the person.

Another example of the application of a social skills training package is provided by Karlan and Rusch (1982), who investigated a relationship between acknowledgement (e.g., saying "okay" or "yes") and compliance (i.e., initiation of action in response to a request) in a vocational training site. The study's results indicated that verbal prompts to acknowledge the receipt of an instruction (a trainer said, "Tell me okay") affected acknowledgement negatively but compliance positively; that is, when the participants were verbally prompted to say "okay", they complied with the instruction previously given rather than acknowledging it. Token points (in this case, plus marks redeemable for a special privilege such as a diet soft drink) resulted in great improvement on compliance. No follow-up was conducted.

Hall, Sheldon-Wildgen, and Sherman (1980) also used a social skills training package (instruction, modeling, role-playing, and positive, corrective feedback) for increasing job application and interview skills of six mildly and moderately retarded adults. The result of the study showed a substantial increase in participants' performance in each job interview skill along with generalization to untrained, structured situations.

Gibson, Lawrence, and Nelson (1976) made a comparison of the elements of social skills training packages with three mildly and moderately retarded adults for three social responses: verbalization (e.g., talking directly to peers), recreation (e.g., playing cards or games), and cooperation (e.g., sweeping floor with others). Different training procedures were provided: (1) modeling, (2) instructions and feedback, and (3) modeling, instruction, and feedback. In modeling, videotapes of nonretarded adults were employed. The most effective procedure was a combination of modeling, instruction, and feedback, followed by a combination of instruction and feedback. Modeling alone was the least effective procedure of the three. Neither maintenance nor generalization effects were assessed.

Other techniques.　Four studies employed techniques other than a social skills training package in social skills interventions with moderately retarded individuals. A study by Dwinell and Connis (1979) used social feedback to reduce the inappropriate verbalization of a moderately retarded male in a restaurant that served as the vocational training site. The treatment procedure included the following components: praise for not verbalizing inappropriately, reprimands, and instruction. The result of the study showed a decrease in appropriate verbalization, but no generalization effect was assessed.

Rusch, Weithers, Menchetti, and Schutz's study (1980) investigated different treatment effects with different agents delivering contingencies. Verbal feedback was used to reduce the topic repetition of a moderately retarded male. During training, either the experimenter or co-workers, at different times, told the participant that he repeated the same topic too often and that several of his co-workers had expressed the wish he not do so. The study's results indicated that a combination of co-worker feedback plus an experimenter feedback was the most effective in reducing topic repetition. Experimenter feedback alone was the least effective. A strength of this study was the introduction of social validation in the identification of target behavior, training, data collection, and criterion level. Co-workers and supervisors identified a target behavior. Co-workers were preinstructed to deliver verbal feedback and were interviewed regarding the participant's frequency of repetitions. Of most importance was the assessment of the criterion level of nondisabled co-workers' topic repetition in comparison with that of the participant. This comprised the first instance of the use of normative data as criterion in studies with moderately and severely retarded individuals. Of particular interest was the finding that co-workers believed that the participant was not reducing the topic repetition even though a direct measurement indicated the opposite result.

Stanford and Wehman (1980) employed verbal prompts and reinforcers to increase the level of social interactions between two moderately retarded employees and their nondisabled co-workers during their lunch breaks. In addition, Stanford and Wehman coached the nondisabled co-workers to be receptive to interacting with the mentally retarded employees. The study result showed a marked increase in the participants' social interaction with their co-workers.

Breen, Haring, Pitts-Conway, and Gaylord-Ross (1985) conducted a study in which nondisabled high school co-workers taught social break-time behaviors to four high school students with autism. The training occurred in a simulated break time at a work site between pairs of autistic and nondisabled students. Generalization was then assessed with the actual co-workers during real break times. In training, social behaviors required during a break (e.g., making coffee and chatting with co-workers) were task analyzed and taught using a level of prompt hierarchy, contingent reinforcement, and a massed trial method for the steps that proved difficult to learn. A multiple exemplar strategy (Horner, Sprague, & Wilcox, 1982; Stokes & Baer, 1977) was used; that is, if the disabled youth did not generalize to the co-worker after training with a given peer, training with a second (or additional) peer was introduced until generalization appeared. All four participants succeeded in learning skills with three or more co-workers in the natural break setting (mean = 4.0 different co-workers). When the participants initiated social interaction, natural co-workers typically responded by saying "Oh, that's nice" and by attending to the participants. However, they did not reciprocally extend the interaction. The authors drew the inference that it might be necessary to modify the receptor culture (in this case the natural co-workers) as well as to modify the behavior of disabled persons so that a greater proportion of extended social exchanges between the disabled and the nondisabled persons would occur. For example, a dyadic training with both potential interactants could be conducted. In addition, the disabled person could be placed in receptor groups that might be more responsive to bids from disabled persons.

Critical Issues

As shown in Table 4.2, a variety of social skills training packages have been found to be effective intervention procedures for inducing social responses in employment settings. Notably, none of the studies assessed the

Text continues on p. 220.

TABLE 4.2 Summary of Social Skills Interventions for Persons with Severe Handicaps

Authors	*Subjects*	*Target Behaviors*	*Setting*
Bates (1980)	16 moderately retarded adults	small talk, asking for help, differing with others, & handling criticism	analogue setting
Breen et al. (1984)	4 autistic high school students	social interaction	restaurant
Chadsey-Rusch et al. (1984)	3 moderately retarded kitchen laborers	question-asking	analogue setting
Dwinell & Connis (1979)	1 moderately retarded male	reducing inappropriate verbalization	restaurant
Gibson et al. (1976)	3 mildly/moderately retarded adults	verbalization, recreation, & cooperation	residential setting
Hall et al. (1980)	6 mildly & moderately retarded adults	job application & interview	analogue setting
Karlan & Rusch (1982)	2 moderately retarded kitchen laborers	acknowledgment & compliance	kitchen
Rusch et al. (1980)	1 moderately retarded kitchen laborer	reproducing topic, repetition	dining hall
Rusch & Menchetti (1981)	1 moderately retarded kitchen laborer	following instruction	kitchen
Shafer et al. (1985)	1 moderately retarded custodian	handling criticism, soliciting help	analogue setting
Stanford & Wehman (1980)	2 moderately retarded adults	socialization	dining hall

Note: All studies reported training effects. Maintenance was measured only by Dwinell & Connis (1979), who reported treatment effects continued at 4 weeks.

Intervention	Agent	Generalization	Social Validation
Social Skills Training Package (SSTP)	experimenter	not occurred	no
task analysis, multiple exemplar strategy	co-workers	yes, to natural co-workers	no
SSTP	trainer	not measured	yes
social feedback	experimenter	not measured	no
SSTP	experimenter	not measured	no
SSTP	experimenter	*natural setting:* not measured; *untrained situations:* yes	no
SSTP	experimenter	not measured	no
verbal feedback	co-worker, experimenter, & supervisor	not measured	yes
SSTP	co-worker & supervisor	yes, to a non-treated group	yes
SSTP	experimenter	partial, in a natural setting	yes
verbal prompt & feedback	experimenter	not measured	no

maintenance of treatment effects. Further, in most instances, treatment effects were shown only for the trainer or co-workers who were involved in the study. The majority of studies either did not assess, or failed to demonstrate, generalization effects across different agents (i.e., other people besides the trainer) in different natural settings. It is interesting to note, however, that generalization effects were demonstrated to occur in some studies that involved co-workers, supervisors, and employers. For example, in Rusch and Menchetti's (1981) study where supervisors and kitchen laborers were involved in collecting data and delivering consequences, treatment effects were generalized to a nontreated group. Also in Breen et al.'s (1985) study, in which nondisabled high school students taught social break-time behaviors to students with autism, a generalized treatment effect to natural co-workers was observed. Among the studies that employed a social skills training package, Shafer et al. (1985) was the only study to demonstrate a partial generalization of treatment effects to a natural setting: the other studies failed to demonstrate cross-setting generalization effects in natural settings. In Shafer et al.'s (1985) study the participant showed a generalization of learned social behaviors to untrained role-play scenes, but demonstrated only a partial generalization to his work supervisor.

Generalization of social behaviors. Generalization has become a critical issue in social skill research with moderately and severely disabled individuals (Gaylord-Ross, Stremel-Campbell, & Storey, 1986; Gresham, 1981; Horner, McDonnell, & Bellamy, 1986; O'Leary & Drabman, 1971; Stokes & Baer, 1977). The generalization of learned social skills across co-workers, supervisors, and employers becomes crucial in job retention since these are the persons who will make the ultimate judgment about the effectiveness of skills demonstrated by the disabled employee. Many studies have clearly shown that failure to demonstrate appropriate social skills is directly related to job termination.

While there is no study available to demonstrate that generalization may be facilitated by including co-workers or supervisors compared to studies without inclusion of co-workers, it can still be said that the inclusion of significant other persons during intervention seems effective in promoting generalization effects. Among all the studies reviewed, only two studies that included co-workers and supervisors have demonstrated generalization effects, Breen et al. (1985), and Rusch and Menchetti (1981). It must be said, however, that certain issues arise when including co-workers and/or supervisors in social skills intervention for a disabled worker. How can these workers be utilized effectively? If these individuals are used, how will their participation affect future interactions and attitudes toward workers with disabilities? (Chadsey-Rusch, 1986). How will their inclusion affect the disabled workers themselves? These are very sensitive issues, which can affect the relationship between disabled workers and nondisabled workers. Therefore, any intervention procedure including co-workers and supervisors should be carefully planned.

Process training. Another way of promoting the generalization of learned skills is to teach the generative process of social behavior rather than a specific component of behavior (Trower, 1984). All of the studies on social skills intervention have taught specific component behaviors. Trower (1984) points out that the major limitation of teaching specific molecular behavior is that it will not lead to a clinically significant change (e.g., maintenance and generalization of social skills). For example, a person may be taught a molecular behavior (e.g., saying "hi") in different situations and with different persons (e.g., co-workers). On the other hand, when a person is taught a process of understanding a social situation and his resulting behavior, it increases his chances of using the behaviors in many settings. Stokes and Baer (1977) referred to this process as self-mediated generalization. Trower (1984) has delineated process training to include decoding a situation, generating alternative responses, selecting and performing a best-fit response, and evaluating the response (e.g., why and how to greet persons in a workplace). The application of reasoning in social situations should enhance social effectiveness in many settings. For example, a worker is more likely to say "hi" to different co-workers and supervisors. Gambrill and Richey (1986) refer to training of the generative process governing the production of behavior in social interaction as a process model, and training of component behaviors (e.g., verbal and nonverbal behavior) as a component model. Process approaches include McFall's model (McFall, 1982) and Trower's model (Trower, 1982, 1984; Trower, Bryant, & Argyle, 1978) while the component approach includes behavioral social skills training packages (such as those reviewed here).

Besides teaching the reasoning process, the process model utilizes self-monitoring techniques that can promote the generalization of learned skills. If an individual is trained to monitor and direct his or her own social behavior, it is likely that the person will use self-monitoring skills to perform adequately on a social task in the absence of a trainer or in a variety of settings. This ability becomes paramount in the employment setting because the continuing presence of the trainer in the work setting is not considered as natural, and because the person being trained is likely to encounter new social situations other than those taught by the intervention program. Several studies have confirmed that self-monitoring skills can be taught to mentally retarded individuals (Connis, 1979; Sowers, Rusch, Connis, & Commings, 1980; Sowers, Verdi, Bourbeau, & Sheehan,

1985; Wacker & Berg, 1983). Instruction in self-monitoring techniques holds promise for improving the social performance of disabled persons in work settings. Future research in the area of social skills intervention might move toward the application of the process approach (cf. Park & Gaylord-Ross, in press.)

Studies published thus far have concentrated on modifying a disabled person's social skills. Future research should look into the modification of the receptor culture as suggested by Breen et al.'s study (1985). Social competence is primarily defined by the overall judgment of significant others in the work setting. In keeping with the meaning of this term as it has been used in an eco-behavioral perspective, social competence or incompetence is a matter of congruence or incongruence between a person and the environment (Chadsey-Rusch, 1986). Therefore, any intervention effort can focus either on a person or on his/her environment. The modification of the environment (e.g., altering a co-worker's and/or supervisor's expectation) could be particularly effective for some disabled persons in developing a positive interpersonal relationship with their co-workers and/or supervisors.

SELF-MANAGEMENT

Since self-management is such an important emerging goal in special education, let us give further attention to its conceptual characteristics, as well as illustrate its further applications to vocational settings. Many employment training programs for persons with mental retardation use a job coach as an external change agent (Rusch, Martin & White, 1985; Wehman, Schutz, Bates, Renzaglia, & Karan, 1978). In this type of setting, the generalization of treatment gains is restricted as the trainer takes on the properties of a cue or discriminative stimulus (S^D). Following training, the target behaviors will occur only in the presence of the S^D, limiting maintenance and generalization of the newly acquired skill. Appropriate strategies must be employed that allow stimulus control to be transferred from external to internal sources. In addition, the ethical, legal, and philosophical implications of externally controlling behavior has caused increased investigation of alternative methods of behavioral treatments (Gardner, Cole, Berry, & Nowinski, 1983). Self-management procedures internalize stimulus control, thus facilitating the maintenance and generalization of behavior change (Bandura, 1986; Fowler, 1984; Gifford, Rusch, Martin, & White, 1984; Mank & Horner, 1987; O'Leary & Dubey, 1979; Rosenbaum & Drabman, 1975; Rusch & Schutz, 1981; Wacker & Berg, 1983). Self-management techniques with mentally retarded persons have been used to increase the individual's performance in different aspects of his vocational training (Bates, Renzaglia, & Clees, 1980; Fowler, 1984; McNally, Kompik, & Sherman, 1984; Sowers, Rusch, Connis, & Cummings, 1980; Sowers, Verdi, Bourbeau, & Sheehan, 1985) in a cost-effective manner (Fowler, 1984; Storey & Gaylord-Ross, 1987). Self-management training has taken many forms; from the use of picture cues (Sowers et al., 1980; Sowers et al., 1985), to the use of self-instructional talk (Agran, Fodor-Davis, & Moore, 1986; Agran, Salzberg, & Stowitschek, in press).

Definition

Under the general rubric of "self-management" falls a variety of different terms (Shapiro, 1981). Kanfer and Gaelick (1975) have proposed a three-stage model of self-management. Self-monitoring is the process in which the individual observes and records the occurrence of a specific behavior. Self-evaluation is the process by which individuals compare the observed behaviors with the criterion they have set up for themselves. Self-reinforcement is the process by which individuals either positively or negatively reinforce their own behavior as a result of the self-monitoring and self-evaluative processes.

McFall (1982) discusses two basic uses of self-management techniques: data collection and as a therapeutic strategy. For the purposes of data collection, the behavior analyst primarily uses the self-monitoring aspect of the self-management paradigm. A major difficulty in the use of self-monitoring for data collection results from the inevitable interaction between components of the self-management procedure; that is, the heightened awareness of a behavior while measuring it may reactively cause it to increase or decrease. Thus, self-monitoring for assessment purpose may yield inaccurate data.

Therapeutic uses of self-management use all four components of the self-management process (self-monitoring, self-evaluation, self-reinforcement, and self-instruction). Nelson and Hayes (1981) propose that benefits of the self-management process are not solely connected to the actual physical act of self-monitoring; they argue that the training of the self-monitoring response, comments from others about the self-monitoring device, and the self-monitoring responses all influence the target behavior through a reactive interaction.

Shapiro (1981) has pointed out two reasons why self-management procedures have not been used more extensively with mentally retarded persons. First, it may be too difficult to learn the abstract qualities of the self-management processes. Second, mentally retarded persons are often kept dependent by society. This dependency precludes the individual's attempts to guide his or her own behaviors through the use of self-management procedures. These obstacles notwithstanding, Mank and Horner (1987) have shown that the mentally retarded client can learn self-management strategies without excessive training. In addition, professionals are concerned that the mentally retarded client has only limited control over his or her own behavior change process (Gardner et al., 1983; Kazdin, 1975) and are actively working towards the development of client-originating, self-management procedures (Gardner et al., 1983; Kazdin, 1975; Shapiro, 1981).

Self-management in Vocational Settings

Picture cues. A major advantage of self-management techniques is that mentally retarded vocational trainees with limited academic abilities can benefit from these training strategies. The use of picture cards and other visual prompts has been shown to be effective for training individuals with limited academic abilities (Connis, 1979; Sowers et al., 1985; Wacker & Berg, 1983; Wacker, Berg, Berrie, & Swatta, 1985).

Wacker and Berg (1983) studied the effects of picture prompts on the acquisition of complex vocational tasks by mentally retarded adolescents. Picture prompts were used to teach five moderately and severely mentally retarded high school students to do four complex vocational tasks. The training in picture prompts (consisting of teaching the students to sequentially turn pages in a picture book and then selecting the correct picture of a specific value) was found to be successful in teaching trainees to assemble complex objects. Following training, all students were able to perform without errors. In addition, Wacker and Berg (1983) found that the training results generalized across time. The Wacker and Berg (1983) study demonstrated that mentally retarded workers can learn complex vocational tasks using self-management strategies. It also proved that the trainee need not possess reading skills, that picture-cue prompts can serve as effective S^Ds for maintaining learned behaviors.

Sowers et al. (1985) studied the use of picture cues in teaching moderately and severely retarded workers to be more independent and flexible on the job site. The study included four males (18–21 yrs.) from classes for moderately and severely retarded persons, none of whom could read. In the picture-cue training system all students were trained to use picture-cue prompts. The system had two major components: a picture-cue apparatus and the four self-management elements outlined above. Picture-cue cards were put on a photo album page and hung in an accessible location at the work site. Pictures representing the day's tasks were inserted in the sheet in the assigned order. The sheet was attached to a clipboard with a water-based pen. Using picture cues the students were trained to sequence job tasks correctly. They were required to go through the following sequence of events: (a) return to picture cue following completion of a task, (b) mark off the picture corresponding to the task, (c) touch the picture of the next task, and (d) begin that task.

Training to use the picture cues and self-management behaviors was instituted in three phases. In Phase A the trainer presented each picture to the student, named the task, and escorted the trainee to the task. After being introduced to the picture-cue apparatus, each student observed the trainer model the appropriate self-management behaviors; was then given the picture-cue apparatus, with seven pictures inserted; and was prompted through the self-management steps.

In Phase B the same procedures were used as in the previous phase, but the students were not prompted through each of the self-management steps. Phase B was continued until a student achieved two consecutive days of 100% independent task change. During Phase C the students were reminded to do each of the self-management steps. Praise was given only after successful completion of the four self-management steps. Corrective feedback was given after any error. Maintenance and generalization probes were conducted in simulated settings modeled after settings in a competitive job situation.

As a result of the training, the number of independent task changes improved immediately after the student entered Phase B of the treatment. The results showed that the use of picture-cue, self-management procedures is an effective, efficient, and practical procedure in employment settings. These results further support the results of previous studies using picture cues (Connis, 1979; Sowers et al., 1985; Wacker & Berg, 1983).

Job productivity. Self-management techniques can also be used to increase the mentally retarded worker's job productivity. An exemplary study using self-management techniques to increase worker productivity rates is McNally et al. (1984). Using a three-part treatment package, coupled with a changing criterion design, the researchers were able to increase the work productivity of mentally retarded workers. The training program, consisting of a combination of self-monitoring, self-reinforcement, and performance feedback, substantially increased the clients' work productivity. The clients ranged in age from 23 to 49 years and were mildly to moderately retarded.

On the first day of the treatment phase each client was given a stack of pink and blue tokens. The number of pink tokens was determined for each client to be $N-1$, where N was the number of production units completed in an average time period during the baseline phase of the experiment. During the work period of the experiment's treatment phase, as the clients completed a unit of production they would take a pink token from a dispenser. After self-administering all the pink tokens (achieving baseline production rates) the worker would self-administer blue tokens. Self-administration of the first blue token signified the exceeding of baseline performance. Clients reported taking the first blue token to the shift supervisor who then lit up a sign with the client's name on it. Any client whose name was lit up received 30 minutes' leisure time at the end of the work day. In addition, at the end of each work day, all blue tokens were attached to a bar graph on a wall in the work area. Clients who earned the most blue tokens on different days were treated to lunch.

After the second, fifth, and sixth treatment day, individual mean production rates were recalculated. The results of this calculation determined the ratio of the pink and blue chips for the following days. This procedure allowed the training strategy to remain dynamic in terms of the demands put on the performance levels of the client through the implementation of a changing criterion design.

McNally et al. (1984) report that these self-management procedures significantly increased the production rates of the mentally retarded workers participating in the study. They also report that the study was time- and cost-effective and required only approximately 20 minutes of the supervisor's time each work day. Although there was an improvement in production rates, no client achieved a normative industrial rate of production.

The investigation of self-reinforcement with mentally retarded persons has been investigated extensively (Baer, Fowler, & Carden-Smith, 1984; Coleman & Whitman, 1984; Horner & Brigham, 1979; Mank & Horner, 1987; Rudrud, Rice, Robertson, & Tolson, 1984). The self-reinforcement of tokens or edibles has been found to maintain or improve vocational performance with mildly or moderately mentally retarded individuals (Bates, Renzaglia, & Clees, 1980; Helland, Palluck & Klein, 1976; Horner, Lahren, Schwartz, O'Neill, & Hunter, 1979; Jackson & Martin, 1984; Srikameswaran & Martin, 1984; Zohn & Borstein, 1980).

Job task sequencing. Agran et al. (in press) have investigated the use of self-instruction to improve job-task sequencing. Self-instruction training consisted of supplying the trainees with a rationale for using the treatment strategy, modeling, behavioral rehearsal, verbal rehearsal, corrective feedback, and contingent reinforcement. Agran et al. (in press) trained mentally retarded workers to make three types of verbalizations: statements that describe a problem, statements that describe what is needed to rectify the problem, and statements describing the actions taken to rectify the problem. They found that self-instructions may facilitate the acquisition and later generalization of work skills for persons with severe handicaps. In addition, they found that self-instructional strategies promote the maintenance and generalization of treatment gains.

Self-reinforcement.   Another self-management procedure is self-reinforcement. This strategy involves the self-determination and self-administration of reinforcement (Jones, Nelson, & Kazdin, 1977). In a study by Helland, Palluck, and Klein (1976), the effects of self-reinforcement and external reinforcement on production rates were compared. Participants in the self-reinforcement group were trained to reinforce themselves (i.e., compliment themselves and select a reinforcer) upon the completion of assigned tasks. The participants in the external reinforcement group were given supervisor-delivered reinforcement following successful completion of assigned work. While results indicated that both reinforcement conditions were effective in raising production levels, it is to be noted that the participants in the self-reinforcement group worked independently of direct supervision.

Social skills in the work setting.   Self-management procedures need not be used only to increase the accuracy or production rates of the mentally retarded worker. Storey and Gaylord-Ross (1987) found that contingent reinforcement and self-monitoring could maintain substantial rates of positive social behaviors during the worker's break. By using a series of sophisticated research designs in their experiments, Storey and Gaylord-Ross (1987) were able to isolate the salient components of their treatment plan. Self-monitoring and contingent reinforcement could maintain normative rates of performance.

Students were trained to use a tally procedure to self-monitor the number of positive verbal statements made during break time at an office complex. The treatment package consisted of role-playing, self-monitoring of positive statements, modeling, contingent reinforcement, and graphic feedback. As the clients played pool during break time, they were given cards to check off a predetermined number of positive statements that they were required to make to their companions who were also playing pool. For the self-monitoring aspect of the treatment, each client was supplied with a 3" × 5" index card with numbers (e.g., 1, 2, 3). The worker knew that he had to make that number of positive statements during the game of pool in order to receive the contingent reinforcement.

Results showed that the clients significantly increased the amount of positive social statements to their peers. However, genealization probes across settings failed to show any carry-over of the newly acquired responses.

An advantage of self-management procedures is the cost- and time-effectiveness of these procedures (Fowler, 1984; Storey & Gaylord-Ross, 1987; Wacker and Berg, 1983). Cost- and time-effectiveness can be measured by the degree to which staff at the vocational setting are freed from the constant instruction involved in the vocational training of the mentally retarded worker. Fowler (1984) writes that reinforcing the use of self-management strategies at times of caretaker absences can promote greater client participation in an unsupervised activity. Researchers have found that self-administered reinforcements can equal the effectiveness of externally administered reinforcements in vocational settings (Connis, 1979; Helland, Palluck, & Klein, 1976; Wacker, & Berg, 1983). Wehman et al. (1978) have written that one of the major advantages of self-management in the vocational setting is that it frees staff for other duties.

Summary

The use of self-management procedures with mentally retarded workers in a vocational setting has been found useful in increasing the frequency of a large variety of positive behaviors. Complex tasks, complex task sequences, rates of production, and work-related social skills have all been increased through the use of the self-management techniques of self-monitoring, self-evaluation, and self-reinforcement. In addition, through the use of picture cues and other visual prompts, the self-management procedures need not rely on the worker's reading abilities.

As is clear from the research outlined in this section, self-management strategies involve a great variety of different behavior techniques, ranging from self-monitoring to self-reinforcing behaviors. All of the studies cited used a combination of one or more of these self-management techniques with other behavioral training techniques (i.e., contingent reinforcement, corrective feedback, and modeling). It will be difficult to determine the role of each of the different components of self-management techniques. However, this should not dissuade the behavioral analyst from using these techniques. We remain concerned with the development of independent and generalizable vocational skills in our clients and so should be aware of the high potential these techniques have for helping our clients attain their goals.

CONCLUSION

There is a growing body of research supporting the effectiveness and promise of vocational special education practices. Follow-up research has indicated that some employment training programs have been successful. Yet the definition of success may depend upon the measurement criteria used, e.g., job retention or quality of life. It would be useful to include more qualitative or ethnographic measures in follow-up studies in order to obtain a more experiential sense of the employment process. Follow-up research may also be criticized as being conducted in a political-economic vacuum. Social action research may wish to examine the effects of substantive employer–business involvement in the job hiring and retention process.

There has been a rapidly emerging literature demonstrating the effectiveness of techniques that promote generalization in vocational contexts. Outcome measures need to include more long-term indicators of maintenance effects. A critical research issue will be what proportion of simulated versus *in vivo* training is needed to produce generalized responding. Preliminary findings indicate that the individual's level of functioning may correlate with the need for more or less community-referenced training.

Although social skills training in the workplace has shown promise, there has been limited evidence demonstrating generalization and maintenance effects. Process models of social skills training have been advanced to enable individuals to decode the social environment, make behavioral choices, and evaluate their performance. Such process approaches, with their cognitive orientation, hold promise for inducing more extensive and lasting generalization effects.

Both social skill training and social support network analyses of the workplace offer an eco-behavioral approach. Rather than simply focusing on the individual and the person's skill deficits, the eco-behavioral perspective examines the social context of interactions and friendships. This may mean including peers in social skills training. It may also entail drafting a co-worker into a benefactor role. Such reciprocal notions of social interaction and social support are innovative ways to promote successful vocational adjustment.

Finally, the self-management process appears to underlie a number of the latest developments in vocational special education. Self-management techniques have been used to increase production performance of job tasks. The techniques have promoted generalization across settings, persons, and materials. Their utility in social skills training has already been cited. Most important, self-management has promoted independence in the workplace. Early research showed how picture cues can be used to prompt disabled employees from one task to the next. More recently, workers have first self-monitored their performance and subsequently recruited reinforcement feedback. In all cases, self-management encourages independent performance as the individual relies less on supervision from others.

We have attempted to review a sample of the most important research topics in vocational special education. Undoubtedly we have left some topics out, for example, the new developments in vocational assessment identifying critical behaviors in an efficient and situationally valid manner. Other research topics, such as vocational education in the primary grades, have been largely ignored and are in need of further investigation. We hope to have given the reader a sense of the critical topics in this field. The ultimate purpose of vocational special education is to facilitate the transition of disabled students into successful employment. Research in this field must thereby document those instructional procedures that lead to the acquisition, generalization, and maintenance of a wide range of occupational and social skills.

REFERENCES

Agran, M., Fodor-Davis, J., & Moore, S. (1986). The effects of self-instructional training on job-talk sequencing: Suggesting a problem solving strategy. *Education and Training of the Mentally Retarded, 21,* 273–281.

Agran, M. Salzberg, C. L., & Stowitschek, J. J. (in press). An analysis of the effects of a social skills training program using self-instructions on the acquisition and generalization of social work behaviors in a work setting. *Journal of the Association of Persons with Severe Handicaps.*

Baer, M., Fowler, S. A., & Carden-Smith, L. (1984). Using reinforcement and independent grading to promote and maintain task accuracy in a mainstreamed class. *Analysis and Intervention in Developmental Disabilities, 4,* 157–169.

Ballantyne, D., McGee, M., Patton, S., & Cohen, D. (1984). *Report on cooperative programs for transition from school to work* (Contract no. 300-83-0158). Waltham, MA: Harold Russell Associates.

Baller, W. R. (1936). A study of the present social status of a group of adults who when they were in elementary schools were classified as mentally deficient. *Genetic Psychology Monographs, 18,* 165–244.

Bandura, A. (1986). *Social foundations of thought and action: A social cognitive approach.* Englewood Cliffs, NJ: Prentice Hall.

Bates, P. (1980). The effectiveness of interpersonal skills training on the social skill acquisition of moderately and mildly retarded adults. *Journal of Applied Behavior Analysis, 13,* 237–248.

Bates, P., Renzaglia, A., & Clees, T. (1980). Improving the work performance of severely/profoundly retarded young adults: The use of the changing criterion procedural design. *Education and Training of the Mentally Retarded, 15,* 95–104.

Baumeister, A. A. (1969). More ado about operant conditioning—or nothing? *Mental Retardation, 7,* 49–51.

Becker, W. C., & Engelmann, S. E. (1978). Systems for basic instruction: Theory and applications. In A. Catania & T. Brigham (Eds.), *Handbook of applied behavior analysis: Social and instructional processes* (pp. 325–377). New York: Irvington.

Becker, W. C., Engelmann, S. E., & Thomas, D. R. (1975). *Teaching 2: Cognitive learning and instruction.* Chicago: Science Research Associates.

Blalock, J. W. (1981). Persistent problems and concerns of young adults with learning disabilities. In W. M. Cruickshank & A. A. Siler (Eds.), *Bridges to tomorrow: The best of ACLD* (Vol. 2, pp. 35–55). Syracuse, NY: Syracuse University Press.

Bolton, B., Rowland, P., Brookings, J., Cook, D., Taperek, P., & Short, H. (1980). Twelve years later: The vocational and psychological adjustment of former rehabilitation clients. *Journal of Applied Rehabilitation Counseling, 11,* 113–123.

Borus, M.E. (Ed.). (1984). *Youth and the labor market: Analyses of the national longitudinal survey.* Kalamazoo, MI: W. G. Upjohn Institute for Employment Research. (ERIC Document Reproduction Service no. ED 242 914)

Breen, C., Haring, T., Pitts-Conway, V., & Gaylord-Ross, R. (1985). The training and generalization of social interaction during breaktime at two job sites in the natural environment. *Journal of the Association for Persons with Severe Handicaps, 10,* 41–50.

Brickey, M., Browning, L., & Campbell, K. (1982). Vocational histories of sheltered workshop employees placed in projects with industry and competitive jobs. *Mental Retardation, 20* (2), 52–56.

Brickey, M., & Campbell, K. (1981). Fast food employment for moderately and mildly mentally retarded adults: The McDonald's project. *Mental Retardation, 19,* 113–116.

Brown, L., Nietupski, J., & Hamre-Nietupski, S. (1976). The criterion of ultimate functioning and public school services for severely handicapped students. In L. Brown, N. Certo, & T. Crowner (Eds.), *Papers and programs related to public school services for secondary-age severely handicapped students* (Vol. 6, pp. 2–15). Madison: WI: Madison Metropolitan School District.

Caplan, G. (1976). The family as a support system. In G. Caplan & M. Killilea (Eds.), *Support systems and mutual help: Multidisciplinary explorations* (pp. 19–36). New York: Grune & Stratton.

Caplan, G., & Killilea, M. (Eds.). (1976). *Support systems and mutual help: Multidisciplinary explorations.* New York: Grune & Stratton.

Catterall, J., & Stern, D. (1986). The effects of alternative school programs on high school completion and labor market outcomes. *Educational Evaluation and Policy Analysis, 8, 1,* 77–86.

Certo, N. J., Brown, L., Belmore, K., & Crowner, T. (1977). A review of secondary level educational service delivery models for severely handicapped students in the Madison Public Schools. In E. Sontag (Ed.), *Educational programming for the severely and profoundly handicapped* (pp. 111–127). Reston, VA: The Council For Exceptional Children.

Chadsey-Rusch, J. (1986). Identifying and teaching valued social behaviors. In F. R. Rush (Ed.), *Competitive employment issues and strategies* (pp. 273–287). Baltimore, MD: Paul H. Brookes, Publisher.

Chadsey-Rusch, J., Karlan, G. R., Riva, M., & Rusch, F R. (1984). Competitive employment: Teaching conversation skills to adults who are mentally retarded. *Mental Retardation, 22,* 218–225.

Chadsey-Rusch, J., & Rusch, F. R. (1988). The ecology of the workplace. In R. Gaylord-Ross (Ed.), *Vocational education for persons with special needs* (pp. 234–255). Palo Alto, CA: Mayfield.

Cheney, D., & Foss, G. (1984). An examination of the social behavior of mentally retarded workers. *Education and Training of the Mentally Retarded, 19,* 216–221.

Clark, G. R., Kivitz, M., & Rosen, M. (1968). *A transitional program for institutionalized adult retarded* (Research and Demonstration Grant No. RD 1275P). Washington, DC: Vocational Rehabilitation Administration, U.S. Department of Health, Education and Welfare.

Clemmons, D. C., & Dodrill, C. B. (1983). Vocational outcomes of high school students with epilepsy. *Journal of Applied Rehabilitation Counseling, 14,* 49–53.

Close, D. W., & Keating, T. J. (1988). Community living and work. In R. Gaylord-Ross (Ed.), *Vocational education for persons with handicaps* (pp. 67–108). Palo Alto, CA: Mayfield.

Cobb, H. V. (1972). *The forecast of fulfillment.* New York: Teachers College Press.

Cobb, H. V. (1976). Social support as a moderator of life stress. *Psychometric Medicine, 38,* 300–312.

Coleman, R. S., & Whitman, T. L. (1984). Developing, generalizing and maintaining physical fitness in mentally retarded adults: Toward a self-directed program. *Analysis and Intervention in Developmental Disabilities, 4,* 109–128.

Connis, R. T. (1979). The effects of sequential pictorial cues, self-recording, and praise on the job task sequencing of retarded adults. *Journal of Applied Behavioral Analysis, 12,* 355–361.

Cook, J. J. (1976). *Follow-up study of the visually impaired, 1976.* Washington, DC: Bureau of Education for the Handicapped. (ERIC Document Reproduction Service No. ED 176 489).

Coon, M., Volgelsberg, R., & Williams, W. (1981). Effects of classroom public transportation instruction on generalization to the natural environment. *Journal of the Association for the Severely Handicapped, 6,* 46–53.

Cordero, I. (1975). *Study of reading disorders in relation to poverty and crime.* Santa Barbara, CA: Work Training Program.

Dalton, R. F., & Latz, A. (1978). Vocational placement: The Pennsylvania Rehabilitation Center. *Rehabilitation Literature, 39,* 336–339.

Delp, H. A., & Lorenz, M. (1953). Follow-up of 84 public school special class pupils with I.Q.'s below 50. *American Journal of Mental Deficiency, 58,* 175–182.

Dinger, J. (1961). Post-school adjustment of former educable retarded pupils. *Exceptional Children, 27,* 353–360.

Drabman, R. S., Hammer, D., & Rosenbaum, M. S. (1979). Assessing generalization in behavior modification with children: The generalization map. *Behavior Assessment, 1,* 203–219.

Dwinell, M. A., & Connis, R. T. (1979). Reducing inappropriate verbalizations of a retarded adult. *American Journal of Mental Deficiency, 84,* 87–92.

Edgar, E. (1987). Secondary programs in special education: Are many of them justifiable? *Exceptional Children, 53,* 555–561.

Edgar, E., & Hayden, A. H. (1985). Who are the children special education should serve and how many children are there? *Journal of Special Education, 18,* 523–539.

Edgerton, R. B. (1967). *The cloak of competence: Stigma in the lives of the mentally retarded.* Berkeley: University of California Press.

Edgerton, R. B. (Ed.). (1984). *Lives in process: Mildly retarded adults in a large city.* Washington, DC: American Association of Mental Deficiency.

Edgerton, R. B. & Bercovici, S. M. (1976). The cloak of competence: Years later. *American Journal of Mental Deficiency, 80,* 485–497.

Edgerton, R. B., & Langness, L. L. (1978). Observing mentally retarded persons in community settings: An anthropological perspective. In G. P. Sackett (Ed.), *Observing behavior: Vol. 1. Theory and applications in mental retardation* (pp. 109–133). Baltimore, MD: University Park Press.

Falvey, M., Brown, L., Lyon, S., Baumgart, D., & Schroeder, J. (1980). Strategies for using cues and correction procedures. In W. Sailor, B. Wilcox, & L. Brown (Eds.), *Methods of instruction for severely handicapped students* (pp. 107–133). Baltimore, MD: Paul H. Brookes.

Fardig, D. B., Algozzine, R. F., Schwartz, S. E., Hensel, J. W., & Westling, D. L. (1985). Postsecondary vocational adjustment of rural mildly handicapped students. *Exceptional Children, 52,* 115–121.

Fernald, W. E. (1919). After-care study of the patients discharged from Waverly for a period of twenty-five years. *Ungraded, 5*(2), 25–31.

Flynn, R. J. (1982). National studies of the effectiveness of conventional vocational education: A research review. In K. P. Lynch, W. E. Kiernan, & J. A. Stark (Eds.), *Vocational education for special needs youth: A blueprint for the 1980's* (pp. 15–34). Baltimore, MD: Paul H. Brookes.

Ford L., Dineen J., & Hall, J. (1984). Is there life after placement? *Education and Training of the Mentally Retarded, 19,* 291–296.

Forte, J., Storey, K., & Gaylord-Ross, R. (1985). The social validation of community vocational training. In R. Gaylord-Ross, V. Forte, K. Storey, A. Wershing, C. Gaylord-Ross, S. Siegel, D. Jameson, & V. Pomies (Eds.), *Community vocational training for handicapped youth.* San Francisco: San Francisco State University.

Foss, G., & Bostwick, D. (1981). Problems of mentally retarded adults: A study of rehabilitation service consumers and providers. *Rehabilitation Counseling Bulletin, 25* (2), 6–73.

Fowler, S. A. (1984). Introductory comments: The pragmatics of self-management for the developmentally disabled. *Analysis and Intervention in Developmental Disabilities, 4,* 85–89.

Gambrill, E. D., & Richey, C. A. (1986). Criteria used to define and evaluate socially competent behavior among women. *Psychology of Women Quarterly, 10,* 183–196.

Gardner, W. I., Cole, C. I., Berry, D. L., & Nowinski, J. M. (1983). Reduction of disruptive behaviors in mentally retarded adults. *Behavior Modification, 7,* 76–96.

Gaylord-Ross, R. J., Haring, T. G., Breen, C., & Pitts-Conway, V. (1984). The training generalization of social interaction skills with autistic youth. *Journal of Applied Behavioral Analysis, 17,* 229–247.

Gaylord-Ross, R., Stremel-Campbell, K., & Storey, K. (1986). Social skill training in natural contexts. In R. H. Horner, L. H. Meyer, & H. D. B. Fredericks (Eds.), *Education of learners with severe handicaps: Exemplary service strategies* (pp. 161–187). Baltimore, MD: Paul H. Brookes.

Giangreco, M. F. (1983). Teaching basic photography skills to a severely handicapped young adult using simulated materials. *Journal of the Association for the Severely Handicapped, 8,* 43–50.

Gibson, F. W., Lawrence, P. S., & Nelson, R. O. (1976). Comparison of three training procedures for teaching social responses to developmentally disabled adults. *American Journal of Mental Deficiency, 81,* 379–387.

Gifford, J., Rusch, F., Martin, J., & White, D. (1984). Autonomy and adaptability: A proposed technology for maintaining work behavior. In N. Ellis & N. Bray (Eds.), *International review of research on mental retardation* (Vol. 12, pp. 285–314). New York: Academic Press.

Gill, H. (1984). *An employment related follow-up of former special education students in Pierce County, Washington.* Tacoma, WA: Vocational/Special Education Cooperative. (ERIC Document Reproduction Service No. ED 250 854)

Gold, M. W. (1975). Vocational training. In J. Worth (Ed.), *Mental retardation and developmental disabilities: An Annual Review* (Vol. 7, pp. 254–264). Washington, DC: Developmental Disabilities Office, U.S. Department of Health, Education, and Welfare.

Goldfried, M. R., & D'Zurilla, T. J. (1969). A behavior-analytic model for assessing competence. In C. D. Spielberger (Ed.), *Current topics in clinical and community psychology* (Vol. 1, pp. 151–196). New York: Academic Press.

Goldstein, H. (1964). Social and occupational adjustment. In H. A. Stevens & R. Herber, *Mental retardation: A review of research from all the major disciplines* (pp. 214–258). Chicago: University of Chicago Press.

Goodfellow, H. D. L. (1947). The mental defective in the community and the philosophy which has resulted in the plan for training defectives at the Ontario Hospital School, Orillia. *American Journal of Mental Deficiency, 51,* 495–501.

Goros, D. L., & Kowalski-Glickman, M. (1983). *Advancements: An implementation guide to a community-based vocational training program for deaf-blind youth* (USDE #300-80-0642). Boston: Perkins School for the Blind.

Gottlieb, B. H. (1983). *Social support strategies.* Beverly Hills, CA: Sage Publications.

Greenspan, S., & Shoultz, B. (1981). Why mentally retarded adults lose their jobs: Social incompetence as a factor in work adjustment. *Applied Research in Mental Retardation, 2,* 23–38.

Gresham, F. M. (1981). Social skills training with handicapped children: A review. *Review of Educational Research, 51*(1), 139–176.

Habeck, R. V., Galvid, D. E., Frey, W. D., Chadderden, L. M., & Tate, D. G. (1985). *Economics and equity in employment of people with disabilities: International policies and practices.* Proceedings from the symposium, April 28–May 2, 1984, Michigan State University Center for International Rehabilitation, East Lansing. (ERIC Document Reproduction Service No. ED 261 209)

Hall, C., Sheldon-Wildgen, J., & Sherman, J. A. (1980). Teaching job interview skills to retarded clients. *Journal of Applied Behavior Analysis, 13,* 433–442.

Halpern, A. S. (1978). The impact of work/study programs on the employment of the mentally retarded: Some findings from two sources. *International Journal of Rehabilitation Research, 1,* 167–175.

Halpern, A. S. (1985). Transitions: A look at the foundations. *Exceptional Children, 51,* 6, 479–486.

Hardy, M. I. (1968). *Clinical follow-up study of disabled readers.* Unpublished doctoral dissertation, University of Toronto, Toronto.

Harnisch, D. L., Chaplin, C. C., Fisher, A. T., & Tu, J. (1986). *Transition literature review on educational, employment, and independent living outcomes.* Champaign: University of Illinois, Secondary Transition Intervention Effectiveness Institute.

Hasazi, S., Gordon, L., & Roe, C. (1985). Factors associated with the employment status of handicapped youth exiting high school from 1979 to 1983. *Exceptional Children, 51* (6), 455–469.

Hasazi, S., Gordon, L., Roe, C., Hull, M., Finck, K., & Salembier, G. (1985, December). A statewide follow-up on post high school employment and residential status of students labeled, "mentally retarded." *Education and Training of the Mentally Retarded, 20,* 222–234.

Helland, C. D., Palluck, R. J., & Klein, M. A. (1976). A comparison of self and external reinforcement with the trainable mentally retarded. *Mental Retardation, 14,* 22–23.

Hill, M., Hill, J. W., Wehman, P., & Banks, P. D. (1985). An analysis of monetary and nonmonetary outcomes associated with competitive employment of mentally retarded persons. In P. Wehman & J. Hill (Eds.), *Competitive employment for persons with mental retardation: From research to practice* (Vol. 1, pp. 110–133). Richmond: Virginia Commonwealth University, Rehabilitation Research Training Center.

Hill, J. W., Hill, M., Wehman, P., Banks, D. P., Pendleton, P., & Britt, C. (1985). Demographic analyses related to successful job retention for competitively employed persons who are mentally retarded. In P. Wehman & J. Hill (Eds.), *Competitive employment for persons with mental retardation: From research to practice* (Volume 1, pp. 65–93). Richmond: Virginia Commonwealth University, Rehabilitation Research Training Center.

Hill, J. W., Wehman, P., Hill, M., & Goodall, P. (1985). Differential reasons for job separation of previously employed mentally retarded persons across measured intelligence levels. In P. Wehman & J. Hill (Eds.), *Competitive employment for persons with mental retardation: From research to practice* (Volume 1, pp. 94–109). Richmond: Virginia Commonwealth University, Rehabilitation Training Center.

Hirsch, B. J. (1981). Social networks and the coping process. In B. H. Gottlieb (Ed.), *Social networks and social support* (pp. 149–170). Beverly Hills, CA: Sage.

Hobbs, N. (1983). *The troubled and troubling child.* San Francisco: Jossey-Bass.

Horn, W., O'Donnell, J., & Vitulano, A. (1983). Long-term follow-up studies of learning-disabled persons. *Journal of Learning Disabilities, 16,* 542–555.

Horner, R. H., & Brigham, T. A. (1979). Self-management and on-task behavior in two retarded children. *Education and Training of the Mentally Retarded, 14,* 18–24.

Horner, R. H., Eberhard, J. M., & Sheehan, M. R. (1986). Teaching generalized table bussing: The importance of negative teaching examples. *Behavior Modification, 10,* 457–471.

Horner, R. H., Lahren, B., Schwartz, T. P., O'Neill, C. T., & Hunter, J. D. (1979).

Considerations in dealing with low production rates of severely retarded workers. *AAESPH Review, 4,* 202–212.

Horner, R. H., & McDonald, R. S. (1982). A comparison of single instance and general case instruction in teaching a generalized vocational skill. *Journal of the Association for the Severely Handicapped, 7,* 7–20.

Horner, R. H., McDonnell, J. J., & Bellamy, G. T. (1986). Teaching generalized skills: General case instruction in simulation and community settings. In R. H. Horner, L. H. Meyer, and H. D. Fredericks (Eds.), *Education of learners with severe handicaps: Exemplary service strategies* (pp. 289–314). Baltimore, MD: Paul H. Brookes.

Horner, R. H., Sprague, J., & Wilcox, B. (1982). Constructing general case programs for community activities. In B. Wilcox & T. Bellamy (Eds.), *Design of high school programs for severely handicapped students* (pp. 61–98). Baltimore, MD: Paul H. Brookes.

House, J. S., Wells, J. A. (1978). Occupational stress, social support, and health. In A. McLean, G. Black, & M. Colligan (Eds.), *Reducing Occupational Stress* (pp. 8–29). Washington, DC: U.S. Department of Health, Education and Welfare. HEW (NIOSH) No. 78–140.

Jackson, D., & Martin, G. (1984). Additive effects of components of a self-control package for improving the production of mentally handicapped workers. *Journal of Practical Approaches to Development Handicaps, 7,* 17–21.

Jones, R. (1983). *Reflections on growing up disabled.* Reston, VA: Council for Exceptional Children.

Jones, R. T., Nelson, R. E., & Kazdin, A. E. (1977). The role of external variables in self-reinforcement. *Behavior Modification, 1,* 147–178.

Kanfer, F. H., & Gaelick, L. (1975). Self-management methods. In F. Kanfer & A. P. Goldstein (Eds.), *Helping people change* (pp. 283–345). New York: Pergamon.

Karan, O. C., & Knight, C. B. (1986). Developing support networks for individuals who fail to achieve competitive employment. In F. R. Rusch (Ed.), *Competitive employment issues and strategies* (pp. 241–255). Baltimore, MD: Paul H. Brookes.

Karlan, G. R., & Rusch, F. R. (1982). Analyzing the relationship between acknowledgement and compliance in a non-sheltered work setting. *Education and Training of the Mentally Retarded, 17,* 202–208.

Kaufman, S. (1984). Friendship, coping systems and community adjustment of mildly retarded adults. In R. B. Edgerton (Ed.), *Lives in process: Mildly retarded adults in a large city* (pp. 73–92). Washington, DC: American Association on Mental Deficiency.

Kazdin, A. E. (1975). *Behavior modification in applied settings.* Homewood, IL: Worsey Press.

Kazdin, A. E. (1977). Assessing the clinical or applied importance of behavior change through social validation. *Behavior Modification, 1*(4), 427–449.

Kernan, K. T., & Koegel, P. (1984). Employment experiences of community-based mildly retarded adults. In R. B. Edgerton (Ed.), *Lives in process: Mildly retarded adults in a large city* (pp. 9–26). Washington, DC: American Association on Mental Deficiency.

Kirchner, C., & Peterson, R. (1979). Employment: Selected characteristics. *Journal of Visual Impairment and Blindness, 73*, 239–242.

Kochany, L., & Keller, J. (1981). An analysis and evaluation of the failures of severely disabled individuals in competitive employment. In P. Wehman (Ed.), *Competitive employment: New horizons for severely disabled individuals* (pp. 181–198). Baltimore, MD: Paul H. Brookes.

Kraus, J. (1972). Supervised living in the community and residential and employment stability of mentally retarded male juveniles. *American Journal of Mental Deficiency, 62*, 481–495.

Landesman-Dwyer, S., & Berkson, G. (1983). Friendship and social behavior. In J. Wortis (Ed.), *Mental retardation and developmental disabilities: Annual review* (Vol. 13, pp. 129–154). New York: Plenum Press.

LaRocco, J. M., House, J. S., & French, J. R. P. (1980). Social support, occupational stress, and health. *Journal of Health and Social Behavior, 21*, 202–218.

LaRocco, J. M., & Jones, A. P. (1978). Coworker and leader support as moderators of stress/strain relationships in work situations. *Journal of Applied Psychology, 63*, 629–634.

Lehtinen-Rogan, L. E., & Hartman, L. D. (1976). *A follow-up study of learning disabled children as adults* (Final Report, Grant #OEG-0-74—7453). Washington, DC: U.S. Department of Health, Education, and Welfare, Office of Education.

Lehtinen, H., & Tuomisto, J. (1978). On the construction and application of an activation variable in the planning of adult education systems. *Adult Education in Finland, 13*, 3–30.

Levin, E., Zigmond, N., & Birch, J. (1985). A follow-up study of 52 learning disabled students. *Journal of Learning Disabilities, 13*, 542–547.

Linden, B. E., & Forness, S. R. (1986). Post-school adjustment of mentally retarded persons with psychiatric disorders: A ten-year follow-up. *Education and Training of the Mentally Retarded, 21*(3), 157–164.

Lurie, L. A., Schlan, L., & Freiberg, M. (1932). A critical analysis of the progress of fifty-five feebleminded children over a period of eight years. *American Journal of Orthopsychiatry, 2*, 58–69.

Madison, H. L. (1964). Work placement success for the mentally retarded. *American Journal of Mental Deficiency, 69*, 50–53.

Mank, D. M., & Horner, R. H. (1987). Self-recruited feedback: A cost-effective procedure for maintaining behavior. *Research in Developmental Disabilities, 8*, 91–112.

Mathews, M. A. (1922). One hundred institutionally trained male defectives in the community under supervision. *Mental Hygiene, 6*, 332–342.

McCarver, R. B., & Craig, E. M. (1974). Placement of the retarded in the community: Prognosis and outcome. In N. R. Ellis (Ed.), *International review of research in mental retardation* (Vol. 7, pp. 146–207). New York: Academic Press.

McCormick, W. J., & Clarke, M. (1986). *Work ability's post-school employment effects.* Sacramento: California State Department of Education, Employment Preparation Division.

McDonnell, J. J., & Horner, R. H. (1985). *Effects of in vivo versus simulation plus in vivo training on the acquisition and generalization of grocery item selection by high school students with severe handicaps.* Unpublished manuscript, University of Oregon, Eugene.

McDonnell, J. J., Horner, R., & Williams, J. A. (1984). A comparison of three strategies for teaching generalized grocery purchasing to high school students with severe handicaps. *Journal of the Association for Persons with Severe Handicaps, 9,* 123–124.

McFall, R. M. (1982). A review and reformulation of the concept of social skills. *Behavioral Assessment, 4,* 1–33.

McNally, R. J., Kompik, J. J., & Sherman, G. (1984). Increasing the productivity of mentally retarded workers through self-management. *Analysis and Intervention in Developmental Disabilities, 4,* 129–135.

Mertens, D. M., & Seitz, P. (1982). *Labor market experiences of handicapped youth.* Columbus: Ohio State University, National Center for Research in Vocational Education.

Mithaug, D. E. (1981). *Prevocational training for retarded students.* Springfield, IL: Charles C. Thomas.

Mithaug, D. E., Horiuchi, C. N., & Fanning, P. N. (1985). A report on the Colorado statewide follow-up survey of special education students. *Exceptional Children, 51,* 5, 397–404.

Neef, N. A., Iwata, B. A., & Page, T. J. (1978). Public transportation training: In vivo versus classroom instruction. *Journal of Applied Behavior Analysis, 11,* 331–344.

Nelson, R. O., & Hayes, S. C. (1981). Theoretical explanations for reactivity in self-monitoring. *Behavioral Modifications, 5,* 3–14.

Nietupski, J., Welch, J., & Wacker, D. (1983). Acquisition, maintenance, and transfer of grocery item purchasing skills by moderately and severely handicapped students. *Education and Training of the Mentally Retarded, 18*(4), 279–286.

O'Connor, G. (1983). Social support of mentally retarded persons. *Mental Retardation, 21*(5), 187–196.

O'Leary, C. G., & Dubey, D. R. (1979). Application of self-control procedures by children: A review. *Journal of Applied Behavioral Analysis, 12,* 449–466.

O'Leary, K. D., & Drabman, R. S. (1971). Token reinforcement programs in the classroom: A review. *Psychological Bulletin, 75,* 379–398.

Page, T. J., Iwata, B. A., & Neef, N. A. (1976). Teaching pedestrian skills to retarded persons: Generalization from the classroom to the natural environment. *Journal of Applied Behavior Analysis, 9,* 433–444.

Pancsofar, E. L., & Bates, P. (1985). The impact of the acquisition of successive training exemplars on generalization by students with severe handicaps. *Journal of the Association for Persons with Severe Handicaps, 10,* 95–104.

Park, H. S., & Gaylord-Ross, R. (in press). Process social skills training with mentally retarded youth in employment settings. *Journal of Applied Behavior Analysis.*

Peterson, L., & Smith, L. (1960). The post-school adjustment of educable mentally retarded adults with that of adults with normal intelligence. *Exceptional Children, 26,* 404–408.

Phelps, L. A. (1986, April). *Transitional programming for special needs youth.* Paper presented at the 1985–86 Distinguished Lecture Series on Employment-Related Education and Training for Special Populations, Long Beach, CA.

Public Law 94–142: The education of all handicapped children act of 1975. (1975). Washington, DC: U.S. Government Printing Office.

Radar, B., Shapiro, H., & Rodin, E. A. (1978). On placement of multiply handicapped clients into the open job market. *Rehabilitation Literature, 39,* 299–302.

Richardson, N. R., & Hill, J. (1980). An evaluation of vocational placement success at a comprehensive rehabilitation center: A third measurement. *Rehabilitation Literature, 41,* 19–22.

Richardson, N., & Krieger, N. (1976). An evaluation of vocational placement success at a comprehensive rehabilitation center. *Rehabilitation Literature, 37,* 237–241.

Romer, E., & Heller, T. (1983). Social adaptation of mentally retarded adults in community settings: A social-ecological approach. *Applied Research in Mental Retardation, 4,* 303–314.

Rose, M. (1985). *Re-working the work ethic.* London: Batsford.

Rosenbaum, M., & Drabman, R. (1975). Self-control training in the classroom: A review and critique. *Journal of Applied Behavior Analysis, 12,* 467–485.

Rosenberg, J. (1978). The relationship of types of post-high school education to occupation and economic independence of physically handicapped adults. *Rehabilitation Literature, 38,* 45–49.

Ross, R. T., Begab, M. J., Dondis, E. H., Giampiccolo, J. S., & Meyers, C. E. (1985). *Lives of the mentally retarded: A forty-year follow-up study.* Palo Alto, CA: Stanford University Press.

Rudrud, E. H., Rice, J. N., Robertson, J. N., & Tolson, N. M. (1984). The use of self-monitoring to increase and maintain production rate. *Vocational Evaluation and Work Adjustment, 17,* 14–17.

Rumberger, R. W., & Daymont, T. N. (1984). The economic value of academic and vocational training acquired in high school. In M. Borus (Ed.), *Youth and the labor market: Analyses of the national longitudinal survey* (pp. 157–192). Kalamazoo, MI: W.G. Upjohn Institute for Employment Research. (ERIC Document Reproduction Service no. ED 242 914)

Rusch, F. R., Martin, J. E., & White, D. M. (1985). Competitive employment: Teaching mentally retarded employees to maintain their work behaviors. *Education and Training of the Mentally Retarded, 20,* 182–189.

Rusch, F. R., & Menchetti, B. M. (1981). Increasing compliant work behaviors in a non-sheltered work setting. *Mental Retardation, 19* (3), 107–111.

Rusch, F. R., & Schutz, R. P. (1981). Vocational and social behavior research: An evaluative review. In J. L. Matson & J. R. McCartney (Eds.), *Handbook of behavior modification with the mentally retarded* (pp. 247–280). New York: Plenum Press.

Rusch, F. R., Schutz, R. P., & Agran, M. (1982). Validating entry-level survival skills for service occupations: implications for curriculum development. *Journal of the Association for the Severely Handicapped, 8,* 32–41.

Rusch, F. R., Weithers, J. A., Menchetti, B., & Schutz, R. P. (1980). Social validation of a program to reduce topic repetition in a non-sheltered setting. *Education and Training in Mental Retardation, 15(3),* 187–194.

Saenger, G. (1957). *The adjustment of severely retarded adults in the community.* Albany: New York State Interdepartmental Health Resources Board.

Sailor, W., & Guess, D. (1983). *Severely handicapped students: An instructional design.* Boston: Houghton Mifflin.

Salzberg, C. L., Agran, M., & Lignugaris/Kraft, B. (1985). *Behaviors that contribute to entry-level employment: A profile of five jobs.* Logan: Department of Special Education, Utah State University.

Salzberg, C. L., McConaughy, K., Lignugaris/Kraft, B., Agran, M., & Stowitschek, J. J. (1987). Behaviors of distinction: The transition from acceptable to highly valued worker. *Journal for Vocational Special Needs Education, 10(1),* 23–28.

Saunders, M. R., & James, J. E. (1983). The modification of parent behavior: A review of generalization and maintenance. *Behavior Modification, 7,* 3–28.

Schalock, R. L., & Harper, R. S. (1978). Placement from community-based mental retardation programs: How well do clients do? *American Journal of Mental Deficiency, 83,* 240–247.

Semmel, D. S., Cosden, M. A., & Konopak, B. (1985). *A comparative study of employment outcomes for special education students in a cooperative work placement program.* Santa Barbara, CA: University of California, Special Education Program.

Shafer, M. S. (1986). Utilizing co-workers as change agents. In F. R. Rusch (Ed.), *Competitive employment issues and strategies* (pp. 215–224). Baltimore, MD: Paul H. Brookes.

Shafer, M. S., Brooke, V., & Wehman, P. (1985). Developing appropriate social-interpersonal skills in a mentally retarded worker. In P. Wehman & J. W. Hill (Eds.), *Competitive employment for persons with mental retardation: From research to practice* (Vol 1, pp. 358–375). Richmond: Virginia Commonwealth University, Rehabilitation Research and Training Center.

Shapiro, E. S. (1981). Self-control procedures with the mentally retarded. In M. Hersen, R. M. Eisler, & P. M. Miller (Eds.), *Progress in behavior modification* (Vol. 12, pp. 265–297). New York: Academic Press.

Skaarbrevik, K. J. (1971). A follow-up study of educable mentally retarded in Norway. *American Journal of Mental Deficiency, 75,* 560–565.

Sleeter, C. (1986). Learning disabilities: The social construction of a special education category. *Exceptional Children, 53,* 46–54.

Sowers, J., Rusch, J., Connis, R., & Cummings, L. (1980). Teaching mentally retarded adults to time manage in a vocational setting. *Journal of Applied Behavior Analysis, 13,* 119–128.

Sowers, J., Verdi, M., Bourbeau, P., & Sheehan, M. (1985). Teaching job independence and flexibility to mentally retarded students through the use of self-control package. *Journal of Applied Behavior Analysis, 18,* 81–85.

Sprague, J. R., & Horner, R. H. (1984). The effects of single instance, multiple instance and general case training on generalized vending machine use by moderately and severely handicapped students. *Journal of Applied Behavioral Analysis, 17,* 273–278.

Srikameswaran, S., & Martin, G. (1984). A component analysis of a self-management program for improving work rates of mentally handicapped persons. *Mental Retardation and Learning Disability Bulletin, 12,* 39–52.

Stanfield, J. (1973). Graduation: What happens to the retarded child when he grows up? *Exceptional Children, 39,* 548–552.

Stanford, K., & Wehman, P. (1980). Improving the social interactions between moderately retarded and nonretarded coworkers: A pilot study. In P. Wehman & M. Hill (Eds.), *Vocational training and placement of severely disabled persons, Vol. 3.* Richmond: Virginia Commonwealth University.

Stokes, T. F., & Baer, D. M. (1977). An implicit technology of generalization. *Journal of Applied Behavioral Analysis, 10,* 349–367.

Storey, K., & Gaylord-Ross, R. (1987). Increasing positive social interactions by handicapped individuals during a recreational activity using a multicomponent treatment package. *Research in Developmental Disabilities, 8,* 627–649.

Tarjan, G., Dingman, H. F., Eyman, R. K., & Brown, S. J. (1960). Effectiveness of hospital release programs. *American Journal of Mental Deficiency, 64,* 609–617.

Thomson, T. L., & Lucas, J. A. (1981). *Follow-up study of former hearing impaired students at Harper College, 1977–1980.* Palatine, IL: Office of Planning and Research. (ERIC Document Reproduction Services No. ED 217 923)

Tisdall, W. J. (1958). *A follow-up study of trainable mentally handicapped children in Illinois.* Unpublished master's thesis, University of Illinois.

Trower, P. (1982). Toward a generative model of social skills: A critique and synthesis. In J. P. Curran & P. M. Monti (Eds.), *Social skills training* (pp. 399–427). New York: Guilford.

Trower, P. (1984). A radical critique and reformulation: From organism to agent. In P. Trower (Ed.), *Radical approaches to social skills training* (pp. 47–88). New York: Croom Helm.

Trower, P., Bryant, B., & Argyle, M. (1978). *Social skills and mental health* (pp. 1–36). Pittsburgh, PA: University of Pittsburgh Press.

Wacker, D., & Berg, W. (1983). Effects of picture prompts on the acquisition of complex vocational tasks by mentally retarded adolescents. *Journal of Applied Behavior Analysis, 16,* 417–433.

Wacker, D., Berg, W., Berrie, P., & Swatta, P. (1985). Generalization and maintenance of complex skills by severely handicapped adolescents following picture prompt training. *Journal of Applied Behavioral Analysis, 18,* 329–336.

Wehman, P., & Hill, J. W. (Eds.). (1985). *Competitive employment for persons with mental retardation: From research to practice* (Volume 1). Richmond: Virginia Commonwealth University, Rehabilitation Research Training Center.

Wehman, P., Hill, M., Goodall, P., Cleveland, P., Brooke, V., & Pentecost, J. H. (1982). Job placement and follow-up of moderately and severely handicapped individuals after three years. *Journal of the Association for the Severely Handicapped, 7,* 5–16.

Wehman, P., Kregel, J., & Seyfarth, J. (1985). Employment outlook for young adults with mental retardation. *Rehabilitation Counseling Bulletin, 29,* 2, 90–99.

Wehman, P., Schutz, R., Bates, P., Renzaglia, A., & Karan, O. (1978). Self-management programs with mentally retarded workers: Implication for developing independent vocational behavior. *British Journal of Social and Clinical Psychology, 17,* 57–64.

Wehman, P., Seyfarth, J., & Kregel, J. (1985). Transition from school to work for individuals with severe handicaps: A follow-up study. *Journal of the Association for the Severely Handicapped, 10,* 132–136.

Weiss, R. (1974). The provision of social relationship. In Z. Rubin (Ed.), *Doing unto others: Joining, molding, confirming, helping, and loving* (pp. 17–26). Englewood Cliffs, NJ: Prentice Hall.

White W. J., Schumaker, J. B., Warner, M. M., Alley, G. R., & Deshler, D. D. (1980). *The current status of young adults identified as learning disabled during their school career* (Research report no. 21). Lawrence: University of Kansas, Institute for Research in Learning Disabilities.

Wilcox, B., & Bellamy, G. T. (1982). *Design of high school programs for severely handicapped students.* Baltimore, MD: Paul H. Brookes Publishing Co.

Will, M. (1984). Bridges from school to working life. *Programs for the handicapped.* Washington DC: Office of Special Education and Rehabilitative Services, Office of Information and Resources for the Handicapped.

Wilson, R. J., & Rasch, J. D. (1982). The relationship of job characteristics to successful placements for the psychiatrically handicapped. *Journal of Applied Rehabilitation Counseling, 13,* 30–33.

Wolf, M. M. (1978). Social validity: The case for subjective measurement or How applied behavior analysis is finding its heart. *Journal of Applied Behavior Analysis, 11,* 203–214.

Wolfe, B. L. (1979). *Impacts of disability and some policy implications.* Madison: University of Wisconsin–Madison, Institute for Research on Poverty. (ERIC Document Reproduction Service no. ED 175 956)

Wolfensberger, W. (Ed.). (1972). *The principle of normalization in human services.* Toronto, Canada: National Institute on Mental Retardation.

Workfare tests find weakness in the 3 r's. (1987, April 28). *San Francisco Chronicle,* p. 8.

Ysseldyke, J. E., Algozzine, B., Shinn, M. R., & McGue, M. (1982). Similarities and differences between low achievers and students classified learning disabled. *Journal of Special Education, 16,* 73–85.

Zigmond, N., & Thornton, H. (1985). Follow-up of postsecondary age learning disabled graduates and drop-outs. *Learning Disabilities Research, 1*(1), 50–55.

Zohn, J. G., & Borstein, D. H. (1980). Self-management of work performance with mentally retarded adults: Effect upon work productivity, work quality and on-task behavior. *Mental Retardation, 18,* 19–24.

CHAPTER 5

Building Initial Communicative Repertoires for Individuals with Severe Developmental Disabilities

JOE REICHLE
MARK MIZUKO
SCOTT DOSS

JEFF SIGAFOOS
HOLLY BENSON
KATHLEEN BYKOWSKY

Persons with developmental disabilities often exhibit deficient communicative repertoires. Approximately 50% of individuals described as having autism (Carr, 1982) and 75% of a sample of adolescents with severe to profound mental retardation (Naor & Balthazar, 1975) were described as having deficient communicative skills. Increasingly, as persons with developmental disabilities move into integrated community environments, functional communicative behavior is necessary to promote normalized social interaction. There is a growing data base suggesting that a significant number of persons with severe developmental disabilities, in the absence of an adequate communication repertoire, may express their wants and needs by using an existing behavioral repertoire that may include a variety of excess behaviors, such as aggression, tantrum, self-injurious, or bizarre behavior (verbal and/or nonverbal). Other learners with developmental disabilities may rarely exhibit social overtures or responses; these learners are characterized as passive, engaging in little discrete voluntary behavior. Frequently, these learners are very prompt-dependent and, because of the low expectations of their caregivers, have been required to engage in few independent social emissions. Consequently, they have been described as exhibiting the phenomenon of *learned helplessness* (Guess, Benson, & Siegel-Causey, 1985). The prevalence of such problems as socially motivated excess and learned helplessness has resulted in the development and implementation of a new generation of communication intervention programs. These programs have had the collateral effect of promoting the acquisition of desirable socialization skills supportive of increased community participation. Consequently, communication intervention is now being regarded less as a science of remediation and more as a science of prevention with respect to problems of social competence.

Within the past 20 years, remarkable progress has been made in generating efficient intervention protocols to teach social-communication skills to persons with developmental disabilities. In spite of this progress, there remain a number of unresolved issues facing professionals charged with implementing communication intervention programs. Traditionally, communication intervention programs focused on establishing the ability to comprehend and produce speech (e.g., Bricker, Dennison, & Bricker, 1976; Guess, Sailor, & Baer, 1977). More recently, the recognition that communication intervention may proceed prior to the production and comprehension of intelligible words has had a profound impact on the intervention process. Additional advances in the area of incidental instructional strategies (Hart, 1985) and stimulus control procedures, along with advances in our conceptualization of generalized use as an acquisition rather than post-acquisition issue, have taken the intervention process to the environments in which new skills are to be used.

This chapter will review the various areas of communicative study by providing for each an overview of our current knowledge. A discussion of important research issues that remain unresolved will follow.

ESTABLISHMENT OF AN INITIAL COMMUNICATIVE REPERTOIRE

The Origins of Communication Production

Intentional communication production has been described as "signaling behavior in which the sender is aware a priori of the effect that a signal will have on his/her listener" (Bates, Benigni, Bretherton, Camioni, & Volterra, 1979). Prior to the onset of intentional communicative behavior, learners may emit discrete voluntary behavior that was not intended for the benefit of a listener even though it is interpreted by the listener as intentional. For example, by approximately 24 weeks of age, learners cry shortly prior to their normal feeding time (Caplan, 1973). Typically, adults in the child's environment treat these cries as requests for food. At the same point in development, if a nipple delivering nutriment is withdrawn from an infant's lips, the infant begins fussing and crying, which parents typically interpret as a protest. These examples are referred to as examples of *perlocutionary* behavior. McLean and Snyder-McLean (1988) have pointed out that during instances of perlocutionary communicative behavior, the learner focuses on a single object or event without referencing his or her communicative partner. By 8 to 9 months of age, normal learners begin to alternate their focus between the referent of interest and their communicative partner. If they engage in fussing at the withdrawal of a desired object and there is an adult present to receive a message, they may be persistent in fussing in addition to alternating their gaze between the referent object or event of interest and their communicative partner. At this point, the learner is described as engaging in *illocutionary* communicative production.

During the initial year of life, both motor and vocal modalities play an important role in the learner's ability to establish intentional (illocutionary) communication production. Gestures represent such an important part of normal children's communicative repertoire that as late as 13 months of age they exhibit no clear-cut preference for either verbal or gestural communicative emissions (Bates et al., 1979). Others, including Murphy (1978), have reported that it is not until approximately 12.5 months of age that children begin coordinating their use of motor and vocal behavior. Initial evidence of integrated use can be seen as children begin to produce motor behaviors such as pointing, showing, and giving with vocalizations.

Initial gestural repertoire. Several sequences of motor behaviors, including ritualized showing-off, showing, giving, pointing, and ritualized requests and ritualized refusals, have been referred to as composing the initial repertoire of gestural communicative intent in normal developing children. "Showing off" and "giving" objects to others appear to emerge between 9 and 11 months of age while communicative pointing, and ritualized requests and rejects become more and more prevalent between 9 and 13 months of age.

All of the preceding behaviors have in common a shift in reference between the object/event of interest and the learner's communicative partner. Several investigators (Murphy, 1978; Murphy & Messer, 1977) have examined the development of pointing and the influence that subtle environmental variations may have on this behavior. Murphy (1978), for example, found that one-fourth of her subjects used pointing gestures at 9 months while 66% used pointing by 14 months. Although the frequency of pointing was roughly similar among those who pointed, older children tended to use their point with more distal objects than the young group of children.

Carter (1973), while studying the progression of children's acquisition of a communicative requesting competency, suggested that as children's ability to produce sounds and sound combinations becomes more sophisticated, children begin to use a smaller proportion of gestures as part of their requesting overture. Consequently, one must examine the development of both vocal mode production and gestural mode development to obtain a comprehensive picture of a child's initial communicative repertoire.

Initial vocal repertoire. Oller (1980) has suggested that the initial 4 months of a learner's vocal production is characterized by the adoption of a particular pattern of repetitious vocal behavior. This pattern appears to be related to a growing oral motor sophistication rather than to variables that include position in space or time of day. During the initial 90 days of life, the bulk of vocal behavior involves nasal vowel-like sounds of short duration. The second half of the child's first year is heralded by a number of advances. By around 6 months of age or so, a young child is able to produce "raspberries," a forceful yet constant push of air through pursed lips much as a trumpet player produces. Additionally, a phenomenon referred to by Oller (1980) as "squeal and growl," is made possible by the descent of the larynx into the child's neck, which makes the vocal folds more susceptible to the forces of the supralaryngeal muscles. Toward the conclusion of the first year of life, Miller, Netsell, and Rosen (1979) report that the child can produce combinations of vowels and consonants (VCVC). Between 7 and 10 months, children begin to produce strings of repeated vowel consonant productions without intervening pauses (Ba-Ba-Ba). Around 10 months, the child begins to vary the topography of the consonants included within the repeated segment, which Oller referred to as *variegated babbling*. This babbling frequently appears just prior to the emergence of the child's intelligible first word.

The Uses of an Initial Communicative Repertoire

The vocal and motor advances just described culminate in the coordinated use of motor and vocal behavior used to obtain goods/services and a second class of behavior aimed at obtaining attention. Bates, Benigni, Bretherton, Camioni, and Volterra (1976) referred to the former as a *protoimperative* and the latter as a *protodeclarative*. It is somewhat unclear from the literature whether there is a developmental order in the emergence of these classes of behavior or whether they emerge somewhat simultaneously in a normal developing population. However, there is evidence to suggest differences in the emergence of these two classes of behavior among persons with developmental disabilities. Curcio (1978) observed 12 autistic learners in the context of natural interactions within their home environment. Although he reported instances of protorequesting behavior, he observed no emission of a describing-like function. Cirrin and Rowland (1985) observed the communicative behavior emitted by 15 individuals with severe intellectual delay. Three groups of learners were observed: those who used primitive acts (proffers cup to request more), those who used conventionalized acts (pointing gestures), and those who used conventional referential communicative behavior. Cirrin and Rowland (1985) reported that the use of describing behavior was associated with advancements in the type of communicative signal used; that is, little describing behavior was observed in the primitive act group, but approximately 43% of utterances produced by the referential group corresponded to a describing function. Although the conclusion is still quite tenuous, it appears that protoimperatives might represent a more viable initial intervention target based on the preceding observations. Data from Cirrin and Rowland (1985) imply that there may be a correlative relationship between the sophistication of the form emitted and the emergence of protodeclaratives in persons with severe intellectual delay.

The observation that "requesting-like" and "describing-like" behavior may not emerge simultaneously among developmentally disabled individuals has resulted in the speculation that early intervention programs aimed at establishing new vocabulary cannot assume that a word taught as a request will necessarily be used to encode other instrumental communicative functions. The roots for this logic are based in the work of Skinner (1957), who described a number of functional uses of communication behavior, including tacts and mands. An utterance is described as a "mand" when it serves to result in the provision of a reinforcer that directly matches the speaker's utterance. For example, if a learner requests an apple and is provided with an apple, an exact match exists between the communicative utterance and the reinforcer. Tacts, on the other hand, represent communicative behavior emitted in the presence of objects or events that typically recruit generalized reinforcement. For example, commenting on the fact that it's a sunny day recruits a social response (e.g., "Yes, it is!") from a listener. There is no specific reinforcer delivered contingently upon the emission of such a comment. Among early production skills typically taught, providing information (a response to a "What is this?" question) is viewed as a tact while a request is viewed as a mand.

Skinner (1957) argued that mands and tacts, even when incorporating identical lexical items, are functionally independent. Lamarre and Holland (1985) investigated the acquisition of prepositional phrases in normal preschoolers (3.5 to 5 years of age). Initially, subjects learned to mand or tact the experimenter's placement of objects with the prepositional phrases "on the left" and "on the right." At regular intervals during acquisition, learners received probes to determine the collateral acquisition of a corresponding tact or mand repertoire. Results demonstrated that mands and tacts were functionally independent during acquisition. A similar result was obtained by Hart and Risley (1968) in an investigation that involved 15 disadvantaged preschoolers. After the children had been taught to tact (describe) play materials using color adjectives (The car is red), the established tacts failed to be used as mands. Similar findings have been reported among persons with severe intellectual delay. Hall and Sundberg (1987) reported that after acquiring a signing repertoire of tacts controlled by various objects (e.g., a can opener, a cup) and the signed "What's that?" such persons failed to emit the acquired vocabulary when establishing stimuli that rendered those objects as effective reinforcers were arranged. Similar results have been obtained with learners having severe handicaps who were using a graphic communication system (Glennen & Calculator, 1985; Reichle & Yoder, 1985; Romski, Sevcik, & Pate, 1988; Sigafoos, Doss, & Reichle, 1989) and with learners taught in the vocal mode (McCook, Cipani, Madigan, & LaCampagne, 1988).

The communication intervention literature is replete with examples of successful procedures to teach tacts. Most of these examples, however, involve the production of tacts given the verbal instruction, "What's this?" Less emphasis has been placed on developing more spontaneous tacting (Halle, 1987). Part of the reason for this phenomenon may be that tacts tend to benefit the listener while mands tend to benefit the speaker (Skinner, 1957). It may be very difficult to maintain a tacting repertoire under purely social contingencies, particularly in those persons with developmental disabilities who actively avoid contact with other individuals in their environment.

Reichle (1987) suggested a tacting intervention procedure for use with learners who displayed little interest in learning to tact. He described an intervention task in which learners were taught to present line-drawn symbols representing completed work in order to cue a teacher to check their work. It is likely that, at least during the early stages of the program, the learners showed teachers their symbols representing work tasks in order to obtain primary reinforcers (a manding function). However, because the teacher had discretionary power to choose the reinforcer, the learners' communication emission contained some characteristics of a tact. The preceding strategy may ease the task of introducing tacting behavior to those individuals who typically do not relish opportunities to exchange information with others.

McLean and Snyder-McLean (1988) have suggested that normal infants communicate prelinguistically for at least four reasons: (a) to obtain relief from discomfort, (b) to attain desired goods, (c) to re-establish proximity to a caregiver, and (d) to terminate an interaction. Three of these reasons tend to result in brief conversational exchanges. Only re-establishing proximity to a caregiver (and keeping the caregiver present) leads to extended chains of turn-taking among participants that approximate conversational exchanges that occur among adults. It appears, therefore, as though there are two distinct patterns of interaction that emerge early on. In one, the child is seeking to obtain an object or escape and avoid the presentation of an undesirable object or event. These situations call for a brief communicative emission and for others in the environment to honor the request or reject. In the second pattern, the focus of the exchange (conversation) appears to be more socially motivated, the one important objective being to keep the interaction going.

Beginning Conversational Skills

Maintaining communicative interactions. Turn-taking rules in conversation and discourse allow for interchanges between the participants and for the coordination of communication so that all participants can exchange their information. In adult-adult interactions, it appears that the primary aim is to be "obtaining a turn"; however, in adult-child interactions, the adult's primary aim appears to be getting the child to take a turn. The adult's bombardment of interrogatives, tag questions, and greetings seems to be intended to promote the child's practice of turntaking. At first, the child's repertoire is extremely limited. Consequently, in early interactions adults seem to accept a wide range of child behavior as the content of an acceptable turn.

Lewis and Cherry (1977) reported that 12-week-old infants were twice as likely to vocalize if their mother verbally responded to the child's initial vocalization. Trevarthen and Hubley (1979) have described rituals and games such as "peek-a-boo" and "this little piggy" and "I'm gonna get you" as examples in which there is a clear repeated exchange of turns with specific and predictable slots for words and actions. These socially motivated routines provide opportunities for young normal children to learn more about the rules of conversation. The propensity to sustain interactions using motor and vocal behavior is exhibited early in life.

MacDonald (personal communication, 1987) has suggested that the basis for communication intervention with developmentally disabled populations rests in the ability to create situations in which interactional routines can be established between the learner and those significant others around him or her. Further, MacDonald has stated that to work exclusively on the establishment of instrumental communicative functions such as requesting and rejecting in short, interactional exchanges may be detrimental to the learner's future communicative development; that is, the learner may gain little or no experience in emitting topic maintenance and topic additions that are required of competent communicators. On the other hand, for those persons with developmental disabilities who show little inclination to interact with others more conversationally, establishing the instrumental function of leave-take exit[1] might be the most efficient manner to demonstrate the usefulness of communicative behavior. Reichle (1987) has suggested that interventionists concurrently address the two general interaction patterns we have identified. Among individuals with an established desire to interact socially, intervention in both types of interaction should proceed smoothly. However, among those who show little interest in sustained interaction, substantial effort may be required to cultivate other individuals as reinforcers. From the standpoint of assessment and intervention, it is important to describe objectively motor and vocal repertoires that represent initial attempts at interactional exchanges that go beyond a single turn.

Persons with severe disabilities frequently exhibit difficulty in maintaining a social interaction. Reasons for this difficulty are numerous. Some individuals may not enjoy the company of other individuals, perhaps because in the past the majority of interactions have been unpleasant or void of reinforcement. The desire to escape such interaction outweighs any potential benefits that may be derived from the interaction. Other individuals may be interested in continuing a communicative interaction but do not have an adequate command of vocabulary required to sustain an interaction short of engaging in strategies that include echolalia, untruthful descriptions, or frequent repeated topics. Other individuals are capable and interested in maintaining an interactional exchange as long as they remain in the role of a responder. This interactional style places a tremendous burden on one's partner to keep an interaction going. Sometimes conversations encounter a maintenance problem because one of the participants is particularly slow, as in the case of many users of augmentative communication aids.

Problems for an augmentative aid user in maintaining a conversation can become very involved. Communication board users are most likely to assume a conversational turn after the production of an obligatory question from a peer. However, even during this condition, communication board users have been reported to produce utterances during only 15% to 16% of the opportunities provided (Calculator & Luchko, 1983; Harris/ Vanderheiden & Vanderheiden, 1980). In part, this failure may occur because normal speakers fail to allow adequate time for the augmentative system user to formulate a message. Lossing (1981) reported that slowing up an interaction increased the production of maintaining utterances by

---

[1] *Leave-take exit* is the emission of a discrete voluntary behavior designed to escape or avoid participation in an ongoing activity.

communication board users. Unfortunately, even when communication board users do assume the speaking floor, their attempts may often go unheeded. Calculator and Dollaghan (1982) reported that 61% of utterances produced by communication board users in institutional settings were ignored. Two strategies are often used to maintain a conversational interaction. In one, the person tags a question to the end of an answer ("I'm fine, and you?"). In the other, a communicative partner has requested clarification (e.g., "What?", "Huh?", "I don't understand."). This instance requires the learner to clarify his or her original message. There are data to suggest that augmentative system users seldom use either of these strategies (Buzolich, 1984; Yoder & Kraat, 1983). Maintaining an interaction with a communication board user may be complicated further as a result of competing topics; for example, after asking a question, a verbal mode speaker may initiate a second topic while waiting for the communication aid user's response. This practice complicates the conversation because the augmentative user is presented with a menu of topics in which to participate.

In summary, the majority of the empirical information dealing with the establishment of conversational maintenance skills addresses the nature of the interaction at a relatively superficial level. We know relatively little about teaching the learner to infuse a prior topic with new information to keep the topic viable. We also know very little about the relative effect of teaching instrumental communicative functions that offer only brief conversational exchanges (such as rejecting) on the learner's propensity to learn to participate in more extended conversational sequences. In augmentative modes, problems in the timing of the turns within an exchange appear to create demands that complicate the establishment of the topic maintenance skills.

Initiating communicative sequences. The bulk of available information suggests that very young children and persons with more severe intellectual delays are not particularly adept at initiating communicative interactions. Initiation has often been characterized as the emission of language in the absence of a verbal cue from another. However, more recently, other antecedent stimuli have been addressed in the analysis of self-initiated communication. Halle (1987) characterized initiated social-communicative behavior as that which is uncued by another individual. Any definition of initiated sociocommunicative behavior must consider several critical variables, including the proximity of the learner to others in the environment, the proximity of the learner to objects of interest, and the familiarity of the activities in which the learner is engaged. In addition, the "function" of the skill being taught must be considered because it has direct bearing on the antecedent stimuli that exert control over initiated behavior. A "spontaneous" tact, for example, would be controlled by environmental events or objects. Mands, in contrast, would be more "spontaneous" when under the control of interoceptive states such as hunger controlling a request for food. Some of the earliest initiated utterances reported among normal developing children involve calls to obtain goods or attention, to express joy, to seek comfort, to express excitement at someone's arrival, and to reject some attention directed at them (Muma, 1986).

In the area of establishing communicative behavior, there is a limited literature that addresses initiating. Carr and Kologinsky (1983) examined the use of initiated requests by three persons with autism. These learners had sign repertoires that ranged from 25 to 50 expressive signs (used as requests). The authors believed that the learners' requests were prompted by the sight of objects. During initiation intervention, no verbal prompts were used by interventionists. Additionally, objects were not visible during intervention procedures. At the conclusion of the investigation, the learners' rate and variety of spontaneous signs had increased. Carr and Kologinsky (1983) concluded that initiated signing was facilitated as a result of a shift in stimulus control from imitative prompting to the simple presence of an attending adult.

Halle, Baer, and Spradlin (1981) taught six retarded individuals to request assistance and materials required to participate in a variety of daily activities. A constant 5-second time delay was used to fade the use of a verbal instructional prompt. Charlop, Schreibman, and Thibodeau (1985) also used a progressive time-delay that increased in 2-second increments in teaching seven verbal individuals with autism to request desired objects spontaneously. These investigators reported that spontaneous requests generalized across settings, persons, and to objects that had not been originally taught. Gobbi, Cipani, Hudson, and Lapenta-Neudeck (1986) implemented a procedure that they described as "quick transfer" to establish spontaneous requesting among two learners with severe handicaps. The instructional procedure consisted of the use of a 30-second time-delay procedure incorporated with the use of graduated levels of stimulus prompts. The authors reported high rates of spontaneous requesting as a result of the intervention procedure.

For some learners, initiating a request in the absence of either a verbal cue or the presence of the requestable item seems an insurmountable obstacle. Some requesting intervention procedures rely heavily on the immediate prior experience of the learner with a reinforcer. For example, suppose that at snack time a learner requests juice and is offered a small quantity that is subsequently consumed. In this case, the disappearance of the reinforcer may serve as the discriminative stimulus for another request for juice. Initially, juice may have to be present as part of the discriminative stimulus. Across successive opportunities, the serving pitcher of juice may be absent and only the consumption of juice by peers (who are also seated at the table) serves as the discriminative stimulus. The systematic removal of these antecedent events may result in the presence of a cup in the absence of juice serving as the discriminative stimulus for a juice-requesting episode. In these examples of recurrence (a request for a greater quantity or another instance), the probability of a self-initiated response is enhanced by the potential for repeated trials over a relatively short period of time; that is, an immediately preceding request may come to serve as part of the discriminative stimulus for the emission of a subsequent request.

Some investigators have suggested a related but slightly different application of the preceding intervention strategy. Goetz, Gee, and Sailor (1985) suggested the use of an interrupted chain of actions within a routine as an opportunity to engage the learner in a request. In an interrupted chain procedure, opportunities for communicative emission are embedded in the context of daily routines. For example, a learner may be engaged in a breakfast routine in which toast is being made. Just after the toast has been buttered, the interventionist may interrupt the routine to ask the learner what he or she wants or needs. In order to resume the routine, the learner must provide a correct approximation of the targeted response. Interrupted chain training is hypothesized to be efficient because it uses naturally occurring events that are part of a chain as discriminative stimuli for the targeted communicative behavior; that is, buttering toast becomes the discriminative stimulus to talk about buttering toast. These investigators caution that in order for interrupted chain training to be effective (a) the learner must be highly motivated to complete the task that has been interrupted, and (b) the level of anxiety created by interrupting the task must not be great.

Requesting assistance is a communicative behavior that allows the natural application of an interrupted chain procedure in an effort to establish initiated use. The learner comes to the portion of a task that he or she cannot complete independently. This problem creates a natural interruption in the task for teaching the use of a generalized requesting assistance symbol. Our experience suggests that many passive individuals engage in substantial repertoires of idiosyncratic behavior that could be interpreted by others as requests for assistance. Getting one's finger stuck in the small opening of a toy, getting twisted in an uncomfortable position in bed, or having one's head fall forward out of a stabilized position may all result in instances of crying or fussing behavior. In these instances, a request for assistance may be taught just as teaching a request for desired objects was described earlier. The main difference is that requests for assistance typically occur with less frequency and require the use of a more incidental teaching paradigm because the conditions that require assistance are less predictable and more difficult to engineer than opportunities to request objects.

One of the primary rationales for teaching a learner to initiate communicatively is to minimize the influence of learned helplessness. Unfortunately, unless this is done carefully, the interventionist's plans may result in strengthening the helplessness. The learner may fail to discriminate when to refrain from using his or her communicative behavior to request in lieu of acting independently.

Typically, initiated communicative requests for objects are taught under the conditions that available object choices are visible and in fairly close proximity to the learner. An intervention history may be established in which the learner acquires the rule that "whenever you see the object and you want it, emit a communicative request." Although adherence to this rule results in the establishment of desirable behavior, it does not necessarily lead to normalized social behavior. While eating family style, for example, serving oneself a nearby food item without requesting it is considered socially acceptable. When the food item is beyond reach, a request is required. An extreme example of the failure to engage in the "conditional," more normalized use of an established repertoire occurs with a learner who requests food between each successive spoonful.

The need to establish the conditional use of communicative behavior is critical to the social acceptability of initiated requests; that is, if a learner is taught to request assistance in order to remove a tightly affixed lid on a peanut butter jar, it is unlikely that the learner will independently remove the jar lid unless that condition is addressed directly. Reichle, Schermer, and Anderson (1987) taught a learner with severe handicaps to remove a twist tie from a loaf of bread. On some occasions, the twist tie was very loosely affixed, in which case the learner was reinforced for continuing on in the task without making a request. On other opportunities, after trying to remove a tightly affixed twist tie, the learner was reinforced for emitting a generalized requesting assistance symbol. This conditional use is critical if the social intent of requesting assistance is to be preserved in the establishment of this particular self-initiated communicative emission. Ensuring that newly established communicative behavior is used to initiate interactions represents a critical area for research. It is insufficient for the interventionist simply to identify the variables that serve as discriminative stimuli for the emission of communicative behavior. Additionally, the influence of the relative status of that variable in relation to other potential discriminative stimuli must be considered (e.g., proximity of learner to potential speaking partner, proximity of learner to object of interest, etc.). The potential interaction among relevant stimulus variables would seem to lend itself to a general case intervention application, in which the intervention establishes a matrix reflecting the critical variables and their interactions. Over a sampling period, the interventionist could identify which cells in the matrix account for the greatest number of self-initiated opportunities across environments that the learner accesses. This frequency would establish the critical variables to be addressed in instructional opportunities. Interventionists are only beginning to consider the subtleties of self-initiated behavior as being more than responding in the absence of an instructional cue.

Terminating interactions.   Termination of a conversational interaction may occur for a variety of reasons that include (a) a desire to avoid the presentation of an undesired object/event, (b) a need to end an ongoing pleasurable experience because of schedule demands, or (c) a desire to end a neutral interactional experience when a topic has been exhausted. Being communicatively competent requires that the learner be able to terminate an interaction under each of the preceding conditions. To date, there is little empirical data describing the acquisition of these competencies.

Often persons with developmental disabilities emit classes of behavior used to terminate ongoing interactions that are not socially progressive. For example, some more passive learners may simply slow down their food intake as the end of a meal occurs. Many individuals who are developmentally disabled are placed in the role of a responder during a conversational interaction. Even though they may produce the last word, it is the normal partner who ends the conversation by leave-taking. Kraat (1983), for example, reported that the majority of conversations between verbal mode speakers and communication board users are terminated by the verbal mode user. She speculated that many individuals with severe handicaps are not physically able to leave an interaction. Hence, using normal cues to terminate an interaction such as beginning to move away from the listener are compromised. Because attention directed to a person with severe communicative handicaps may be limited to begin with, the handicapped individual may be reluctant to terminate a behavior (conversation) that is viewed as being very infrequent; that is, persons with a communicative system who have limited capability of initiating a conversation may be reluctant to terminate a conversation once it has grown stale for fear of not being able to start another conversation in a few minutes with the same individual. A more simplistic explanation is that because severely handicapped individuals may receive less conversational attention when they are recipients, they tend to satiate at a much different rate than their communicative partner. As a result, the partner typically terminates the interaction.

Other individuals with developmental disabilities may actively terminate social interactions using highly idiosyncratic and sometimes socially unacceptable behavior. Carr and Durand (1985) have documented carefully the use of excess behavior (aggression, tantrum, self-injurious behavior) as signs to gain termination from an interaction. The use of these more active communication strategies will be addressed more thoroughly in our discussion of the relationship between an initial social-communication and the emission of excess repertoires later in this chapter.

Research Issues

There are a number of issues pertaining to the establishment of an initial communicative repertoire whose resolution will serve to enhance the efficiency of intervention procedures. These issues involve (a) determining the prerequisites, if any, to the establishment of beginning communication skills; (b) developing criteria to determine the most efficient intervention sequence to teach specific instrumental communication functions (such as requesting, rejecting, and providing information) and interactional skills; (c) validating procedures to establish early conversational skills; (d) transitioning from less sophisticated communicative forms to more sophisticated communicative behavior; and (e) identifying conditions most likely to result in the generalized use of early communicative topographies that allow a full range of conversational skills, including initiating, maintaining, and terminating interactions. Each of these areas will be explored further in the sections that follow.

Prerequisites and communicative acquisition. Thus far, we have described early communicative behaviors that emerge in normal developing children. A logical question for a service professional to ask is whether there are any prerequisite skills that a learner must emit prior to the implementation of initial communicative intervention. The most frequently proposed prerequisites to the establishment of a communicative repertoire focus on cognitive skills (particularly Piagetian-referenced domains that emerge during the first two years of life).

Siegel, Katsuki, and Potechin (1985) concluded that it is improbable that the relationship between cognition and communication can be clarified by reviewing existing empirical work. One difficulty in interpreting relationships between cognition and communication involves the failure to define communication and cognition as two separate constructs. For example, a protoimperative communicative utterance defined by Bates et al. (1976) involves the emission of vocal and motor behavior directed at procurement of a good or service. That description also meets the requirements of a description of an instance of means-end behavior at sensorimotor stage V (Piagetian perspective) provided the learner's behavior was directed to another. If mutually exclusive definitions between classes of cognition and communication cannot be made, it makes little sense to explore correlative and/or causal relationships between the two. If independence in definition cannot be made, "we end up asserting that language causes language or that cognition causes cognition" (Siegel et al., 1985, p. 302).

Chapman and Miller (1980) suggested that for a learner functioning between 1 and 8 months of age, a focus on caregiver-child interaction and the establishment of social bonds represented the most desirable communication intervention strategy. As mentioned earlier, MacDonald (1985) has elaborated on this strategy. He suggests that initially it is important that learners acquire the ability to participate in interactive routines with others in their environment. Games, such as "peek-a-boo," "so big," and "I'm gonna get you," and greeting routines represent early targets. Although the games may be built around specific pragmatic intents, such as requesting, the primary focus is on the establishment of an interaction. Chapman and Miller's (1980) strategy suggests that prior to sensorimotor stage IV, intervention directed at the establishment of formal communicative symbols should not be attempted (although their criteria seem to have been softened somewhat; see Miller & Chapman, 1984). With respect to the implementation of augmentative communication systems (communication board and signing), Shane and Bashir (1980) cited sensorimotor stage V performance as a prerequisite for augmentative communication system implementation (mental age of 18 months, ability to recognize objects represented by photos).

Clearly, there are discrepancies regarding the point at which communication intervention could be implemented successfully. Miller, Chapman, Branston, and Reichle (1980) examined the role of sensorimotor cognitive skills in the areas of means end, causality, space, object permanence, and object schemas in relation to the development of language comprehension skills. A summary of this study led Miller and Chapman (1984) to conclude that

> nonverbally measured cognitive level becomes a reasonable baseline for identifying specific language delays in mentally retarded children. At the same time, these studies cast doubt on approaches to therapy that require the teaching of specific cognitive prerequisites for the purpose of readiness for communicative skills. (p. 538)

The critical question seems to be "Have children acquired language in the absence of proposed cognitive prerequisites?" To date, few interventionists have addressed this issue (see Reichle & Yoder, 1985). There is a critical need for research that attempts to establish an initial communicative repertoire in the absence of hypothesized cognitive prerequisites. The majority of data addressing the issue of cognitive prerequisites involves examinations of the correlative relationship among cognitive prerequisites and emerging language behavior in normally developing populations.

Sequencing the implementation of pragmatic intervention. The available literature suggests that persons with severe mental retardation as well as at least some individuals with autism either fail to acquire the use of protodeclaratives or begin to acquire them well after the emergence of protoimperatives (McLean & Snyder-McLean, 1988). This observed sequence must be investigated further. It seems reasonable to hypothesize that protodeclaratives, for some learners, may emerge later or never because the learners have not learned to cultivate the company of others as a generalized class of reinforcement. That is to say, if you don't enjoy the company of others, you may be less likely to recruit attention. For those learners who eventually do begin emitting protodeclaratives, there may be several plausible explanations. Eventually, sufficiently powerful primary reinforcers may be located to "make it worth the learner's while" to chain an attention-getting topography to an object request. A second possibility is that, as more protoimperatives are emitted, a more extensive history of other persons delivering social reinforcers is established. Consequently, social interactions with others (typically focused around the receipt of primary reinforcers) become conditioned reinforcers. If any of the preceding explanations are true, one would expect to see early protodeclarative behavior tending to occur in close proximity to and immediately preceding requesting response directed at obtaining a good or service. Further, the preceding scenario might translate easily to an intervention strategy aimed at establishing an early repertoire of protodeclaratives.

The second issue related to the preceding topic involves the sequencing of instructional objectives to teach requesting and describing communicative intents. As mentioned earlier, there is some literature to suggest that teaching the use of a specific vocabulary item as a mand may create difficulties if the interventionist attempts to obtain generalized use of that vocabulary item as a tact (Savage-Rumbaugh, 1984). There are few empirical data addressing the best strategy to use in sequencing the introduction of intervention to establish initial instrumental communicative intents. Possibilities include the concurrent establishment of describing and requesting behavior using the same vocabulary, establishing tacts first, establishing mands first, or establishing concurrent tacts and mands with different vocabulary being assigned initially to each communicative intent.

Of course, it is also possible that the problems reported by Savage-Rumbaugh (1984) do not represent significant problems when applied to the population as a whole. However, as reviewed earlier, it seems likely that children and persons with severe handicaps do not immediately generalize newly acquired language skills across different instrumental communicative intents. The few investigations that have examined the functional relationship between tacting and manding repertoires have not considered the potential influence of language comprehension skills. It is unclear what effect teaching a learner to "find a cookie" in a comprehension task with a consequence of some reinforcing event other than a cookie might have on the learner's ability to tact or mand in production. It is possible that the "nonspecific" reinforcement history established in the comprehension task (where the reinforcer delivered does not match the referent) would make it much easier to establish the same reinforcement strategy in a tact. At the outset, this alternative may be risky because of the literature supporting the independence of comprehension and production as response classes (to be discussed later in this chapter). The best strategy to use in implementing instruction in a range of communicative intents and the relationship between these intents remains an area of critical research importance.

Validating intervention procedures that promote early conversational skills. We know remarkably little about the emergence of early conversational skills. We do have extensive information regarding the development of imitation in both normal populations and those with developmental disabilities. However, we know very little about methods to establish interactive chains of behavior that go beyond a single turn. This is particularly true of populations with significant developmental disabilities. In order to become more sophisticated in our approach to this topic, we must address a number of issues.

As discussed earlier, MacDonald (J. MacDonald, personal communication, 1987) emphasizes the turn-taking aspects of cooperative play as being critical to the establishment of an initial conversational repertoire. While there are limited empirical data to support this position, it is unclear to what extent the ability to participate in extended play routines serves to predict advancing conversational performance. One would assume, for example, that a child who was capable of integrating newly offered toys into an ongoing play routine might be more adept in adding to a topic introduced by a speaking partner. Unfortunately, there are few data pertaining to populations with developmental delay that address this issue.

Another critical area relates to the sequencing of communication objectives designed to teach instrumental communication functions and early conversational (turn-taking) skills. As mentioned earlier, MacDonald feels that the latter must be the focus of initial intervention efforts. Further, he suggests that to concentrate on instrumental communication functions as initial intervention targets may create difficulty. Presumably, the difficulty would result from the fact that instrumental communicative intents such as requesting and rejecting typically result in short interactions in which the communicative function is emitted and then consequated without any particular need for further conversation. Karlan (G. Karlan, personal communication, 1987) suggested that an initial communication intervention protocol should focus on initial repertoires of instrumental functions *and* opportunities for extended turn-taking episodes.

Pursuing research on Karlan's suggestion is not easy. Reichle and Keogh (1986) outlined procedures that could be used to establish instrumental communication functions in both structured and more incidental instructional formats. In a massed opportunity structured format, a learner might be seated at dinner. After requesting and consuming dessert, he or she may wait quietly until another individual attends to him or her and asks "How are you doing?" At this point, the learner again requests. This episode repeated represents one example of what MacDonald (personal communication, 1987) refers to as early conversational teaching opportunities. Over time, when the learner is more apt to self-initiate the request, the interventionist may force a second learner's turn within the interaction by requiring that he or she choose between a large or small dessert serving. At the same time, opportunities to initiate and respond conversationally are provided in massed opportunities; the learner might receive practice in other settings where there is no attempt to extend turn-takings around the instrumental communicative function.

Moving from less sophisticated to more sophisticated forms of communication. Initially, young normal developing children tend to cry or fuss when they are requesting an object/event. Over time, the conditions of the environment make it advantageous for the learner to acquire more sophisticated methods to request (i.e., "want" or "that" as the child points). Even though words are acquired, children may continue to use old forms of behavior to communicate under certain specific environmental circumstances; for example, if a desired object is visible and nearby, the learner may simply point and say "that." However, if the object is not visible, he or she may produce the explicit name of the object. This more sophisticated form is used conditionally. Among individuals with severe communicative deficits, there appears to be a tendency to teach a new form of behavior as a replacement for an earlier produced form. Frequently, when the new form is emitted in only some settings and not others, the assumption is that the behavior failed to generalize. An alternative explanation is that the new behavior is being used conditionally. If a learner is taught, for example, to use a communication board at school, failure to extend its use into the home may be because the learner's marginally intelligible verbal behavior is understood quite well in the home environment.

The crux of the conditional use issue raised in the preceding paragraphs is the instance of teaching the learner when it is and is *not* appropriate to use a newly established initial communicative behavior. Teaching the learner, say, to produce a protoimperative (motor + vocal behavior used to obtain a good or a service) is most easily accomplished by placing an array of desired items near the learner and asking what he or she wants. Ultimately, the student learns that when objects are near, there is an opportunity to request and be reinforced. Unfortunately, he or she may have failed to learn that there are some situations in which it is socially acceptable to take an object without requesting. The majority of the early communication intervention literature addresses only the stimulus conditions in which the target behavior should be emitted, and rarely addresses the stimulus conditions under which no communicative behavior is required (i.e., at mealtime when salt is directly in front of one, it is unnecessary to request it). Many communication intervention programs promote the overgeneralized use of newly established communicative intents. When this occurs, a new communication repertoire may serve to establish a level of learned helplessness. Horner, Bellamy, and Colvin (1984) have argued forcefully for including training on when not to respond as an aspect of generalization. As mentioned earlier, Reichle, Schermer, and Anderson (1987) reported that teaching a learner to request assistance (help), in the context of a difficult task, resulted in the learner's continuing to use the request even though under some conditions he or she could independently complete the task. Conditional use of the "help" request was not established until the conditions of the intervention program were rearranged so that the learner had to attempt the task first. If it was an instance where he or she could be independent, reinforcement was contingent on refraining from requesting help. During other opportunities, the activity was arranged to require assistance, and a request for assistance was reinforced. Establishing conditioned use of a communicative repertoire is particularly important in the case of an individual who uses a communication board and/or signing to supplement or replicate verbal mode communication. Several investigations (Kraat, 1983; Light, Collier, & Parnes, 1985) have reported that once a graphic mode augmentative is established, most learners continue to use other modes during a substantial portion of their communicative interactions. Of critical concern to interventionists should be identifying those communicative contexts that more clearly support the use of a particular communicative mode over another. As an example, for the learner at home with other individuals who sign, sign will have distinct portability and speed advantages over the graphic mode (communication board). On the other hand, in a community setting where few individuals sign, a graphic mode system will have the distinct advantage of being more readily deciphered. Reichle and Ward (1985) described a procedure used to teach a moderately handicapped individual to use sign and an electronic communication aid conditionally as a function of the setting in which he or she was attempting to communicate.

Traditionally, interventionists have established repertoires of new communicative behavior under the singular condition in which it is to be used and have not taught learners when to refrain from using the behavior (or when to use an alternative behavior). However, it is the conditional use of communicative behavior that, in a large measure, defines social appropriateness for an individual who engages in communicative exchanges.

Establishing a generalizable communicative repertoire. For the most part, the topic of generalized communicative use has addressed stimulus variables that include persons, settings, and materials. It is becoming increasingly obvious that these variables represent only the tip of the iceberg. For example, as mentioned earlier, persons with developmental disabilities typically do not use newly established vocabulary across different pragmatic intents (i.e., use of the same word to request and provide information) unless the vocabulary was taught in a variety of situations that required different pragmatic intents. Consequently, the interventionists must provide clear discrete opportunities to use a newly established vocabulary item across a range of different pragmatic intents using a general case instructional form or a matrix training paradigm. This area of generalization has been addressed in detail most recently by Stremel-Campbell and Campbell (1985).

Another frequently overlooked area of generalized use in the establishment of an initial communicative repertoire involves self-initiated communication. If a communicative behavior is taught exclusively for the purpose of maintaining an ongoing interaction, there is little reason to believe that it will be used as a strategy to initiate an interaction. The bulk of the existing literature addresses situations in which one first establishes communicative behavior in response to a verbal instruction (e.g., "What is this?" or "What do you want?") and only later transfers instructional control to functional attributes of the learner's environment. There is a critical need to establish some initial repertoire of communicative behavior under the control of nonverbal characteristics of the environment from the start of the intervention process. A question of particular interest is whether it is easier to generalize from the self-initiated use of a communicative behavior to a responding use than vice versa.

With respect to learners whose repertoire was first established as a response to the verbal antecedent delivered by a speaking partner in close proximity, it is important to examine systematically the relative influence that variables such as referent proximity, listener proximity, and an interaction of the two might leave on a learner's propensity to self-initiate. Halle (1987) has some particularly enlightening approaches to this issue.

A final, rather subtle, aspect of generalized use of one's communicative repertoire involves the ability to emit each of several different communicative intents in the presence of the same referent. At breakfast, say, when asked whether one wants coffee, an appropriate response is to emit an accepting communicative response. However, by midmorning, after the learner has had five cups, when coffee is offered, a state of satiation dictates the use of a rejecting communicative response. There is virtually no literature regarding this aspect of generalized communicative behavior. Yet it is critical when one addresses the issue of establishing the use of pragmatic classes of behavior that are context determined rather than solely referent determined.

COMMUNICATION AND EXCESS BEHAVIORS

The Relationship Between Social-communication and the Emission of Excess Repertoires

Some persons with developmental disabilities have learned extensive repertoires of intentional communicative behavior to express instrumental communicative functions. Unfortunately, the modes used may consist of socially maladaptive behavior. Carr and Durand (1985) reported that high rates of excess behavior (tantrums, aggression, stereotypic behaviors) among persons with developmental disabilities may be motivated by the desire to communicate instrumental pragmatic intents such as leave-take exit, rejection, requesting goods and services, and requesting attention.

The social-communicative hypothesis posits that excess behavior may be acquired and maintained as a result of the social consequences it produces ("social" in that the consequence requires the mediation of others in order to occur). Inherent in the social communicative hypothesis is the caution that some excess behavior appears to be maintained by social reinforcement for individuals with developmental disabilities (Carr & Durand, 1985; Favell, McGimsey, & Schell, 1982; Lovaas, Newsom, & Hickman, 1987; Rincover, Cook, Peoples, & Packard, 1979; Rincover & Devany,

1982). For example, if obtaining adult attention serves as an important motivator for an individual, *delivering* attention contingent upon the emission of excess behavior increases the likelihood that she or he will emit excess behavior in the future (constituting an example of a positive social reinforcement paradigm). Other individuals may emit excess behavior whenever a difficult task or undesired object/event is presented. Contingent upon the emission of excess behavior, the teacher may develop a history of withdrawing the task. If the task is aversive for the student, withdrawing it increases the likelihood of the emission of excess behavior (constituting an example of negative reinforcement). The preceding episodes suggest an expanded role for the mediator in an intervention paradigm, from that of an agent delivering reinforcement to that of a party in an interaction. The social-communicative hypothesis emphasizes that some excess behavior may be a learned operant that influences the actions of others. This shift has some significant ramifications for both communication assessment and intervention. At issue is whether all socially motivated excess behavior can be explained using the original escape/avoidance (negative reinforcement) versus attention-seeking (positive reinforcement) motivational scheme or if some expanded scheme is desirable. It also suggests that communication interventionists can no longer consider only the absence of, delay in, or deviance of language as a condition warranting intervention. The status of a learner's language must be viewed in the larger context of the individual's social competence.

Demonstrating that some excess behaviors are socially instigated. Approaches to the experimental analysis of the negative reinforcement hypothesis have been to compare the level of the target behavior in the presence of high versus low social demands (Carr & Newsom, 1985; Carr, Newsom, & Binkoff, 1976; Carr, Newsom, & Binkoff, 1980; Durand, 1982) or to compare levels in the presence of easy versus difficult tasks (Carr & Durand, 1985; Iwata, Dorsey, Slifer, Bauman, & Richman, 1982; Weeks & Gaylord-Ross, 1981). In the context of experimental analogues to naturally occurring situations, increased levels of excess behavior in the presence of high demands/difficult tasks across repeated assessments are used to infer an escape-avoidance motivation. This escape-avoidance motivation, in turn, has been treated by teaching an appropriate request for assistance or a request to leave-take exit, which in turn is assumed to reduce the aversiveness of demands/difficult tasks, thus removing the discriminative stimuli for excess behavior.

Carr, Newsom, and Binkoff (1980) found that severe aggressive behavior emitted by two children with mental retardation was maintained by the opportunity to escape from tasks that were educationally demanding. Further, they demonstrated that excess behavior was most apt to be emitted in situations in which greater task demands were placed on the learners.

Usually, tests of the positive reinforcement hypothesis are arranged by making adult attention contingent upon the emission of excess behavior (Iwata et al., 1982; Lovaas, Freitag, Gold, & Kassorla, 1965; Lovaas & Simmons, 1969). Levels of excess behavior in the presence of an adult when the behavior obtains attention is compared to situations in which the adult uses no such contingency. Higher levels of the excess behavior when the contingency is in effect across repeated assessments are used to infer the behavior is maintained by positive social reinforcement.

As with the assessment of the negative reinforcement hypothesis, at least two conditions have typically been constructed. One condition approximates the naturally occurring evocative context for the excess. The remaining condition usually includes frequent noncontingent attention, as this will be associated with low levels of the excess if the excess serves as an attention-seeking function for the learner.

The influence of pragmatics on socio-communicative approaches to the management of excess. Pragmatics is the study of the relationship between meaning and the context in which the meaning is produced (Hart, 1981; Prutting, 1982). Prutting (1982) emphasized that all behavior which occurs in a social context has properties of perlocution (the effects of the behavior on the receiver) and illocution (the intention of the sender). As mentioned earlier, these properties can be independent of one another; that is, behavior occurring in a social context influences the receiver regardless of the communicative intent of the sender (Donnellan, Mirenda, Mesaros, & Fassbender, 1984). An intriguing implication of this is that socially unacceptable behaviors may serve as effective communication devices without one's having to assume communicative intent on the part of the individual emitting them. Further, an operant model suggests that frequent pairing of perlocutionary emissions with the matching consequence may serve to establish illocutionary behavior (Reichle & Keogh, 1986).

Epidemiological studies on the emergence of language in infants and on the inverse relationship between excess behavior and communication skills in persons with developmental disabilities also indirectly support the view that excesses may serve communication functions. While such studies do not directly implicate excess behaviors as communication devices, they provide correlational evidence that substantiates the social-communicative hypothesis (Carr & Durand, 1985).

Talkington, Hall, and Altman (1971) compared measures of aggression in matched groups of noncommunicating and communicating institutionalized persons with comparable mental retardation. The noncommunicating group evidenced significantly higher levels of aggression, suggesting less aggression for the group with more normal communication skills. Other studies involving individuals with developmental disabilities have suggested an inverse relationship between excess behavior and communication instruction, although this evidence is anecdotal (Rowe & Rapp, 1980).

Crying in very young normal infants occurs reliably in certain social contexts (Wolff, 1969). In a longitudinal study of infant behavior in the first year of life, Bell and Ainsworth (1972) found that as more developmentally advanced forms of communication began to appear in infants, crying decreased. In a study of aggression by toddlers toward peers, Brownlee and Bakeman (1981) showed that some forms of aggression were emitted to terminate an interaction. Other aggression, much milder in intensity than this, seemed to denote the message, "Hey, wanna play?" Thus, aggression was emitted as an instrumental device to communicate more than one social intent.

Empirical data suggest a connection between "normal" communication skills and behaviors that would be construed as excessive if emitted by a learner with severe handicaps (the more you have of one, the less you have of the other). The nonverbal behaviors reviewed (crying and aggression) are typical of behaviors characterized as excesses in this population. The major implication of these findings for a population that does not develop normal skills rapidly or extensively is clear: If new (more socially acceptable) communication skills do not develop, then behavioral tactics presently in the repertoire must suffice to communicate needs and desires.

Several assessment tools emphasizing communicative functions of excess behavior have been developed (Donnellan et al., 1984, Prizant & Duchan, 1981; Prizant & Rydell, 1984; Schuler & Goetz, 1981). "Function," used in a pragmatic sense, means purpose rather than "behavior is a function of" as in the case of operant conditioning (Meyer & Evans, 1986). For some of these assessment tools, the categories used to attribute communicative intent are parallel to or isomorphic with the positive reinforcement/negative reinforcement dichotomy established by Carr (1977). However, in some instances, these instruments have expanded, and in other instances subdivided Carr's (1977) original descriptive scheme.

Up to this point, examples of socially motivated excess have involved nonverbal topographies of behavior. However, Prizant and Duchan (1981) observed that among developmentally disabled individuals who exhibit childhood autism, there may be several verbal excess topographies that are socially motivated. Echolalia has been described as the most frequently mentioned characteristic of verbal autistic children, occurring in at least

75% of these individuals (Prizant & Rydell, 1984). Typically, echolalic behavior is differentiated as being either immediate or delayed. Traditionally, language interventionists viewed echolalia as a nonfunctional verbal topography (Lovaas, Schreibman, & Koegel, 1974), representing a language disorder in and of itself. Others (Prizant & Duchan, 1981; Prizant & Rydell, 1984) hypothesized that the emission of delayed echolalia might be used as a strategy to maintain social interactions, compensating for comprehension disorders. Most recently, Prizant and Duchan (1981) found that immediate echolalia can express a variety of communicative intents, including requesting, regulating one's own behavior, confirming, labeling, and rehearsing. Prizant and Rydell (1984) found similar patterns with delayed echolalia.

There appears to be ample evidence to support the hypothesis that some socially maladaptive behavior may be acquired and maintained in an effort to communicate. Further, it appears that the establishment of a socially acceptable communicative repertoire may serve to decelerate an existing repertoire of socially unacceptable behavior.

Research Issues

It is clear that communication intervention represents a viable component of an intervention package designed to decelerate socially motivated excess behaviors. However, there remain a number of unanswered issues. Some individuals are difficult to begin communication training with because their excess emissions are not easily predicted. When an emission cannot be anticipated easily, it becomes difficult to prompt the communicative behavior prior to the emission of the excess behavior. Once the excess behavior has been emitted, the interventionist has been placed in a teaching dilemma. On one hand, he or she could complete the prompt to the target communicative topography. Doing so, however, will only serve to strengthen the chain of emitting the excess behavior followed by the emission of the communicative topography. While the communicative topography may be established, the excess may also be strengthened.

One alternative to the dilemma is to identify low-level approximations of the excess that may be emitted by the learner. For example, some learners who wish to leave an ongoing event may begin an episode of excess hand-tapping on a table. If no intervention follows, he or she may then stand and begin to rock. If no intervention is forthcoming, the learner may finally overturn a table. When an escalating hierarchy of excess can be identified, it may be most efficient to utilize the lowest level approximation of the excess sequence as a cue to intervene. Doing so will, no doubt, strengthen the low-level approximation, but it will also serve to interrupt the chain of socially unacceptable behaviors before the individual arrives at the most socially maladaptive step of the chain.

Not only may some learners be somewhat unpredictable in their emission of socially motivated excess, they may also fail to engage in an escalating hierarchy of excess. For these persons, an intervention strategy may focus on establishing the form of the replacement behavior under more natural stimulus conditions. It is possible, say, that a learner is willing to engage in watching a home video for 10–15 minutes. However, at the end of that period, he or she may become satiated and exit. This event might be targeted as an opportunity to prompt a leave-take response at the end of 10 minutes. Because excess is an improbable behavior, it allows the interventionist to prompt the target response in the absence of excess. However, it seems unlikely that the socially acceptable leave-take established in this situation would generalize to leave-take situations that involved even less preferred activities that tended to recruit more vehemently emitted excess repertoires. On the other hand, because the leave-take symbol/gesture topography has been established under a neutral stimulus condition, it may require less effort to prompt in a situation in which excess is more likely to occur. Currently, there are few data to suggest whether the preceding strategy would result in an increased likelihood of providing an instructional prompt prior to the emission of an excess behavior.

Some persons use the same excess repertoire for different social intents (bite as an attempt to obtain attention but also in an effort to leave an undesired activity). Others may use pragmatic function-specific excess behavior (hitting to escape or avoid undesired events and self-injury to obtain attention). Finally, some individuals may use several different excess behaviors to encode the same social intent (hit to obtain attention on some occasions but engage in bizarre mannerisms to obtain attention in other situations). Few investigations have attempted to examine the influence that the preceding types of emission histories may have upon developing a "general case" intervention strategy for preceding existing repertoires. Although much discussion is provided addressing the design of "simple to use" assessment protocols to document the pattern of excess emission described above, there are few empirical investigations that have gone beyond a more traditional laboratory-setting/controlled-task identification of social events likely to evoke an excess repertoire.

Virtually all investigations examining the implementation of communicative behaviors as an alternative to excess repertoires have assumed that a normal adult is the recipient of the learner's communicative overture. Frequently, however, other clients may be the recipient of a learner's socially motivated excess. Doss (1988), for example, reported that unauthorized removal of objects (stealing) may represent socially motivated excess directed at other clients. An ecological analysis of stealing may result in determining which of several social intents is being communicated. Learners may steal in order to (a) obtain staff attention, (b) escape or avoid an ongoing activity, or (c) obtain a desired good or service. Doss (1988) reported on a procedure designed to teach self-initiated requesting as a replacement for stealing resulting from a simple desire to obtain a good or service. His procedure involved first teaching self-initiated requesting under a continuous reinforcement schedule in which each request resulted in providing the desired object. A second phase of the intervention procedure involved teaching the learner to refrain from stealing in response to a verbal utterance "no" produced by the recipient of the self-initiated request. In effect, self-initiated requests were placed on an intermittent schedule of reinforcement. Unfortunately, when subjects invoke a requesting strategy directed at their peers, the peers may almost always indicate "no." If this is the case, the interventionist must ensure that the listeners are taught to share occasionally if self-initiated requesting is expected to decelerate stealing. Ecologically evaluating the influence of the environment of the communicative alternative to excess is an area in great need of exploration. In many respects, investigations examining the relationship between excess and communication are at the same level as early communication studies in the early 1970s. Investigators are so intent on demonstrating that communicative behavior can serve as an alternative to excess repertoires that ecological issues such as those raised above are not yet being considered.

INITIAL SEMANTIC PRODUCTION

Thus far, the communicative emissions discussed need not convey specific meaning even though they display explicit communicative intent. Sometime between approximately 9 and 14 months of age, most normally developing children produce their first intelligible word. Prior to this time, children may produce idiosyncratic words referred to by Reich (1984) as *idiomorphs*. Idiomorphs are relatively stable combinations of consonants and vowels used to represent an object or action class. For example, a bottle of milk may come to be called "ba ba," juice may be referred to as "du du," etc.

Difficulties with Generalization

One of the great difficulties in attributing early meaning to the child is a result of his or her propensity to overgeneralize and/or undergeneralize meanings. Overgeneralization occurs when the learner uses a word to refer to the appropriate referent class but also uses the word to refer to items that are not members of the referent class. For example, a child may label a black-and-white rat terrier a "dog" but also label a black-and-white cat of approximately the same size a "dog." Undergeneralization occurs when the learner fails to refer to all members in a given semantic class with the same vocabulary item. For example, a learner may refer to a rose as a flower but consistently fail to refer to a daisy as a flower. Both overgeneralization and undergeneralization occur as part of a developing production repertoire in intellectually delayed populations as well as normal children. Further, many children exhibit both overgeneralization and undergeneralization at the same item, making the job of assessing and teaching early vocabulary skills even more challenging.

Vocabulary Selection Strategies

Unfortunately, some vocabulary selection strategies used by language interventionists may encourage the use of the production strategies described above. Keogh and Reichle (1985) reasoned that if a learner initially calls a cookie by the name "food," he or she may become confused when asked at a later point to learn to produce the word "cookie." Further, Keogh and Reichle (1985) suggested that double-function words like "drink," which can be used as either an object or an action, can be more specifically represented as an object by using words such as juice, Coke, milk, etc. Bowerman (1978) summarized it best when she suggested that object names that represent the initial vocabulary taught should correspond directly to the objects that they represent. Unfortunately, utilizing this strategy may mean that the learner would have fewer situations in which explicit vocabulary can be used (early on) than would be the case if a more generalized vocabulary item (drink other than Diet Coke) had been selected. The criteria used to select initial vocabulary to teach a learner can become particularly complex.

In the area of augmentative communication systems, factors including motoric difficulty of signs and iconicity (transparency and translucency) of both signs and graphic mode systems have been addressed as critical factors in the selection of an initial vocabulary. Iconicity refers to the degree to which the elements of a sign or symbol are related to the visual aspects of what is denoted (Bellugi & Klima, 1976). At one end of the iconicity continuum are symbols considered highly suggestive of their referents. As such, their gloss or meaning can be readily guessed by naive viewers. These symbols are considered to be *transparent*. In the center of the continuum scale are those symbols that may not be readily guessable, but the viewer is able to perceive a relationship between the symbol and its meaning. These symbols are considered *translucent*, that is, ideographic symbols that represent a concept. At the other end of the scale are those abstract symbols not guessable. These are considered *opaque*, that is, arbitrary symbols that have no apparent relationship to its referent.

Although transparency and translucency refer to iconicity, they represent two distinctly different characteristics. Transparency has been defined as guessing the symbol when given the gloss or guessing the gloss when shown the symbol. Translucency, on the other hand, has been defined as agreement regarding the relationship between a symbol and its referent (Bellugi & Klima, 1976).

Currently, there is little empirically based information regarding the influence of iconicity and graphic symbol system use among handicapped persons. To date, a few cross-system investigations of iconicity have provided evidence supporting the contention that pictographic systems, such as Pictogram-Ideogram Communication (PIC) and Rebus are more transparent (Goossens, 1983; Leonhart & Maharaj, 1979) than Blissymbols. There is limited evidence to indicate that iconicity of different relational symbol systems are consistent across different word categories: Rebus, for example, was found to be the most translucent system across three-word classes: nouns, verbs, and modifiers (Bloomberg, 1984). The translucency ratings of different word categories by normal adults were consistent across different representational systems; that is, nouns were the most translucent word category across five representational symbol systems. This trend in translucency ranking parallels what we know about children's acquisition of words; i.e., that nouns and verbs are easier to acquire than modifiers (Bloom, 1970). Like the translucency data, there may be transparency differences among the word categories as the symbols from different word categories may be represented differently for each symbol system. For example, Blissymbols and Picsyms consist of three types of symbols: pictographic symbols (drawings that resemble their referents), ideographic symbols (drawings that symbolize the idea rather than the name of a referent), and arbitrary symbols (drawings which do not have a perceptual or conceptual relationship to its referent), whereas the Pictorial Communication System (PCS) consists of mainly pictographic symbols. This consistency across word categories occurs with relational symbol system acquisition and is supported by recent research of normally developing 3-year-old children (Mizuko, 1987). It is not currently clear to what extent, if any, these consistencies across word categories are similar for the handicapped population. It seems reasonable to assume, however, that the same trends found with the normal subjects would be replicated with the handicapped subjects.

To date, cross-system investigations of recall among individuals with disabilities have provided some empirical evidence supporting the notion that "Rebus-like" symbols (Hurlbut, Iwata, & Green, 1982), Rebus (Goossens, 1983) and Picture Ideogram communication (Leonhart & Maharaj, 1979; Maharaj, 1980) are easier to learn than Blissymbols. It also has been difficult to generate the differences found with certain relational systems to specific word categories since the production of nouns, verbs, descriptors, etc. have not been reported or tested in these cross-system investigations and since ease of acquisition may vary from symbol to symbol or from word category to word category. In general, nonspeech symbols judged *a priori* to be high in iconicity were more easily learned (Goossens, 1983; Hurlbut, Iwata, & Green, 1982) by individuals with mental retardation and/or autism than were nonspeech symbols judged to be low in iconicity. Clark (1984) suggested that nonspeaking individuals with apparent cognitive delays may need a system that is iconic and easily learned. Conversely, when little or no cognitive delay is present in a nonspeaking individual, ease of learning and iconicity may not be critical factors.

Considerations in selecting an initial repertoire of vocabulary appears to involve much more than considering what vocabulary normally developing children use. Great care must be taken to consider the influence that vocabulary selection will have on establishing discriminative and generalized use of the vocabulary. Additionally, when an augmentative mode is considered, additional considerations such as iconicity appear to be of lesser significance in the verbal mode.

The Relationship Between Semantics and Pragmatics

Words can express a variety of meanings. Substantive semantic functions refer to the names of things. Relational semantic functions encode a class of meaning that can be represented using a variety of different specific vocabulary. Agency, for example, is a relational semantic function. The doer of an action is referred to semantically as an agent. Obviously, a number of nouns can serve as agents.

A semantic function such as recurrence (a relational semantic class of behavior that refers to an additional instance or greater amount of a referent object or activity) can be used for each of several distinctly different reasons (pragmatic intents). Upon eating a cookie, a learner can say "more." In this instance, the semantic function of recurrence is produced to encode a request pragmatically. In a second instance, however, a learner may comment on a deepening snowfall by looking out the window and saying "more snow." In this instance, the relational semantic function of recurrence is used to pragmatically encode a provision of information.

There is some evidence to suggest that both normal children as well as individuals with developmental disabilities have difficulty using an isolated semantic function to encode each of several distinctly different pragmatic intents: Miller (1981) reported that initial uses of recurrence are observed only in the expression of requests among normal developing children in their second year.

Research Issues

The role of idiomorphs. Idiomorphs have been of interest to communication interventionists because they herald the child's representation of specific referents with unique sounds or sound combinations. In effect, having learned to match a characteristic symbol to a referent, all the child has to do is adhere to the rules imposed by his or her native language. It seems plausible to suggest that among persons with handicaps, the ability to produce idiomorphs represents a predictor of success in vocal mode production programs. Procedurally, the acquisition of idiomorphs seems to suggest that the learner benefits either from vocal models presented by others or the object itself. Or it suggests that by the child's (perhaps accidentally at first) pairing a distinctive sound with a referent, over time a form of stimulus control forms so that seeing the object serves as a prompt to produce the sound.

Most of the research regarding the emergence of idiomorphs has focused on segmental (speech sound) features rather than prosodic characteristics (e.g., loudness, duration, pitch, etc.). It may be that some children come to begin producing idiomorphs such as "vroom-vroom" to represent a car and "moooo" to represent a cow because of distinctive features of the sound or sound combination, involving pitch, loudness, or duration. Reichle, Siegel, and Rettie (1985) reported that some Down syndrome preschoolers were more likely to imitate prosodic features than discrete sounds. Among those who use augmentative communication systems (communication board and sign), there are behaviors that correspond somewhat to the use of idiomorphs in the vocal mode. In the graphic mode, children may use objects to represent specific needs. For example, each time a child is thirsty, he or she may travel to a counter, retrieve a glass, and offer it to a listener. In the gestural mode, a learner who wants gum from a vending machine may approach another and twist their wrist as if activating the machine. There is a significant need to examine the conditions under which children come to acquire idiomorphs. Because they frequently correspond with the onset of semantic production, attempting to harness the naturalistic intervention procedures that established their use may prove beneficial.

Vocabulary selection criteria.   Criteria used in selecting initial semantic vocabulary is a particularly troubling use for the language researcher. On one hand, the suggestion of Bloom and Lahey (1978) to begin instruction at a level of intermediate specificity makes perfect sense. Teaching a child "drink" rather than "milk" affords him or her the opportunity to communicate in a variety of situations with some hope of being understood. On the other hand, Bowerman's (1978) suggestion of being as explicit as possible makes sense in terms of establishing discrete discriminative use of new symbols. Interestingly, Bloom (1970) has proposed that at least some overgeneralizations in most children's initial semantic repertoire may be emitted intentionally; that is, the child, realizing that he or she doesn't have the correct word to fit a referent situation, uses the word in his or her repertoire that represents a best fit. If this is true, the vocabulary selection strategy suggested by Bloom and Lahey (1978) prompts the strategy of overgeneralization. Reinforcement of this response strategy may not be bad, if it is able to be remediated efficiently as new stimuli are introduced. However, for some learners, eliminating overgeneralized use of vocabulary may be particularly difficult to overcome. If this is the case, Bowerman's (1978) strategy of representing referents as specifically as possible may be more suitable. If one wanted to adhere to Bloom and Lahey's (1978) vocabulary selection strategy but minimize its problems, one could establish a "general level of specificity" vocabulary item such as "drink." Once this level was established, when new, more explicit beverage vocabulary was introduced, the learner would be taught to produce a chained utterance "drink + Coke" rather than to attempt to eliminate the use of the word "drink" in the presence of Coke. This strategy has the potentially pleasing advantage of allowing the learner to refer to unknown beverages using the term "drink" in isolation, but referring to known beverages with an explicit term "drink + Coke."

Of course, the use of a more general vocabulary selection strategy with a word like "drink" presents a second potential difficulty. "Drink" can be used semantically as an action in addition to its use as an object. Little work has been done to examine the nature of generalizing a single double function vocabulary word, such as "drink" across semantic classes, and represents an important area for future examination. Keogh and Reichle (1985) suggested using, exclusively double function words such as "drink" as actions. Their strategy thus minimizes the need for the learner to use a single word across semantic classes.

Sequencing initial intervention.   The selection of initial vocabulary to teach also depends on the extent to which one adheres to developmental data in determining when to introduce certain vocabulary items. Between the mid-1960s and mid-1970s, a plethora of data emerged describing early semantic intents used by normally developing children. Miller and Yoder (1974) suggested using frequency of occurrence in the normative data base as a criterion for sequencing the introduction of initial semantic functions. While this strategy seems logical, it presumes that all learners have a commonality of experience and common desires to communicate about those experiences. It seems quite possible that, when one considers persons with developmental disabilities, such may not be the case.

The use of available developmental data describing the acquisition of semantic production skills must be tempered with the ecologically driven communication needs of persons with developmental disabilities. Up to this point, many speech and language pathologists have been willing to accept the use of frequently occurring semantic classes as reasonable definitions of behavior to teach. Frequency of use by a normal developing population may have relatively little to do with ease of acquisition or usefulness of the behavior to any particular learner. The identification of and criteria for sequencing initial semantic production skills to teach could benefit from a systematic analysis.

Generalization and initial semantic classes. This area is ripe for systematic investigation. The evidence available suggests that when a learner is taught a specific vocabulary item in the context of one specific pragmatic intent (i.e., requesting), the use of that vocabulary item tends not to be generalized readily to encode other pragmatic intents (i.e., providing information). A logical prediction is that if one teaches a semantic class such as recurrence, using each of a variety of specific vocabulary, that vocabulary not specifically used in the context of recurrence training will not be used to encode recurrence.

A second hypothesis that needs to be studied systematically is that if a semantic function such as a recurrence is always taught in the context of a request, it (recurrence) will not be used to encode a different pragmatic intent such as commenting. Issues such as these are directly applicable to establishing communicative behavior that approximates the flexibility required to communicate in a generalized manner.

The two areas mentioned above represent far more sophisticated applications than traditionally have been associated with generalization issues in language acquisition. To date, there have been minimal attempts to address either of these areas in the applied intervention literature. However, if a learner is to learn to separate differentially pragmatic from semantic applications, if these aspects of generalized use can be addressed successfully, the learner will have tremendously greater communicative power with the vocabulary at his or her disposal.

ESTABLISHMENT OF INITIAL COMPREHENSION REPERTOIRES

The Origin of Language Comprehension

Being able to understand language requires that the learner correspond a current event to (a) his or her prior knowledge and (b) the discourse that has been emitted in the context of the interaction at hand. Out
of this correspondence, the learner must decipher propositional meaning
and the communicative intents of others with only gestures and accompanying context to assist in this process (Chapman, 1981). Initially, evidence that children comprehend communicative acts addressed to them
seems to be based more on the arrangement of the environment and the
gestures of others than on the verbal behavior of the communication.
What Chapman (1978) referred to as "comprehension strategies" represent a usable first step in assessing and teaching an initial repertoire of
language comprehension. There are a variety of interpersonal games that
children learn relatively early in life. For example, in "peekaboo," there is
a well-documented sequence of development. In this game, the adult approaches the child, covers his or her [the adult's] eyes, and then quickly
removes hands from eyes while saying "peekaboo." Sometime around 3
months of age, children begin to react to an adult-initiated game of peekaboo by smiling. Around 5 or 6 months of age, children, through repeated
practice, have come to anticipate the game such that as soon as the adult
approaches and begins the game, the child immediately responds as if the
adult had already withdrawn his or her hand and said "peekaboo." At this
point, the child clearly understands the sequence of events that make up
the peekaboo game. There is something about the interventionist's approach that cues the child that he or she should react in a particular way.

The learner's anticipatory behavior offers the basis for a valid assessment task and later an intervention strategy designed to move the child
from understanding "the game" to understanding the vocabulary associated with the game. Initially, the interventionist can focus on whether
the child's anticipations were under the instructional control of the gestures or the verbal behavior associated with the game. On some occasions
during assessment, the interventionist approaches the learner without
emitting any of the gestural cues associated with the game and says "peekaboo." If the learner responds as usual, it is possible that the interventionist's vocal behavior is being utilized as an instructional cue. Of course, in
our example, the spoken word "peekaboo" is usually offered in a characteristic singsong fashion. Consequently, it is possible that the intonation

pattern of the phrase results in the learner's identification of the game. During subsequent assessment opportunities, the word "peekaboo" can be offered in using an intonation pattern that is unique to the one that has been used predictably in "the game." To ensure that the simple presence of the adult is not serving as the cue, on some occasions he or she would approach without vocalizing. Finally, to ensure that it is the phrase "peek-aboo" controlling learner behavior, when the adult approaches and says something distinctively different from "peekaboo," the learner should refrain from responding. Once a different spoken word becomes the controlling cue for each of two separate games, the learner is beginning to engage in initial vocabulary comprehension.

There are far more empirical data describing the acquisition of semantic production than there are pertinent to the acquisition of semantic comprehension skills. Miller, Chapman, Branston, and Reichle (1980) reported that by 10–12 months of age, normal developing children comprehend the spoken names of a number of familiar persons and objects in their environment. Between approximately 13 and 15 months, children begin to understand the names of actions that the learner may emit without applying the action to an object (e.g., run, jump, dance, etc.). At approximately the same point in time, the learner begins to understand possession references such as "find Mom's hat" versus "find (child's name) hat."

The presence of the referent seems to be particularly important in the development of an initial repertoire. Miller et al. (1980) reported that when objects of which learners comprehended the spoken name were not visible, the learner's comprehension performance deteriorated greatly. This differential performance continues until children approach their second birthday. This observation is particularly important when one considers the generalizability of comprehended language.

It is not unusual for initial comprehension repertoires to be taught with referents present. Rarely do acquisition procedures (with the exception of Kent, 1974) address the generalized use of comprehension in the absence of a referent. This later emission involves the integrated use of several separate classes of behavior. Suppose, for example, that the learner is asked to get a Coke when both the learner and his or her communicative partner are in the living room and the Coke is in the refrigerator. To be successful, learners must remember the instruction as they transport themselves to the refrigerator. Further, they must correspond the referent named to the storage location of the referent. Among more handicapped learners, it may be necessary to address each of these discrete skills to ensure generalized emission of a targeted comprehension skill.

Critical Issues

The transition from "situational" to "language" comprehension. The conditions under which comprehension skills are taught represent a particularly important area for future scrutiny. Traditionally, interventionists have been interested in controlling for any contextual variables that may influence learner performance during a comprehension task. This strategy has represented an attempt to utilize comprehension assessment information as a criterion reference against which the implementation of intervention procedures can be judged. As such, traditional comprehension intervention formats require that the interventionist eliminate as many of the nonlinguistic cues as possible from the intervention task.

An alternative approach requires establishing natural contextual variables that exert control over the learner's behavior and that can be paired with a verbal utterance directed to the learner. After a history of pairing verbal utterances with contextual cues, attempts are made to separate systematically the verbal cue from the controlling contextual variables. Assume that initially the interventionist's performing the action of "standing up" results in the learner's also standing up. After a history is established in which the interventionist says "stand up" followed by actually standing (with the learner then contingently standing), he or she may begin delaying the delivery of the contextual cue (standing up). This approach represents an effort to shift stimulus control from the contextual cue of standing up to the verbal cue of saying "stand up." Although stimulus control features have been demonstrated to be highly efficient in teaching new repertoires of behavior, they have been used rather sparingly in the language comprehension intervention literature.

For some learners, it may be a reasonable instructional objective to establish situational comprehension skills that are under the control of consistently occurring nonverbal environmental cues. For example, when teachers give learners a verbal directive to move from one activity to another, they frequently accompany their directive with a pointing cue. This pointing cue represents a salient nonverbal gesture that would be of great use if learners consistently made use of it. Following a pointing cue is a form of "line of regard." It requires to look where the partner has directed his or her attention. Although pointing prompts are used frequently by teachers/parents, and although there is a literature describing the emergence of this skill, there is virtually no empirically based intervention literature regarding the establishment of this behavior.

Following a pointer to direct learner movement is but one application of situational comprehension. A number of other situational cues are nonverbal but serve to direct the learner's social behavior. Some of these, such as getting one's coat as others in a room prepare to exit, influence the learner's ability to terminate an ongoing activity and, no doubt, are affected by the learner's ability to imitate. Often, however, opportunities for situational comprehension as a prompt to terminate an activity, such as seeking out an adult to check one's performance at the end of a task, do not necessarily involve imitative behavior. There have been few reported empirical efforts that address systematically implemented intervention procedures to establish situational comprehension.

Comprehending suprasegmental aspects of utterances. Traditionally, language interventionists consider the segmental aspects of a speech signal (sounds and sound combinations) as elements to address in comprehension intervention tasks. Suprasegmental aspects of utterances involve combinations of pitch, duration, and loudness used in conjunction with segmental features of speech. There are some data to suggest that young children may utilize suprasegmental information in their initial attempts to decipher communicative behavior addressed to them.

Chapman (1981) reported that young normal children demonstrate the ability to discriminate between utterances directed to them versus others in the immediate environment; that is, when two adults are conversing and in the middle of the interaction, one adult addresses the child, even very young children shift attention from the activity at hand to the adult. Chapman surmised that this attentiveness may be due to the adult's use of significantly higher pitched verbal behavior with young children than they use in addressing older children or adults (Garnica, 1977). Around the time that normal children begin producing a variety of one-word utterances, they begin differentiating when an adult's utterance addressed to them demands an action versus a verbal response even though it may be sometime later (depending on the type of adult-produced utterance) before they are capable of comprehending the exact semantic content of the message.

Some persons with developmental disabilities may be more apt to attend to and discriminate among suprasegmental than segmental aspects of language addressed to them. Reichle, Siegel, and Rettie (1985) reported that some preschoolers with Down Syndrome were more apt to imitate suprasegmental features of pitch change, loudness change, and duration change than segmental features of consonant plus vowel. Currently, there are few data on teaching learners to utilize suprasegmental cues in comprehension tasks. For learners who have significant difficulty learning to discriminate among segmental features of language, the utilization of suprasegmental features may be an alternative in teaching initial vocal mode discriminations.

The order of difficulty among semantic classes. The developmental literature suggests that normal individuals begin to comprehend the names of objects before they begin to comprehend the names of actions (Miller et al., 1980). As a result, interventionists, for the most part, have chosen to teach object-name comprehension prior to action-name comprehension. This vocabulary-sequencing decision represents a leap of logic in the absence of strong empirical support. Even if action vocabulary proved to be more difficult to teach, it is not clear that requiring comprehension of object names first would accelerate the rate at which action vocabulary were acquired.

A critical area for research involves comparing the relative difficulty in establishing comprehension of object and action vocabulary. An investigation employing two serial sequences and one concurrent sequence of introducing vocabulary could be used. One serial sequence would require teaching a repertoire of comprehended object vocabulary prior to the introduction of procedures to teach the learner to comprehend action vocabulary. A second serial intervention sequence would involve teaching the comprehension of a repertoire of action vocabulary prior to initiating object vocabulary. The concurrent strategy would involve teaching both object and action vocabulary concurrently. This concurrent strategy could be further divided to explore the relative efficiency of teaching homogeneous sets of object vocabulary and separate sets of action vocabulary compared to training sets that consisted of one action vocabulary.

The relative difficulty of object and action vocabulary may be somewhat different when the interventionist considers an augmentative communication mode such as signing. Because of the inherent ability to represent movement in sign, it may be that action vocabulary was somehwat more guessable in sign, which in turn might tend to lessen differences in difficulty between object and action vocabulary. Most recently, Ratner (1988) demonstrated that among adult normal listeners, action vocabulary was significantly more guessable than action vocabulary represented via line-drawn representation.

Although it is accepted that comprehension of object vocabulary is easier to establish than comprehension of action vocabulary, there is a scarcity of literature addressing relative differences in difficulty in terms of intervention. This difference, along with the most efficient sequence in which to introduce object and action vocabulary, needs to be further explored.

Variables influencing generalization. A functional command of a repertoire of comprehended vocabulary requires that learners be able to act on information received event though action may not occur immediately and may occur in an environment other than that in which the utterance was directed to the learner. Undoubtedly, there are a large number of variables that influence the learner's ability to extend his or her language comprehension skills across time and settings. Even the more obvious factors, however, have received relatively little attention in the intervention literature.

One evidence of comprehension is the ability to respond to the verbal directive of another with a contingent action. Sometimes the contingent action is to the advantage of the requester as in "Get [speaker's name] a Coke." At other times, following a directive benefits the listener: "Get [listener's name] a Coke." Aside from understanding the language in each of these utterances, the listener must (a) be able to match the referent "Coke" with its storage location, (b) remember the instruction during travel to (and in some cases from) the storage location, and (c) refrain from being distracted along the way. The learner's competency in dealing with each of these variables influences greatly the learner's ability to use his or her language comprehension abilities. For persons who have developmental disabilities, there are virtually no empirical data validating assessment strategies that systematically explore each of these areas in the context of a language comprehension task. This knowledge gap is particularly troublesome given our extensive knowledge of technologies that could have a significant impact on the establishment of intervention options.

For example, the application of time-delay procedures applied to the interval of time passing prior to the delivery of a prompted reminder of an instruction or the application of a shifting criterion design applied to the distance traveled prior to the delivery of an instructional reminder could be ways to teach learners to remember instructions. In another example, matching storage location to object is a variable that lends itself to a number of functional program activities. For example, in the case of "Coke," a learner could engage in putting groceries away from a shopping activity to develop a history of pairing an object to its storage location.

The bulk of curricula currently available that address beginning comprehension skills focus more on the use of more traditional intervention procedures to establish comprehension under more tightly controlled stimulus conditions. There is a significant need to match the ecological demands with the conditions under which comprehension is taught.

INTEGRATION OF COMPREHENSION AND PRODUCTION SKILLS INTO CONVERSATIONAL EXCHANGES

As mentioned earlier, research in the area of mother-child interaction suggests that during a child's first year, mothers structure their utterances to follow their child's vocalizations in order to develop interactive turn-taking (Snow, 1977). During the second year, children demonstrate comprehension of turn-taking responsibilities by responding to adult speech with actions (Shatz, 1978). It is also at the beginning of the second year that children begin to produce speech contingent to their mother's utterances. The early 1970s resulted in detailed investigations of correlative relationships between classes of child and parent communicative behavior. More recently, interest has focused upon the conditions that prompt children to use particular interactional strategies. One of these conditions involves the adult listener's request for clarification when the child's preceding utterance is in need of repair. There is limited literature regarding the effect that a child's unsuccessful turn in conversation has on his or her subsequent utterances.

Repair Strategies

Gallagher (1977) examined the repair strategies employed by 18 children, 6 each at Brown (1973) Stages I, II, and III[2] when an adult listener provided feedback to suggest that their preceding utterance has not been understood. An adult experimenter visited the subjects in their homes and spontaneous language samples were obtained. Approximately 20 times during a 1-hour session, the experimenter pretended not to understand the child's message and asked "What?" The examiner's query did not follow any specific child utterance. Results indicated a significantly greater use of revisions (phonetic change, elaboration, reduction, or substitution) than either repetitions or no responses, by all children. Additionally, the structure of the revisions suggested the use of strategies consistent within language stages, but different across stages of linguistic development. The Brown Stage I children made significantly more phonetic change revisions and significantly less reduction revisions than did the Brown Stage II or III children. Additionally, the Brown Stage III subjects made significantly more substitution revisions than did the Brown Stage I or II children.

Gallagher and Darnton (1978) partially replicated Gallagher (1977) with language-disordered children. The researchers found that children with language disorders also used revisions as their repair strategy significantly more often than they used repetitions or no responses. However, unlike Brown Stage I, II, and III normal children, the pattern of revision behavior among children with language disorders was similar across stages but qualitatively different from that reported with normal children. Results indicated that there were no significant differences in the proportions of

---

[2] Brown Stages refer to mean length of utterance in morphemes ranges among normal developing children. Stage I children have a mean length of utterance between 1.0 and 2.0; Stage II children have MLU between 2.0 and 2.5; Stage III have MLU between 2.5 and 3.0.

the four revision types (phonetic change, elaboration, reduction, and substitution) across language stages.

Wilcox and Webster (1980) used a design similar to that of Gallagher (1977). However, experimenter-initiated requests for clarification followed the child's requesting behavior only. Subjects included 16 normal children between 17 and 24 months (all of whom were operating in Brown Stage I). Based upon spontaneous language samples and interviews with mothers, experimenters placed each subject in one of four categories: (a) high syntax–low vocabulary, (b) high syntax–high vocabulary, (c) low syntax–high vocabulary, or (d) low syntax–low vocabulary. The experimenter provided two types of feedback to indicate that the child's message wasn't understood: (a) "What?" indicated the request was not accurately received, and (b) "Yes, I see it" indicated the intent of the request was misunderstood. Feedback was directed to each child's single-word requests only. Results indicated that the children of all subjects revised (by expansion, substitution, or gesture) their utterances significantly more often in the misunderstood condition and repeated their utterances significantly more often in the "What?" condition. Additionally, children classified as "low vocabulary" used repetition significantly more often as their repair strategy than did children classified as "high vocabulary." Choice of revision type varied as a function of syntactic ability. Overall, children categorized as "low syntax" employed gestural revisions significantly more often than children classified "high syntax." Additionally, the "high syntax" children used elaborations and multiword substitutions significantly more often than the "low syntax" children. The authors concluded that type of listener feedback influenced the repair strategies chosen in response to communicative failure, thus demonstrating the discriminative use of different responses for different listener feedback.

Collectively, the available literature suggests that children learning language demonstrate a sensitivity to the responsibilities of conversation maintenance by repairing their message when listener feedback indicates it was not accurately received. The literature also suggests that the extent of learners' language skills influences significantly the repair strategies that they will select.

Research Issues

Very little information is available regarding the repair strategies used by individuals with language deficits. As a result, there have been few efforts to examine systematically how to teach developmental disabled populations to invoke conversational repair strategies. While it seems perfectly logical that individuals' ability to comprehend language would influence significantly their ability to participate in a conversational exchange, there is surprisingly little empirical information regarding this issue. The problem of comprehension deficit may be a particular problem for individuals who rely on the use of electronic communication aids.

Electronic communication aid technology makes it possible to store a lengthy and complex message that can be generated via synthesized or digitized speech. In order to produce the message, the learner may have to select a single logograph displayed among a matrix of logographs. For example, to communicate that the utterance "If you'd like to, we could go to McDonald's and order an exquisitely prepared meal" the learner might select a single logo of the McDonald golden arches. To an unfamiliar listener, the impression would be given that the augmentative system user had an extensive productive repertoire and was probably capable of comprehending the message that was produced. Consequently, the language addressed to the augmentative system user has a good chance of being matched to the sophistication of the synthesized/digitized message that he or she produced. The potential problem is that augmentative communication systems may impose conversational difficulties by giving the impression that a learner is a more sophisticated communicator than he or she really is.

Some learners may have difficulty participating in a socially satisfying communicative exchange because they don't have an adequate vocabulary to support conversational demands. It has been speculated that echolalic behavior may be emitted in an attempt to hold a speaking partner's attention. More subtle examples of strategies to hold a conversational partner may include overusing a topic (for example, saying "I went fishing" several times within a short conversational exchange). A variation of this strategy involves using a stereotypic phrase as a conversational opener. For example, each time the learner engages in a conversational exchange, his or her first utterance is "I went fishing." In an effort to maintain an interaction, learners may produce speech that does not actually correspond to their actions. For example, a learner may always begin an interaction by saying "I sure worked hard today," when in fact it is the weekend and the learner watched TV all day.

For the most part, the problem described above may represent communicative mismatches between speaker and listener in which the learner either comprehends a speaker's utterance but has inadequate production skills to respond, or has adequate production skills but, because he or she cannot understand the partner's utterances, cannot respond relevantly. There are little empirical data that address comprehension and production deficits as a contributor to conversational deficits. There is even less empirical information regarding conversationally based intervention strategies to deal with these communicative deficits.

The Relationship Between Comprehension and Production

Traditionally, it was believed that comprehension of a given language form preceded production of that same form, although more current research has challenged this assumption (Chapman & Miller, 1975; Guess, 1969; Guess & Baer, 1973). Chapman and Miller (1975) studied the subject-verb-object construction with 15 intellectually normal subjects who ranged in age from 1.5 to 2.5 years. Each subject was presented with a comprehension task in which he or she was to perform tasks described by the investigator. Additionally, each learner was required to engage in a production task in which the investigator performed an action and the learner was asked to describe what had happened. The dependent variable was correct assignment of the subject and object role. Data suggested that events in which the expected roles of animate and inanimate objects were reversed (such as "the table pushes the boy") tended to be described expressively just as accurately as those that conformed to normal expectations ("the boy pushes the table"). In comprehension, there was a tendency for children to associate animate objects with agents and inanimate objects with recipients of action. Thus, the data suggest that young normal children may use word order rules to convey some meanings expressively before they use those rules to decode meaning expressed by others. Evidence from earlier points in language development are equally compelling. Miller and Chapman (1984) reported that children who overgeneralize words in production (calling all adult females "Mommy") still understood the word to mean *their* mothers.

Related to the preceding findings are several studies with developmentally disabled populations. Leonard, Camarata, Rowan, and Chapman (1982) investigated language impaired children who were not intellectually delayed. Subjects showed comprehension deficits at least 6 months below levels predicted by chronological age. They computed the proportion of words that the children produced to the words that the children comprehended. This proportion was then compared to the same proportion computed for younger but language-normal children. No differences were reported between the two groups. Both groups produced approximately 30% of the words that they comprehended. The observation that children typically produce a subset of the words that they comprehend is what may lead many to believe that comprehension is easier than or even a prerequisite to production. However, Leonard (1988) reported that he had observed both normal and language impaired children who produced words that they were not capable of comprehending.

There is an intervention literature that addresses the relationship between comprehension and production. Guess and Baer (1973) reported that in training severely intellectually delayed learners to comprehend and produce plural morphemes, there was no generalization from comprehension to production or vice versa. They also reported, however, that training in one modality may facilitate the acquisition of the other; that is, teaching a learner to produce a pluralization rule may speed the acquisition in learning to comprehend that rule and vice versa. Cuvo and Riva (1980) reported some transfer across the modalities of comprehension and production in teaching coin names to persons with intellectual delay. After teaching four children with moderate intellectual delays to comprehend and produce plurals, Siegel and Vogt (1984) concluded that teaching plurals on one mode facilitates acquisition in the remaining mode. The data in their investigation provided modest support for teaching production mode first; learners who first received production training required fewer instructional opportunities than those learners receiving comprehension training first.

The relationship between comprehension and production has significant implications for interventionists attempting to design efficient intervention protocols. Most recent evidence suggests that comprehension and production might best be viewed as separate but intertwined classes of behavior. If this is true, the traditional intervention practice of teaching comprehension of a given communication form prior to production may not be necessary. Several important issues regarding the sequencing of comprehension and production targets remain. Siegel and Vogt (1984) reported modest evidence for teaching production skills prior to comprehension. Intervention programs designed for persons with severe handicaps focus primarily on production as an initial communicative repertoire. Guess, Sailor, & Baer (1977) suggested that teaching production first allows clients to learn that they can control their environment through the use of language. They propose that once clients learn what communicative behavior can do for them, they will be more motivated to acquire additional language skills. To date, however, there have been few intervention efforts that have systematically compared the relative effect of ordering comprehension and production intervention targets on the acquisition of new communicative skills.

CONCLUSIONS

Our knowledge of best practices in the area of communication intervention with persons who have severe developmental disabilities is growing at an unprecedented rate. Still, this very positive conclusion must be tempered by the qualification that there are a large number of critically important questions that remain unresolved. In spite of our ability to describe the earliest emergence of communicative behavior among normally developing populations, relatively little headway has been made in identifying classes of behavior that are necessary to establish an initial communicative repertoire. Once communicative targets are identified for a prospective recipient of communication, interventionists must consider the relative emphasis to place on each of the three communication modes (verbal, gestural, and graphic systems). For persons with developmental disabilities who have the most severe handicaps, this decision may be particularly difficult. Currently, there are few empirically validated guidelines to assist the interventionist.

Initial vocabulary selected for intervention usually represents items in which the learner has great interest. Most interventionists serving people with developmental disabilities agree that requesting represents a initial pragmatic intent to teach. Unfortunately, we know relatively little about the wisdom of that decision. Limited evidence available suggests that assigning a specific vocabulary item to a single pragmatic intent may set the occasion for the learner to fail to use the vocabulary item taught to express a variety of other communicative intents. One might question which communicative intent (e.g., requesting, providing information) to address in the earliest phase of an instructional program. One must also ask whether a vocabulary item eventually to be used across several different pragmatic intents should be targeted for one particular intent first.

A growing literature suggests that the selection of initial pragmatic intents to teach should be influenced by those intents of greatest interest to the learner. Some learners who engage in high rates of socially unacceptable methods of communicating have been shown to benefit greatly from the establishment of a program that focuses on more socially appropriate methods of communicating. These successful demonstrations have broadened tremendously the role of communication intervention in the educational planning process. Clearly, the utilization of communication intervention is an important element of behavior management protocols. Determining the most efficient methods of establishing new repertoires of communicative behavior with individuals who engage in high rates of socially motivated excess behaviors, however, remains an important area for further empirical scrutiny.

Another issue in initial vocabulary selection introduced addresses the level of specificity at which to target initial vocabulary. For example, the vocabulary items "apple," "fruit," and "food" could all be used to represent a real apple. Communication interventionists fall into two separate camps on this issue. Using a less specific vocabulary item creates a greater number and variety of instructional opportunities for the interventionist; for example, "fruit" can be used to describe or request apples, bananas, peaches, and any other fruit. On the other hand, if the word "apple" is taught, the learner can only correctly use his or her new vocabulary in the presence of apples, thereby limiting the utility. This issue of vocabulary specificity has not been addressed sufficiently to render helpful advice to the planning team responsible for decisions regarding the selection of vocabulary.

If the intervention is implemented sufficiently, learners will acquire more sophisticated methods of representing thoughts and ideas than they once expressed using simpler forms. For example, initially the learner may have pointed to obtain an apple. After learning the vocabulary "apple," the learner now has a more explicit, exacting method to request it. Many communication intervention curricula treat only the establishment of the new behavior and ignore specifying the conditions under which it might be desirable for the learner to continue to use his or her pointing. This issue seems particularly important when one considers the issue of speed and effort that may be required for a person with multiple handicaps to participate in a communicative exchange. To date, there has been a very limited infusion of relevant literature on establishing the conditional discrimination to the actual establishment of communicative behavior.

The trend among communication interventionists is to treat the establishment of conversational skills at the outset of the intervention process. Interestingly, establishing initial interaction, maintenance, and termination competencies requires relatively little understanding of the language being used. More sophisticated conversations, however, require the integrated use of comprehension and production skills. For individuals with developmental disabilities, there are a large number of rather subtle skills to be acquired such as being able to judge when to request and/or provide clarifying utterances in order to keep a conversation progressing. Compared to our knowledge of language production, we know relatively little about comprehension. The bulk of the available literature has not addressed comprehensively the variety of situational variables that influence the learner's ability to exhibit language comprehension in natural settings.

In spite of our limited knowledge, the research questions that challenge the communication interventionist today are encouraging in that they reflect a certain confidence and optimism. No longer are researchers concerned with highly controlled demonstrations that communicative behavior can be taught. Instead, the concern has shifted toward addressing the variables that will be most critical if we are to ensure that the recipients of intervention use their newly established communication behavior optimally.

REFERENCES

Bates, E., Benigni, L., Bretherton, I., Camioni, L., & Volterra, V. (1976). From gesture to first word: On cognitive and social prerequisites. In M. Lewis & L. Rosenblom (Eds.), *Origins of behavior: Language and communication* (pp. 247–308). New York: John Wiley & Sons.

Bates, E., Benigni, L., Bretherton, I., Camioni, L., & Volterra, V. (1979). *The emergence of symbols: Cognition and communication in infancy.* New York: Academic Press.

Bell, S. M., & Ainsworth, M. D. S. (1972). Infant crying and maternal responsiveness. *Child Development, 43,* 1171–1190.

Bellugi, U., & Klima, E. (1976). Two faces of sign: Iconic and abstract. In S. Harnad, H. Steklis, & J. Lancester (Eds.), *Origins and evolution of language and speech* (pp. 514–538). New York: New York Academy of Sciences.

Bloom, L. (1970). *Language development: Structure and function in emerging grammars.* Cambridge, MA: MIT Press.

Bloom, L., & Lahey, M. (1978). *Language development and language disorders.* New York: Wiley.

Bloomberg, K. (1984). *The comparative translucency of initial lexical items represented by five graphic symbol systems.* Unpublished master's thesis, Purdue University, West Lafayette, IN.

Bowerman, M. (1978). Semantic and syntactic development: A review of what, when and how in language acquisition. In R. L. Schiefelbusch (Ed.), *Bases of language intervention* (pp. 97–189). Austin, TX: PRO-ED.

Bricker, D., Dennison, L., & Bricker, W. (1976). *A language intervention program for developmentally young children* (MCCD Monograph Series I). Miami, FL: University of Miami, Mailman Center for Child Development.

Brown, R. (1973). *A first language.* Cambridge, MA: Harvard University Press.

Brownlee, J. R., & Bakeman, R. (1981). Hitting in toddler-peer interaction. *Child Development, 52,* 1076–1079.

Buzolich, M. (1984). *Interaction analysis of augmented and normal adult communicators.* Unpublished doctoral dissertation, University of California, San Francisco, CA.

Calculator, S., & Dollaghan, C. (1982). The use of communication boards in a residential setting: An evaluation. *Journal of Speech and Hearing Disorders, 47,* 281–287.

Calculator, S., & Luchko, C. (1983). Evaluating the effectiveness of a communication board training program. *Journal of Speech and Hearing Disorders, 48,* 185–191.

Caplan, F. (1973). *The first twelve months of life.* New York: Dunlap.

Carr, E. G. (1977). The motivation of self-injurious behavior: A review of some hypotheses. *Psychological Bulletin, 84*(4), 800–816.

Carr, E. G. (1982). Sign language. In R. Koegel, A. Rincover, & A. Egal (Eds.), *Educating and understanding autistic children* (pp. 142–157). San Diego, CA: College Hill Press.

Carr, E. G., & Durand, V. M. (1985). Reducing behavior problems through functional communication training. *Journal of Applied Behavior Analysis, 18,* 111–126.

Carr, E., & Kologinsky, E. (1983). Acquisition of sign language by autistic children, II: Spontaneity and generalization effects. *Journal of Applied Behavior Analysis, 16,* 297–314.

Carr, E. G., & Newsom, C. D. (1985). Demand-related tantrums: Conceptualization and treatment. *Behavior Modification, 9*(4), 403–426.

Carr, E. G., Newsom, C. D., & Binkoff, J. A. (1976). Stimulus control of self-destructive behavior in a psychotic child. *Journal of Abnormal Child Psychology, 4*(2), 139–153.

Carr, E. G., Newsom, C. D., & Binkoff, J. A. (1980). Escape as a factor in the aggressive behavior of two retarded children. *Journal of Applied Behavior Analysis, 13,* 101–117.

Carter, A. (1973, March). *Development of presyntactic communication system: A case study.* Paper presented at SRCD meeting, Philadelphia, PA.

Chapman, R. (1978). Comprehension strategies in children. In J. Cavanaugh & W. Strange (Eds.), *Speech and language in the laboratory school and clinic* (pp. 308–327). Cambridge, MA: MIT Press.

Chapman, R. (1981). Mother-child interaction in the second year of life: Its role in language development. In R. Schiefelbusch & D. Bricker (Eds.), *Early language: Acquisition and intervention* (pp. 201–250). Baltimore, MD: University Park Press.

Chapman, R., & Miller, J. (1975). Word order in early two and three word utterances: Does production precede comprehension? *Journal of Speech and Hearing Research, 18,* 355–371.

Chapman, R., & Miller, J. (1980). Analyzing language and communication in the child. In R. L. Schiefelbusch (Ed.), *Nonspeech language and communication: Analysis and intervention* (pp. 159–196). Baltimore, MD: University Park Press.

Charlop, M., Schreibman, L., & Thibodeau, M. (1985). Increasing spontaneous verbal responding in autistic children using a time delay procedure. *Journal of Applied Behavior Analysis, 18,* 155–166.

Cirrin, F., & Rowland, C. (1985). Communicative assessment of nonverbal youths with severe, profound mental retardation. *Mental Retardation, 3,* 52–62.

Clark, C. R. (1984). A close look at the standard Rebus system and Blissymbolics. *Journal of the Association for Persons with Severe Handicaps, 9,* 37–48.

Curcio, F. (1978). Sensorimotor functioning and communication in mute autistic children. *Journal of Autism and Childhood Schizophrenia, 3,* 281–292.

Cuvo, A., & Riva, M. (1980). Generalization and transfer between comprehension and production: A combination of retarded and nonretarded persons. *Journal of Applied Behavior Analysis, 13,* 315–331.

Donnellan, A. M., Mirenda, P. L., Mesaros, R. A., & Fassbender, L. L. (1984). Analyzing the communicative functions of aberrant behavior. *Journal of the Association for Persons with Severe Handicaps, 9*(3), 201–212.

Doss, L. S. (1988). *The effects of communication instruction on food stealing in adults with developmental disabilities.* Unpublished doctoral dissertation, University of Minnesota, Minneapolis, MN.

Durand, V. M. (1982). Analysis and intervention of self-injurious behavior. *Journal of the Association for the Severely Handicapped, 7*(1), 44–53.

Favell, J. E., McGimsey, J. F., & Schell, R. M. (1982). Treatment of self-injury by providing alternate sensory activities. *Analysis and Intervention in Developmental Disabilities, 2,* 83–104.

Gallagher, T. (1977). Revision behaviors in the speech of normal children developing language. *Journal of Speech and Hearing Research, 20,* 303–318.

Gallagher, T., & Darnton, B. (1978). Conversational aspects of the speech of language disordered children: Revision behaviors. *Journal of Speech and Hearing Research, 21,* 118–136.

Garnica, O. (1977). Some prosodic and paralinguistic features of speech to young children. In C. Snow & C. Ferguson (Eds.), *Talking to children* (pp. 63–88). Cambridge, MA: Cambridge University Press.

Glennen, S. L., & Calculator, S. N. (1985). Training functional communication board use: A pragmatic approach. *Augmentative and Alternative Communication, 1,* 134–142.

Gobbi, L., Cipani, E., Hudson, C., & Lapenta-Neudeck, R. (1986). Developing spontaneous requesting among children with severe mental retardation. *Mental Retardation, 24,* 357–363.

Goetz, L., Gee, K., & Sailor, W. (1985). Using a behavior chain interruption strategy to teach communication skills to students with severe disabilities. *Journal of the Association for Persons with Severe Handicaps, 10,* 21–30.

Goossens̀, C. (1983). *The use of gestural communication systems with nonspeakers.* Workshop presented at Mayer Children's Institute, Omaha, NE.

Guess, D. (1969). A functional analysis of receptive language and productive speech: Acquisition of the plural morpheme. *JABA, 2,* 55–64.

Guess, D., & Baer, D. (1973). An analysis of individual differences in generalization between receptive and productive language in retarded children. *Journal of Applied Behavior Analysis, 6,* 311–329.

Guess, D., Benson, H., & Siegel-Causey, E. (1985). Concepts and issues related to choicemaking and autonomy among persons with severe disabilities. *Journal of the Association for Persons with Severe Handicaps, 10,* 79–86.

Guess, D., Sailor, W., & Baer, D. (1977). Children with limited language. In R. L. Schiefelbusch (Ed.), *Language intervention strategies* (pp. 360–377). Baltimore, MD: University Park Press.

Hall, G., & Sundberg, M. L. (1987). Teaching mands by manipulating conditioned establishing operations. *Analysis of Verbal Behavior, 5,* 41–53.

Halle, J. (1987). Teaching language in the natural environment: An analysis of spontaneity. *Journal of the Association for Persons with Severe Handicaps, 12,* 28–37.

Halle, J., Baer, D., & Spradlin, J. (1981). An analysis of teachers' generalized use of delay in helping children: A stimulus control procedure to increase language use in handicapped children. *Journal of Applied Behavior Analysis, 14,* 389–409.

Harris/Vanderheiden, D., & Vanderheiden, G. (1980). Enhancing the development of communicative interaction in non-vocal severely physically handicapped children. In R. Schiefelbusch (Ed.), *Non-speech language intervention processes* (pp. 227–257). Baltimore, MD: University Park Press.

Hart, B. (1981). Pragmatics: How language is used. *Analysis and Intervention in Developmental Disabilities, 1,* 299–313.

Hart, B. (1985). Naturalistic language training techniques. In S. Warren & A. Rogers-Warren (Eds.), *Teaching functional language* (pp. 63–88). Baltimore, MD: University Park Press.

Hart, B., & Risley, T. (1968). Establishing use of descriptive adjectives in the spontaneous speech of disadvantaged preschool children. *Journal of Applied Behavior Analysis, 1,* 109–120.

Horner, R. H., Bellamy, G. T., & Colvin, G. T. (1984). Responding in the presence of nontrained stimuli: Implications of generalization error patterns. *Journal of the Association for Persons with Severe Handicaps, 9,* 287–295.

Hurlbut, B., Iwata, B., & Green, J. (1982). Nonvocal language acquisition in adolescents with severe physical disabilities: Blissymbol versus iconic stimulus formats. *Journal of Applied Behavior Analysis, 15,* 241–258.

Iwata, B. A., Dorsey, M. F., Slifer, K. J., Bauman, K. E., & Richman, G. S. (1982). Toward a functional analysis of self-injury. *Analysis and Intervention in Developmental Disabilities, 2,* 3–20.

Kent, L. (1974). *Language acquisition program for the retarded or multiply impaired.* Champaign, IL: Champaign Research Press.

Keogh, W., & Reichle, J. (1985). Communication intervention for the "difficult-to-teach" severely handicapped. In S. Warren & A. Rogers-Warren (Eds.), *Teaching functional language* (pp. 157–194). Baltimore, MD: University Park Press.

Kraat, A. (1983). Communication interaction between aid users and others: An international perspective. *Proceedings of the 2nd International Conference on Rehabilitation Engineering.* Ottawa, Canada.

Lamarre, J., & Holland, J. G. (1985). The functional independence of mands and tacts. *Journal of the Experimental Analysis of Behavior, 43,* 5–19.

Leonard, L. (1988). Lexical development and processing in specific language impairment. In R. Schiefelbusch & L. Lloyd (Eds.), *Language perspectives: Acquisition, retardation, and intervention* (2nd ed.) (pp. 69–90). Baltimore, MD: University Park Press.

Leonard, L., Camarata, S., Rowan, L., & Chapman, K. (1982). The communicative functions of lexical usage by language impaired children. *Applied Psycholinguistics, 3,* 109–125.

Leonhart, I., & Maharaj, S. (1979). *Pictogram ideogram communication.* Regina, Canada: George Reed Foundation for the Handicapped.

Lewis, M., & Cherry, L. (1977). Social behavior and language acquisition. In M. Lewis & L. Rosenblum (Eds.), *Interaction, conversation and the development of language* (pp. 227–246). New York: John Wiley.

Light, J., Collier, B., & Parnes, P. (1985). Communicative interaction between young nonspeaking physically disabled children and their primary care givers: Part 1, Discourse patterns. *AAC, 1,* 74–83.

Lossing, C. (1981). *A technique for the quantification of non-vocal communicative performance by listeners.* Unpublished master's thesis, University of Washington, Seattle, WA.

Lovaas, O. I., Freitag, G., Gold, V. J., & Kassorla, I. C. (1965). Experimental studies in childhood schizophrenia: Analysis of self-destructive behavior. *Journal of Experimental Child Psychology, 2,* 67–84.

Lovaas, O. I., Newsom, C. D., & Hickman, C. (1987). Self-stimulatory behavior and perceptual reinforcement. *Journal of Applied Behavior Analysis, 20,* 45–68.

Lovaas, O. I., Schreibman, L., & Koegel, R. L. (1974). A behavior modification approach to the treatment of autistic children. *Journal of Autism and Childhood Schizophrenia, 4,* 111–129.

Lovaas, O. I., & Simmons, J. Q. (1969). Manipulation of self-destruction in three retarded children. *Journal of Applied Behavior Analysis, 2,* 143–157.

MacDonald, J. (1985). Language through conversation: A model for intervention with language-delayed persons. In S. Warren & A. Rogers-Warren (Eds.), *Teaching functional language* (pp. 89–122). Baltimore, MD: University Park Press.

Maharaj, S. (1980). *Pictogram ideogram communication.* Regina, Canada: George Reed Foundation for the Handicapped.

McCook, B., Cipani, E., Madigan, K., & LaCampagne, J. (1988). Developing requesting behavior: Acquisition, fluency, and generality. *Mental Retardation, 26,* 137–143.

McLean, J., & Snyder-McLean, L. (1988). Application of pragmatics to severely mentally retarded children and youth. In R. Schiefelbusch & L. Lloyd (Eds.), *Language perspectives: Acquisition, retardation, and intervention* (2nd ed.) (pp. 255–290). Austin, TX: PRO-ED.

Meyer, L. H., & Evans, I. M. (1986). Modification of excess behavior: An adaptive and functional approach for educational and community contexts. In R. H. Horner, L. H. Meyer, & H. D. Fredericks (Eds.), *Education of learners with severe handicaps: Exemplary service strategies* (pp. 315–350). Baltimore, MD: Paul H. Brookes.

Miller, J. (1981). *Assessing language production in children: Experimental procedures.* Baltimore, MD: University Park Press.

Miller, J. F., & Chapman, R. S. (1984). Disorders of communication: Investigating the development of language of mentally retarded children. *American Journal of Mental Deficiency, 88,* 536–545.

Miller, J., Chapman, R., Branston, M., & Reichle, J. (1980). Language comprehension in sensorimotor stages V and VI. *Journal of Speech and Hearing Research, 23,* 284–311.

Miller, J., Netsell, R., & Rosen, P. (1979). Unpublished manuscript, University of Wisconsin-Madison, WI.

Miller, J., & Yoder, D. (1974). An ontogenetic language teaching strategy for retarded children. In R. Schiefelbusch & L. Lloyd (Eds.), *Language perspectives: Acquisition, retardation, and intervention* (pp. 505–528). Baltimore, MD: University Park Press.

Mizuko, M. (1987). *Transparency and recall of symbols among intellectually handicapped adults.* Unpublished manuscript, University of Minnesota—Duluth, MN.

Muma, J. (1986). *Language acquisition: A functionalistic perspective.* Austin, TX: PRO-ED.

Murphy, C. (1978). Pointing in the context of a shared activity. *Child Development, 49,* 371–380.

Murphy, C., & Messer, D. (1977). Mothers, infants and pointing: A study of gesture. In H. R. Shaffer (Ed.), *Studies in mother-infant interaction* (pp. 325–354). New York: Academic Press.

Naor, E., & Balthazar, E. (1975). Provision of language index for severely and profoundly retarded individuals. *American Journal of Mental Deficiency, 79,* 717–725.

Oller, K. (1980). The emergence of the sounds of speech in infants. In G. Yeni-Komshsian, J. Kavanaugh, & C. Ferguson (Eds.), *Child phonology: Production* (pp. 93–112). New York: Academic Press.

Oller, D., & Smith, B. (1977). Effect of final syllable position on vowel duration in infant babbling. *Journal of the Acoustical Society of America, 67,* 994–997.

Prizant, B. M. (1983). Language acquisition and communicative behavior in autism: Toward an understanding of the "whole" of it. *Journal of Speech and Hearing Disorders, 48,* 296–307.

Prizant, B. M., & Duchan, J. F. (1981). The functions of immediate echolalia in autistic children. *Journal of Speech and Hearing Disorders, 46,* 241–249.

Prizant, B. M., & Rydell, P. J. (1984). Analysis of functions of delayed echolalia in autistic children. *Journal of Speech and Hearing Research, 27,* 183–192.

Prutting, C. A. (1982). Pragmatics as social competence. *Journal of Speech and Hearing Disorders, 47,* 123–134.

Ratner, H. (1988). *Translucency and transparency of graphic and gestural mode communication systems.* Unpublished manuscript, University of Minnesota, Minneapolis, MN.

Reich, R. (1984). *Language development.* Columbus, OH: Charles Merrill.

Reichle, J. (1987). *Establishing a tacting repertoire among persons with severe handicaps.* Unpublished manuscript, University of Minnesota, Minneapolis, MN.

Reichle, J., & Keogh, W. (1986). Communication instruction for learners with severe handicaps: Some unresolved issues. In R. Horner, L. Meyer, & H. Fredericks (Eds.), *Education of learners with severe handicaps: Exemplary service strategies* (pp. 189–220). Baltimore, MD: Paul H. Brookes.

Reichle, J., Schermer, G., & Anderson, H. (1987). *Teaching the discriminative use of a requesting assistance symbol to an adult with severe handicaps.* Unpublished manuscript, University of Minnesota, Minneapolis, MN.

Reichle, J., Siegel, G., & Rettie, M. (1985). Matching prosodic and sound features: Performance of Down's preschoolers. *Journal of Communication Disorders, 18,* 149–159.

Reichle, J., & Ward, M. (1985). Teaching discriminative use of signed English and encoding graphic modality to an autistic adolescent. *Language, Speech, and Hearing Services in Schools, 16,* 58–63.

Reichle, J., & Yoder, D. E. (1985). Communication board use in severely handicapped learners. *Language, Speech, and Hearing Services in Schools, 16,* 146–157.

Rincover, A., Cook, R., Peoples, A., & Packard, D. (1979). Sensory extinction and sensory reinforcement principles for programming multiple adaptive behavior change. *Journal of Applied Behavior Analysis, 12,* 221–233.

Rincover, A., & Devany, J. (1982). The application of sensory extinction procedures to self-injury. *Analysis and Intervention in Developmental Disabilities, 2,* 67–81.

Romski, M., Sevcik, R., & Pate, J. (1988). Establishment of symbolic communication in persons with severe mental retardation. *Journal of Speech and Hearing Disorders, 53,* 94–107.

Rowe, J. A., & Rapp, D. L. (1980). Tantrums: Remediation through communication. *Child Care, Health, and Development, 6,* 197–208.

Savage-Rumbaugh, E. S. (1984). Verbal behavior at a procedural level in a chimpanzee. *Journal of the Experimental Analysis of Behavior, 41,* 223–250.

Schuler, A. L., & Goetz, L. (1981). The assessment of severe language disabilities: Communicative and cognitive considerations. *Analysis and Intervention in Developmental Disabilities, 1,* 333–346.

Shane, H., & Bashir, A. (1980). Election criteria for the adoption of an augmentative communication system: Preliminary considerations. *Journal of Speech and Hearing Disorders, 45,* 408–414.

Shatz, M. (1978). On the development of communicative understandings: An early strategy for interpreting and responding to messages. *Cognitive Psychology, 10,* 271–301.

Siegel, G., Katsuki, J., & Potechin, G. (1985). Comment on Mabel Rice's "Contemporary accounts of cognition/language relationship." *Journal of Speech and Hearing Disorders, 50,* 302–303.

Siegel, G., & Vogt, M. (1984). Pluralization instruction in comprehension and production. *JSHD, 49,* 128–135.

Sigafoos, J., Doss, S., & Reichle, J. (1989). Developing mand and tact repertoires in persons with severe developmental disabilities using graphic symbols. *Research in Developmental Disabilities, 10,* 183–200.

Skinner, B. F. (1957). *Verbal behavior.* New York: Appleton-Century-Crofts.

Snow, C. (1977). *Talking to children: Language input and acquisition.* New York: Cambridge University Press.

Stremel-Campbell, K., & Campbell, R. (1985). Training techniques that may facilitate generalization. In S. Warren & A. Rogers-Warren (Eds.), *Teaching functional language* (pp. 251–285). Baltimore, MD: University Park Press.

Talkington, L. W., Hall, S., & Altman, R. (1971). Communication deficits and aggression in the mentally retarded. *American Journal of Mental Deficiency, 76,* 235–237.

Trevarthen, C., & Hubley, P. (1979). Secondary intersubjectivity: Confidence confiding and acts of meaning in the first year. In A. Lock (Ed.), *Action, gesture and symbol* (pp. 183–229). London: Academic Press.

Weeks, M., & Gaylord-Ross, R. (1981). Task difficulty and aberrant behavior in severely handicapped students. *Journal of Applied Behavior Analysis, 14,* 449–463.

Wilcox, M., & Webster, E. (1980). Early discourse behavior: An analysis of children's responses to listener feedback. *Child Development, 51,* 1120–1125.

Wolff, P. H. (1969). The natural history of crying and other vocalizations in early infancy. In B. M. Foss (Ed.), *Determinants of infant behavior* (Vol. 4, pp. 81–108). London: Methuen.

Yoder, D. E., & Kraat, A. (1983). Intervention issues in non-speech communication. In J. Miller, D. Yoder, & R. Schiefelbusch (Eds.), *Contemporary issues in language intervention. ASHA Reports, 12,* 27–51. Rockville, MD: American Speech-Language-Hearing Association.

CHAPTER 6

Education and
Community Integration Experiences
of Deaf Adolescents and Young Adults

MICHAEL BULLIS   **BRUCE BULL**
JOHN FREEBURG   **JOSEPH SENDELBAUGH**

Deaf adolescents and young adults form a substantial subgroup of all persons with disabilities in this country (Edgar & Hayden, 1984/1985; Schein & Delk, 1974). In the 1982–83 school year, between 75,000 and 90,000 students received special educational services in the United States because of hearing loss (Karchmer, 1985). Analysis of data files from the state/federal system of vocational rehabilitation revealed that 25,000 to 29,000 persons with mild to severe hearing impairments received services in 1981 (El-Khiami, 1986). Despite the prevalence of deaf adolescents and young adults in society, however, few research reviews have been compiled on their education and community integration experiences.

This chapter provides such a synthesis of available empirical information. The discussion focuses on persons who are deaf and devoid of serious, secondary disabilities (e.g., deaf-blindness); and the age range from middle teens to middle twenties is emphasized. This slice of life is termed the "transition years" (Coleman, 1974), and currently is the subject of intense interest relative to all persons with disabilities (Clark & Knowlton, 1987). Indeed, the concept of school-to-community transition has been identified as a major national priority in the field of special education and rehabilitation (Will, 1984). Thus, a distinct "transition" flavor is maintained in this chapter. We do not deal with personality and social development; instead, the reader is referred to an excellent publication by Greenberg and Kushé (in press) for coverage of this topic. The first section of the chapter provides background information on this population; the

The preparation of this chapter was supported in part by Grant # G008635209 from the National Institute on Disability and Rehabilitation Research. However, no official endorsement of this manuscript by that agency should be inferred.

second focuses on assessment and educational interventions, and the third discusses the experience of people in the community who are deaf.

BACKGROUND INFORMATION

This part of the chapter provides an overview of certain characteristics of persons who are deaf. The first section describes the demographics of the population, and the second discusses commonly used communication systems.

Demography

Inferences about groups of people are of little value without awareness of who belongs to a particular unit and who does not. This awareness is of particular importance when looking at the population of hearing-impaired persons in the United States. The complex task of defining the population opens this section, followed by some general characteristics of the group and a description of common etiologies.

Definitions. The term "hearing impairments" covers a deceptively wide range of handicaps due to hearing loss. When we speak of those who are hearing impaired, we often mean people of all ages and hearing abilities. Such gross categorization can be incorrect or at least misleading. Accordingly, it is necessary to define more clearly the parameters of the population.

There are three major types of hearing loss (Breadle, 1982). *Conductive impairments* are localized in the outer or middle ear. Hearing loss in the inner ear, or between the inner ear mechanism and brainstem, is termed *sensorineural loss*. Impairments resulting from damage to the brainstem or the brain itself are categorized as *central processing hearing losses*. The result of any of these three types of impairments can vary from a mild unilateral (one-sided loss) to a profound bilateral (two-sided) hearing loss. National and international definitions of hearing impairments differ dramatically: Some embody functional criteria, and others emphasize hearing threshold via clinically assessed decibel (dB) levels (dB is a unit for measuring sound volume). One widely used definition in this country was adopted by the Conference of Educational Administrators Serving the Deaf (CEASD) (Frisina, 1974):

> Deafness refers to the condition of individuals whose hearing is disabled and is expressed in terms of speech or other sounds calibrated for frequency and intensity. Such individuals are classified according to the following categories of deafness. There is substantial variability among individuals in all categories,

and any diagnosis must be a functional one. The stated requirements in communication and education associated with these levels are to be assumed necessary for each infant/child/adult until proved otherwise:

1. Level I, 35–54 dB. Individuals in this category routinely do not require special class/school placement; they routinely do require special speech and hearing assistance.
2. Level II, 55–69 dB. These individuals occasionally require special class/school placement; they routinely require special speech, hearing, and language assistance.
3. Level III, 70–89 dB. Individuals in this category of deafness routinely require special class/school placement; they also routinely require special speech, hearing, language, and educational assistance.
4. Level IV, 90 dB and beyond. These individuals routinely require special class/school placement; they also routinely require special speech, hearing, language, and educational assistance. (p. 8)

Generally speaking, persons with the severest hearing loss (i.e., Level IV and often Level III) are considered "deaf" and people at the other end of the continuum (i.e., Level I and Level II) are referred to as "hard of hearing." CEASD differentiated further between levels of impairment by defining a hard-of-hearing person as one whose hearing is disabled to an extent that makes it difficult, but does not rule out, the understanding of speech through the ear alone, with or without a hearing aid. A deaf person, then, is one whose hearing is disabled to an extent that precludes the understanding of speech through the ear alone, with or without the use of a hearing aid. It should be noted that this chapter focuses on this latter group. A similar, functional definition was used by Schein and Delk (1974), who described deafness as the inability to hear and understand speech. A related description was presented in 1979 by the Rehabilitation Services Administration (RSA) for use in describing the hearing impairments of rehabilitation clients (Jacobs, 1979). A person was considered deaf when hearing was impaired to the extent that he or she depended primarily on visual communication such as writing, lipreading, manual communication, and gestures. A person was considered hard-of-hearing when hearing was impaired, but not to the extent that manual communication systems were necessary to interact with others.

These three definitions demonstrate movement away from classifying hearing impairments strictly by virtue of quantitative hearing ability. Instead the focus is on the way in which an individual functions pragmatically, although some reference to hearing loss in terms of dB level may be included. Obvious quantitative differences exist between the hearing abilities of persons on opposite ends of the continuum of hearing impairments.

The *qualitative* differences between the groups, however, often dictate divergent lifestyles. Switzer and Williams (1967) write, "The hard of hearing population differ only in degree from the general population, while deaf people stand apart psychologically and socially" (p. 249).

Such variations create problems in describing the entire population in a succinct manner. Some of the research in this area includes heterogeneous samples; inferences from results of these studies are difficult to make. Definitions of hearing ability alone, moreover, do not take into consideration other important variables. Age at onset, type of communication system(s) utilized, etiology, and hearing aid use are all important factors in the communication and functioning of individuals with hearing loss.

A crucial variable is the age at which an individual first experiences the hearing impairment, or the "age at onset." For example, an individual may be born deaf (congenital) or acquire the condition later in life (adventitious). This dichotomy may be taken even further. Persons who are deafened prelingually (deafness occurring before the development of fluent spoken language, usually before age 3) typically find it difficult to become proficient in written and spoken language, since their exposure to the spoken word has been so limited. On the other hand, postlingually deafened individuals (deafness experienced after the age of 3) have generally had some exposure to and experience with language that may foster the ability to communicate. In addition, the postlingually deafened population can be divided by age of onset with respect to vocation. In general, prevocational deafness occurs before the 19th birthday, and postvocational deafness occurs after that age.

Hearing aid use is an important communication factor for thousands of persons. Essentially, hearing aids are any wearable instrument(s) for assisting those with impaired hearing to hear (Sinclair, 1979). By amplifying sounds within the speech range, hearing aids can, in many cases, improve a person's ability to hear spoken language. People with conductive losses typically experience an improvement in hearing due to the amplification afforded by hearing aids (Breadle, 1982). However, people with sensorineural and central processing hearing losses are less likely to benefit. Unlike conductive loss, where sound waves are reduced before entering the inner ear, these impairments involve a problem with the reception or transmission of sounds (Breadle, 1982). A relatively new advancement in technology, the cochlear implant, may benefit some persons with a profound sensorineural hearing loss. This device is implanted in the cochlea, and can help the wearer recognize environmental sounds.

Population parameters.   "Elusive" aptly describes the numerical estimates of the number of hearing impaired persons and, specifically, of those who are deaf. Statistics from the 1971 National Health Survey showed that hearing impairment was the largest single handicapping condition of persons in the United States (Wilder, 1975). An average of 7,160 persons per 100,000 or over 14 million people, were affected with some type of hearing loss. Of these 14 million hearing-impaired people, only 322,000 (2.3%) were considered to be deaf (Wilder, 1975). The National Health Survey in 1977 categorized the data in a somewhat different fashion (Feller, 1981), finding an average of about 7,640 persons per 100,000 to be hearing impaired. In this study the category of deafness was combined with all bilateral hearing impairments so the percentage of people considered to be deaf was not available.

Probably the most widely known investigation of persons who are deaf in the United States was the National Census of the Deaf Population (NCDP) conducted in 1974 (Schein & Delk, 1974). This study attempted to determine the size and configurations of the population, and looked at characteristics of these persons compared to individuals without hearing disabilities. Prevalence figures of 6,603 persons who are hearing impaired per 100,000 were found. Also, 873 people per 100,000 were identified as deaf; of those, roughly 100 per 100,000 were deafened prelingually and 203 per 100,000 were deafened prevocationally.

Though prevalence has been the subject of discussion, there is greater certainty when dealing with other population characteristics. Among those deafened adventitiously, it is well documented that a positive correlation exists between age and severe hearing impairment (Gentile, 1975; Moss & Parsons, 1986; Ries, 1982). In other words, it is more common to have impaired hearing as one grows older; further, the chance of that loss being severe increases with age. It is important to realize that a geriatric population with postvocational hearing impairments will possess needs different from younger people deafened prelingually or prevocationally.

Another finding that has repeatedly shown up in studies is the higher prevalence of males then females who are deaf. Several studies (Schein & Delk, 1974; Moss & Parsons, 1986) report that males comprise from 52 to 57% of the deaf population. Schein (1979) stated that the rate of females who are deaf is less before age 55 but, because women tend to live longer than men, the number of deaf women may exceed that of males in the older segments of the population.

One of the most extensively examined segments of the population is school-age children. This is due, in large part, to the fact that demographic data are compiled for determining educational services and programs. Sontag, Smith, and Certo (1977) estimated that approximately 377,000 school-age children were eligible for special education services due to hearing impairments. Of these, 49,000 were deaf and the remainder, hard-of-hearing. Craig and Craig (1977) stated that 58,468 children who were hearing impaired were enrolled in special school programs. Rawlings and Trybus (1978) reported that 60,231 students who were deaf were supplied special education programs, and a total enrollment of about 69,000 was estimated. The U.S. Department of Education (1984) reported 74,279 hard-of-hearing or deaf children, ages 3 to 21, were served in the 1983–84 school year. For the 1982–83 school year, Karchmer (1985) reported that about 75,000 students received special education services nationally because of hearing loss. He estimated that the actual number of students who were hearing impaired and served by special education services was between 75,000 and 90,000. Finally, Craig and Craig (1985) reported that 49,552 hearing impaired students were enrolled in special education programs as of October 1984. Discrepancies clearly exist between reported figures; most probably, these fluctuations are due to the different reporting systems along with real difference in prevalence over time.

Etiology.   Certain types of etiologies tend to cause a more profound hearing impairment than others. In the 1982–83 Survey of Hearing Impaired Children and Youth (Karchmer, 1985), 64% of the students who had experienced meningitis were found to have a profound hearing loss, as compared with only 38% of students with unknown causes experiencing a similar level of impairment. Other causes of hearing impairments may lead to the presence of additional disabilities. For example, 40% of students whose hearing impairment was caused by maternal rubella in the 1982–83 survey had other disabilities. Early knowledge of a person's etiology may assist in the determination of the best medical, educational, or rehabilitation approach to use with that individual (Karchmer, 1985). Unfortunately, many investigations find the largest single cause of hearing loss to be "unknown" (Ries, 1973; Vernon, 1968; Karchmer, 1985). Nevertheless, common etiologies of prelingual deafness such as heredity, maternal rubella, cytomegalovirus (CMV), Rh-factor incompatibility, meningitis, and complications of prematurity have been identified (Moores, 1987).

Heredity/genetics may well be the largest cause of deafness. Vernon (1987) estimated that 40% to 60% of deafness is related to genetic determinants. With advancements in research, over 150 distinct forms of genetic hearing loss have been determined (McKusick, 1983).

Maternal rubella was a major cause of sensory impairments for children born in the 1960s. A pregnant woman exposed to this viral infection would typically experience a mild illness, though her developing fetus could be seriously affected. Sensory damage was especially likely if rubella was contracted during the first trimester. The "rubella bulge" (a disproportionately high number of hearing impaired persons in public schools in the

1970s and early 1980s) was due to the rubella epidemic of 1963–1965. An efficient vaccine has been developed to minimize this disease and its consequences.

Cytomegalovirus (CMV), an etiology for which there is no effective vaccine, has only recently received wide attention. CMV is a herpes-type virus posing a serious risk to developing fetuses. The effects of CMV, like rubella, can be quite varied, but it is a common cause of mental retardation as well as hearing and vision loss. It is estimated that 5,000 children per year will be born in the United States with some type of disability caused by CMV (Gehrz, 1984).

Hearing impairments due to negative Rh-factor incompatibility result when the blood type of the mother is Rh negative and that of the fetus is Rh positive. Due to this incompatibility, the mother's antibodies destroy the blood cells of the fetus. Typically, the first born child is not affected but subsequent children are increasingly at risk. Technological advancements in in-utero blood transfusions have been perfected recently, reducing the effect of the Rh-negative factor on the fetus. Moreover, Rh-immune globulin can be given to the Rh-negative mother after the first child, thereby destroying the antibodies and giving the mother's next child no more increased risk than that of the first (Vernon, 1987).

Meningitis, the inflammation of the meninges (the covering of the brain), is estimated to be responsible for 10% of childhood hearing loss (Pappas, 1985). The disease typically strikes young children at an age that makes it difficult to detect the early symptoms of headache and stiff neck. Recent use of antibiotics has improved the survival rate, though it is not uncommon for children who were affected with meningitis to experience additional disabilities in conjunction with deafness.

Finally, premature birth appears to be a cause of deafness. Vernon (1987) stated that prematurity is more common among deaf persons than in the hearing population; specifically, 17% of all persons who are deaf were born prematurely. Moores (1987) has predicted that, as advancements are made in techniques to save babies born prematurely, the number of deaf children and children who are deaf with multiple disabilities will increase.

Secondary handicapping conditions. A portion of the hearing impaired population has additional disabilities, though the actual percentage of these individuals is a subject of some discussion (e.g., Stewart, 1978). Of the estimated 75,000 to 90,000 school-age children and young adults who were deaf and eligible for special education in 1982–83, 31% were found to have additional disabilities (Karchmer, 1985). Craig and Craig (1985) reported that just over 20% of students who were hearing impaired had multiple disabilities. And, in a later report, Craig and Craig (1986) indicated that 8,390 students, or just over 19% of the total number receiving special education services, had additional handicapping conditions. Schlidroth (1987) found that of students 12 to 20 years of age, 32% of those served in residential schools had multiple handicaps, as compared to 26% of students served in mainstreamed settings.

Despite the disparity between these figures (some of which can be attributed to the different school years when the data were gathered and differences in reporting procedures), there is little doubt that a sizable segment of the hearing-impaired population has secondary disabilities. A discussion of these individuals and their specific needs is not within the scope of this chapter, although some sections touch on issues affecting this group. It is imperative, though, to realize that the presence of a secondary disability requires considerations over and above the needs mandated by partial or total hearing loss.

Communication

Of the issues that span the history of education of deaf children, none has been more prevalent than the debate on the most appropriate method of communication to be used in the classroom. Parents, teachers, and adults who are hearing impaired eventually find themselves aligned with a philosophy that supports one of two broad communication approaches: the oral method and the manual communication method. This section reviews briefly the characteristics of both as they are used by school programs for deaf students. Included are descriptions of American Sign Language, Pidgin Sign English, and some related Manually Coded English systems. Also presented is a review of communication devices commonly employed in education and in service programs.

Common terms. Before proceeding, we shall give definitions of the principal terms related to the communication options available to deaf people: oralism, total communication, fingerspelling, American Sign Language, Pidgin Sign English, and Manually Coded English.

"Oralism" or the "oral-aural" method refers to the communication approach that places emphasis on the child's expression and reception of spoken language. Educators who employ this approach stress the development of speech and speechreading (lipreading) skills and the use of any residual hearing through the amplification of sound. Gestures and signs are prohibited (Moores, 1978).

"Total Communication" (TC) was defined by the Conference of Executives of American Schools for the Deaf (Gannon, 1981) as follows: "Total Communication is a philosophy incorporating appropriate aural, manual, and oral modes of communication in order to insure effective communication with and among hearing impaired persons" (p. 369). This orientation allows instructors to select whatever communication modalities, in their opinion, most effectively convey information to the student (Benderly, 1980; Mayberry & Wodlinger-Cohen, 1987). The philosophy also enforces the students' right to choose to pursue the development of any and all communication skills (i.e., auditory training, lipreading, sign language, etc.).

"Fingerspelling" refers to manually representing the words of a spoken language by using a separate handshape for each letter of the alphabet (Baker & Cokely, 1980). It is often used in manual communication to represent words that have no sign such as people's names and other proper nouns.

"American Sign Language" (ASL) has been referred to as Ameslan, Sign, or Sign Language. It is the visual/gestural language that was developed naturally by deaf people in the United States (Cokely, 1975). It is often the first language of deaf children born to deaf parents (Baker & Cokely, 1980) and it has its own unique grammatical structure (Fant, 1974; Stokoe, 1972). Each ASL sign indicates a concept rather than a specific word. ASL has no written form and the use of fingerspelling is minimal. It is the preferred mode of communication among the majority of adults who identify themselves as part of the "Deaf Culture." Indeed, ASL is considered an entry requirement for full membership into the Culture (Jacobs, 1980). For most persons who are deaf, except the 5% to 10% born to deaf parents, ASL is learned later in life, during their education if they attend a residential school, or after leaving school if they attended a mainstream education program (Padden & Markowicz, 1982).

"Manually Coded English" (MCE) is a general term for all artificially developed communication systems that may use signs and fingerspelling to represent English (Baker & Cokely, 1980). Within most of these systems, each sign is used to convey a single word rather than a concept. Both the sender and receiver of the message must have an understanding of English grammar and syntax in order to communicate using this method. Clearly, then, MCE lends itself to the sender's simultaneous production of signs and spoken English; this is an advantage if the receiver has any degree of residual hearing or if he or she possesses lipreading talent. Education programs using these methods share the belief that through early exposure to a manual form of English, one can enhance a child's language development, educational achievement, speech production, and speech-reading proficiency (Wilbur, 1979).

"Pidgin Sign English" (PSE) is described by Baker and Cokely (1980) as "varieties of signing used by deaf and hearing people which combine certain elements of both ASL and English. The varieties of PSE found in deaf people's signing often include more of the features of ASL, whereas the varieties of PSE found in hearing people's signing often include more English-like structures" (p. 461).

Oral communication in the classroom. Essentially, the oral method is a communication approach that places major emphasis on the child's speech and speechreading development; classroom instruction is in spoken English only. The primary motivation for stressing the development of oral communication lies in the hope of giving the student skills to communicate in the dominant language mode: speech. As an instructional method, however, the oral-only approach presents the risk that the student may receive only a portion of the information sent. In essence, the oral approach focuses on the student's weakest receptive area (hearing) rather than on his or her most receptive mode (vision). Moores (1978) pointed out that the use of oral instruction to develop speech and lipreading ability has had little empirical investigation. Accordingly there has been a shift to incorporate manual communication in most school programs (Mayberry & Wodlinger-Cohen, 1987). In 1970, fully 85% of programs for children with severe or profound deafness used oral-only instruction; however, in 1985 only 5% of all programs still used an oral-only approach (Nober, 1985).

Use of manual communication in the classroom. The communication systems that currently predominate in educational settings are those that would be classified as Manually Coded English (MCE). Educational programs support the learning of English (Wodlinger-Cohen, 1986); and, as pointed out earlier, MCE lends itself to the simultaneous use of spoken English and signs. This dual usage allows students to take advantage of any residual hearing they may possess while also receiving English in a visual and more accessible mode. It has been reported that the majority of youths who are deaf receive their instruction through the use of MCE (Bornstein, 1973), and that 95% of adolescents who use signs to communicate all or part of their needs use an MCE system (Nober, 1985). Following are brief descriptions of two of the more common systems that embrace an MCE focus: Signing Exact English and Signed English.

1. *Signing Exact English.* Fundamental to Signing Exact English (SEE II) is the use of only one sign for each English word. In order to understand SEE communication, one must be able to associate an English term with its appropriate referent. For example, when using the word "run"

the sign for "run" is the same in all situations. In the sentences, "Please run to the corner," and "Run the water for me," the same sign is used. Thus, the receiver of the communication must understand the structure of the phrases in order to gain full understanding of their meaning.

Also, each base or root word (sometimes referred to as a morpheme) is treated as a single unit. Examples of such words would be "fish," "play," "who," and "what." These words cannot be broken down into smaller units of meaning. Complex words are simply root words to which suffixes are added; therefore, "play" becomes "plays" by adding a sign that represents "s."

Another method used to distinguish words with similar conceptual bases involves initializing (taking the first letter of an English word and incorporating it into the sign for that word). For example, the letter "e" is formed on both hands as the hands are pushed forward in front of the body to indicate "effort." Likewise, "t" is used to indicate "try" and "a" for attempt.

There is difficulty in the use of SEE II when conveying irregular verbs. For instance, it is somewhat awkward when the past-tense indicator "-ed" is applied to this special group of words. To clarify, if the verb "skip" were to be changed to past tense, it would be signed "skip + -ED" to form the word "skipped." When an irregular verb is encountered, past tense is also indicated by the "-ED" ending; therefore, "run" becomes "runned."

2. *Signed English.* Signed English refers to a system consisting of approximately 2,500 signs that represent English words: 1,700 traditional signs and 800 signs that were borrowed from other sign systems (Bornstein, 1973). In Signed English, emphasis is placed upon the production of specific signs to represent specific English words. Some special signs have been developed to indicate tense, possessives, plurals, and so on. Signed English has an advantage in that the vast majority of signs in this system use the same conceptual base as ASL, yet the system can parallel spoken English in grammatical structure. Signed English is most often used by members of The Deaf Culture when in communication situations with hearing persons who sign (Bolton, 1976).

Both Signing Exact English and Signed English are examples of Manually Coded English systems that are a visual representation of spoken English. Indeed, the great advantage of employing a visual English system is the potential for every word to be seen. Conversely, if a communicator does not sign each word as it is said, the receiver misses that bit of the English sentence (Mayberry & Wodlinger-Cohen, 1987). Further, these systems represent efforts to incorporate traditional ASL signs into a manual communication system based on English order. Some professionals and institutions, however, prefer to create new signs arbitrarily, rather than determine first if there is a traditional sign that exists for the desired term. Bornstein (1973) has estimated that only 75 to 80% of MCE vocabulary is standardized across educational programs in the United States. If this estimate is correct, students could be required to relearn as much as one-fourth of their vocabulary in order to communicate with individuals from other school districts.

Despite their long history, the use of MCE systems in the school environment is generally considered to be in need of further development. Early European educators assumed that the use of signs interfered with the development of reading, writing, and spoken language skills. Recent empirical evidence suggests that the use of signs with speech (simultaneous method) increases language and speech production skills as compared with instruction using oral/aural presentation only (Delaney, Stuckless, & Walter, 1984; Meadow, 1980; Montgomery, 1966; Newell, 1978; Quigley, 1969; Schlesinger & Meadow, 1972; Stevenson, 1964; Stuckless & Birch, 1966). Schlesinger and Meadow (1972) reported that in studies of young children (19 months of age or younger) who were deaf the subjects were capable of developing proficiency in English through the use of signs. In cases where a child who is deaf is born to deaf parents, the use of ASL in the preschool years correlated positively to the child's ability to learn English language structure. Further, children involved in experimental TC programs have consistently shown higher levels of performance on standard English language usage tests and tests of speech reading ability when compared to individuals without such exposure (Mayberry & Wodlinger-Cohen, 1987).

Use of interpreters in education.　Nober (1985) notes that 74% of all deaf children in 1984 received their school instruction in programs close to their home. Because of increased enrollments in public school programs and the mainstreaming of deaf children in the general school population (Karchmer, 1985), the demand for interpreters in educational settings has increased rapidly. To meet this need, college-level programs preparing sign language interpreters flourished throughout the 1970s. By 1984, there were 54 postsecondary interpreter-training programs in existence (Craig & Craig, 1985).

The majority of all full-time interpreting positions are now in the public classroom setting (Gustason, 1985). Classroom interpreters are now recognized as essential to the application of the mainstreaming concept. They provide a vehicle for hearing and deaf students to interact (Newmann-Solow, 1981) and they allow access to public education, especially in settings where the regular classroom instructor does not hold certification in deaf education. Postsecondary training institutions at every level now admit deaf students to their programs. According to Frishberg (1986), those that have been successful at maintaining their enrollment of deaf students offer support personnel that include counselors, notetakers, tutors, and interpreters. Today over 55 colleges and universities offer comprehensive support services. In 1985 these institutions awarded a total of 422 degrees and certificates to hearing-impaired students, largely through the benefit of interpreted instruction (Rawlings, Karchmer, DeCaro, & Egelston-Dodd, 1986).

Assistive communication devices. The broad population of people who are hearing impaired can be assisted to reach their ultimate communication potential through recent advancements in communication technology (Leavitt, 1987). The devices developed can be categorized as those that either enhance sound (for people who can benefit from amplification) or those that offer a visual representation of an auditory signal (for people who are more severely deafened). Four assistive communication technologies are used commonly and shall be described here.

Electromagnetic Induction Systems, also known as "loop systems," are designed to improve the hearing-aid user's speech discrimination. The loop system requires the listener to have no special equipment other than a hearing aid with a telephone or "T" switch. Only those sounds transmitted through the system are heard. With all extraneous background noise blocked out, the hearing-aid user can achieve the best possible understanding of speech. The loop system allows a student, for example, to hear an instructor speaking softly in the front of the room.

Telecommunication Devices for the Deaf (TDD) and their related signaling equipment provide deaf people with instantaneous communication by telephone to all others who have TDDs, thereby overcoming what has been a traditional barrier to full communication for this population. The telephone ring is relayed to a light that flashes to signal the incoming call. As TDD users type their message, a signal representing each letter is electrically transmitted over phone lines to the receiving TDD where the signal is converted and the corresponding message is printed. The conversation is limited only by the typing speed of the users. A 1984 study (TDI, Inc.) reported that over 100,000 people in the United States use TDDs. To foster the use of this technology among people with hearing impairments, 13 states have legislated support of a free TDD loan program. Most of these states also employ a third-party relay service for TDD users who wish to contact hearing individuals who do not have the necessary equipment (Klinefelter, 1986).

Signal-alerting devices are often adapted to be of benefit to people who are deaf. These devices include visual fire and emergency alarms, wireless vibrating pagers, and strobe-light alarm clocks. Several organizations have also been successful in training dogs to assist people who are deaf to become more communicatively independent. The dogs visually or tactually alert their owners to a variety of sounds including doorbells, baby cries, and the sound of a potential intruder.

Closed-captioned television programming provides a printed representation of the television sound track at the bottom of the television screen, enabling an individual to read what is not heard. Currently, more than 250,000 telecaption decoders are connected to the television sets of people who are deaf, providing over 250 hours per week of visually accessible programming (National Captioning Institute, personal communication, October 31, 1988). Several hundred home video titles have also been captioned for entertainment and educational purposes. After the purchase of the decoder (about $200), there is no charge for receiving captions, as the cost of the service is shared by networks, program sponsors, corporations, foundations and by the U.S. Department of Education. Developers of the caption service are promoting its benefits as an education tool with potential to assist people to learn English as a second language and to help both deaf and hearing children practice reading. One study (Jensema, 1985) concluded that "severe to profoundly deaf students learn and retain sight words better when closed captioned T.V. is used as a medium for instruction that when traditional print medium is used" (p. 11). In this research the pairing of a picture stimulus with printed English appeared to facilitate reading comprehension and promote motivation, lending support to use of captions in teaching reading.

To summarize, it appears that the philosophy of Total Communication, which encourages the use of all oral, aural, and manual communication methods, is the overwhelming system of preference in the educational setting. Signs, many of which are borrowed from the language of the Deaf Culture (ASL), are produced simultaneously with spoken language, utilizing the student's visual and auditory channels in order to achieve the optimum transmission of thought. Although fewer in number, strong oral-only programs continue to offer the hope that lipreading and speaking talents can be developed sufficiently. However, evidence suggests that early exposure to simultaneous sign and speech may in fact foster the growth of spoken language as effectively as a strictly oral approach. Setting the issue of speech skills aside, proponents of the use of sign language respect the Deaf Culture and the visual language that they share: ASL. Finally, technological advances such as TDDs and telecaptioning appear to enhance the development of students' language and facilitate the teaching of school subjects.

ASSESSMENT PROCEDURES AND EDUCATIONAL INTERVENTIONS

In recent years the functional preparation (e.g., vocational and independent living skill training) of persons with disabilities has received great attention (e.g., Brolin & Kokaska, 1979). This type of educational orientation has been emphasized in the field of deafness, as well (Dwyer, 1985; Munson & Egelston, 1975; Ouellette & Dwyer, 1985). Accordingly, two topics are discussed in this section: assessment procedures and education practices. An overview of a research project currently in progress is also provided.

Assessment

Data derived from assessment and evaluation procedures form the cornerstone of career and vocational education programs. These results provide fundamental information on the initial status of the person, on ways to instruct or train that individual, and on the impact of intervention programs. Nowhere on the continuum of educational and community services is the gathering of measurement data so important as during the time of transition from secondary school to community. It is imperative that services at this juncture be focused and powerful enough to facilitate community placement (Clark & Knowlton, 1987; Will, 1984) and thus paramount that this subject be reviewed for deaf persons. We offer here an overview of traditional psychometric assessment techniques and problems, academic testing procedures, and career/vocational evaluation approaches. The reader is referred to recent volumes by Elliott, Glass, and Evans (1987); Heller, Flohr, and Zegans (1987); and Stewart (1986a) for a more complete treatment of this topic.

Traditional assessment. Traditional assessment techniques, or psychometric methods (Critchfield, 1986), include those procedures designed to gather information on an individual's intelligence or social/personality structure (Halpern & Fuhrer, 1984). By and large, these methods, which embody a product-oriented assessment orientation (How smart is an individual? How much does the person know? How does the subject feel?) predominate in the field of deafness (Elliott et al., 1987; Heller et al., 1987; Levine, 1974; Stewart, 1986a). It should be stressed that this discussion is directed toward the use of these instruments and their results in planning and evaluating transition and rehabilitation efforts. The utility of these tools in therapeutic situations lies outside of the scope and purpose of this chapter.

Substantial effort has been devoted to both the development and/or adaptation of traditional, product-oriented measures for deaf persons. To illustrate, the following tests have been the object of such research:

16PF (Jacobs, in press; Jensema, 1975; Trybus, 1973)
Tennessee Self Concept Scale (Gibson-Harman & Austin, 1985)
Hiskey-Nebraska Test of Learning Aptitude (Watson & Goldgar, 1985)
Meadow/Kendall Social-Emotional Assessment Inventory (Meadow, 1980)
Wechsler Intelligence Scales (Evans, 1980; Miller, 1984; Ray, 1982; Sullivan, 1982)
Behavior Problem Checklist (Hirshoren & Schnittjer, 1979)
Locus of Control Inventory for the Deaf (Dowaliby, McKee, & Maher, 1983)
Rorschach (Acree, Orr, & Schleisenger, 1986)
House-Tree-Person Projective Drawing Technique (Ouellette, in press)

The bulk of these studies, though, have failed to establish acceptable psychometric levels for these instruments (Holm, 1987; Stewart, 1986b; Watson, 1979).

In lieu of population-specific instruments, the most common method of assessing either the intelligence or social/personality status of deaf individuals is to use standard tests (e.g., Wechsler Scales, Bender-Gestalt) administered by the clinician in the client's communication modality (e.g., sign language), or through an interpreter who acts as a conduit for information between the clinician and the client (Levine, 1974). Inherent in this approach are two beliefs. When using measures standardized on a general population, one assumes that the test results for a deaf individual will have similar meaning as for a peer without such a condition. Second, because the testing is conducted in the client's usual mode of communication (e.g., manual communication, ASL), the results are valid.

There is some credence to the belief that instruments standardized on a hearing population have relevance for persons who are deaf; that is, these results give an idea of how individuals compare with their peers without disabilities. This information is important, as a primary goal of the service system is to assist persons with disabilities to function similarly to the general public. However, it is clear that many who are deaf experience widespread problems in performing on intelligence and personality tests, problems that result in poor scores irrespective of the individual's actual ability on the particular trait (Allen, 1984; Critchfield, 1986; Evans, 1980; Hirshoren, Hurley, & Kavale, 1979; Hurley, Hirshoren, Hunt, & Kavale, 1979; Jensema, 1975; Miller, 1984; Ray, 1982; Rudner, 1978; Stewart, 1986b; Sullivan, 1982; Yandell, 1986). Does a full-scale intelligence score of 65 *really* mean that the client falls into the mildly retarded range of intelligence and should be treated accordingly? Or does it mean that he or she could not understand the test questions and scored poorly, rendering the diagnosis of mental retardation inappropriate? Addressing this issue, Watson (1979) stated:

> The unique communications systems and cultural characteristics of deaf persons pose very real problems to the assessment process. . . . Because of the lack of standardization on a deaf population and inadequate adaptations, what appear to be valuable tools in the evaluation on some disabled persons become only gross approximations of a deaf person's skills. Often these tools become a deterrent rather than a facilitator of rehabilitation services. (p. 53)

General guidelines to follow in the interpretation of these types of test results may alleviate these problems (e.g., Heller & Harris, 1987; Orr, DeMatteo, Heller, Lee, & Nguyen, 1987; Stewart, 1986a; Yandell, 1986). For example, it is a recommended practice to gather considerable information on the client's sociodemographic history, communication skills, and scores on other tests in addition to examining performance on primary measures. And, when testing a client's IQ, it is recommended that the Wechsler Scales be used and that the Performance Score be regarded as a true indicator of the person's intelligence (e.g., Elliott et al., 1987; Heller et al., 1987; Stewart, 1986a). All of this information is then weighed carefully to gain a comprehensive overview of the individual before drawing final diagnostic conclusions.

The second assumption relates to using the native language of the client (e.g., ASL) in the testing situation, either by the clinician or an interpreter. Because the person will understand the questions, it can be reasoned that the outcome is truly reflective of actual skill or status in the test area. There is evidence that performing testing in the client's usual mode of communication can improve scores on intelligence tests (Dillon, 1980). However, many clinicians do not possess manual communication skills appropriate for interacting with deaf clients (Levine, 1974; Stewart, 1986a). Also, the use of an interpreter in these exchanges and that person's effect on the testing outcomes not been examined extensively (Stansfield & Veltri, 1987; Stewart, 1986b).

The mere transfer of information on a measure like the Wechsler scales to sign language does not ensure that the test is truly applicable for the client who is deaf. It is generally agreed that traditional intelligence tests maintain a high cultural orientation toward white, middle-class values and weigh heavily on a verbal factor (e.g., Gould, 1979; Olmedo, 1981; Reschley, 1981). As deaf persons have limited opportunities and capabilities to learn from incidental and social situations (Moores, 1987), they may not pick up on the nuances of the dominant (hearing) culture. Also, as mentioned earlier, many deaf persons maintain a close-knit subculture, that is, the Deaf Culture (Barnum, 1984; Reagan, 1985); it is possible then that, because of cultural influences, at least some individuals would not perform well on traditional, psychometric instruments.

Finally, the validity of results obtained from tests standardized on a hearing population may be questioned when the instrument's administration procedures are not followed, that is, when substituting instructions in manual communication for verbal instructions. Gerweck and Ysseldyke (1979) stated that such an administration procedure violates elementary rules of psychological measurement:

> When an examiner substitutes nonverbal instructions for the verbal instructions employed in the standardization procedure, he is not adhering to standard procedures, rendering the results of the test invalid. . . . One of the consequences of violating the standard administration procedures of a test is that reliability estimates obtained with the standardized presentation of the test can no longer be assumed to apply. When one considers the likelihood of varying administration procedures, the question of test reliability and, hence, validity becomes a major concern. (p. 246)

To conclude this section, results from traditional psychometric instruments are discussed in terms of planning and evaluating transition and rehabilitation programs. Sullivan (1986) states that measures of this type that are properly administered and interpreted will yield important information for the individual's functional training and school-to-community transition. On the other hand, professionals within the general special education and rehabilitation field or who specialize in other disability groups question the value of traditional psychometric tests for this purpose (e.g., Halpern & Fuhrer, 1984; Salvia & Ysseldyke, 1987). Various studies have found only low correlations between IQ scores and community placement success for mentally retarded persons (e.g., Bruininks, Meyers, Sigford, & Lakin, 1981), and in a recent review (Cohen & Anthony, 1984) of psychometric test results with mentally ill persons, little relationship was found between test scores and rehabilitation success. As the usefulness of traditional psychometric measures to the transition of deaf adolescents and young adults has not been examined through extensive research, the value of such information in assessing, planning, and evaluating functional skills and training efforts must be questioned. Testing situations are individual in nature and the skills of different clinicians vary; nonetheless, in many instances such data may be helpful in the education and transition process. Of course, this information may also play a central role in clinical/ therapeutic interventions, a subject not treated in this chapter.

Academic assessment. Academic assessment techniques can be grouped into four areas: communication skills, achievement testing, learning style, and measurement procedures. Measures of speech intelligibility specific to the target population are described here, but not general measures of spoken language. The reader is referred to Klein (1981) for a review of these types of instruments.

Communication issues assume primary importance in the education of adolescents and young adults. In line with this emphasis, some investigations have been conducted to develop measures of functional communication ability, that is, the ability to function in an educational environment. Three assessment tools of special note have applicability for use with deaf adolescents and young adults: Central Institute for the Deaf Everyday Sentence Lists (Caccanise, 1979), Speech Intelligibility Evaluation (Monson, 1981), and the National Technical Institute for the Deaf Communication Profile (Johnson & Kadnuc, 1980). These instruments are promising and focused toward pragmatic communication for adolescents and young adults. Regrettably, to our knowledge, no measures are available that are designed to assess communication skills in employment settings. Such measures would be important, as interactions in these contexts may be far different from those in the educational setting. Moreover, it seems that the ability to communicate effectively with supervisors and coworkers is a key part of job success (Emerton, Foster, & Royer, 1986; Foster, 1986). Also, no measures focused on communication skills in independent living situations are available—an unfortunate omission, as the fundamental skill to communicate, in some way, bears relevance for success in living in the community.

Achievement testing refers to the use of national academic tests with secondary and postsecondary students. Rudner (1978) investigated the use of the Stanford Achievement Test, Intermediate I Battery with 618 students with normal hearing and 2,821 deaf students. Using regression analysis, it was found that numerous items in the test appeared biased against the latter group. Allen (1984) scrutinized the test performance of college students on the System for Comprehensive Assessment of Learning Experiences. Through Rasch Analysis, he found evidence that the measure was not valid for deaf students. Based on these studies some doubt is raised regarding the valid use of available standardized academic tests with many persons in the target population.

An encouraging line of research is in the area of assessment of learning potential and learning style, stemming from the pioneering work of Feuerstein and his colleagues (Feuerstein, 1979, 1980; Feuerstein et al., 1986). Essentially, this assessment process focuses on the way in which a client learns to complete tasks, rather than simply finding out if the person *can* complete the task. The approach is based on the assumption that many persons will perform poorly on a test due to cultural differences; for example, a poor, black child may score in the retarded range on an intelligence test, not because of some intellectual problem, but because the test items are grounded in content from the white, middle-class culture. If the testing process is altered, though, to examine the way in which that individual learns to perform assessment tasks (e.g., block assembly) through a standardized administration process, important profile data specific to the individual's learning style can be gathered. With such information it is possible to develop individualized interventions, rather than merely to classify individuals or summarize their ability through an aggregate score, based on what assessment tasks can or cannot be completed successfully.

Generally, studies conducted on the learning potential method supports its use with deaf persons (Davey & LaSasso, 1984; Dowaliby, Burke, & McKee, 1980; Katz & Buchhom, 1984; Keane, 1987; LaSasso, 1980; Long, Conklin & Garrison, 1978; Luetke-Stahlman & Waver, 1982). Given the general test performance problems of this group on psychometric and achievement measures, it seems that this assessment approach would be a reasonable alternative for gathering educationally relevant test data. Logically, this assessment model could also be integrated into tests of vocational and independent living skills to yield important intervention information and guidelines in these functional, applied areas (e.g., How does a person best learn to balance a checkbook?).

The area of measurement procedures deals with the way tests are administered. Surprisingly little research has been conducted on the way this population should be tested; thus, it is difficult to state how assessment instruments should be structured to elicit accurate data (e.g., should visual, manual, or a combination of communication modalities be used in administering tests?) or to verify what type of response format is most appropriate (e.g., true/false or multiple choice). Existing investigations suggest that the use of answer sheets separate from a test booklet is valid (Rogers, 1983), that students who are deaf do not respond well to "WH" questions (e.g., who, when, where) (LaSasso, 1979), and that multiple choice questions appear more valid than true/false questions for deaf college students (McKee & Lang, 1982). Much inquiry is needed to identify precise testing procedures and processes for this population. Such investigations will help in constructing measures that provide performance data reflecting the individual's actual knowledge or skill in an area, rather than an artifact of the testing tool.

Vocational/career evaluation. In recent years there has been a general call for assessment to be directly relevant to both education (Bennett & Maher, 1986; Salvia & Ysseldyke, 1987) and habilitation/rehabilitation

(Halpern & Fuhrer, 1984) intervention and training efforts. Paralleling the growth of vocational and career training options for deaf students in secondary and postsecondary institutions has been the concomitant expansion of vocational and career assessment, including commercially available work samples (Marut & Innes, 1986; Ouellette & Dwyer, 1985). It is intuitively appealing to use work samples or measures of career aspirations and maturity as measures of relevant career interests and vocational skills, and these approaches are, indeed, used widely in the field of deafness (Shiels, 1986; Sligar, 1983; Watson, 1979). However, empirical documentation to substantiate these practices is scarce. Sligar (1983) correctly points out that reliability and validity indices on major work-sample testing systems are not generally available for deaf clients. Few studies describe the development of vocational/career instruments for these people (e.g., Bolton & Brown, 1971), and little research has focused on developing standardized procedures to evaluate job-related behavior, job-seeking skills, or independent living skills.

Available investigations are not fully supportive of the current use of vocational and career assessment instruments with deaf persons. Bullis and Marut (1986) found only weak statistical relationships between categories of vocational evaluation recommendations (job placement, work adjustment training, job training, academic training) and eventual placement decisions of adolescents in a residential school or adults in a rehabilitation facility. A statistically significant relationship was found, though, between the percentage of recommendations followed and eventual work success. In essence, these results question the validity of recommendations for specific job placements and training programs, but offer positive support for the use of the vocational evaluation approach.

A second study (White & Slusher, 1978) examined the validity of several career maturity tests designed for a hearing population (Assessment of Career Development, New Mexico Career Education Test Series, Career Development Inventory, and the Career Maturity Inventory) with a group of college students who were deaf. The students were administered each test and extensive face-to-face interviews were conducted with each student to determine career aspirations, results of which served as the criterion in this investigation. Correlations between the test scores and the interview results were uniformly low, indicating little relationship between test performance and the criterion awareness. The authors stated:

> The findings and conclusions of this study place the deaf educator between a rock and a hard place. Clearly, the assessment of students' career related knowledge and the quality of their career decisions is an important part in successful career educational program development, implementation and

evaluation. The evidence presented here suggests that commercially available tests are not very useful in obtaining this information. (p. 18)

To our knowledge, there is only one standardized measure of independent living skills for deaf persons, the recently completed National Independent Living Skills Assessment Instruments (NILS) (Dunlap & Sands, 1987). NILS is comprised of seven rating scales in the areas of (a) health/ hygiene, (b) family responsibility, (c) money management, (d) community awareness, (e) legal awareness, (f) social/interpersonal skills, and (g) maladaptive behavior. NILS represents a fine start in the assessment of functional skills for this population, but more work and development in this general subject area are necessary.

Public Education

The first part of this section provides a brief overview and history of the educational system for deaf children and youth. The second presents a review of career education for adolescents and young adults. In the third part the concept of transition is discussed.

Overview of the educational system. The first school for deaf students was established in Connecticut in 1817 under the direction of Thomas Gallaudet. The second school was established in New York City in 1818, and the third in Pennsylvania in 1820. Twenty-nine other schools were developed during the period between 1820 and 1860. Most of these programs were residential, requiring the student to live on the school grounds. Today there are 63 residential schools in the United States.

Initially, most residential schools and educational programs maintained a clear emphasis on manual rather than oral communication methods for their students. In the middle 1850s, the oral approach gained favor, as it was felt that persons who could learn the English language would be of more value to society and be more successful in life than those who could not. This oral-versus-manual issue was bitterly debated in the field in the late 1800s and through the years, similar debates have raged over the merits of the two communication approaches. Today the philosophy of Total Communication, which, as already noted, encourages the development of speech and language while permitting the use of sign language by both the teacher and student, appears to have been adopted by the majority of educators (Mayberry & Wodlinger-Cohen, 1987). Schools that maintain an oral-only approach, however, do exist in the United States, and many programs in public schools embrace an oral orientation.

A recent educational trend is the mainstreaming movement. This approach instigated by PL 94–142, "The Education for All Handicapped Children Act of 1975," calls for the education of all children with handicaps in the least restrictive environment possible. To date, the law's impact has been dramatic. To illustrate, in 1974 (the year of PL 94–142's passage) Schein and Delk (1974) found that approximately 55% of all deaf students were educated in residential schools. Later, in the 1982–83 school year, Karchmer (1985) noted that only 28% of all deaf students were educated in residential schools. Further, 48% of the total number of students received at least some instruction in regular classroom settings with hearing peers.

The movement toward mainstreamed programs has not been viewed in a totally positive light by many persons in the field of deafness. Since the passage of PL 94–142, controversy has existed over the correct educational placement for these students. The part of the law that has caused concern relates to the requirement that children with handicaps receive a *free and appropriate public education in the least restrictive environment.* Does this mean that all deaf students must be placed in mainstreamed programs, or is the most appropriate placement the residential school? At one extreme, residential schools are viewed as institutions that warehouse students, keeping them away from society and limiting their educational opportunities. At the other end of the spectrum, residential schools are considered as the most appropriate educational placement for deaf students as they purport to foster "normal" social and communication development. Consider the following quotes from the position statement of the International Association of Parents of the Deaf on Public Law 94–142 (cited in Jacobs, 1980):

> Public Law 94–142 is a commendable law, however, problems arise as a result of different interpretations of the law and insufficient understanding of the specific needs of hearing-impaired children. The basic intent of P.L. 94–142 is not simply to mainstream (integration of handicapped children in the least restrictive environment) but to diversify, expand and improve educational opportunities for individual handicapped children.
>
> [Discussing mainstreaming] This concept is very appealing, but its implementation in present day local public school will constitute a challenge. If handicapped children are placed in regular classes without appropriate support, they are subjected to blatant discrimination and are almost sure to withdraw or fail. Currently many local and public schools lack needed special services. (pp. 63–65)

In a related vein, Jacobs (1980) stated:

> With the stigma of failure and the term, "most restrictive environment," automatically connected with special schools, it becomes most difficult for par-

ents of deaf children to accept the concept that deafness is a unique handicap which affects communication channels rather than physical ability. Deaf students, therefore, require different consideration than the other disabled groups. Because of this, the thinking has to be completely reversed for deaf children. That is, mainstreamed situations are easily the most restricted environment for our special children because they are for most purposes isolated from the regular school population; and special schools for them are the least restrictive environment, where everybody is specially trained to communicate and work with deaf children. Indeed, these special facilities may be regarded as miniature communities where deaf children can interact in a very normal manner and thereby achieve the usual rate of growth and maturity. (p. 66)

In a review of literature conducted on the mainstreaming issue from 1959 to 1977, Farrugia and Austin (1980) stated that the research data indicate "academic performance is probably enhanced by attendance in public schools, but social and emotional development may be adversely affected" (p. 535). Several studies have examined this issue empirically. An investigation conducted in New Zealand (Witheford & Wilton, 1978) found that students in public schools performed better than students in residential schools on measures of social-emotional adjustment. Ladd, Munson, and Miller (1984) in a 2-year follow-along study of students in a secondary-level mainstreamed program, found that the individuals adjusted well to the placement and were accepted by their hearing peers. Conversely, Lytle and Jonas (1985) found that students from mainstreamed programs were more apt to experience social maladjustment and to require mental health services when they attended college. Quarrington and Solomon (1975) found that students in residential programs were rated as more mature than students in other settings (e.g., public school programs). Farrugia and Austin (1980) found that students in public schools demonstrated lower levels of social, emotional, and mature behaviors than students in residential schools. Based solely on these few studies, it is impossible to reach firm conclusions regarding the "best" educational placement for all deaf students.

Career education.   This section contains three objectives. First, a brief history of the career education movement is presented. Second, research on this education approach specific to students who are deaf is reviewed. Third, implications of the recent emphasis on the school-to-community transition of persons with disabilities are drawn for deaf adolescents and young adults. For a more complete review of career education issues the reader is referred to Bullis and Watson (1985). It must be pointed out that career education does not occur only during the years one is in public school. This educational approach should originate at the elementary level and continue through the secondary years, but it may also carry on into many postsecondary programs. Thus, much of what is said here will be applicable to the section of this chapter where postsecondary education programs are discussed.

Career education is, basically, an instructional philosophy and approach that emphasizes preparing an individual to make mature career decisions and to engage in a lifelong pattern of rewarding work and community integration. It embodies the notion that persons gain a maturity toward work through a developmental process (Holland, 1966; Super, 1957; Tiedemann & O'Hara, 1963); one that can be fostered through the introduction of appropriate educational procedures. This instructional model has its roots in the 1960s, when career education began to be emphasized due to weaknesses in the academic training approach for many students (e.g., lack of content relevance, lack of work preparation, etc.) (Marland, 1974; Reinhart, 1979). At that time career education focused on students without disabilities, but the movement instigated career education programming for students with special needs (e.g. Brolin, 1978; Brolin & Kokaska, 1979), including the deaf population (Dwyer, 1985).

The genesis of the career education movement for this population can be traced back to an institute held in 1970 by the National Technical Institute for the Deaf (NTID). The purpose of that institute was to develop, from the "grass roots up," a working model of the general concept. Career education was stressed as an important part of the educational curriculum from elementary through high school levels. In this same year an important study (Lerman & Guilfoyle, 1970) found that students in residential schools had a much lower level of vocational development than did hearing peers and that they exhibited poor vocational awareness and planning. These results further stimulated interest in career preparation.

Several projects were initiated during the 1970s and early 1980s as a consequence of this early work. In 1971 a project entitled Cooperative Research Endeavors in the Education of the Deaf (CREED) was initiated to develop and implement career education materials applicable to the school setting. It was evaluated in a quasi-experimental design in 12 school programs in the state of New York (Munson & Egelston, 1975). Statistically significant differences on two career language measures were found between students in the experimental group and those in the control group, suggesting the positive impact of the program.

The largest project, and the one with the widest dissemination, was the National Project on Career Education (NPCE) (Updegraff & Egelston-Dodd, 1982; Updegraff, Bishop, Steffan & Egelston-Dodd, 1979). NPCE provided training to educators who served deaf students in 60 school programs across the nation in career education methods. These professionals then worked in their institutions setting up career education programs and providing training to other staff. Extensive follow-up was also offered by NPCE personnel. Products from this project include career education modules and approaches (Egelston-Dodd, 1980; Young, Lutz, Lichty, & Egelston-Dodd, 1980). To date, the effect of this program on the participating educators has been demonstrated as positive (Egelston-Dodd, Young, Lutz, & Lichty, 1983), but the effect on the students involved has not been established.

In 1980, the Conference of Executives of American Schools for the Deaf developed a position paper that recommended that career education be included in educational programs (Bishop et al., 1980). This document basically reiterates the process set forth by NPCE and denotes a significant commitment to the concept and practice of career education.

An outgrowth of this developmental process has been the establishment of a comprehensive model of career preparation, the Comprehensive Career Education Model (CCEM); see Figure 6.1. Originally developed to incorporate training from birth through the secondary years, the model has been modified to include postsecondary training (Galloway, 1978). This theoretical paradigm is significant in that it presents a clear, lifelong blueprint for intervention: Specifically, career awareness begins early in one's life, followed by exploration of various career avenues around the seventh grade, preparation for work at about the eleventh grade, and job specialization training during the postsecondary years. Recognition is given post–high school training and the fluctuating nature of employment by extending the model past the public school years. The educational thrust is expanded further to include three instructional environments: home, school, and community. Finally, eight career education content elements are delineated, ranging from self-awareness to employability skills, and attitudes and appreciations. This "grounding" of career education practice provides a firm starting point for program development and individual training efforts.

In 1983 a national survey (Ouellette & Dwyer, 1985) of career education programs in 177 rehabilitation or community service programs, postsecondary educational settings, residential schools, and day school programs outlined the dramatic growth of career education for deaf persons. First, it was clear that the career education movement had become firmly entrenched in the service system; that is, many programs had been developed and career education was being offered to deaf students. Most programs were offered in the secondary grades, but some schools began career programming at an earlier stage in the educational process. Second, emphasis was placed on developing student awareness of career and self through a counseling approach; that is, students were understood to need maturity and basic work habits and attitudes more than job-specific skills. Third, most programs used teacher-designed training materials and only a few employed commercially available curricula. Fourth, many programs utilized career and vocational testing. Fifth and last, many rehabilitation and postsecondary education programs provided career education services on a regular basis.

Other than the projects mentioned above, few efforts have focused on the empirically based, programmatic development of career education materials. The exception to this rule relates to career decision making. Several publications (DeCaro & Arenson, 1983; DiFrancesca, 1980; Lang & Stinson, 1982) suggest that college students who are deaf are weak in this skill. In one needs assessment (Bullis, 1985a), lack of decision-making skill was

FIGURE 6.1 The CCEM

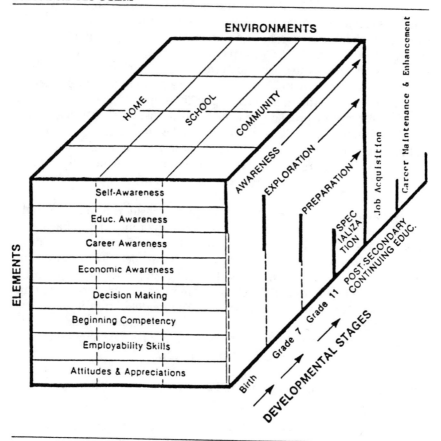

Source: Developed by the Ohio State University and modified by Galloway (1978)

identified as the greatest career education deficit for students at the secondary level. A well-designed and popular curriculum in this area is *The Step Method: Learning and Practicing Thinking Skills* (DiFrancesca, 1978). The Step method is structured to teach critical thinking skills within the school, society, and vocational contexts. It is clearly written and organized, but its effect on students has not been documented at this point (Bullis, 1985b). Another program used to train persons in career decision making is the Career Awareness Summer Program (CASP) (Egelston-Dodd & Young, 1984; Low & Egelston-Dodd, 1984). CASP is a two-week-long program designed to expose students to different educational and vocational options and to introduce the fundamentals of career decision-making skills.

Research that examines the efficacy of specific job placement techniques (such as the Job Club [Azrin & Besalel, 1980]) is not widely available. This is not to say that programs of this nature do not exist in the field. Indeed, excellent descriptions of programs that use a Job Club model are available (Long & Davis, 1986; Torretti & Hendrick, 1986), but these efforts have not—at this point—been subjected to empirical examination (Amrine & Bullis, 1985). Also, there is little research that addresses independent living skills (Woodrick, 1980), and there is only scant evidence to specify the types of problems encountered by persons with deafness in community settings. It follows that there are few research-based programs and/or materials on this subject. Instead, most of the writing in this area is devoted to the description of service programs (eg., Ouellette & Loyd, 1980).

Transition.[1]   In one sense the concept of transition is not new to the field of deafness. As discussed previously, career/vocational training of deaf persons has a relatively long history. Also, there exists a close relationship between residential schools and many state departments of vocational rehabilitation (Sendelbaugh & Bullis, 1987). On the other hand, given the lack of research inquiry and development in this area, the concept of transition demands a fresh and intense look. The model of transition for deaf persons shown in Figure 6.2 is offered to assist in that reconsideration. The paradigm borrows from Will (1984), Fairweather (1984), Halpern (1985), Brolin (1978), and Wilcox and Bellamy (1982).

It is clear that a person's ultimate success in life is influenced significantly by personal characteristics and attributes (e.g., intelligence) and by

---

[1] Much of this section is taken from Bullis, M., Bull, B., Sendelbaugh, J., & Freeburg, J. (1987). *Review of research on the school-to-community transition of adolescents and young adults with hearing impairments.* Washington, DC: National Rehabilitation Information Center, Catholic University.

family background and support. Family influence is regarded as a powerful variable in the school to community transition process (Egelston-Dodd, O'Brien & Bondi-Wolcott, 1987; El-Khiami, 1987a).

School experience is another potent force that shapes the individual. It is logical to assume that the type of education provided has a powerful impact on the knowledge and skills of the student and, subsequently, on how well prepared the individual is upon exit from the school system. To illustrate, a highly academic instructional program may prepare a student to succeed in college but he or she may not do well in a blue-collar vocational placement. Conversely, a student who receives instruction only in blue-collar work may not succeed in a demanding college setting.

The movement from the secondary school level to the community is what is typically called transition (e.g., Halpern, 1985; Will, 1984). This process involves the joint planning and interaction of the educational agency and adult service agencies (e.g., vocational rehabilitation, Social Security). The end result of the endeavor should be the integration of the individual into the community as evidenced by successful employment, adequate housing and independent living experiences, and appropriate social/interpersonal outlets. Of course, varying levels of competence may be reached in any or all three of these domains. Stated differently, some degree of external support may need to be afforded the individual in a time-limited or continuous manner for success to be achieved in community integration. By delineating the outcomes of transition as career/vocational, independent living, and social/interpersonal, a "blueprint" for education is provided. Students should receive instruction in these content areas, and again, varying intensities and content of instruction in the three domains will be required by different students.

What makes the transition experience unique for deaf students is that

FIGURE 6.2 Conceptual model of transition

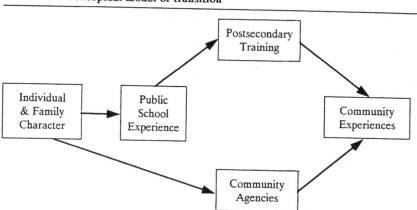

so many go on to some type of postsecondary education (El-Khiami, 1986, 1987b; Ouellette, 1986a; Schroedel, 1986, 1987; Stewart, 1986c). This option has the potential to affect dramatically the transition the student makes from the secondary grades *and* ultimate community integration. The decision to engage in postsecondary training requires the establishment of three separate transition links: between the public schools and the postsecondary institution as regards enrollment; between the public schools, the postsecondary institution, and adult service agencies as regards sponsoring the student; and between the postsecondary institution and the adult service agency as regards supporting the student when he or she completes training and moves from school to a community placement. As the same general community outcomes are possible for students who receive postsecondary education, it makes sense that they too receive individualized instruction in the content areas of career/vocational development, independent living skills, and social/interpersonal skills. Of course, offerings may range from academic to functional in nature.

Inherent in this model are two features. The first can be termed administrative policies. The interactions of diverse groups from public education, postsecondary education, and adult service agencies must be carefully orchestrated (Corthell & Van Boskirk, 1984). These cooperative agreements can improve the service system and ultimately the school-to-community transition of students. The second relates to evaluation or assessment of individuals. Evaluation is necessary to diagnose and structure interventions and placements; also, the long-term follow-up of these students is essential to gauge the success of their work and living experiences. This type of data can be used to judge the success of the program and to guide program modifications to strengthen the service structure.

In sum, the school-to-community transition of persons who are deaf is a multidimensional process that is both enhanced and complicated by the fact that so many go on to some type of postsecondary education. General educational offerings should relate to instruction in the employment, independent living, and social/interpersonal domains. Of course, different students will require programs ranging from academic to functional in nature, and varying levels of support (e.g., counseling, agency services) will be needed. Inherent in the process is the interaction of the public school, postsecondary institution, and community service agencies. An ongoing evaluation of the student is recommended to structure effective transition programs and monitor the success of the system.

Research Study

This section provides a brief review of an empirical investigation of deaf adolescents and young adults. The project focuses on the transition experiences of this group and is being conducted through a grant received from the National Institute on Disability and Rehabilitation Research (Bullis & Freeburg, 1986). At this writing, the first year of a 3-year funding cycle is being completed. Therefore, the discussion deals primarily with method and project design instead of results.

As noted earlier in this chapter, there are few existing studies that chart and describe the school-to-community transition of persons who are deaf or hearing impaired. Thus, the purpose of this project is to gather data related to the personal and family characteristics of this population; their high school preparation; their postsecondary and community agency involvements; and their vocational, independent living, and social experiences in the community.

To construct a representative subject sample for the project, the model presented in Figure 6.3 was developed. It was assumed that persons from either residential school programs, or programs in rural, urban, or metropolitan regions could have different types of transition experiences. Accordingly, schools from these locales in the states of Oregon, Washington,

FIGURE 6.3 **Population parameters**

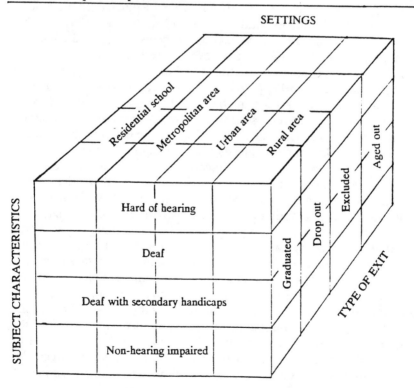

and Idaho were recruited to participate in the study. Second, as a requirement of the project, hard-of-hearing, deaf, and deaf/multiply handicapped
students were included as the target population for investigation. Finally,
it must be realized that students can exit educational programs through
four distinct channels: They may graduate by earning a diploma or certificate, they may "age out" of a program (reach 21 years of age and no
longer be eligible for public education), they may "drop out" prior to completion of their education, and they can be excluded or expelled from
school. Every effort was made to identify those students involved in the
project who left school through any of these four channels. During the first
year, 8 research sites were involved in the research. During the second and
third years, 14 other sites will be added, for a total of 22 school programs
in the project.

A primary question to be addressed in this study is, "How well do
these persons do in their transition into the community?" It follows that
one must also ask, "In relation to what?" Thus, the experiences of students
without disabilities must be gathered and used as the standard of such
competence and success. In essence, these persons comprise the comparison or "control" group (Fairweather, 1984) for the investigation.

Two research components for the project were devised. In the follow-
along component, students who leave school during the 1986–87 and
1987–88 school years are involved. Those students are queried while still
in school and then at regular intervals over the rest of the project to monitor their transition experiences. In the follow-up component, persons who
left school 3 to 4 years earlier (1983–84 school year, 1984–85 school year,
and 1985–86 school year) are queried one time only to gather data on
their lives since leaving high school. In both cases questions are asked
regarding vocational, independent living, social, and continuing education
experiences as well as their involvement with community agencies.

A major issue in conducting a research project of this type relates to
the method of data collection. There is reason to believe that at least some
individuals in the hearing-impaired population would have trouble completing a written, mailed survey form (Schroedel, 1979). Accordingly, data
collection efforts start with the parents of all identified students. These persons are interviewed by data collectors via a structured phone interview.
For deaf parents the interviews are carried out in a face-to-face interview
by a data collector skilled in manual communication and familiar with the
interview protocol. Once parents have been interviewed, data collection
efforts turn to their son or daughter. Students without disabilities are interviewed on the phone through a structured protocol similar to that administered to parents. Students who are hearing impaired (i.e., hard of
hearing, deaf, deaf and multiply handicapped) are interviewed directly by
data collectors skilled in manual communication. Finally, information

from school records for both groups of students is gathered on hearing loss, IQ, GPA, classes completed, involvement in extracurricular activities, and so forth.

The first year of the project served primarily as a pilot test for the data collection procedures. During this period data were gathered on approximately 100 hearing impaired students and a comparable number without disabilities. Constant reliability checks were made on all phone interviewers and face-to-face interviewers, with interjudge agreement indices ranging from .90 to 1.0. Also, all coding and data entry problems were resolved.

By the end of the project, information will be gathered on a subject pool of about 150 hearing impaired subjects in the follow-along study and about 400 hearing impaired subjects in the follow-up study. This data will be analyzed descriptively, comparatively (in contrast with data from control students), and through correlational analysis to examine relationships among groups of variables (e.g., analysis of covariance structures [Kerlinger, 1986]). It is to be hoped that these procedures will lead to a greater awareness and understanding of the transition process for deaf persons.

COMMUNITY EXPERIENCES

This section provides an overview of the young adult's experiences in the community after leaving the public school. As mentioned earlier, individuals moving from these programs may enroll in postsecondary education programs, or seek work and living placements in the community. Accordingly, discussion of these areas comprises this part of the chapter.

Postsecondary Education

Postsecondary education options for deaf persons have increased in number and scope in the past two decades (Nash & Castle, 1980). Until 1964, the only postsecondary program for these people was Gallaudet College (now, University), a liberal arts institution in Washington, DC. In 1965 the National Technical Institute for the Deaf was established as one of nine colleges of the Rochester Institute of Technology to provide technology training to the population. Since that time, there has been an explosion of other programs, available to students who are deaf, in community colleges, junior colleges, and four-year colleges and universities. By 1978 more than 55 such programs existed (Stuckless, 1973), serving more than 4,000 students (Rawlings, Trybus, & Biser, 1978). Currently, there are at least 61 postsecondary educational programs that operate through state and federal funding (Rawlings, Karchmer, DeCaro, & Egelston-Dodd,

1986). It has been estimated that the federal government spends nearly 60 million dollars yearly in programs serving deaf persons. Tens of millions of state dollars are allocated for community colleges, and about five million dollars is spent yearly by vocational rehabilitation agencies to sponsor students in postsecondary education (Ouellette, 1986a).

Despite this dramatic expansion, there have been no intensive investigations of the educational system until recently. In 1983 the University of Arkansas Rehabilitation Research and Training Center in Deafness and Hearing Impairment was awarded a 3-year project to examine the postsecondary education network and its effect on students who are deaf (Watson, 1983). Research reports from this project provide an excellent overview of postsecondary educational opportunities for this group. Selected results from these manuscripts follow.

Ouellette (1986a) conducted a survey of 46 postsecondary programs to gain a general description of cost and funding issues for 5,018 students served in those institutions in 1983. This group was split almost equally in terms of gender. Minorities, particularly blacks, were underrepresented in this group; 83% were Caucasian. Roughly 35% of the total population were enrolled in nondegree programs (high school equivalency or vocational training), 17% were pursuing associate-level degrees, and 48% were enrolled in bachelor's or graduate degree programs. More than half of the 46 programs received federal funding; 80% of the institutions received state funding, and about 65% of all students in the study received some funding from vocational rehabilitation. On the average, it cost $5,000 per year to educate a deaf student in these programs, about $1,000 more than to educate a student without hearing loss. The author stated that this difference is due most probably to cost of support services (interpreters, notetakers) necessary for the students to succeed in the educational environment.

Since many persons who are deaf and in postsecondary education receive at least some financial assistance from vocational rehabilitation (VR) agencies, it was necessary to investigate the policies of these service programs. Stewart (1986a) queried all 53 VR agencies in the states and territories of the United States. Seventy percent of the 53 agencies sponsored students at any level of academic preparation and 3,984 students were receiving funding for postsecondary education from 42 VR programs. Stewart (1986a) found that, "There is a pronounced relationship between the number of training programs for deaf students within a region and the number of students sponsored in training by the state VR agency in that region" (p. 289) and "it appears that the more programs for deaf students there are within a state, the more inhibiting factors there are for the VR agency in sponsoring a student out-of-state" (p. 290). These two points carry direct relevance for students selecting a program; availability of a program in a region may preclude attending a different, but better, program out of the region. General uniformity between the funding policies of the 53 programs was noted.

Schroedel (1986) conducted a survey of 371 students graduating in 1984 from 37 programs across the United States to gain direct input from the group on why certain programs were selected, the scope of VR contact, and the extent of financial aid. Half of the students were profoundly deaf, 86% were prelingually deafened, 10% had secondary disabilities, 82% were white, and 85% considered themselves to be proficient in manual communication. The major reason that most gave for selecting their post-secondary program was to receive a good education or job training. The second most important reason related to the reported quality of the program. The third strongest reason was recommendation by a significant other, with 57% of the sample indicating that their parents encouraged them to go on to school. There was a clear sex-related influence in choosing a major: Females tended to be involved in secretarial, data processing, liberal arts, or education programs, while males chose skilled crafts or technological fields. Over 75% expected to complete degrees below the baccalaureate level. The author suggested that these tendencies (assumption of traditional roles and pursuit of lower academic degrees) among both deaf women and men are crucial problems that must be remedied. Finally, most students (73%) stated that they saw their VR counselors only one to five times per year; 65% received funding from VR, 40% from Social Security, 36% from their families, and 31% received support from scholarships or grants.

In a second manuscript, Schroedel (1987) described a study of 743 graduates of 41 postsecondary education programs and a follow-up of the 1984 group included in the earlier investigation. Of particular interest is the follow-up of the 193 alumni (from a total of 371) from the class of 1984. These graduates completed a survey one year after completing their postsecondary training. It was found that 81.5% were working and 18.5% were not, as compared to 6.8% unemployment in the general labor force. Also, 28% of alumni from community colleges were unemployed as compared to 15% of the alumni from four-year colleges. Of the total number of students working, 30% were employed in professional and technical positions, and 28% were clerical workers. When asked to name the most important change necessary in their educational program, many indicated a need to increase the emphasis on work skills.

Last, El-Khiami (1987b) examined employers' perceptions of graduates of 21 postsecondary education programs. Employers ($n = 123$) from across the country who had experience in hiring graduates of these programs participated in the study. Of the participants, 77% dealt predominantly with the hearing public and about half were private businesses. Most of the employers (80%) indicated that the graduates they hired were in white-collar jobs, and 20% hired graduates in blue-collar positions. The majority (61%) reported hiring graduates of 4-year colleges, but there appeared to be a distinct increase in the hiring of graduates from community colleges and rehabilitation/vocational-technical programs. Only 20% of the respondents indicated a concern with job safety for deaf employees, 80% rated these workers as average or above average in overall performance, 93% of the employers rated the social interaction skills of the group as good or very good, 88% rated the worker's ability to follow instructions as good or very good, and 97% stated that they would hire other deaf workers. Conversely, 32% of the employers noted that workers should be better prepared in nontechnical aspects of work and communication deficits were identified as the principal employment barrier.

In summary, the growth of postsecondary programs for deaf persons has been rapid and expansive. The series of studies conducted under the aegis of the Rehabilitation Research and Training Center on Deafness and Hearing Impairment provide an excellent review of the system and its impact. In general, this effect has been positive. It is also apparent that students tend to choose traditional work roles and that unemployment rates for these persons are higher than for the general population. Specific issues related to employment are discussed next in more detail.

Employment

There is no question that securing and maintaining a vocation is a primary goal for most persons. Indeed, work is a medium through which monetary rewards are received and provides intangible reinforcement relating to self-concept and happiness. Accordingly, an overview of employment statistics for deaf people is provided, and variables related to successful employment are discussed.

Employment statistics. Any discussion of vocational success should address the rate of unemployment experienced, the types of jobs secured, and the wages earned. These issues have received a great deal of attention in the research literature, but some discrepancy exists between findings. We examine here two probable reasons for this discrepancy.

First, conceptualizing unemployment issues in terms of only one index, or percentage, for all deaf persons is both incorrect and misleading. This is an extremely heterogeneous population; consequently, the unemployment rate for a particular subgroup (e.g., college graduates) may be very different from that experienced by another (e.g., high school dropouts). For example, in a review of the research literature in this area (Bullis, Bull, Sendelbaugh, & Freeburg, 1987) it was found that, of 43 studies published since 1975 on the employment experiences of deaf persons, 23 were conducted with individuals affiliated with college programs. Clearly, the experiences of this subset may not reflect experiences of persons who do not continue their education past high school or who drop out.

Second, most investigations of employment experiences survey research procedures with written data collection forms that required the respondent to read and answer questions. Although many deaf persons would have no problem with such tasks, those with limited verbal abilities may not be able to complete such instruments in a valid fashion (Schroedel, 1979). Thus, respondents to written surveys may be more proficient in English presumably of higher ability levels, and not representative of the population as a whole. Similarly, studies that follow only graduates of an institution(s) as an initial subject pool may be biased toward a higher functioning group. It is not too farfetched to believe that graduates are more able than students who leave programs by dropping out, aging out (i.e., becoming older than 21 in a public school program), or by being excluded.

In spite of these cautions, it is possible to draw some conclusions regarding the employment status of four groups of persons: college graduates, graduates of other postsecondary education programs, graduates of high school, and persons completing rehabilitation programs. First, the majority of studies on persons from college programs have been conducted under the auspices of the National Technical Institute for the Deaf (NTID) and Gallaudet University, as part of their institutional research and evaluation units. Complete discussion of all these documents is beyond the scope of this chapter; only information from recent publications is summarized here. Reports from NTID (Grant, Marron & Welsh, 1980; Martin, 1983; Welsh, 1982, 1986; Welsh & Parker, 1982a, 1982b) demonstrate that graduates of this program can work and earn salaries in the competitive labor market at a rate comparable to that of hearing peers. Also, comparisons with program dropouts revealed differences favoring graduates in employment successes. Interestingly, unemployment rates among graduates tend to decrease over time. Welsh (1986) found that 13.7% of graduates of 1984 or 1985 were unemployed compared to 8.1% of graduates from 1981 to 1983; unemployment was 3.9% for graduates from 1975 to 1980 and 2.1% for graduates before 1975. Research from Gallaudet (Brown, 1987; Rawlings, Karchmer, King, & Brown, 1985) documents that its graduates tend to do very well in the work force, both earning and being employed at a rate commensurate with members of the general population who have the same level of education. For both groups of graduates, however, it seems that there is an overrepresentation in blue-collar jobs, and an underrepresentation in white-collar and managerial positions.

Second, in the examination of 146 graduates of postsecondary educational programs discussed earlier, Schroedel (1987) found an initial unemployment rate of 18.5% for the total sample, and a direct relationship with the type of program completed and the unemployment index. Unemployment was lower for graduates of 4-year colleges (15.4%) than for graduates of community college programs (27.8%), technical programs (21.4%), and rehabilitation facilities (22.2%). Members of this group pursued some 75 different types of occupations mainly in the technical, clerical, service, and craft fields. Again, the absence of graduates in managerial and white-collar jobs was highlighted.

A series of surveys conducted by MacLeod (1983, 1984, & 1985) describes some employment experiences of graduates of residential and public school programs. Persons responding to her surveys experienced rates of unemployment higher than norms for hearing persons; if employed they earned a lower salary, demonstrated little upward mobility, tended to stay at a job for a long period of time, and found work in blue-collar occupations. As in the NTID investigations, though, the unemployment rate for the respondents diminished over time. Whether this is due to persons finding work, or leaving the work force and not being included as part of the unemployment group, is speculative. In other studies, De Paolo (1976) and Fraser and Owlsey (1981) found unemployment rates of 16% and 29% respectively, in groups of students who completed secondary programs and entered employment.

Two follow-up studies give some indication of what happens to persons from rehabilitation programs. Wootton and Mowry (1986) contacted 95 former clients of vocational rehabilitation three years after case closure. They found that individuals classified as hard of hearing experienced slightly higher rates of unemployment than deaf persons, 32% to 25%. Persons in both groups who did work were employed in manufacturing, processing, and fabrication and, on the average, earned about one-third less than hearing peers. Ouellette (1986b) investigated the employment status of 39 persons who had received training in a rehabilitation facility 8 years before data collection. She found an unemployment rate of 56% and that only 15% of those persons working were employed on a job related to training received in the facility.

Finally, El-Khiami (1986) studied selected characteristics of 29,000 clients of general state/federal rehabilitation agencies with all levels of hearing impairments by reviewing the federal Rehabilitation Service Administration's R-300 data file. It was found that the former clients who were classified as hard of hearing tended to be employed in different types of jobs than former deaf clients; specifically, they were placed in professional, technical, and service occupations. Conversely, deaf persons had a greater representation in higher income brackets than did persons who were hard of hearing. There were, however, higher percentages of persons from this latter group at the middle-income level.

To conclude, given the heterogeneity of the deaf population, it is incorrect to believe that there is one unemployment figure to describe the entire group. From the studies reviewed here it seems that unemployment rates may range from below national average to around 50%. It is clear, also, that the unemployment rate declines over time. Overall, those who do find work earn less than their hearing peers, tend to work in blue-collar positions, and have limited upward mobility.

Variables related to successful employment. From investigations reviewed in this chapter (e.g., Schroedel, 1987), it is apparent that persons who completed higher levels of education and who, presumably, function at a higher cognitive level are more successful in employment. Are there other variables that influence vocational behavior and outcomes? This question has been discussed in the research literature through survey methodology and correlational analysis (path analysis), and recently some effort has been made to examine the topic through qualitative approaches. In this section we discuss the relationship of several major variables to employment status: communication, age of onset of disability, sex, race, and family influence.

Phillips (1975) and Foster (1986) pointed out that the quality of an individual's communication may reduce employer concerns about hiring deaf people. All 25 persons in Foster's qualitative study felt that communication on the job was extremely important and that their opportunities for advancement were minimal due to communication difficulties. It is very likely, too, that these individuals understand the competitive disadvantage of their disability and develop the "right attitude" for coping in an often difficult environment, resulting in a level of acceptance, but not total satisfaction, with the "manageable" job. For example, Emerton, Foster, and Royer (1986) interviewed 17 deaf workers to determine the impact of changing technology on their employment. Regarding the impact of communication, the authors state:

> To be forced to depend on the good will of others to accept and accommodate hearing impairment is handicapping far beyond the physical limitations of deafness. And, as our respondents have repeatedly shown, it is most frustrating because it is beyond the deaf individual's sphere of direct control. (p. 25)

The investigation of employers by El-Khiami (1987b) stands somewhat in contrast to these views. She found that employers in her study viewed communication as an important issue, but not one that was insurmountable through job modification and/or special accommodations. However, these employers tended to hire graduates of college programs in white-collar jobs. Although communication was not a major obstacle to employment for these persons, the situation may be different for others with lower levels of education.

Research examining the impact on employment of the age of onset of the hearing impairment yields discrepant results, as well. Schein and Delk (1974) reported that earnings were directly related to the period in life when one becomes deaf; that is, those who were congenitally deafened received the lowest personal earnings as compared to those who became deaf after the age of 6. They suggest that this finding may be a function of better oral communication skills possessed by those deafened after the acquisition of spoken language. On the other hand, Fiaz and Fiaz (1977) found no significant relationship between the age of onset of a person's deafness and occupational status. Brown (1987), in his study of income determinants of Gallaudet alumni, reported that age of onset of hearing loss was not significant in predicting income attainment. He cautioned that this finding may not be generalizable to all deaf persons; students at Gallaudet are predominantly prelingually deafened and, thus, do not mirror the population as a whole.

Drawing from studies examining the influence of sex on occupational status (Barnett, 1982; Egelston-Dodd, 1977; Schroedel, 1987), it seems that deaf women are "doubly disadvantaged" (Barnett, 1982). Overall, this group earns significantly less than women in general and deaf males, and many are employed in blue-collar or clerical jobs. Welsh and Schroedel (1982), though, found that gender was unrelated with the occupational status of graduates from NTID, a result that may be associated with the educational level of the group. Last, it is important to note that many deaf women enter traditional occupations (e.g., secretarial) (Egelston-Dodd, 1977; Schroedel, 1987), rather than training for careers in historically male dominated roles (e.g., management).

Even though examinations of race as a factor in employment for deaf persons are sparse, there is some indication that individuals from minority groups experience higher rates of unemployment, earn lower wages, and work in menial jobs (Lombardo, 1976; Taft, 1983). Conclusions on this subject must be tentative due to the relative absence of empirical investigations.

Finally, it seems that family influences play a major role in the employment success of persons who are deaf. Welsh and Schroedel (1982) found that, for graduates of NTID, the father's socioeconomic status was related significantly to the student's socioeconomic status. Schroedel

(1987) and El-Khiami (1987a) indicated that parental involvement and encouragement were major factors in students' choice of and entry into postsecondary education programs. As completion of such training is related strongly to eventual vocational outcomes, parental participation in the life of the adolescent or young adult appears significant.

To reiterate, deficits in communication and social skills may limit vocational advancement of persons who are deaf. It is possible, however, that among persons completing postsecondary degrees communication issues are less important. Also, it appears that sex and race are related to employment outcomes, and family background and family support are very important to vocational success.

Living and Social Status

A discussion of what is known about the living and social status of deaf people cannot take place without extensive reference to the National Census of the Deaf Population (NCDP) (Schein & Delk, 1974). We provide here a cursory sampling of the NCDP findings that may be relevant to the profile of adolescents and young adults leaving school and entering society today. Despite the wealth of data provided by the NCDP, little information is available about the community experiences of this population. Where possible, information from NCDP is supplemented with more recent investigations.

The NCDP demonstrated that the proportion of deaf individuals who marry was far smaller than that of the general population. The proportion of never-married single males was more than double for persons who were deaf than the rate for people without disabilities. Twenty-eight percent of deaf females, aged 25 to 34, were single as compared to 15% of women in the same age group in the general population. Fiaz and Fiaz (1977) studied 380 young (mean age 27 years), urban (Toronto, Canada) deaf high school graduates. They found that 78% of the male subjects and 63% of females had never married. In both the NCDP and the Fiaz and Fiaz study it was found that those who do marry do so at a much later age than persons without disabilities.

Schein and Delk (1974) suggest that these marriage rates may be the result of closely supervised heterosexual relationships in the residential school setting, presumably leading to a delay in dating and other opportunities to socialize with the opposite sex. Unfortunately, no current research exists on the marital status of graduates of mainstream education programs who are deaf. Another possible explanation for these marriage rates may be related to the lower socioeconomic status and an older mean age for completion of educational programs for deaf persons.

El-Khiami's (1986) examination of former VR clients included subjects with a broader age range than the participants in the Fiaz and Fiaz
(1977) study, but found a similar picture of marital status. She isolated
persons who were hard of hearing and deaf, and showed that people in
the former group married at a higher rate than those in the latter. In fact,
the proportion of persons considered to be hard of hearing who had never
been married was only half that of deaf individuals.

Schein and Delk (1974) found that an overwhelming majority of respondents in the NCDP study chose mates who were also deaf. This is
particularly true of those having early onset deafness; for example, only
12 to 14% of those deafened before age 19 chose hearing spouses. Those
persons who were deaf and did choose hearing partners, appeared to be
better educated. Still, only one deaf person out of eight chose a spouse
without hearing loss; an even smaller number chose mates who were hard
of hearing. Divorce rates among deaf persons appeared to be identical to
the general population. Schein and Delk (1974) found that rates for divorce and separation were somewhat lower in those marriages in which
both spouses were deaf than in unions where only one partner was deaf.

The average deaf woman in the NCDP bore fewer children than her
counterparts in the general population. The number of children born to
mothers who were deaf was also influenced by the mother's age at onset
of deafness: The median number of children born to mothers who were
congenitally deafened was .4; of mothers deafened in their first to third
year, 1.2 children; third to fifth years, 1.8 children; and fifth to eighteenth
years, 2.3 children.

Also the NCDP found that 88% of all deaf parents gave birth to children with normal hearing. As expected, the rates of offspring with some
level of hearing impairment was appreciably greater in those marriages
where one (12.5%) or both (17.4%) of the spouses were congenitally deafened as compared to those marriages in which both spouses had acquired
their hearing loss later in life (6%). Moreover, 90% of adults in NCDP were
born to hearing parents. The vast majority of parents who were deaf raised
hearing children. Schein (1979) noted:

> Deaf parents are also successful in raising their normally hearing children.
> Many sons and daughters of deaf parents have become eminent entertainers,
> physicians, educators. Their parents have been ingenious in anticipating and
> overcoming problems associated with deafness. The children, in turn, have
> often sought careers in education and rehabilitation serving deaf people.
> (p. 482)

The NCDP data present a picture of persons whose interests parallel
those of the general community. These adults participated in religious or-

ganizations to the same extent as hearing people, usually through the provision of a sign language interpreter. They were involved in legal actions at the same rate as the general population, except that other studies (Emerton & Emerton, 1987) showed them to have better driving records. Leisure-time activities (watching television, etc.) are also like those of hearing people. This is especially true since the advent of telecaptioning decoders. Also, Schein (1979) pointed out that organized sports have a high priority in the lives of deaf people partly because the visual nature of most activities permits the involvement of both spectator and participant.

Finally, a number of deaf persons, as well as professionals serving this population, have begun to view a special segment of these people as belonging to a unique subculture of American society—the "Deaf Culture" (Padden, 1980). Typically, acceptance into the Deaf Culture requires that persons have experienced hearing loss early enough, and at a level severe enough, to require special education services, most often in a residential school. It is congregation in these residential settings that fosters the core of common experiences with which members of the Deaf Culture freely identify. A second factor that qualifies individuals for inclusion in this subgroup is the use of American Sign Language (ASL) as the preferred mode of communication. In the same way as all cultural minorities utilize their native language to interact, members of the Deaf Culture are profoundly drawn together by their use of ASL.

In a related vein, there is a move away from a clinical definition of deaf people as those who possess a measurable hearing loss significant enough to impede normal functioning in hearing society (Myklebust, 1964), and toward a definition of deaf people as persons who share a common means of communication that provides the basis for group cohesion and identity (Schlesinger & Meadow, 1972). Viewing deaf people as a cultural minority, as opposed to a disability group, has profound implications for professionals who serve this population. Acceptance of this perspective presents a situation where most hearing professionals are working cross-culturally with deaf people (Glickman, 1986), rather than dealing with a clientele that is "handicapped."

CONCLUSION AND RECOMMENDATIONS FOR RESEARCH

There is no question that services to deaf persons have expanded greatly in the past 20 years. Many of these programs are excellent, serving and affecting the individual in a positive fashion. But it is also apparent that there is much work to be done to counter the pervasive problems of unemployment and underemployment encountered by these persons. Further, relatively little is known about the community living and social experiences of persons who are deaf. Accordingly, we make the following recommendations for future investigations.

First, a current, accurate, and replicable census of this population needs to be established. This is a difficult task, and some of the inherent difficulties in the task, such as survey response problems and locating subjects, were touched on earlier. Nonetheless, it is imperative that the number of deaf persons be known so that adequate levels of service can be established. Since the extent of the population has important ramifications for state and federal programs, a geographical breakdown of the population is imperative.

Second, augmentative communication systems, such as TDDs or captioning represent an exciting and potentially beneficial development in the field of deafness. There is, however, little research on the actual effect of these instruments or the way they should be employed. There is need for investigations that focus on the practical implementation and impact of these systems on the individual in the community setting.

Third, measures are needed that evaluate functional skills (e.g., job behavior or independent living skills) and that are standardized on a deaf population. Work in this area will require a careful analysis of the criterion environment (the community) to specify key content issues and problems. Similarly, the development of such instruments must include examination of how best to evaluate these persons; test data should assess actual skills instead of reflecting test-taking strengths and/or weaknesses. Also, the application of learning potential procedures in the development of functional measures appears to have a great relevance for this population.

Fourth, it is probable that more research will be generated on the mainstreaming issue, but we are not very optimistic about the value of this line of inquiry for proving that one setting is better than another. Investigations of this type are fraught with inherent methodological problems. The greatest difficulty rests in equating groups of students in different educational settings (residential versus mainstreamed) and making valid inferences regarding the true effect of the respective placement. There is no doubt that some students will do better in mainstreamed settings than in residential schools. On the other hand, there is no doubt that other students will do better in residential schools. Therefore, to facilitate appropriate placements, it makes sense to examine what type of student does better in each educational option (i.e., Aptitude Treatment Interaction, Cronbach & Snow, 1977; Reynolds, 1988) and to improve programs in both settings.

Fifth, research should be conducted to examine the efficacy of different job placement procedures, such as Job Club and techniques to foster employment tenure and advancement. Also, the link between schools and adult service agencies should be examined to foster better transition of the student into the community.

Last, investigations are needed that identify problems in independent living experienced in the community. Drawing from this baseline of data, assessment and instructional materials should be designed, implemented, and evaluated.

We conclude this chapter with one final thought. Deaf persons form a unique and somewhat misunderstood subgroup within the population served under the umbrella of special education and rehabilitation. Their needs, desires, and skills vary dramatically, and they stand apart because of their use of manual/visual systems as opposed to aural/oral communication. Some do extremely well in the hearing world, securing good jobs and having fruitful lives, but others are not so fortunate. Most deaf individuals have unimpaired mental and physical abilities, and their lack of success therefore represents a tragic waste of human resources. It is morally imperative, then, that research and service programs be implemented to improve the lives of these people.

REFERENCES

Acree, M., Orr, F., & Schleisenger, H. (1986). Rorschach testing with deaf adolescents: Clinical issues and research findings. In G. Anderson, D. Watson, & M. Taff-Watson (Eds.), *Integrating human resources, technology, and systems in deafness* (pp. 240–254). Silver Spring, MD: American Deafness and Rehabilitation Association.

Allen, T. (1984). Test response variations between hearing-impaired and hearing students. *Journal of Special Education, 18,* 119–129.

Amrine, C., & Bullis, M. (1985). The job club approach to job placement: A viable tool? *Journal of Rehabilitation of the Deaf, 19*(1 & 2), 18–23.

Azrin, N., & Besalel, V. (1980). *Job club counselor's manual.* Baltimore, MD: University Park Press.

Baker, C., & Cokely, D. (1980). *American Sign Language: A teacher's resource text on grammar and culture.* Silver Spring, MD: T. J. Publishers.

Barnett, S. (1982). The socioeconomic status of deaf women: Are they doubly disadvantaged? In J. Christiansen & J. Egelston-Dodd (Eds.), *Social aspects of deafness: Vol. 4. Socioeconomic status of the deaf population* (pp. 205–239). Washington, DC: Gallaudet College.

Barnum, M. (1984). In support of bilingual/bicultural education for deaf children. *American Annals of the Deaf, 129,* 404–408.

Benderly, B. L. (1980). *Dancing without music: Deafness in America.* Garden City, NY: Anchor Doubleday.

Bennett, R., & Maher, C. (Eds.). (1986). *Emerging perspectives on assessment of exceptional children.* New York: Haworth.

Bishop, M., Hicks, T., Galloway, V., Lauritsen, R., Updegraff, D., & Wykes, H. (1980). *Career education: The position paper of the conference of executives of American schools for the deaf.* Washington, DC: National Association of the Deaf.

Bolton, B. (Ed.). (1976). *Psychology of deafness for rehabilitation counselors.* Baltimore, MD: University Park Press.

Bolton, B., & Brown, K. (1971). The development of an instrument to assess work attitudes of deaf rehabilitation clients. *Journal of Rehabilitation of the Deaf, 4(4),* 18–29.

Bornstein, H. (1973). A discussion of some current sign systems designed to represent English. *American Annals of the Deaf, 118,* 454–463.

Breadle, K. (1982). Communication disorders: Speech and hearing. In E. Bleck & D. Nagel (Eds.), *Physically handicapped children: A medical atlas for teachers* (pp. 133–143). New York: Grune & Stratton.

Brolin, D. (1978). *Life centered career education: A competency based approach.* Reston, VA: Council for Exceptional Children.

Brolin, D., & Kokaska, C. (1979). *Career education for handicapped children and youth.* Columbus, OH: Charles E. Merrill.

Brown, S. (1987). Predictors of income variance among a group of deaf former college students. *Journal of Rehabilitation of the Deaf, 20(4),* 20–29.

Bruininks, R., Meyers, C. E., Sigford, B., & Lakin, K. C. (Eds.). (1981). *Deinstitutionalization and community adjustment of mentally retarded people* (Monograph No. 4). Washington, DC: American Association on Mental Deficiency.

Bullis, M. (1985a). A dilemma: Who and what to teach in career education programs? In M. Bullis & D. Watson (Eds.), *Career education of hearing impaired students: A review* (pp. 55–75). Little Rock, AR: Rehabilitation Research and Training Center on Deafness and Hearing Impairment.

Bullis, M. (1985b). Decision-making: A theoretical frame of reference in the career education of students with deafness. In G. Anderson & D. Watson (Eds.), *The habilitation and rehabilitation of deaf adolescents* (pp. 304–316). Washington, DC: Gallaudet College.

Bullis, M., Bull, B., Sendelbaugh, J., & Freeburg, J. (1987). *Review of research on the school-to-community transition of adolescents and young adults with hearing impairments.* Washington, DC: National Rehabilitation Information Center, Catholic University.

Bullis, M., & Freeburg, J. (1986). *Transition study of persons who are hard of hearing, deaf, or hearing impaired with secondary handicapping conditions.* Funded proposal from the National Institute of Disability and Rehabilitation Research to the Teaching Research Division, Oregon State System of Higher Education.

Bullis, M., & Marut, P. (1986). Evaluation recommendations and rehabilitation outcomes. In L. Stewart (Ed.), *Clinical rehabilitation assessment and hearing impairment: A guide to quality assurance* (pp. 111–118). Washington, DC: National Association of the Deaf.

Bullis, M., & Watson, D. (Eds.). (1985). *Career education of hearing impaired students: A review.* Little Rock, AR: Rehabilitation Research and Training Center on Deafness and Hearing Impairment.

Caccanise, F. (1979). Reliability of CID. Everyday sentence lists for performance assessment of receptive English simultaneous and manual communication skills. *American Annals of the Deaf, 124,* 726–730.

Clark, G., & Knowlton, E. (Eds.). (1987). The transition from school to adult life (special issue). *Exceptional Children, 53,*(8).

Cohen, B., & Anthony, W. (1984). Functional assessment in psychiatric rehabilitation. In A. Halpern & M. Fuhrer (Eds.), *Functional assessment in rehabilitation* (pp. 79–100). Baltimore, MD: Paul H. Brookes.

Cokely, D. (1975). *Varieties of manual communication in readings for sign language instructor certification.* Gallaudet College, Sign Language Programs and the National Association of the Deaf Communication Skills Programs.

Coleman, J. (1974). The transition from youth to adult. *Education Quarterly, 5*(3), 2–5.

Corthell, D., & Van Boskirk, C. (1984). *Continuum of services: School to work.* Menomonie, WI: Stout Vocational Rehabilitation Institute.

Craig, W., & Craig, H. (1977). Directory of services. *American Annals of the Deaf, 122,* 76–130.

Craig, W., & Craig, H. (1985). Directory of services. *American Annals of the Deaf, 130,* 81–129.

Craig, W., & Craig, H. (1986). Directory of services. *American Annals of the Deaf, 131,* 93–153.

Critchfield, A. B. (1986). Psychometric assessment. In L. Stewart (Ed.), *Clinical rehabilitation assessment and hearing impairment: A guide to quality assurance* (pp. 1–8). Washington, DC: National Association of the Deaf.

Cronbach, L., & Snow, R. (1977). *Aptitudes and instructional methods.* New York: Irvington.

Davey, B., & LaSasso, C. (1984). *Relations of cognitive style to assessment components of reading comprehension for deaf adolescents.* Washington, DC: International Symposium on Cognition, Education, and Deafness.

DeCaro, J., & Arenson, A. (1983). Career assessment and advisement of the technical college student. In D. Watson, G. Anderson, P. Marut, S. Ouellette, & N. Ford (Eds.), *Vocational evaluation of hearing impaired persons: Research and practice* (pp. 77–92). Little Rock, AR: Rehabilitation Research and Training Center on Deafness and Hearing Impairment.

Delaney, M., Stuckless, E. R., & Walter, G. G. (1984). Total communication effects—A longitudinal study of a school for the deaf in transition. *American Annals of the Deaf, 129,* 481–486.

De Paolo, A. (1976). *Comparison of hearing impaired to hearing graduates on the high school graduates career survey.* Scranton, PA: Department of Education, Bureau of Vocational Education. (ERIC Document Reproduction Service No. ED 138011)

DiFrancesca, S. (1978). *The Step method: Learning and practicing thinking skills.* New York: Psychological Corporation.

DiFrancesca, S. (1980). Developing thinking skills in career education. *Volta Review, 80,* 351–354.

Dillon, R. F. (1980). Cognitive style and elaboration of logical abilities in hearing impaired children. *Journal of Experimental Child Psychiatry, 29,* 532–538.

Dowaliby, F., Burke, N., & McKee, B. (1980). *Validity and reliability of a learning style inventory for post secondary deaf individuals.* Rochester, NY: National Technical Institute for the Deaf.

Dowaliby, F., McKee, B., & Maher, H. (1983). A focus of control inventory for postsecondary hearing impaired students. *American Annals of the Deaf, 128,* 884–889.

Dunlap, W., & Sands, D. (1987). Development of a set of instruments to assess independent living skills. *Journal of Rehabilitation, 53*(1), 58–67.

Dwyer, C. (1985). Career education: A literature review. In M. Bullis & D. Watson (Eds.), *Career education of hearing impaired students: A review* (pp. 3–25). Little Rock, AR: Rehabilitation Research and Training Center on Deafness and Hearing Impairment.

Edgar, E., & Hayden, A. (1984/1985). Who are the students special education should serve and how many are there? *Journal of Special Education, 18,* 525–540.

Egelston-Dodd, J. (1977). Overcoming occupational stereotypes related to sex and deafness. *American Annals of the Deaf, 122,* 489–491.

Egelston-Dodd, J. (Ed.). (1980). *Trainer's manual career education/planning skills.* Rochester, NY: National Technical Institute for the Deaf.

Egelston-Dodd, J., O'Brien, E., & Bondi-Wolcott, J. (1987). Explore your future: An NTID parent transition workshop. In G. Anderson & D. Watson (Eds.), *Innovations in the habilation and rehabilitation of deaf adolescents* (pp. 84–98). Little Rock, AR: Rehabilitation Research and Training Center in Deafness and Hearing Impairment.

Egelston-Dodd, J., & Young, M. (Eds.). (1984). *Catch tomorrow: Career awareness summer program.* Rochester, NY: National Technical Institute for the Deaf.

Egelston-Dodd, J., Young, M., Lutz, J., & Lichty, D. (1983). Inservice training in career education and planning skills. In G. Tyler (Ed.), *Critical issues in rehabilitation and human services* (Vol. 6, pp. 61–88). Silver Spring, MD: American Deafness and Rehabilitation Association.

El-Khiami, A. (1986). Selected characteristics of hearing impaired rehabilitants of general VR agencies: A sociodemographic profile. In D. Watson, G. Anderson, & M. Taff-Watson (Eds.), *Integrating human resources, technology, and systems in deafness* (pp. 136–144). Silver Spring, MD: American Deafness and Rehabilitation Association.

El-Khiami, A. (1987a). The role of the family in the transition of young hearing-impaired adults: The case of postsecondary graduates. In G. Anderson & D. Watson (Eds.), *Innovations in the habilation and rehabilitation of deaf adolescents* (pp. 99–116). Little Rock, AR: Rehabilitation Research and Training Center on Deafness and Hearing Impairment.

El-Khiami, A. (1987b). Transition from school to work: Employers' perceptions of hearing-impaired graduates of postsecondary programs. In G. Anderson & D. Watson (Eds.), *Innovations in the habilation and rehabilitation of deaf adolescents* (pp. 141–155). Little Rock, AR: Rehabilitation Research and Training Center on Deafness and Hearing Impairment.

Elliott, H., Glass, L., & Evans, J. (Eds.). (1987). *Mental health assessment of deaf clients.* Boston: Little, Brown.

Emerton, R., & Emerton, K. (1987). Crime and delinquency. In J. V. Van Cleve (Ed.), *Gallaudet encyclopedia of deaf people and deafness* (pp. 213–216). New York: McGraw-Hill.

Emerton, R. G., Foster, S., & Royer, H. (1986, June). *Technology and social change: The impact of changing technologies on the employment of a group of older deaf workers.* Paper presented at the Conference on Social Change and the Deaf Community/Deaf Culture, Gallaudet College, Washington, DC.

Evans, L. (1980). WISC performance scale and colored progressive matrices with deaf children. *British Journal of Educational Psychology, 50,* 216–222.

Fairweather, J. (1984). *Alternative study designs and revised conceptual framework for the longitudinal study of handicapped youth in transition.* Menlo Park, CA: SRI International.

Fant, L. (1974, Winter). Ameslan. *Gallaudet Today,* pp. 1–3.

Farrugia, D., & Austin, G. (1980). A study of social-emotional adjustment patterns of hearing-impaired students in different educational settings. *American Annals of the Deaf, 125,* 535–541.

Feller, B. A. (1981). *Prevalence of selected impairments, United States, 1977* (DHHS Publication No. (PHS) 81-1562). Washington, DC: U.S. Government Printing Office.

Feuerstein, R. (1979). *The dynamic assessment of retarded performers: The Learning Potential Device, theory, instruments, and techniques.* Baltimore, MD: University Park Press.

Feuerstein, R. (1980). *Instrumental enrichment: An intervention program for cognitive modifiability.* Baltimore, MD: University Park Press.

Feuerstein, R., Rand, Y., Jensen, M., Kaniel, S., Tzuriel, D., Shachar, N., & Mintzker, Y. (1986). Learning potential assessment. In R. Bennett & C. Maher (Eds.), *Emerging perspectives on assessment of exceptional children* (pp. 85–106). New York: Haworth.

Fiaz, M., & Fiaz, N. (1977). Occupational distribution of the hearing impaired in Ontario: A statistical profile. *Educational Planning, 4,* 11–28.

Foster, S. (1986). *Employment experiences of deaf RIT graduates: An interview study.* Unpublished manuscript, National Technical Institute for the Deaf, Rochester, NY.

Fraser, S., & Owlsey, P. J. (1981). A study of graduates at the Atlantic Provinces Centre for the Hearing Handicapped from 1967–1977. *Association of Canadian Educators of the Hearing Impaired, 7*(3), 86–93.

Frishberg, N. (1986). *Interpreting: An introduction.* Silver Spring, MD: RID.

Frisina, R. (1974). *Report of the committee to redefining deaf and hard of hearing for educational purposes.* Washington, DC: Conference of Executives of American Schools for the Deaf.

Galloway, V. (1978). *Overview of a career development model.* Washington, DC: Gallaudet College.

Gannon, J. R. (1981). *Deaf heritage: A narrative of deaf Americans.* Silver Spring, MD: National Association of the Deaf.

Gehrz, R. C. (1984). *CMV: Diagnosis, prevention and treatment.* St. Paul, MN: Children's Hospital.

Gentile, A. (1975). *Persons with impaired hearing, United States: 1971* (DHEW Publication No. (HRA) 76-1528). Washington, DC: U.S. Government Printing Office. (pp. 10, 101).

Gerweck, S., & Ysseldyke, J. (1979). Limitations of current psychological practices for the intellectual assessment of the hearing impaired: A response to the Levine study. *Volta Review, 77*, 243–248.

Gibson-Harman, K., & Austin, G. F. (1985). A revised form of the Tennessee self concept scale for use with deaf and hard of hearing persons. *American Annals of the Deaf, 130*, 218–225.

Glickman, W. (1986). Cultural identity, deafness, and mental health. *Journal of Rehabilitation of the Deaf, 20*(2), 1–10.

Gould, S. (1979). *The mismeasure of man.* New York: W. W. Norton.

Grant, D. J., Marron, M. J., & Welsh, W. A. (1980). *Beginning a longitudinal analysis: A look at patterns of labor mobility among deaf graduates of the Rochester Institute of Technology* (Report No. 37). Rochester, NY: National Technical Institute for the Deaf.

Greenberg, M., & Kushé, C. (in press). Cognitive, personal and social development of deaf children and adolescents. In M. Wang, M. Reynolds, & H. Walberg (Eds.), *Handbook of special education: Research and practice* (Vol. 1). Elmsford, NY: Pergamon.

Gustason, G. (1985). Interpreters entering public school employment. *American Annals of the Deaf, 130*(4), 265–266.

Halpern, A. (1985). Transition: A look at the foundations. *Exceptional Children, 51*, 479–486.

Halpern, A., & Fuhrer, M. (Eds.). (1984). *Functional assessment in rehabilitation.* Baltimore, MD: Paul H. Brookes.

Heller, B., Flohr, L., & Zegans, L. (Eds.). (1987). *Psychosocial interventions with sensorially disabled persons.* New York: Grune & Stratton.

Heller, B., & Harris, R. (1987). Special considerations in the psychological assessment of hearing impaired persons. In B. Heller, L. Flohr, & L. Zegans (Eds.), *Psychosocial interventions with sensorially disabled persons* (pp. 53–78). New York: Grune & Stratton.

Hirshoren, A., Hurley, O., & Kavale, K. (1979). Psychometric characteristics of the WISC-R performance scale with deaf children. *Journal of Hearing and Speech Disorders, 44*, 73–79.

Hirshoren, A., & Schnittjer, C. (1979). Dimensions of problem behavior in deaf children. *Journal of Abnormal Child Psychology, 7*, 221–228.

Holland, J. (1966). *The psychology of vocational choice.* Waltham, MA: Blaisdell.

Holm, C. (1987). Testing for values with the deaf: The language/cultural effect. *Journal of Rehabilitation of the Deaf, 20*(4), 7–19.

Hurley, O., Hirshoren, A., Hunt, J., & Kavale, K. (1979). Predictive validity of two mental ability tests with black deaf children. *Journal of Negro Education, 48*, 14–19.

Jacobs, R. (in press). Use of the sixteen personality questionnaire form A, with deaf university students. *Journal of Rehabilitation of the Deaf.*

Jacobs, R. (1979). *Report of the ad hoc committee on coding of hearing impaired vocational rehabilitation clients.* Washington, DC: Rehabilitation Services Administration.

Jacobs, L. (1980). *A deaf adult speaks out* (2nd ed.). Washington, DC: Gallaudet College.

Jensema, C. (1975). A statistical investigation of the 16PF form E as applied to hearing impaired college students. *Journal of Rehabilitation of the Deaf, 9*(1), 21–29.

Jensema, C. (1985). *Using closed-captioned television in the teaching of reading to deaf students.* Falls Church, VA: National Captioning Institute.

Johnson, D., & Kadnuc, N. (1980). Usefulness of the NTID communication profile for evaluating deaf secondary-level students. *American Annals of the Deaf, 125,* 337–349.

Karchmer, M. A. (1985). Demographics and deaf adolescents. In G. B. Anderson & D. Watson (Eds.), *The habilitation and rehabilitation of deaf adolescents* (pp. 28–48).Washington, DC: Gallaudet College.

Katz, M., & Buchhom, E. (1984). Use of the LPAD for cognitive enrichment of a deaf child. *School Psychology Review, 13,* 99–106.

Keane, K. (1987). Assessing deaf children. In C. Lidz (Ed.), *Dynamic assessment* (pp. 360–378). New York: Guilford.

Kerlinger, F. (1986). *Foundations of behavioral research* (3rd. ed.). New York: Holt, Rinehart, & Winston.

Klein, E. (1981). Assessment of language. In J. Salvia & J. Ysseldyke (Eds.), *Assessment in special and remedial education* (pp. 387–419). Boston: Houghton Mifflin.

Klinefelter, R. (1986). *Guidelines for the implementation of a TDD distribution program.* Unpublished manuscript, Santa Monica, CA.

Ladd, G., Munson, H., & Miller, J. (1984). Social integration of deaf adolescents in secondary-level mainstreamed programs. *Exceptional Children, 50,* 420–428.

Lang, H., & Stinson, M. (1982). Career education and the occupational status of deaf persons: Concepts, research, and implications. In J. Christiansen & J. Egelston-Dodd (Eds.), *Social aspects of deafness: Vol. 4. Socioeconomic status of the deaf population* (pp. 95–121). Washington, DC: Gallaudet College.

LaSasso, C. (1979). The effect of WH question format versus incomplete statement format on deaf students' demonstration of comprehension of text-explicit information. *American Annals of the Deaf, 124,* 833–837.

LaSasso, C. (1980). The validity and reliability of the cloze procedure as a measure of reliability for prelingually, profoundly deaf students. *American Annals of the Deaf, 125,* 359–363.

Leavitt, R. J. (1987). Dispensing rehabilitation technology for hearing-impaired people. *American Speech and Hearing Association, 29,* 28–31.

Lerman, A., & Guilfoyle, G. (1970). *The development of prevocational behavior in deaf adolescents.* New York: Teachers College Press.

Levine, E. (1974). Psychological tests and practices with the deaf: A survey of the state of the art. *Volta Review, 76,* 298–319.

Lombardo, A. (1976). An examination of the difficulties encountered by the black deaf. *The Deaf American, 28*(7), 23–26.

Long, G., Conklin, O., & Garrison, W. (1978). *The development of a cognitive process based learning strategies questionnaire* (Paper No. 23). Rochester, NY: National Technical Institute for the Deaf.

Long, N., & Davis, G. (1986). Self-directed job seeking skills training: Utilization in a project with industry program. In D. Watson, G. Anderson, & M. Taff-Watson (Eds.), *Integrating human resources, technology, and systems in deafness* (pp. 313–324). Silver Spring, MD: American Deafness and Rehabilitation Association.

Low, W., & Egelston-Dodd, J. (1984). *Catch tomorrow: CASP literature and materials review.* Rochester, NY: National Technical Institute for the Deaf.

Luetke-Stahlman, B., & Waver, F. (1982). Assessing language and/or system preferences of Spanish-deaf preschoolers. *American Annals of the Deaf, 127,* 789–796.

Lytle, R., & Jonas, B. (1985). Predictors of social and emotional adjustment in deaf adolescents at a residential school. In G. Anderson & D. Watson (Eds.), *The habilitation and rehabilitation of deaf adolescents* (pp. 62–80). Washington, DC: Gallaudet College.

MacLeod, J. (1983). *Secondary school graduate follow-up program of the hearing impaired: Fourth annual report.* Rochester, NY: National Technical Institute for the Deaf, Division of Career Opportunities.

MacLeod, J. (1984). *Secondary school graduate follow-up program of the hearing: Fifth annual report.* Rochester, NY: National Technical Institute for the Deaf.

MacLeod, J. (1985). *Secondary school graduate follow-up program of the hearing: Sixth annual report.* Rochester, NY: National Technical Institute for the Deaf.

Marland, S. (1974). *Career education: A proposal for reform.* New York: McGraw-Hill.

Martin, K. (1983). Innovations in the placement of hearing-impaired technical graduates. In D. Watson, G. Anderson, N. Ford, P. Marut, & S. Ouellette (Eds.), *Job placement of hearing impaired persons: Research and practice* (pp. 41–56). Little Rock, AR: Rehabilitation Research and Training Center on Deafness and Hearing Impairment.

Marut, P., & Innes, C. (1986). The delivery of vocational evaluation and adjustment services to deaf people. In D. Watson, G. Anderson, & M. Taff-Watson (Eds.), *Integrating human resources, technology, and systems in deafness* (pp. 135–144). Silver Spring, MD: American Deafness and Rehabilitation Association.

Mayberry, R., & Wodlinger-Cohen, R. (1987). After the revolution: Educational practice and the deaf child's communication skills. In E. D. Mindel & E. M. Vernon (Eds.), *They grow in silence: Understanding deaf children and adults* (2nd ed., pp. 149–185). Boston: College-Hill.

McKee, B., & Lang, H. (1982). A comparison of deaf students' performance on true-false and multiple-choice items. *American Annals of the Deaf, 127,* 49–54.

McKusick, V. (1983). *Mendelian inheritance in man* (6th ed.). Baltimore, MD: Johns Hopkins.

Meadow, K. (1980). *Meadow/Kendall social emotional assessment inventory for deaf students: Manual.* Washington, DC: Gallaudet University.

Miller, M. (1984). *Experimental use of signed presentations of the verbal scale of the WISC-R with profoundly deaf children: A preliminary report of the sign selection process and experimental test procedures.* Washington, DC: International Symposium on Cognition Education and Deafness.

Monson, R. (1981). A usable test for the speech intelligibility of deaf talkers. *American Annals of the Deaf, 126,* 845–852.

Montgomery, G. (1966). Relationships of oral skills to manual communication in profoundly deaf students. *American Annals of the Deaf, 111,* pp. 557–565.

Moores, D. (1978). *Educating the deaf: Psychology, principles, and practices.* Boston: Houghton Mifflin.

Moores, D. F. (1979). Hearing impairments. In M. S. Lily (Ed.), *Children with exceptional needs: A survey of special education* (pp. 279–319). New York: Holt, Rinehart, & Winston.

Moores, D. F. (1987). *Educating the deaf: Psychology, principles and practices* (3rd Ed.). Boston: Houghton Mifflin.

Moss, A. J., & Parsons, V. L. (1986). *Current estimates from the national health interview survey* (DHHS Publication No. (PHS) 86–1588). Washington, DC: U.S. Government Printing Office.

Munson, H., & Egelston, J. (1975). Career education for the deaf: A program model and materials. *Journal of Rehabilitation of the Deaf, 9*(2), 24–35.

Myklebust, H. (1964). *The psychology of deafness.* New York: Grune & Stratton.

Nash, K., & Castle, W. (1980). Special problems of deaf adolescents and young adults. *Exceptional Education Quarterly, 1,* 99–106.

Newell, W. (1978). A study of the ability of day-class adolescents to comprehend factual information using four communication modalities. *American Annals of the Deaf, 123,* 558–562.

Newmann-Solow, S. (1981). *Sign language interpreting: A basic resource book.* Silver Spring, MD: National Association of the Deaf.

Nober, L. (1985, July). *Instructional services to hearing-impaired students in the United States: 1984 update.* Paper presented to the International Congress on Education of the Deaf, Manchester, Great Britain.

Olmedo, E. (1981). Testing linguistic minorities. *American Psychologist, 36,* 1078–1085.

Orr, F., DeMatteo, A., Heller, B., Lee, M., & Nguyen, M. (1987). Psychological assessment. In H. Elliott, L. Glass, & J. Evans (Eds.), *Mental health assessment of deaf clients* (pp. 93–106). Boston: Little, Brown.

Ouellette, S. (1986a). Preliminary results of a descriptive analysis of 46 post-secondary education programs for hearing impaired students in the United States. In D. Watson, G. Anderson, & M. Taff-Watson (Eds.), *Integrating human resources, technology, and systems in deafness* (pp. 255–266). Silver Spring, MD: American Deafness and Rehabilitation Association.

Ouellette, S. (1986b). Selected results of a long-term follow-up study of severely disabled hearing-impaired clients served in a comprehensive rehabilitation facility. In D. Watson, G. Anderson, & M. Taff-Watson (Eds.), *Integrating human resources, technology, and systems in deafness* (pp. 420–428). Silver Spring, MD: American Deafness and Rehabilitation Association.

Ouellette, S. (in press). The use of the House-Tree-Person test with deaf adults. *American Annals of the Deaf.*

Ouellette, S., & Dwyer, C. (1985). A current profile of career education programs. In M. Bullis & D. Watson (Eds.), *Career education of hearing impaired students:*

A review (pp. 27–54). Little Rock, AR: Research and Training Center on Deafness and Hearing Impairments.

Ouellette, S., & Loyd, G. (1980). *Independent living skills for severely handicapped deaf people.* Silver Spring, MD: American Deafness and Rehabilitation Association.

Padden, C. (1980). The deaf community and the culture of deaf people. In C. Baker & R. Battison (Eds.), *Sign language and the deaf community* (pp. 89–102). Silver Spring, MD: National Association of the Deaf.

Padden, C., & Markowicz, H. (1982). Learning to be deaf: Conflicts between hearing and deaf culture. *Quarterly Newsletter of the Laboratory of Comparative Human Cognition, 4*(4), 67–72.

Pappas, D. (1985). *Diagnosis and treatment of hearing impairment in children.* San Diego: College Hill.

Phillips, G. B. (1975). An exploration of employer attitudes concerning employment opportunities for deaf people. *Journal of Rehabilitation of Deaf, 9*(2), 1–9.

Quarrington, B., & Solomon, B. (1975). A current study of the social maturity of deaf students. *Canadian Journal of Behavioral Sciences, 7,* 70–77.

Quigley, S. (1969). *The influence of finger-spelling and the development of language, communication, and educational achievement in deaf children.* Unpublished manuscript, University of Illinois, Champaign-Urbana.

Rawlings, B., Karchmer, M., DeCaro, J. & Egelston-Dodd, J. (1986). *College and career programs for deaf students.* Washington, DC and Rochester, NY: Gallaudet College and the National Technical Institute for the Deaf.

Rawlings, B., Karchmer, M., King, S., & Brown, S. (1985). *Gallaudet College alumni survey, 1984.* Washington, DC: Gallaudet.

Rawlings, B., & Trybus, R. (1978). Personnel, facilities, and services available in schools and classes for hearing impaired children in the United States. *American Annals of the Deaf, 123,* 99–115.

Rawlings, B., Trybus, R., & Biser, J. (1978). *A career guide to college/career programs for deaf students.* Washington, DC and Rochester, NY: Gallaudet College and National Technical Institute for the Deaf.

Ray, S. (1982). Adopting the WISC-R for deaf children. *Diagnostique, 7,* 147–157.

Reagan, T. (1985). The deaf as a linguistic minority: Educational considerations. *Harvard Educational Review, 55,* 265–277.

Reinhart, B. (1979). *Career education: From concept to reality.* New York: McGraw-Hill.

Reschley, D. (1981). Psychological testing in educational classification and placement. *American Psychologist, 36,* 1094–1102.

Reynolds, C. E. (1988). Putting the individual into aptitude-treatment interaction. *Exceptional Children, 54,* 324–331.

Ries, P. (1973). *Reported causes of hearing loss for hearing impaired student, 1970–71* (Series D., No. 11). Washington, DC: Gallaudet College Office of Demographic Studies.

Ries, P. W. (1982). *Hearing ability of persons by sociodemographic and health characteristics.* (DHHS Publication No. (PHS) 82–1568). Washington, DC: U.S. Government Printing Office.

Rogers, W. T. (1983). Use of separate answer sheets with hearing impaired and deaf school age students. *British Columbia Journal of Special Education, 7,* 63–72.

Rudner, L. (1978). Using standardized tests with the hearing impaired: The problem of item bias. *Volta Review, 80,* 31–40.

Salvia, J., & Ysseldyke, J. (1987). *Assessment in special and remedial education* (7th ed.). Boston: Houghton Mifflin.

Schein, J. (1979). Society and culture of hearing impaired people. In L. Bradford & W. Hardy (Eds.), *Hearing and hearing impairments* (pp. 479–487). New York: Grune & Stratton.

Schein, J., & Delk, M., Jr. (1974). *The deaf population of the United States.* Silver Spring, MD: National Association of the Deaf.

Schlesinger, H. S., & Meadow, K. (1972). *Sound and sign.* Berkeley: University of California Press.

Schlidroth, A. (1987). Residential schools for deaf students: A decade in review. In A. Schlidroth & M. Karchmer (Eds.), *Deaf children in America* (pp. 83–104). Boston: Little, Brown.

Schroedel, J. (1979). Surveys on the socioeconomic status of deaf, 1956–1971: Assessing response rates. In J. Christiansen & J. Egelston-Dodd (Eds.), *Social aspects of deafness* (Vol. 4, pp. 271–290). Washington, DC: Gallaudet College.

Schroedel, J. (1986). A national study of the class of 1984 in postsecondary education with implications for rehabilitation. In D. Watson, G. Anderson, & M. Taff-Watson (Eds.), *Integrating human resources, technology, and systems in deafness* (pp. 267–286). Silver Spring, MD: American Deafness and Rehabilitation Association.

Schroedel, J. (1987). The educational and occupational aspirations and attainments of deaf students and alumni of postsecondary programs. In G. Anderson & D. Watson (Eds.), *Innovations in the habilitation and rehabilitation of deaf adolescents* (pp. 117–140). Little Rock, AR: Rehabilitation Research and Training Center on Deafness and Hearing Impairments.

Sendelbaugh, J., & Bullis, M. (1987). *Examination of state level special education and rehabilitation policies on the transition of students with hearing impairments.* Manuscript submitted for publication.

Shiels, J. (1986). Vocational assessment. In L. Stewart (Ed.), *Clinical rehabilitation assessment and hearing impairment: A guide to quality assurance* (pp. 95–110). Washington, DC: National Association of the Deaf.

Sinclair, J. S. (1979). Design and performance of hearing aids. In L. J. Bradford & W. G. Hardy (Eds.), *Hearing and hearing impairment* (pp. 173–192). New York: Grune & Stratton.

Sligar, S. (1983). Commercial vocational evaluation systems and deaf persons. In D. Watson, G. Anderson, P. Marut, S. Ouellette, & N. Ford (Eds.), *Vocational evaluation of hearing impaired persons: Research and practice* (pp. 35–56). Little Rock, AR: Rehabilitation Research and Training Center in Deafness and Hearing Impairment.

Sonnenstrahl, A. (Ed.). (1987). *International phone directory for TDD users.* Silver Spring, MD: Telecommunications for the Deaf, Inc.

Sontag, E., Smith, J., & Certo, N. (1977). *Educational programming for the severely and profoundly handicapped.* Reston, VA: Council for Exceptional Children.

Stansfield, M., & Veltri, D. (1987). Assessment from the perspective of the sign language interpreter. In H. Elliott, L. Glass, & J. Evans (Eds.), *Mental health assessment of deaf clients* (pp. 153–164). Boston: Little, Brown.

Stevenson, E. (1964). *A study of the educational achievement of deaf children of deaf parents.* Berkeley: California School for the Deaf.

Stewart, L. (1978). Hearing impaired/developmentally disabled persons in the United States: Definitions, causes, effects, and prevalence estimates. *American Annals of the Deaf, 123,* 488–495.

Stewart, L. (Ed.) (1986a). *Clinical rehabilitation assessment and hearing impairment: A guide to quality assurance.* Washington, DC: National Association of the Deaf.

Stewart, L. (1986b). Psychological assessment: One perspective. In L. Stewart (Ed.), *Clinical rehabilitation assessment and hearing impairment: A guide to quality assurance* (pp. 9–26). Washington, DC: National Association of the Deaf.

Stewart, L. (1986c). State VR agencies policies for sponsoring deaf students in post-secondary education and training. In D. Watson, G. Anderson, & M. Taff-Watson (Eds.), *Integrating human resources, technology, and systems in deafness* (pp. 287–297). Silver Spring, MD: American Deafness and Rehabilitation Association.

Stokoe, W. (1972). A classroom experiment in two languages. In T. O'Rourke (Ed.), *Psycholinguistics and total communication: The state of the art* (pp. 85–91). Silver Spring, MD: American Annals of the Deaf.

Stuckless, E., & Birch, J. (1966). The influence of early manual communication on the linguistic development of deaf children. *American Annals of the Deaf, 111,* 452–461.

Stuckless, R. (1973). *Principles basic to the establishment of postsecondary education programs for deaf students.* Washington, DC: Conference of Executives of American Schools for the Deaf.

Sullivan, F. (1982). Administration modifications on the WISC-R performance scale with different categories of deaf children. *American Annals of the Deaf, 127,* 780–788.

Sullivan, P. (1986). Characteristics and assessment of students in transition. In L. Stewart (Ed.), *Clinical rehabilitation assessment and hearing impairment: A guide to quality assurance* (pp. 37–48). Silver Spring, MD: American Deafness and Rehabilitation Association.

Super, D. (1957). *The psychology of careers.* New York: Harper & Row.

Switzer, M., & Williams, B. (1967). Life problems of deaf people, prevention and training. *Archives of Environmental Health, 15,* 249–256.

Taft, B. (1983). Employability of black deaf persons in Washington, DC: National implications. *American Annals of the Deaf, 128,* 453–457.

Tiedemann, D., & O'Hara, R. (1963). *Career development: Choice and adjustment.* New York: College Entrance Examination Board.

Torretti, W., & Hendrick, P. (1986). A job club approach with severely disabled deaf clients. In D. Watson, G. Anderson, & M. Taff-Watson (Eds.), *Integrating human resources, technology, and systems in deafness* (pp. 325–339). Silver Spring, MD: American Deafness and Rehabilitation Association.

Trybus, R. (1973). Personality assessment of entering hearing-impaired students using the 16PF form E. *Journal of Rehabilitation of the Deaf, 6*(3), 34–40.

Updegraff, D., Bishop, M., Steffan, R., & Egelston-Dodd, J. (1979). *Career development for the hearing impaired: Proceedings of two working conferences,* Washington, DC: Gallaudet College.

Updegraff, D., & Egelston-Dodd, J. (1982). The National Project on Career Education: Past, present, and future. *Directions, 2*(4), 15–23.

U.S. Department of Education. (1984). *Sixth annual report to Congress on the implementation of the Education of the Handicapped Act.* Washington, DC: U.S. Government Printing Office.

Vernon, M. (1968). Current etiological factors in deafness. *American Annals of the Deaf, 113,* 106–115.

Vernon, M. (1987). The primary causes of deafness. In E. Mindel & M. Vernon (Eds.), *The grow in silence* (2nd ed., pp. 31–38). Boston: College-Hill.

Watson, B., & Goldgar, D. (1985). A note on the Hiskey-Nebraska test of learning aptitude with deaf children. *Language, Speech, and Hearing Services in the Schools, 16,* 53–57.

Watson, D. (1979). Guidelines for the psychological and vocational assessment of deaf rehabilitation clients. *Journal of Rehabilitation of the Deaf, 13*(1), 29–57.

Watson, D. (1983). *Improving vocational rehabilitation in postsecondary education programs for deaf individuals.* Grant from the National Institute of Handicapped Research.

Welsh, W. (1982). Correlates of labor force activities of deaf graduates of the Rochester Institute of Technology. In J. Christiansen & J. Egelston-Dodd (Eds.), *Social aspects of deafness* (Vol. 4, pp. 153–169). Washington, DC: Gallaudet College.

Welsh, W. (1986). *The status of RIT graduates in the work place: 1985.* Rochester, NY: National Technical Institute for the Deaf.

Welsh, W., & Parker, C. (1982a). *The comparative status of deaf RIT graduates: 1978–1980* (Report No. 42). Rochester, NY: National Technical Institute for the Deaf.

Welsh, W., & Parker, C. (1982b). *Employment and occupational accommodation: A longitudinal and comparative analysis of deaf graduates of the Rochester Institute of Technology* (Report No. 49). Rochester, NY: National Technical Institute for the Deaf.

Welsh, W. A., & Schroedel, J. G. (1982). *Predictors of success for deaf graduates of the Rochester Institute of Technology* (Report No. 46). Rochester, NY: Institutional Planning and Research, National Technical Institute for the Deaf.

White, K. (1982). Defining and prioritizing the personal and social competencies needed by hearing-impaired students. *Volta Review, 82,* 226–274.

White, K., & Slusher, N. (1978). *Measuring career development among post-secondary deaf students* (Paper No. 25). Rochester, NY: National Technical Institute for the Deaf.

Wilbur, R. (1979). *American Sign Language and sign systems.* Baltimore, MD: University Park Press.

Wilcox, B., & Bellamy, T. (1982). *Design of high school programs for severely handicapped students.* Baltimore, MD: Paul H. Brookes.

Wilder, C. S. (1975). *Prevalence of selected impairments. United States, 1971* (DHEW

Publication No. (HRA) 75–1526). Washington, DC: Government Printing Office.

Will, M. (1984). *OSERS program for the transition of youth with disabilities: Bridges from school to working life.* Washington, DC: Office of Special Education and Rehabilitation.

Witheford, M., & Wilton, K. (1978). Effects of residential school attendance on the social development of hearing-handicapped children. *New Zealand Journal of Educational Studies, 13,* 40–51.

Wodlinger-Cohen, R. (1986). *The manual representation of speech by deaf children, their mothers and their teachers.* Paper presented at The Conference on Theoretical Issues in Sign Language Research, Rochester, NY.

Woodrick, W. (1980). Introduction to independent living skills and presentation of objectives. *Independent living skills for severely handicapped deaf people.* American Deafness and Rehabilitation Association, 5, 1–3.

Wootton, S. C., & Mowry, R. L. (1986). A follow-up study of hearing impaired VR clients closed successfully by a state VR agency. In D. Watson, G. Anderson, & M. Taft-Watson (Eds.), *Integrating human resources, technology, and systems in deafness* (pp. 410–419). Silver Spring, MD: American Deafness and Rehabilitation Association.

Yandell, D. (1986). Psychological assessment: Another perspective. In L. Stewart (Ed.), *Clinical rehabilitation assessment and hearing impairment: A guide to quality assurance* (pp. 27–36). Washington, DC: National Association of the Deaf.

Young, M., Lutz, J., Lichty, D., & Egelston-Dodd, J. (1980). *Evaluation of an inservice program.* Rochester, NY: National Technical Institute for the Deaf.

CHAPTER 7

Dynamic Assessment:
A Comprehensive Review of Literature

HOWARD R. ROTHMAN
MELVYN I. SEMMEL

In the past two decades there has been growing interest in the area of dynamic assessment as a means of evaluating the intellectual status and learning potential of retarded and other academically disabled individuals (Bransford, Delclos, Vye, Burns, & Hasselbring, 1986; Brown & French, 1979; Budoff, 1965, 1967, 1972, 1974; Campione, Brown & Ferrara, 1982; Feuerstein, 1979; Haywood, 1985). One reason for this interest is the growing dissatisfaction among educators with the use of traditional "static" psychometric tests. The tests' inadequate prescriptive applicability in the classroom, ethnic biases, and reliability in identifying learning disabled populations have all been presented as reasons for considering alternative forms of intellectual assessment (Delclos, 1983).

Bransford and his associates (Bransford, Delclos, Vye, Burns, & Hasselbring 1986) have suggested that dynamic approaches to assessment "might help educators improve the quality of placement, assessment, and instruction and thereby improve learning" (p. 1). In this regard, application of these techniques may help reduce some of the difficulties associated with static measurement (Budoff, 1974; Feuerstein, 1979, 1980). Considering the strong claims that have been made concerning the potential value of dynamic approaches to assessment, it seems timely to conduct a comprehensive review of the literature. We begin by comparing a general dynamic assessment approach with traditional static approaches. Next, we present a discussion of the weaknesses of static assessment as cited in the literature. Then, we compare and contrast empirical endeavors of four primary research groups to evaluate the relative merits of differing approaches to this form of evaluation. Finally, a summary and conclusion of the current review is presented and recommendations for future research needs are discussed.

Authors listed alphabetically.

A COMPARISON OF DYNAMIC AND STATIC CONCEPTS

Dynamic assessment refers to approaches of measuring an individual's receptiveness to instruction (Feuerstein, 1979) or "zone of proximal development" (Vygotsky, 1978). In contrast to static assessment, dynamic procedures require ongoing interaction between the examiner and testee so that specific problem-solving behavior can be assessed. The examiner often uses a systematic approach in modifying specific task components and providing essential information for solving a presented problem. In contrast to static assessment procedures, a student's initial incorrect response is not taken as the final product of the evaluation endeavor. Instead, prompts or other forms of mediation are provided to help evaluate an individual's responsiveness to instruction. In this way, the examiner is able to compare an individual's baseline ability performance with his/her receptivity to instructional intervention. Thus, two students with the same chronological and mental age may yield significantly different results when their responsiveness to learning a specific task is compared.

It has been argued (Brown & French, 1979; Campione & Brown, 1987; Campione, Brown & Ferrara, 1982; Feuerstein, 1979) that traditional, static IQ tests often fail to provide teachers with relevant information helpful in developing appropriate teaching strategies. This failure to link diagnosis and remediation is one of the reasons teachers often give for questioning the time and effort involved in the referral-assessment process (Gerber & Semmel, 1984).

Other areas in which traditional assessment approaches have been questioned are multilingual and multicultural assessment (Rueda, in press) and assessment of groups having low socioeconomic status (Budoff, 1974; Feuerstein, 1979). It has been suggested, and in some cases empirically validated (Budoff, 1974), that dynamic assessment techniques have the potential of differentiating between children of limited intellectual ability and those of higher ability who have been misclassified as "lower functioning" because of limited experience with the predominant language and culture. Budoff (1972) indicates that children from poor or nonwhite homes often score below average on traditional IQ tests. He points out that these children "are often fearful of the testing process, expect to do poorly, are often insensitive to speed requirements, are poor test takers, and are unfamiliar with the problem contents" (p. 1). In fact, many of these apparently lower functioning children are actually adequate problem-solvers in that they can profit from appropriate learning experiences. When an assessment procedure sensitive to training effects is used, these initial discrepancies are often no longer evident.

A significant flaw of the traditional psychometric approach to assessment is its assumption that testing conditions are standardized to ensure that each child is treated equally. In fact, a number of studies examining tester-testee interaction have indicated that there is significant variability in static testing environments (Feldman & Sullivan, 1971; Mehan, 1973; Saigh, 1981). All too often test bias favoring the middle-class child is evident (Campione, Brown, & Ferrara, 1982). Mehan (1973) reported up to a 27% difference between strict and lenient scoring criteria, often in favor of the middle-class child. Studies in which examiners use positive verbal or nonverbal feedback (Feldman & Sullivan, 1971; Saigh, 1981) indicate that test performance is significantly affected by tester feedback. It has been suggested (Burns & Stephens, in press; Campione, Brown, & Ferrara, 1982) that dynamic assessment methods may reduce this bias significantly.

FOUR RESEARCH PROGRAMS FOCUSED ON DYNAMIC ASSESSMENT

Dynamic assessment research has been carried out by four primary research groups: Budoff and his associates, Feuerstein and his associates, Brown and Campione and their research group at the University of Illinois, and Bransford and his associates at Vanderbilt University. A review of these findings will be presented beginning with the work of Milton Budoff and his associates (Budoff & Friedman,1964; Budoff & Corman, 1973; Budoff, 1967, 1972, 1974).

Budoff's Learning Potential Research

Budoff and his associates devised and evaluated test-teach-test strategies to help assess the learning potential of nonretarded, mildly retarded, and more severely retarded children and adults. In a typical pretest session, participants were assessed using traditional IQ problems (for example Kohs Blocks and Raven's Progressive Matrices). In the instructional phase, an incorrect response to a presented problem resulted in a series of progressively explicit hints being provided by the examiner until success was achieved. Budoff (1972) explained the logic to his Learning Potential Assessment approach as follows:

> The intent is to obtain an estimate of general ability derived from reasoning problems of suitable difficulty which the child has had an opportunity to learn how to solve and which permit a comparison with low scholastic aptitude score (e.g., the Binet IQ). If the child can demonstrate, following a short period of training on a nonverbal reasoning task that he can perform at the level approximating his agemates' performance, then clearly he is not men-

tally retarded. We define *intelligence* in this assessment paradigm as the ability to profit from experience. (p. 4)

Budoff and Friedman (1964) used the Kohs Block Design Task (Kohs, 1923) to compare the learning potential of a group of mildly and moderately retarded institutionalized teenagers. Participants were matched according to IQ and assigned to a coaching or noncoaching group. The coaching procedure consisted of encouraging the participants to check their designs against the stimulus card, pointing to specific pattern areas to encourage a systematic problem-solving approach, utilizing a stripe to help outline two-color blocks, and praising and encouraging the subjects. Fifteen test designs were administered to both groups on three occasions: at a pretest session, one week later, and one month later. The experimental treatment of coaching was introduced one day before the second session. Results between groups on analysis of variance measures indicated that (1) mildly retarded subjects performed better on the block design test than the moderately retarded performers, (2) posttest scores improved for both the mildly and moderately retarded groups as a function of the coaching intervention, and (3) most importantly, the improved performances achieved one day after coaching were maintained one month later.

Budoff (1967) attempted to replicate the original study using a different examiner and a sample of 36 previously unstudied subjects. The author also noted that in the earlier study subjects were not matched for their initial performance on the Kohs Test. The resulting analysis of variance (ANOVA) indicated that these baseline levels, in fact, did not significantly differ. An additional feature of this study was Budoff's method of pooling the participants from the original study so that he could compare characteristics concerning coached performance improvement within subject. He indicated that coached participants could be divided into three groups: 17 participants who failed to improve by at least 4 points during the instructional phase (nongainers), 27 subjects who demonstrated at least a 4-point posttest gain (gainers), and 7 individuals who solved the most difficult pretest designs, and therefore could not demonstrate posttest gains because of ceiling effects (high scorers).

Utilizing available psychometric, social history, and problem-solving data, Budoff found gainers to have higher WISC or WAIS performance IQs (omitting block design scores) than nongainers. This group was also more successful on a double alteration task (Hodges, 1956) and a paired associates problem. Budoff interpreted these findings as supporting his delineation of specific learning groups. He also concluded that the ability displayed can be generalized across nonverbal tasks rather than specific to the Kohs measure. In contrast, no significant differences were found between the groups with regard to Wechsler Verbal IQ, Binet IQ, or chronological age.

Budoff (1972) attempted to understand these findings by looking at social history and test correlatates of the three groups. In a sample of 383 mildly retarded subjects in the Massachusetts area, he found that 60% of special-class children attained gainer or high scorer status while the remaining 40% were nongainers. More important, there was a significantly greater number of gainers from lower socioeconomic groups, while the middle class tended to be nongainers. Learning potential was also correlated with chronological age. The percentage of nongainers was significantly higher for 12-year-old adolescents than for 16 to 19-year-olds. Other groups in which gainers exceeded nongainers included community educable mentally retarded persons (EMRs) compared to institutionalized EMRs and individuals scoring higher on the Stanford-Binet and WISC verbal scale.

We are not surprised that individuals with higher WAIS and WISC performance IQs are more likely to fall in the gainer category, considering the nonverbal nature of the training and validation tasks. Of more interest are the findings indicating a greater number of special-class EMR gainers from lower socioeconomic groups than middle-class groups, thus supporting Budoff's (1972) theory concerning traditional test bias.

As noted earlier, Budoff (1972) hypothesized that lower functioning children from poor and/or nonwhite backgrounds were more likely to be misclassified because of test bias than white middle-class EMRs, whose experiential background is congruent with the biases inherent in IQ tests. Additionally, because static psychometric measures are less sensitive to the effects of training, an initially poor test performer is given little opportunity to demonstrate that he or she is responsive to instructional interventions. Budoff's (1972) use of learning potential procedures is an attempt to rectify this problem.

Campione, Brown, and Ferrara (1982) have noted problems with Budoff's approach to classifying subjects. They pointed out that Budoff's classification system is product rather than process oriented. For example, a subject classified as a gainer may have answered only one more question correctly than one classified as a nongainer. Moreover, there are obvious difficulties when comparing a child who scored higher on the pretest but demonstrated little gain during instruction, with one who scored lower on the pretest but demonstrated moderate gain during the instruction period. In this situation, the categorical label does not provide necessary information to help describe the specific learning processes utilized during instruction. Also, psychometric test gains have proved to be negatively correlated to pretest scores, because extreme scores tend to regress toward the mean (Lord, 1963; McNemar, 1969). Thus, a student who scored lower on the pretest is statistically more likely to demonstrate a gain than an individual with a higher initial performance.

Delclos (1983) raises other concerns with Budoff's methodology. First, the primary method of matching groups by IQ was verbal, while the training and posttest tasks were nonverbal, therefore raising questions of external validity. Second, all the measures were product oriented, giving little insight into why subjects' performances differed. Third, the training was task specific and did not attempt to teach general problem-solving strategies.

Despite apparent methodological weaknesses, Budoff and his associates have provided the first extensive empirical effort dealing with dynamic assessment in this country (Delclos, 1983). Moreover, their focus on dynamic procedures as an alternative method for reducing problems associated with traditional IQ test bias, especially in the assessment of minority groups, is an important step closer to truly nondiscriminatory test procedures.

The test-train-retest format employed by Budoff (1972, 1974) represents one of the first efforts to develop quantitative methods for measuring learning potential. In this regard, he saw the importance of acquiring baseline measures and subsequently providing standardized intervention strategies in an attempt to obtain valid and reliable psychometric data. In the next section, we will see how Feuerstein (1979) has developed a learning potential model aimed at obtaining a richer clinical information concerning an individual's underlying cognitive thought processes.

Feuerstein's Learning Potential Assessment Device

Similar to Budoff and Vygotsky, Feuerstein's theory of intellectual development (Feuerstein, 1979, 1980) and its resulting approach to assessment emphasizes the importance of mediated learning, which he contrasts to incidental learning. Incidental learning occurs randomly as a child interacts with his environment, whereas mediated learning is planned instruction, provided to the child by a significant interactive adult. Like Budoff, Feuerstein feels that the primary reason for the poor test performance of many disadvantaged youth is the lack of meaningful parent-child mediated learning experiences. These experiences are an important aspect of an individual's development as he or she progresses from infancy to adulthood. The earlier and more frequently these mediated learning experiences occur, the greater the individual's potential for benefiting from direct experiences. Feuerstein believes that the difference between the cognitive performances of two adolescents of seemingly equal intelligence is due to differences in their mediated experiences. Paralleling Vygotsky (1978), Feuerstein bases his theory on the concept of internalization. By interacting with a focused adult, the child eventually incorporates appropriate learning approaches into his or her own learning style.

Feuerstein (1979) has presented a list of criticisms concerning the use of traditional intelligence tests and the psychometric model that they are based upon. Some of the criticisms have been alluded to earlier, including the emphasis on performance products rather than on processes involved with outcomes, the inherent difficulties and potential biases in testor-testee interactions, and the emphasis upon aggregates of performance data that generally help to mask extremely high and low scores (Sternberg, 1982).

Feuerstein (1979) contrasted two factors that heavily influence cognitive functioning. *Distal factors* include all biological, educational, and sociocultural variables that influence development. A *proximal factor* refers to the amount of mediated learning experience afforded an individual. Feuerstein believes there are four primary deficiencies in cognitive functioning: information-processing impairments occurring during input, elaboration, output, and affective-motivational stages. He also refers to "cognitive maps," which involve guidelines by which a mental act can be analyzed, characterized, and sequenced.

Based on his theory of intelligence, Feuerstein developed two dynamic assessment batteries: the Learning Potential Assessment Device (LPAD) and the Instrumental Enrichment (IE) instructional program. The LPAD consists of a number of tasks that resemble traditional IQ measures. Items such as stencil designs, organization of dots, analytic perception, matrices problems, and numerical progressions are among the tasks included on the LPAD. Using this instrument, the examiner attempts to identify a subject's deficient cognitive functions and thought processes by utilizing individualized mediational techniques (Jensen & Feuerstein, 1987). These testing procedures are in ways quite similar to Budoff's (1974), particularly with respect to the test-intervention-test procedure. However, in contrast to Budoff, Feuerstein (1979) did not provide a pretest condition as a means of providing baseline measures. He indicated that early test failure often results in a negative set occurring between the child and the examiner, thus impeding subsequent learning interactions between them. Unfortunately, the emphasis on establishing rapport in this way comes at the expense of obtaining stronger empirical data.

The Instrumental Enrichment (IE) program (Feuerstein, 1980) contains a comprehensive training curriculum for developing cognitive abilities designed to remediate weaknesses diagnosed by the LPAD. Savell, Twohig, and Rachford (1986) conducted an extensive review of research programs utilizing Instrumental Enrichment techniques. To date, the major studies on IE have been attempted with school-age students in Israel, Canada, Venezuela, and the United States. In most studies reported, an IE group was compared with a control group on a number of dependent measures including nonverbal intelligence, academic achievement, impulsivity, self-esteem, and classroom behavior. The IE training consisted of a minimum of one week of instruction for the IE teachers and 80 or more hours of student training presented over a one- or two-year span. Like the LPAD, the content of IE instruction is made up of materials that are similarly found on standard IQ tests (Campione, Brown, & Ferrara, 1982). These tasks differ from achievement test tasks in that they lack academic content.

The authors reported significant experimental/comparison group differences favoring IE groups (ages 12–18) on a number of nonverbal measures of intelligence. In one study reviewed by Savell et al. (1986), Feuerstein, Rand, Hoffman, Hoffman, and Miller (1979) reported analysis of covariance pretest-posttest findings indicating that a IE group of 12–15-year-old culturally disadvantaged students ($n = 57$) scored significantly higher than a matched general enrichment (GE) group on Thurstone's Primary Mental Abilities Test (PMA) and one of two classroom participation scales. Analysis of posttest data (with PMA as a covariate) demonstrated that the IE subjects also scored higher on two other nonverbal measures of general ability.

Savell et al. (1986) noted the reported findings could be interpreted in more than one way because (1) participants were not randomly assigned to experimental and control conditions, (2) the classroom teachers who completed behavioral rating scales were aware of a student's experimental/comparison group status, and (3) student attrition rates were not specified. They also noted that group intelligence test differences tended to be larger on measures whose content was most similar to the intervention materials employed. In their summary they listed a number of problems associated with the overall research, including conflicting outcomes on various measures, inappropriate experimental controls, and lack of comprehensiveness in the reported information. They also indicated that effects on measures of academic achievement, impulsivity, self-esteem, and classroom behavior were "absent, inconsistent, or difficult to interpret" (p. 402).

Savell et al. (1986) concluded by providing a comprehensive list of recommendations to help eliminate the problems associated with current IE studies. The most important recommendations include:

1. Articulating the goals of the research more clearly.
2. Determining the administrative feasibility of the study.

3. Randomly assigning experimental units, and providing information regarding specific procedures to accomplish this goal.
4. Providing information and controlling for naturally occurring sources of experimental error.
5. Providing statistics on changes in group composition over time.
6. Determining the relative importance of various dependent measures with respect to IE training.

We suggest that individuals interested in the IE program read this excellent review in its entirety.

Other researchers (Campione, Brown, & Ferrara, 1982; Gresham, 1986; Reschley, 1984, 1988) have raised critical issues concerning the LPAD and resulting IE program. Gresham (1986) pointed out that, like traditional IQ devices, the LPAD falls short in linking a cognitive diagnosis to specific academically relevant treatments, because Feuerstein's program trains individuals in what could be described as "metacognitive" aspects of learning rather than content specific instruction. From a theoretical and practical perspective, Feuerstein (1980) assumes that by providing training, the examinee's input, elaborative, and output processes are enhanced, thus improving his or her mental efficiency and underlying academic performance. However, because domain-specific content is missing from the assessment, helpful academic intervention strategies cannot be easily provided. Gresham (1986) calls this a problem of treatment validity. He cites discouraging research on the Illinois Test of Psycholinguistic Ability (Hammill & Larsen, 1974) to demonstrate that improvement on cognitive tasks (in this case psycholinguistic ones) is not necessarily associated with academic gains. The merits of cognitive deficit training versus direct academic instruction is, of course, not a new issue in the area of special education (Mann, 1979; Reynolds, 1986).

In supporting the LPAD and IE, Haywood and Switzky (1986) argue that this cognitive process instruction should be provided in conjunction with, and incorporated into, a teaching program rich in academic content. They also suggest, however, that children who constantly fail at reading may best be served by a change in direction from direct academic teaching to cognitive process instruction: "By separating the concepts of intelligence and cognition, we can concentrate attention on the cognitive processes that may underlie learning to read, integrate those with actual content teaching, and look forward to greater success" (p. 265).

From a psychometric perspective, the validity of any cognitive posttest gains is questionable on the grounds that the mediational procedures and IQ-type tasks provide the student with specific content also present on posttest IQ measures. Thus a "teaching to the test" argument is raised (Campione et al., 1982; Reynolds, 1986). As Gresham (1986) pointed out, "we should not be particularly interested in the fact that children perform better on tasks such as the Raven since there are no schools to my knowledge that use Raven-like tasks as part of the curricula" (p. 262).

To summarize, Feuerstein has developed a learning potential assessment and remediation model based on his theory of mediated learning. Despite noted research weaknesses, the LPAD/IE program remains the most comprehensive dynamic assessment program available. If implemented, the recommendations made by Savell et al. (1986) to improve research methodology should help clarify the status of this program as a viable alternative to traditional approaches to assessment.

University of Illinois Research Program

Influenced by the work of Vygotsky (1978) and other Soviet researchers (Vlasova & Pevzner, 1971; Zabramna, 1971), investigators at the University of Illinois (Campione, Brown & Ferrara, 1982; Campione & Ferrara, in preparation; Campione & Brown, 1987; Campione, Brown, Ferrara, Jones, & Steinberg, 1985; Ferrara, Brown & Campione, 1986) have conducted a major research project in an attempt to examine clinical and psychometric variables associated with dynamic assessment. Before reviewing this research, we present Vygotsky's concept of the "zone of proximal development," and also discuss how some neo-Vygotskian researchers in the Soviet Union have applied these principals.

Vygotsky (1978) was interested in the interactional influences of adults on child development. By observing the processes by which children emulate adult roles, he was better able to understand the effects of social interactions. He believed that a large portion of what a child learns is mediated by this social interplay. He characterized behavioral changes in relation to the variability of control that is transferred from adult to child. Initially, the child and adult work cooperatively on a cognitive task, with the adult acting as an expert role model. The responsibility of control shifts to the child as he or she internalizes the activity, thus becoming more independent. Campione and Brown (1987) indicate that it is this gradual shift of control they attempted to evaluate when utilizing dynamic assessment techniques.

Vygotsky (1978) initially coined the term "zone of proximal development" (ZPD) to describe this transfer of control. ZPD is explained as the distance between a child's unaided performance on a problem-solving task and the performance level of "potential development as determined through problem solving under adult guidance or in collaboration with more capable peers" (p. 86). Thus, the ZPD can be thought of as the disparity between what a student knows at point *A* and what he demonstrates with the assistance of an adult guide at point *B*. As we have noted, two children who appear to be equal when assessed statically may have varying zones when receptivity to instruction is taken into account.

Vygotsky's designing of assessment devices to help determine the zone of proximal development has had a great influence on recent dynamic testing attempts in both the Soviet Union and the United States. Brown & Ferrara (1985) described these basic testing methods as refined by Vlasova and Pevzner (1971) and Zabramna (1971) in the Soviet Union. Traditional static intelligence tests have also been criticized by Soviet psychologists. Some Soviet psychologists, therefore, have designed test batteries that are modifications of traditional IQ measures, for example, matching block designs. The primary difference between this approach and traditional methods involves contrasts in test administration, namely, the instructional intervention process provided by the examiner if the student is unable to initially solve a problem. A system of gradual hints (to be explained later) is employed to identify a child's problem-solving status and responsiveness to instruction.

The Soviet approach to assessment provides diagnostic information related to a student's baseline level of problem-solving competence as well as his or her proficiency in learning the same task with examiner assistance. This diagnostic method is also utilized to measure the extent to which a child can transfer problem-solving skills across tasks. Just as Budoff (1974) found differences between culturally disadvantaged and middle-class EMR children with respect to learning proficiency, the Soviets found performance differences between learning disabled and mildly retarded youngsters, favoring the former group. Although these two groups do not appear to differ on starting IQ measures, they differ significantly in their ability to benefit from graduated clues presented by the examiner (Brown & French, 1979). In other studies in which normal subjects were added as a comparison group, the nondisabled children scored higher on initial learning and transfer measures. Brown and French (1979) point out that there is a lack of information concerning the specific measures used and the resulting data obtained by the Soviet research team. It is within this context that the authors at the University of Illinois began their research to replicate and expand on these findings.

The Illinois research group (Campione, Brown & Ferrara, 1982; Campione & Ferrara, in preparation; Ferrara, Brown & Campione, 1986; Campione, Brown, Ferrara, Jones, & Steinberg, 1985) investigated variables related to the relationship between dynamic assessment and traditional IQ scores. For example, do dynamic measures of receptiveness to learning and transfer relate to static IQ scores? As Brown and Ferrara (1985) state:

> If this were the case, then both the IQ and the [ZPD] measures would be validated and we would add credence to a process theory of intelligence that defines it as speed of learning and efficiency of transfering. If this were so, then it would be imperative that the predictive validity of ZPD scores be compared with IQ measures; that is, does knowing a child's ZPD score tell us more (or less, or something different) about how she will perform in a domain than knowing her IQ score? (pp. 285–286)

In psychometric terms, this question concerns the concurrent validity of the dynamic test instrument.

Campione, Brown, Ferrara, Jones, and Steinberg (1985) used dynamic assessment techniques to compare learning and transfer characteristics of 25 mildly retarded and 25 nonretarded students. The experiment took place in five stages: pretest, training, maintenance, transfer, and posttest. The identical pretest and posttest measures consisted of twenty-four 3×3 matrix problems that were administered without examiner assistance. The research method used subsequently to pretest involved introducing matrix problems to each student via a computer and providing a systematic series of hints to help them. The hints were initiated during the instructional phase and consisted of three basic problem-solving rules involving rotation, imposition, and subtraction. Examples of these problems are illustrated in Figure 7.1.

In the maintenance session, new examples of the same three types of matrix problems were introduced in random order, rather than the sequential order provided during initial training. In the transfer session, the same three types of problems were presented but problems requiring understanding of rule combinations (for example, rotation plus imposition) were also introduced. Instead of emphasizing a final level of performance, the measure of evaluation used was the number of hints needed to solve a particular problem. It is important to note that the hints were provided in a general-to-specific sequence, initially consisting of very general problem-solving information and progressing to explicit hints on how to answer a question (Brown & French, 1979). The authors emphasized that the intervention procedure was "task" rather than "child" oriented in that the hints were given in a fixed sequence, independent of type of incorrect response offered. The rationale provided for this approach is that it helped provide stronger psychometric data than would be obtained by clinical methods; clinical procedures, in which provided information is based on a child's problem-solving approach, may not produce strong quantifiable data (Campione et al., 1985).

Findings indicated that there were no significant group differences during the pretest phase of the experiment. Pretest scores of the non-retarded group averaged 37% correct as compared to the retarded group's 29% success rate. The mean number of hints needed to elicit a correct response during training was also found to be nonsignificant. In contrast, significant mean differences in number of hints needed were found during maintenance and transfer phases, favoring the nonretarded group. Moreover, the retarded group required an increased number of hints and made more errors as the complexity of the task increased. The authors pointed out that the nonretarded children demonstrated greater flexibility in ap-

FIGURE 7.1 **Examples of three types of matrix problems**

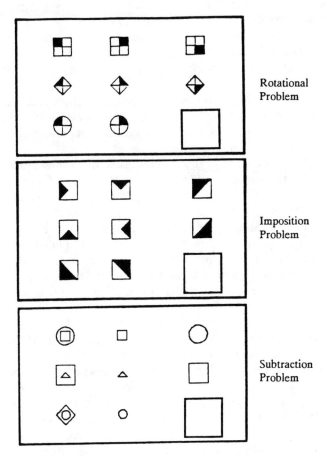

Rotational Problem

Imposition Problem

Subtraction Problem

Source: Campione, Brown, Ferrara, Jones, & Steinberg, 1985, p. 302. Reprinted by permission.

plying learned rules than retarded youngsters. Posttest scores were also significantly higher for the nonretarded group.

In a second study Ferrara, Brown, and Campione (1986) compared third- and fifth-grade children of average and above-average ability using a letter series completion task, a more sensitive measure of transfer distance than the original matrix task. Subjects participated in three sessions: learning, maintenance and transfer, learning and far transfer. Up to 15 prompts were provided to individuals who failed an item.

Results from the learning session indicated that grade and IQ were significantly related to learning: Specifically, third graders required more prompts than fifth graders and average IQ children required more prompts than high-average IQ children. In the second session, there were no IQ or age differences during maintenance and near transfer problems, but reliable group differences on far and very far transfer items. These findings were confirmed in a study conducted by Campione and Ferrara (in preparation) in which retarded and nonretarded children were compared. Again, significant group differences were found between these two groups on learning and transfer tasks.

The overall findings of these studies indicate that brighter children need less help to solve novel problems, and tend to be more flexible in utilizing problem-solving rules. Moreover, the magnitude of performance differences increases as a function of transfer distance.

A second question investigated at Illinois concerned the test measures of predictive validity, or the way dynamic measures of learning and transfer provide additional diagnostic information beyond that obtained from traditional IQ scores. Bryant, Brown, and Campione (in preparation) and Bryant (1982) worked with kindergarten-age youngsters to study the predictive validity of dynamic assessment measures using simplified age-appropriate measures of the progressive matrix task and series completion task. A significant relationship between IQ and learning and transfer scores were obtained supporting the concurrent validity findings of previous research.

The authors used multiple regression procedures to help find the extent to which dynamic techniques added to the predictive value of the assessment procedure. The question to be investigated was which score, or scores in combination, among baseline competence, general ability, and learning and transfer, best predicted future performance. As in previous studies, subjects were administered a pretest (in this case the WPPSI and Raven Coloured Matrices), participated in learning and transfer sessions, and then took a posttest that was a repeat of the pretest measure. A gain score was obtained by comparing the pretest and posttest measures.

Findings presented in Tables 7.1 and 7.2 indicated that static IQ assessment accounted for approximately 60% of the variance in gain scores. Of greater significance was that learning and transfer scores accounted for additional variance after the effects of IQ scores were removed. On the matrix task, learning performance accounted for an additional 22% of the variance while transfer performance accounted for an additional 17% (Campione & Brown, 1987). On the series completion task, an additional 22% of the variance could be predicted by the transfer score. In contrast to the matrix task, learning in the series completion task did not result in improved predictability. Campione and Brown (1987) pointed out that learning and transfer measures were better predictors of performance gains than individual static measures. Results from these studies suggest that

TABLE 7.1 **Multiple Regression Summary Table for Matrices Task**

Dependent variable	Independent variable	Correlation (r)	Multiple R	Increment in R²
Training	Information	-.439*	.439	.193*
	Coding	-.043	.587	.152*
Transfer	Information	-.389*	.389	.151*
Residual gain	Estimated IQ	.485*	.485	.235*
	Raven	.472*	.608	.135*
	Training	-.605*	.770	.224*
	Transfer	-.598*	.876	.173*
	Far transfer	-.698*	.884	.014

*Significant at the 5% level.
Source: Campione & Brown, 1987, p. 99. Reprinted by permission.

TABLE 7.2 **Multiple Regression Summary Table for Series Completion Task**

Dependent variable	Independent variable	Correlation (r)	Multiple R	Increment in R²
Training	Block design	-.476*	.476	.227*
	Vocabulary	-.427*	.677	.153*
Transfer	Block design	-.581*	.581	.338*
	Vocabulary	-.479	.641	.073
Residual gain	Estimated IQ	.521*	.521	.272*
	Raven	.352	.578	.062
	Training	-.461*	.595	.020
	Transfer	-.693*	.745	.221*
	Far transfer	-.558*	.745	.000

*Significant at the 5% level.
Source: Campione & Brown, 1987, p. 99. Reprinted by permission.

dynamic ability measures yield different estimates of learning than static methods.

One major educational implication of these findings is the possibility of providing instruction tailored to the upper limits of a child's zone of proximal development as determined by dynamic performance measures (Brown & Ferrara, 1985). This approach to intervention is contrasted with more traditional methods, in which a child's unaided static IQ performance is often used to determine an appropriate level of instructional difficulty. As Brown and Ferrara (1985) point out: "By concentrating on a level a student can reach with aid, the student is led to levels of success previously not envisaged by either the student or the teacher" (p. 301).

In conjunction with the Illinois dynamic assessment studies, Campione and Brown (1987) are developing and validating a domain-specific academic instructional program, addressing the need of linking assessment to meaningful remediations. As mentioned earlier, a criticism of Feuerstein's approach was his failure to incorporate academically relevant instruction into his IE program. Campione and Brown (1987) note that emphasizing a specific academic domain will enable them to provide a more comprehensive view of the specific skills that help distinguish more and less successful students. Within this context, a reciprocal teaching program (Brown & Palincsar, 1982; Palincsar & Brown, 1984) was developed, based on Vygotsky's theoretical framework.

During reciprocal teaching, the teacher and student alternately lead dialogues on assigned reading with the goal of improving comprehension skills. In each case, the leader of the dialogue is asked to summarize what has been said and develop appropriate questions concerning the main topic. The same Vygotskian principles of transferring control from teacher to student are followed, as the student learns to approach each text segment utilizing comprehension-fostering and comprehension-monitoring strategies initially modeled by the teacher. These specific strategies include (1) summarizing what has been read, (2) developing questions that discern the main idea, (3) clarifying ambiguities, and (4) predicting what the author will subsequently say. Like other dynamic approaches, ongoing diagnosis is also an important part of the reciprocal teaching method (See Palincsar & Brown, 1984, for a more detailed description of the reciprocal teaching approach).

In one study, Palincsar and Brown (1984) compared seventh graders receiving reciprocal teaching (RT) instruction, with students assigned to three comparison groups (a group receiving an alternate treatment; a control group answering daily assessment questions who were tested during the baseline, maintenance, pretest, and posttest phases of the study; and a control group who were administered the baseline, maintenance, pretest, and posttest without answering daily assessment questions). All 24 subjects were slow learners displaying weak reading comprehension skills (one to four years below grade level) and adequate word-decoding skills. Criteria used to compare groups included (1) consistent improvement on the specific training task, (2) independent evidence of improvement on strategies employed, (3) improvement of independent reading, (4) durability of training effects, (5) generalization of effects, and (6) transfer to novel tasks.

The authors reported effects on measures of dialogue change, daily comprehension assessment, and transfer. Findings indicated that the reciprocal teaching group increased their understanding for a story's main idea from 54 to 70%. Moreover, incorrect and incomplete statements were reduced from 19 to 10% and detail summaries reduced from 29 to 4%. The decline in inadequate summaries is contrasted with the significant increase in main idea summaries from 52 to 85% ($z = 2.86, p < .002$).

The RT and two comparison groups were tested on daily reading comprehension measures. Results indicated that the RT group improved to at least a 75% comprehension level, while the other treatment and control groups failed to improve greatly. A 3×4 mixed analysis of variance was attempted with the scores of the three groups receiving daily comprehension assessment used as a between-subject variable and the four phases of the sessions as a within-subject variable. The main effect of Groups and Phase was reliable ($p < .03$ and $p < .001$, respectively). Moreover, a Groups × Phase interaction was also significant, $p < .001$. The authors explained this interaction on the grounds that the difference between the RT and other groups grew larger as the intervention progressed.

Planned comparison measures were carried out during each phase of the RT intervention. The authors report that mean accuracy during training was significantly higher when compared to baseline measures, $p < .001$. Moreover, comprehension improvement held up over time; that is, there were no significant differences found eight weeks subsequent to training. Significant posttest gains were also reported when the third control group was compared with the RT group.

To summarize, Campione, Brown, and their associates have built upon Vygotsky's Zone of Proximal Development principals in developing and validating dynamic testing techniques. Their research findings indicate that there is a significant relationship between static and dynamic measures and that dynamic assessment provides additional predictive information beyond that obtained by static tests.

It is not surprising that IQ is significantly related to learning ability. The fact that brighter children also appear to be more flexible in their thinking also seems to be an obvious finding. Campione, Brown, and their associates attempted to establish these relationships in hope of developing statistically strong dynamic assessment instruments. For similar reasons they employed task-oriented gradual-hint methods in an effort to produce stronger empirical data. Of course the psychometric gains obtained using structured task-oriented procedures must be weighed against the richer clinical information afforded when utilizing mediated clinical approaches. We shall discuss this issue in more depth later.

Campione and Brown (1987) also report that they are extending Vygotskian procedures to other academically rich domains, for example, developing dynamic assessment devices to test early mathematical knowledge (Ferrara, Brown & Campione, 1986). They point out that improvement in mathematics can be tracked longitudinally, whereas long-term improvement on an inductive reasoning task is more restricted by ceiling effects. They also point out that mathematical content is easily adaptable to gradual prompting methods.

Vanderbilt University Research Program

Influenced by the ideas of Feuerstein (1979); Brown, Campione, and their associates (Brown & Ferrara, 1985; Brown & French, 1979; Brown and Palincsar, 1982; Campione et al., 1982, 1985); and Vygotsky (1978), a group of researchers at Vanderbilt University (Vye, Burns, Delclos, & Bransford, 1987) have developed a "continuum of assessment services" model, in which degree of assessment ranged from simple screening methods to more in-depth forms of dynamic assessment. Of interest in this model are the contrasting dynamic approaches employed, depending on an individual's initial test performance. For example, a student who scores within the average range on traditional IQ measures would not receive further assessment. If he or she scores at least one standard deviation below the mean, an assessment procedure based on Brown and Campione's gradual prompting method would be implemented. At this point on the continuum, a child's below-average static score is compared to his or her performance aided by gradual prompting. A student who performs significantly higher on the "graduated hint" dynamic measure would be considered responsive to instruction, and therefore have more potential than initially indicated by static measures. A student who scores below average on graduated hint methods would next be tested using "mediated" dynamic procedures based on a modification of Feuerstein's methods. These mediated procedures differ from the gradual hint methods in that the latter approach uses a set sequence of prompts, while the former provides more in-depth information to the student. We shall now discuss these two intervention methods.

As we have pointed out, gradual prompting procedures were developed and employed by Brown, Campione, and their associates (Brown & Ferrara, 1985; Brown & French, 1979; Brown & Palincsar, 1982; Campione & Brown, 1987; Campione et al., 1982, 1985; Ferrara et al., 1986), while mediational methods were based on the work of Feuerstein and Hoffman (1982) and Feuerstein et al. (1979, 1981), and employed by (among others) Bransford et al. (1986) and Burns (1985). Graduated prompting requires the examiner to provide a series of general-to-specific ordered hints to the child until a specific learning criteria is reached. The procedures were based on a comprehensive task analysis of content to insure that each prompt would provide more explicit information than the previous one (Brown & French, 1979). As previously noted, the method is task rather than examinee oriented in that the information provided is not determined by a child's response. An exception to this rule occurs only when the child has already exhibited information provided in a specific hint. In this situation, the superfluous hint is omitted (Campione & Brown, 1987). Figure 7.2 provides a sample of a prompting sequence used in rotational matrices problems similar to Figure 7.1.

In contrast to gradual hint procedures, the mediational intervention approach devised by Feuerstein (1979) is child rather than task oriented. Thus, during a dynamic test situation, the examiner determines the content and style of the mediational interaction as a result of a child's subtle or explicit needs for assistance rather than his or her answer to a specific test item.

Burns (1985) pointed out that mediational procedures are clinically richer in that they provide more in-depth methods for problem-solving and are contingent on the quality of a child's initial response to a presented problem. Thus, mediational methods enable the amount and form of mediation to vary according to a student's educational needs, while gradual prompt methods are not contingent on specific deficiencies exhibited by the child. Figure 7.3 presents an example of a mediational procedure using the Stencil Design Test.

An interesting study by Burns (1985) was carried out comparing mediational and gradual hint models of assessment. Burns studied 4- to 6-year-old children with "significant" learning problems to compare the effects of these two models, and a third static model of assessment, on ensuing learning and transfer performance. An adaptation of the Arthur Point Scale of Performance Tests (Arthur, 1947) was used as the dynamic cognitive task and the Animal House matching board from the Wechsler Preschool and Primary Scale of Intelligence (Wechsler, 1967) as the transfer task.

Analysis of variance findings indicated that there was a significant main effect difference for groups. A multiple *t*-test indicated that the gradual prompt group scored significantly higher than the static group, while the mediated group scored significantly higher than the graduated prompt group. A significant main effect difference was also found for transfer, and the mediation group scored significantly higher on the posttransfer task than the graduated prompt group.

Using the McCarthy Scales of Children's Ability (McCarthy, 1972) as a static measure and an adapted version of the Arthur Stencil Design Test (Arthur, 1947; Burns, 1985) as the dynamic measure, Vye, Burns, Delclos,

---

FIGURE 7.2 A sample hint sequence for a rotation problem

HINT 1: "This problem is called a turning problem. Think about why it might be called that. . . . Do you know how to solve the problem now or do you want another hint?

HINT 2: "This is row 1. Put picture 1 in the practice box. Touch IN. Touch the picture. Now try to make the picture look like the second picture." (if successful) "You did it. Now make it look like the last picture." (If child cannot make picture 3. PLATO will give hint 2A.)

HINT 2A: "This is row 1. This is picture 1. Watch how it turns. Watch again. Now you do it." (If child cannot repeat the above demonstration, PLATO will give hint 2B.)

HINT 2B: "This is row 1. Let's try to make the last picture in the row. Put picture 1 in the practice box. Touch ∧ . Touch ∧ again. Good. You have made the last picture in row 1. Now try to make the missing picture."

HINT 3: "Now let's look at row 2. Put picture 1 of row 2 in the practice box. Now make it look like picture 2." (If child does not respond correctly PLATO will display TOUCH ∧ .) "You did it. Now make the picture in the practice box look like the last picture in row 2. Now try the problem again." (If child cannot make picture 3 PLATO will give hint 3A.)

HINT 3A: "Touch ∧ . Touch ∧ again."

HINT 4: "You used the turning rule to make the last picture in rows 1 and 2. The last picture in row 3 is missing. Try to use the same rule to make the missing picture in row 3." (If child cannot do so, PLATO will give hint 4A.)

HINT 4A: "This is the shape you work with." (PLATO displays appropriate shape.) "Put it in the practice box. Touch the first picture in row 3. Now touch ∧ . Now touch ∧ again. That is correct. Touch DONE."

EXPLANATION (given with every original learning problem): "Good. Look at all three rows. The turning rule is used in each row. And you used the turning rule to make the missing picture. You turned picture 1 to get picture 2. Then you turned picture 2 to get picture 3."

In original learning, the child continues to solve rotation problems until he or she can do *two* problems in a row without any hints. Then PLATO will move ahead to the first imposition problem.

Source: Campione et al., 1985, p. 307. Reprinted by permission.

FIGURE 7.3 Mediation procedure for Stencil Design Test

Familiarizing the Child with Materials and Relevant Dimensions

1. Point out cut-outs (I CUT THEM OUT).
2. Label shapes. If there is resistance or difficulty learning labels, then tell the child the label, but go quickly to finding shapes that match and say FIND ALL THE CARDS LIKE THIS. Comment on the lack of labels in a report, but do not get bogged down—the matching encourages comparative behavior while establishing shape as a relevant feature.
3. Point out solids (NOT CUT-OUTS—NO HOLES). Note all are in bottom row, near child.
4. Label colors (see notes for label shapes).
5. Have child COUNT THE SOLIDS. Focus here is not on the ability to count, but on the child's conceptualization of "solid" or "not cut-out." If child counts correctly to 6, then the distinction is being made.

* * * WARNING * * *

If child cannot count all the solids, he or she needs more work on the preceding concepts.
6. Compare 2 circles (big, small)/2 white squares (straight, crooked)/2 blue cards (solid, cut-out)/2 yellow cards (solid, cut-out)/yellow and blue crosses (yellow, blue).
7. At some point, put solid and cut-out back in wrong place—again to gauge whether the discrimination is being made.

* * * WARNING * * *

If child cannot see that you put solid back in wrong place, he or she needs more work on preceding concepts.

Combination Rules

1. Demonstrate what happens when a green circle is placed on a yellow solid. Point out 2 colors, made from 1 ± 1.
2. Change solids, showing that the *inside* color changes by changing *solids*. Allow child to try 1 or 2 color changes. Emphasize that it is *solid* that is changing.

* * * WARNING * * *

If child cannot change the color of the solid, he or she needs more work on the preceding concepts.
3. Use white solid with green circle. Change cut-outs (don't reproduce any of the upcoming designs). Show that *outside* color changes by changing cut-outs.
4. Put solid on top of cut-out and establish necessary order rule and reason. Have child repeat the rule "I put a cut-out on top of a solid and the color of the solid is in the middle."
5. End with the sample design formed from stencils, then introduce the sample design model.

FIGURE 7.3 *Continued*

Helping the Child Reproduce the Model

1. Display model while reproduction is still on the table, discussing how a picture was made of it. Point out that there are 2 colors in the picture and 2 colors in the reproduction, but only *1* color on each separate card.
2. Put stencils back in place and request reproduction. Teach search pattern over cut-outs and over solids. Have child say "Is it this one?"
3. When production is made, encourage checking back to model. Go over what is *right* and what is *wrong* about the production.

* * * WARNING * * *

If the child's production is wrong, he or she needs more work on the preceding concepts. Refer to any errors made in route to a correct answer (spontaneous corrections) and discuss why they were wrong. Alternate the correct one and the wrong one. Always end with the correct solution.

4. Repeat Step 3 with each of the remaining training models.

Source: Vye, Burns, Delclos, & Bransford, 1987, pp. 356-357. Reprinted by permission.

and Bransford (1987) calculated correlations between the two tests in an unaided and graduated prompt situation. The McCarthy Scales are made up of a global ability scale (general cognitive index) and three subscales measuring perceptual performance and verbal and quantitative ability.

Findings indicated that there was a significant correlation ($r = .48$, $p < .01$) between the perceptual performance scale and the dynamic assessment measures. This finding is not surprising, since both tasks measure perceptual performance. In contrast, there were no significant differences obtained when the other subscale scores were compared with the dynamic measure. Vye et al. (1987) concluded that the nonperformance measures would not be a reliable indicator of a student's responsiveness to instruction. Also, the correlation between the General Cognitive Index and the Stencil Design Task (SDT) was moderate and nonsignificant. In this case, the authors note that the restriction of test range on the GCI may have resulted in an underestimation in the obtained score.

Combining students from a second study, Vye et al. (1987) divided 77 handicapped students into four ability groups ranging in static IQ from below 37 to 108. The groups consisted of 27 students with IQs below 37, 11 students with IQs between 37 and 52, 28 students with IQs between 58 and 68, and 11 students with IQs between 69 and 108. They then attempted to ascertain what percentage of each group successfully completed the Stencil Design Task following dynamic assessment.

The authors reported the percentages of children in each static IQ group who reached a 75% criterion as follows:

Below 37 IQ group   26%
37–52 IQ group   36%
53–68 IQ group   53%
69–108 IQ group   82%

It is evident from these results that a significant number of students in each group reached the specified criterion following a dynamic assessment session. The authors suggest that dynamic measures provide additional information (specifically demonstrating that a sizeable number of low IQ children are responsive to instruction) not provided by static measures. We are warned of the potential inaccuracy associated with using static test scores to classify children and predict their future school performance.

A broader implication suggested from the data is that classroom failure often attributed to a disorder within the child may primarily reflect problems related to the quality of instruction. This is most readily displayed when a child that initially appears "unteachable" demonstrates responsiveness to effective instruction within the context of dynamic assessment. Moreover, research conducted by Delclos, Burns, and Kulewicz (1985) has been presented to help support the position that dynamic assessment can affect teacher opinions concerning a child's learning potential: Specifically, a group of teachers surveyed rated their expectations of children's learning potential higher after viewing their videotaped dynamic assessment performance than when viewing their static test performance. As Bransford, Delclos, Vye, Burns and Hasselbring (1987) stated:

> The ability to shift the teachers' conceptualization of the locus of failure from the child to the instructional techniques is an important first step toward changing the educational assessment and delivery system and can be seen as one valuable role of dynamic assessment (p. 485).

In a second phase of their study, Vye et al. (1987) investigated dynamic assessment and degree of transfer within and across task domains. In one study, subjects were assessed dynamically on the Stencil Design Task, with either graduated prompting or mediation procedures employed. Their unassisted or independent performance on three within-domain transfer tasks and SDT task was then measured.

Findings indicated that subjects who were successful on the SDT with graduated prompting scored significantly higher on three within-domain transfer tasks than subjects who scored poorly on the same SDT test. In contrast, there was less than significant transfer differences found between the high and low SDT groups when mediated strategies were employed. The authors suggest that these results can be explained in terms of the relatively good transfer obtained when mediation methods are employed with lower functioning children, because mediation instruction is a better method for facilitating generalization than graduated prompting approaches. Moreover, they indicate that the differences between the strategies might relate to the greater emphasis that mediational methods place on teaching metacognitive skills. For example, they note that the mediational approach they employed included training in search and self-checking strategies.

The Vanderbilt group also used a single-subject design to study within and across task transfer with more severely handicapped children. Using mediational procedures, they reported that within-task transfer was demonstrated on two stencil transfer tasks. In contrast, there was no indication of spontaneous across-task transfer, thus supporting the position that responsiveness to instruction on one task does not help predict responsiveness to instruction on a task in a different domain.

Like the Illinois group, researchers at Vanderbilt have also seen the necessity of using tasks closely related to specific content areas. In this regard, Bransford, Delclos, Vye, Burns, and Hasselbring (1986) are devising dynamic approaches for understanding the learning strategies of mathematically delayed fifth- and sixth-grade students. They note that the strategies students employ to solve specific math problems can significantly influence their performance, as well as their ability to benefit from practice. Their initial findings indicate that content-specific dynamic assessment provides teachers relevant diagnostic information helpful in developing successful teaching strategies.

In summary, Vye et al. (1987) have presented data supporting the concurrent and predictive validity of their dynamic assessment methods. A significant correlation between static and dynamic perceptual measures was reported. While responsiveness to instruction was predictive of transfer within the perceptual domain, however, the relationship across domains was less apparent.

The Vanderbilt group has also reported data indicating that dynamic measures provide objective and qualitative information not available when static test instruments are used. It is noteworthy that a substantial number of moderate and severely handicapped children were able to complete tasks not suggested by their static test performance. We are further encouraged by the research findings reported by Delclos et al. (1985) concerning the positive impact that viewing a dynamic assessment test situation may have on teacher expectations.

SUMMARY AND CONCLUSIONS

Although relatively scant, the findings emerging from the current review suggest that dynamic intellectual assessment may provide educators with alternative methods for evaluating the learning status of normal and difficult to teach children. As suggested earlier, these procedures may help identify a class of students whose potential for learning has previously been underestimated. While studies cited by Brown, Budoff, Feuerstein, and others have provided some promising results in the area of identification, dynamic assessment methods have not as yet been definitively tested to prove their effectiveness in bridging the gap between diagnosis and resulting remedial academic prescriptions. We will begin by summarizing the more conclusive research findings and then highlight some areas of concern.

As we have noted, questions of concurrent and predictive validity have led to research demonstrating a relationship between static and dynamic measures. For example, Campione et al. (1985) have shown that individuals who score higher on traditional measures of intelligence also display a propensity for learning and transferring their newly acquired skills in divergent situations. A highly reliable correlation between traditional and dynamic measures is apparent when tasks of far and very far transfer are considered. In their research on concurrent validity, Vye et al. (1987) found that there was a significant correlation between static and dynamic measures only when the task domain was the same, and concluded that a single static subscale score would be a poor predictor of a child's response to instruction. Of more relevance is the data presented by the same authors demonstrating that a significant number of children who scored low on static IQ tests are responsive to instruction. These findings taken together with the results reported by Budoff (1967, 1974), Brown and associates (Brown & Ferrara, 1985; Brown & French, 1979; Brown & Palincsar, 1982; Campione & Brown, 1987; Campione et al., 1982, 1985; Ferrara et al., 1986) and Feuerstein (1979) help support the position that dynamic procedures can help psychologists and educators discern learning differences among children otherwise homogeneously grouped according to traditional psychometric measures.

The extent to which dynamic measures provide additional diagnostic information not readily derived by static assessment has also been demonstrated (Brown & associates; Vye et al., 1987). Using multiple regression analyses, these researchers have found that dynamic learning and transfer scores account for sizeable proportions of variance not predicted from static IQ tests.

Research findings indicate that teachers may change their perceptions toward lower functioning students after viewing their dynamic assessment performance. The literature reviewed suggests that higher expectations concerning a child's intellectual potential often result in improved teacher instruction and higher pupil performance. As previously noted, Brown and Ferrara (1985) suggest that classroom instruction should be provided that is difficult enough to tap a child's upper zone of proximal development. Traditional assessment methods do not provide this needed information.

Another implication is drawn from the results presented by Budoff and Feuerstein and their associates concerning the misdiagnosis of poor and nonwhite children. These researchers have demonstrated that a significant number of lower functioning lower SES students performed similarly to nonretarded youngsters when assessed dynamically. Among its provisions, Public Law 94–142 (1975) requires that psychoeducational assessment be nondiscriminatory. Moreover, a recent court decision (Larry P. v. Wilson Riles, 1979) has resulted in banning the use of IQ tests with black children for the purpose of special education placement because of test bias. In this regard, a number of efforts have been made to develop tests that more appropriately meet this provision (Mercer, 1979). A number of authors (Budoff, 1972; Reuda, in press; Sewell, 1987) have suggested that dynamic methods may provide a promising alternative to this assessment issue. Sewell (1987) has concluded that static IQ measures may provide a more valid measure of learning potential for middle-class children, than for poor or nonwhite populations, but the reverse may be true when dynamic measures are utilized. More extensive research using dynamic measures with lower SES and minority populations will have to be carried out before definitive conclusions can be made in this area.

Initial data has been presented (Burns, 1985) indicating that mediational procedures are more effective for promoting transfer than gradual prompting methods. In this regard, Vye, Burns, Delclos, and Bransford (1987) point out that these two methods may be employed for different purposes. They indicate that the scripted gradual prompt method may be more appropriately used for prediction while the mediational approach may be more applicable within a diagnostic-prescriptive system. It would appear that the scripted nature of the graduated prompting method makes it easier to acquire reliable and valid quantitative information than the mediational approach offers. Conversely, the mediated method provides richer clinical information not obtainable through gradual prompting procedures.

In contrast to these encouraging findings, many questions remain concerning the prescriptive applicability of dynamic assessment techniques in the classroom. For example, the current validation studies have generally failed to utilize predictive measures within a specific academic performance domain, but instead have continued to focus on specific psychological test constructs and other nonacademic factors. Ironically, problems associated with educational treatment validity have been one of the primary weaknesses attributed to static assessment techniques. As indicated earlier, intelligence tests have generally failed to provide relevant information on which to base effective teaching strategies. A number of researchers, including Bransford et al. (1986) and Campione and Brown (1987), indicate that they are currently exploring the issue of curriculum applicability, although to our knowledge, the empirical evidence has not yet been reported.

Similarly, utilizing dynamic assessment techniques to teach cognitive thinking strategies has not necessarily resulted in improved academic performance. Favorable findings attributed to Feuerstein's Instructional Enrichment (IE) program, while encouraging, have been difficult to interpret because of various design and other methodology inconsistencies (Savell, Twohig, & Rachford, 1986). Also, the validity of cognitive posttest gains have raised "teaching to the test" arguments (Reschley, 1984, 1988).

Viewing dynamic assessment within the context of time- and cost-effectiveness raises other potential problems inherent in this approach. In contrast to traditional assessment, dynamic techniques require additional time to implement because their assessment process is ongoing rather than a one-shot endeavor. The psychometric gains that these new techniques might offer will have to be weighed against the increased costs for additional personnel and added time requirements.

Designating specific personnel to conduct these evaluations presents a potentially controversial problem. The ongoing factors as well as the diagnostic-prescriptive nature of the dynamic process will probably render the classroom teacher the likely candidate to carry out the major portion of the resulting evaluation. This potential alteration in service delivery roles will impact heavily on current school psychology practices and training programs. We look favorably at the data presented by Palinscar and Brown (1984) concerning reciprocal teaching, in which ongoing diagnosis of student comprehension strategies in the classroom is a large part of the resulting remedial program.

To what extent will these new methods help alleviate chronic classification and placement problems associated with current psychometrically based procedures? Gerber and Semmel (1984) have pointed out that LD placement decisions are more strongly influenced by economic and political factors than by valid psychometric findings. From this perspective, the improvement of assessment procedures, at least with regard to LD populations, will not necessarily result in improved identification practices.

SUGGESTIONS FOR FUTURE RESEARCH

While we are encouraged by research demonstrating the validity of specific dynamic assessment methods in helping to evaluate diverse learning populations, there remain a number of questions that need to be explored. We suggest that additional research exploring the concurrent and predictive validity of various dynamic measures should be attempted. In this regard, modifications to assessment instruments commonly used in traditional IQ evaluation (for example the Wechsler Intelligence Scale for Children—Revised) may be made in order to validate their use for dynamic assessment purposes.

If dynamic assessment techniques are going to be utilized effectively with the LD population, extensive research will need to be undertaken, exploring curriculum applicability. Dynamic assessment test strategies that combine cognitive thinking skills and specific reading, language and math content need to be tested empirically. Studying the feasibility of utilizing existing assessment systems (for example, curriculum-based assessment, Deno, 1985) to enhance the prescriptive applicability of current dynamic procedures might also be considered.

Research exploring other factors related to gradual prompting and mediated learning methods is also needed. From a psychometric perspective, it would be informative to compare the number of prompts as a metric of learning with measures of gain. Is one method better for prediction or generating prescriptions than the other? Validation of the continuum of services model presented by Vye et al. (1987) would of be help in understanding the relative strengths of these two methods.

It is recommended that other conceptual dynamic assessment models and intervention strategies be developed and validated with existing clinical and psychometric models. We argue that a student's superior posttest performance following dynamic intervention may be due to the social quality of examiner-examinee interaction rather than a specific strategy or teaching method.

Single-subject design studies of the type presented by Vye et al. (1987) hold promise for studying the use of dynamic measures with more severely handicapped populations: in particular, questions of within- and across-task transfer as it relates to this population. Again, the nature of the task presented and the type of dynamic method implemented need to be studied with regard to effect on specific task performance.

Current and future research efforts in the areas of multicultural dynamic assessment are necessary within the context of recent litigation and PL 94–142 (1975) provisions calling for unbiased assessment of individuals with exceptional needs. Research exploring the most appropriate and cost-effective dynamic assessment delivery system should be initiated. In this context, a number of economic, administrative, and social variables will have to be weighed before school districts will be willing to change dramatically the process by which they evaluate and educate difficult-to-teach youngsters.

As we noted earlier, Delclos, Burns and Kulewicz (1985) reported that teachers may change their expectations of lower functioning children after viewing their dynamic assessment performance. However, like traditional assessments, dynamic test findings will also need to be communicated in written form. Accordingly, research exploring the most effective ways of writing and presenting dynamic assessment reports is needed, so that teachers may learn to apply appropriate content-based interventions.

REFERENCES

Arthur, G. (1947). *A point scale of performance tests.* New York: Psychological Corporation.

Bransford, J. D., Delclos, V. R., Vye, N. J., Burns, M. S., & Hasselbring, T. S. (1986). Improving the quality of assessment and instruction: Roles for dynamic assessment. (Working paper No. 1, Alternative Assessments of Handicapped Children). Nashville, TN: John F. Kennedy Center for Research on Education and Human Development, Vanderbilt University.

Bransford, J. D., Delclos, V. R., Vye, N. J., Burns, M. S., & Hasselbring, T. S. (1987). State of the art and future directions. In C. S. Lidz (Ed.), *Dynamic assessment: Foundations and fundamentals* (pp. 479–496). New York: Guilford Press.

Brown, A. L., & Ferrara, R. A. (1985). Diagnosing zones of proximal development. In J. Wertsch (Ed.), *Culture, communication, and cognition: Vygotskian perspectives* (pp. 273–305). Cambridge, MA: Cambridge University Press.

Brown, A. L., & French, L. A. (1979). The zone of potential development: Implications for intelligence testing in the year 2000. *Intelligence, 3,* 253–271.

Brown, A. L., & Palincsar, A. S. (1982). Inducing strategic learning from texts by means of informed, self-control training. *Topics in Learning and Learning Disabilities, 2*(1), 1–17.

Bryant, N. R. (1982). *Preschool children's learning and transfer of matrices problems: A study of proximal development.* Unpublished master's thesis, University of Illinois.

Budoff, M. (1965). *Learning potential among the educable mentally retarded.* Progress report to the National Institute of Mental Health. Mimeographed.

Budoff, M. (1967). Learning potential among institutionalized young adult retardates. *American Journal of Mental Deficiency, 72,* 404–411.

Budoff, M. (1972). Measuring learning potential: An alternative to the traditional intelligence test. *Studies in Learning Potential, 3* (39), entire issue.

Budoff, M. (1974). *Learning potential and educability among the educable mentally retarded* (Final Report Project No. 312312). Cambridge, MA: Research Institute for Educational Problems, Cambridge Mental Health Association.

Budoff, M., & Corman, L. (1973). The effectiveness of a group training procedure on the Raven Learning Potential Measure with children from diverse racial and socioeconomic backgrounds. *Studies in Learning Potential, 3* (entire issue 58).

Budoff, M., & Friedman, M. (1964). "Learning potential" as an assessment approach to the adolescent mentally retarded. *Journal of Consulting Psychology, 28,* 434–439.

Burns, M. S. (1985). *Comparison of "Graduated Prompt" and "Mediational" dynamic assessment and static assessment with young children.* Nashville, TN: John F. Kennedy Center for Research on Human Development, Vanderbilt University.

Burns, M. S., & Stephens, D. K. (in press). *Tester child instructional interactions during dynamic assessment.* Nashville, TN: John F. Kennedy Center for Research on Human Development, Vanderbilt University.

Campione, J. C., & Brown, A. L. (1987). Linking dynamic assessment with school achievement. In C. S. Lidz (Ed.), *Dynamic assessment: Foundations and fundamentals* (pp. 82–115). New York: Guilford Press.

Campione, J. C., Brown, A. L., & Ferrara, R. A. (1982). Mental retardation and intelligence. In R. J. Sternberg (Ed.), *Handbook of human intelligence* (pp. 392–490). Cambridge, MA: Harvard University Press.

Campione, J. C., Brown, A. L., Ferrara, R. A., Jones, R. S., & Steinberg, E. (1985). Differences between retarded and non-retarded children in transfer following equivalent learning performance: Breakdowns in flexible use of information. *Intelligence, 9,* 297–315.

Delclos, V. R. (1983). *Differential error analysis in the group administration of the representational stencil design test.* Unpublished doctoral dissertation, George Peabody College for Teachers, Vanderbilt University.

Delclos, V. R., Burns, S., & Kulewicz, S. J. (1985). *Effects of dynamic assessment on teachers' expectations of handicapped children* (Technical Report No. 3, Alternative Assessments of Handicapped Children). Nashville, TN: John F. Kennedy Center for Research on Education and Human Development, Vanderbilt University.

Deno, S. (1985). Curriculum-based measurement: The emerging alternative. *Exceptional Children, 52,* 219–232.

Feldman, S. E., & Sullivan, D. S. (1971). Factors mediating the effects enhanced rapport on children's performance. *Journal of Consulting and Clinical Psychology, 36*(2), 302.

Ferrara, R. A., Brown, A. L., & Campione, J. C. (1986). Children's learning and transfer of inductive reasoning rules: Studies in proximal development. *Child Development, 57,* 1087–1099.

Feuerstein, R. (1979). *The dynamic assessment of retarded performers: The learning potential assessment device, theory, instruments, and techniques.* Baltimore, MD: University Park Press.

Feuerstein, R. (1980). *Instrumental enrichment: An intervention program for cognitive modifiability.* Baltimore, MD: University Park Press.

Feuerstein, R., & Hoffman, M. B. (1982). Intergenerational conflict of rights: Cultural imposition and self-realization. *Journal of School Education, 58,* 44–61.

Feuerstein, R., Rand, Y., Hoffman, M., Hoffman, M., & Miller, R. (1979). Cognitive modifiability in retarded adolescents: Effects of instrumental enrichment. *American Journal of Mental Deficiency, 83,* 539–550.

Feuerstein, R., Rand, Y., & Jensen, M. R. (1981). Can evolving techniques better measure cognitive change? *Journal of Special Education, 15,* 201–219.

Gerber, M. M., & Semmel, M. I. (1984). Teachers as imperfect tests: Reconceptualizing the referral process. *Educational Psychologist, 19,* 137–148.

Gresham, F. M. (1986). On the malleability of intelligence: Unnecessary assumptions, reifications, and occlusion. *School Psychology Review, 15,* 261–263.

Hammill, D. D., & Larsen, S. (1974). The effectiveness of psycholinguistic training. *Exceptional Children, 41,* 5–15.

Haywood, H. C. (1985). *The malleability of intelligence: Cognitive processes as a function of polygenic-experential interaction.* Paper presented at Keynote Address to the National Association of School Psychologists.

Haywood, H. C., & Switzky, H. N. (1986). Transactionalism and cognitive processes: Reply to Reynolds and Gresham. *School Psychology Review, 15,* 264–267.

Hodges, A. (1956). Double alternation: A measure of intelligence. *Journal of Consulting Psychology, 20,* 59–62.

Jensen, M. R., & Feuerstein, R. (1987). The learning potential assessment device: From philosophy to practice. In C. S. Lidz (Ed.), *Dynamic assessment: Foundations and fundamentals* (pp. 379–402). New York: Guilford Press.

Kohs, S. C. (1923). *Intelligence measurement.* New York: Macmillan.

Larry P. v. Wilson Riles, (1979). N. CO-71–2270 RFP, U.S. District Court for Northern District of California.

Lord, F. M. (1963). Elementary models for measuring change. In C. Harris (Ed.), *Problems in measuring change* (pp. 21–38). Madison, WI: University of Wisconsin Press.

Mann, L. (1979). *On the trail of process.* New York: Gune & Stratton.

McCarthy, D. (1972). *Manual for the McCarthy scales of children's abilities.* New York: Psychological Corporation.

NcNemar, Q. (1969). *Psychological statistics.* New York: John Wiley.

Mehan, H. (1973). Assessing children's language using abilities: Methodological and cross-cultural implications. In M. Armer & A. D. Grimshaw (Eds.), *Comparative social research: Methodological problems and strategies* (pp. 309–343). New York: Wiley.

Mercer, J. (1979). *SOMPA technical manual.* New York: Psychological Corp.

Palincsar, A. S., & Brown, A. L. (1984). Reciprocal teaching of comprehension-fostering and comprehension monitoring activities. *Cognition and Instruction, 1,* 117–175.

Public Law 94–142. The education of all handicapped children act of 1975. (1975). Washington, DC: U.S. Government Printing Office.

Reschley, D. J. (1984). Beyond IQ test bias: The national academy panel's analysis of minority EMR overrepresentation. *Educational Researcher, 13,* 15–19.

Reschley, D. J. (1988). Minority overrepresentation and special education reform. *Exceptional Children, 54,* 316–323.

Reynolds, C. R. (1986). Transactional models of intellectual development, yes. Deficit models of process remediation, no. *School Psychology Review, 15,* 256–260.

Rueda, R. (in press). Special education: Dynamic and multicultural assessment of mildly handicapped students. In T. Husen (Ed.), *International encyclopedia of education.* Oxford: Pergamon Press.

Saigh, P. A. (1981). The effects of positive nonverbal examiner comments on the WISC-R performance of Americans in Lebanon. *Journal of Psychology, 104,* 165–169.

Savell, J. M., Twohig, P. T., & Rachford, D. L. (1986). Empirical status of Feuerstein's instrumental enrichment (FIE) technique as a method of teaching thinking skills. *Review of Educational Research, 56,* 381–409.

Sewell, T. E. (1987). Dynamic assessment as a nondiscriminatory procedure. In C. S. Lidz (Ed.), *Dynamic assessment: Foundations and fundamentals* (pp. 426–443). New York: Guilford Press.

Sternberg, R. J. (1982). *Handbook of human intelligence.* Cambridge, MA: Harvard University Press.

Vlasova, T. A., & Pevzner, M. S. (1971). *Children with temporary retardation in development.* Moscow: Pedagogika.

Vye, N. J., Burns, M. S., Delclos, V. R., & Bransford, J. D. (1987). Dynamic assessment of intellectually handicapped children. In C. S. Lidz (Ed.), *Dynamic assessment: Foundations and fundamentals* (pp. 327–359). New York: Guilford Press.

Vygotsky, L. S. (1978). *Mind in society: The development of higher psychological processes* (M. Cole, V. John-Steiner, S. Scribner, & E. Souberman, Eds. and Trans.). Cambridge, MA: Harvard University Press.

Wechsler, D. (1967). *Preschool and primary scale of intelligence.* New York: Psychological Corporation.

Zabramna, S. D. (1971). *Otbor detei vo vspomogatel'nye shkoly* [The selection of children for schools for the mentally retarded]. Moscow: Prosveshchenie.

About the Contributors

HOLLY BENSON received her master's degree in special education from the University of Vermont. Currently she is completing a doctoral degree in social work at the University of Kansas. Ms. Benson has served as a teacher of students with multiple handicaps and has extensive experience in individual educational plan review for legal advocacy in Vermont.

BRUCE BULL received his master's degree in special education from Western Oregon State College in 1985. He is an instructor at the Teaching Research Division of the Oregon State System of Higher Education and Coordinator of the Follow-up and Follow-along Transition Study of Hearing Impaired Adolescents in the Northwest. Mr. Bull's research interests include programs for persons with severe/multiple disabilities and phone survey research methods.

MICHAEL BULLIS received his doctorate in special education and rehabilitation from the University of Oregon in 1983. He is an associate research professor and the Assistant Director of Secondary, Transition, and Adult Programs at the Teaching Research Division of the Oregon State System of Higher Education. Dr. Bullis has been employed as a vocational rehabilitation counselor, a work evaluator, and a research associate at the University of Arkansas' Rehabilitation Research and Training Center on Deafness and Hearing Impairment. He currently directs two federally funded projects on the school-to-community transition of deaf adolescents. His research interests include functional assessment, social skills training, and job placement strategies.

KATHLEEN BYKOWSKY received her master's degree in communication disorders from the University of Minnesota. Currently she is a speech and language pathologist in private practice.

SCOTT DOSS received his Ph.D. in educational psychology from the University of Minnesota, where he is currently a postdoctoral fellow in the Department of Communicative Disorders. Dr. Doss's research focuses on the relationship between socially unacceptable repertoires of behavior and communicative intent among populations with severe intellectual deficits.

JOHN FILLER is Professor of Special Education at the University of Nevada, Las Vegas. He received his Ph.D. in developmental psychology in

1974 from George Peabody College of Vanderbilt University. Dr. Filler has authored numerous research articles and textbook chapters as well as co-edited two texts, all in the area of early childhood education for children with handicaps. A continuing interest is early intervention for children with severe multiple disabilities.

JERRY FORD is a graduate student in the joint doctoral program in special education between San Francisco State University and the University of California, Berkeley. He has considerable experience in providing in-service training of teachers of students with severe disabilities.

JOHN FREEBURG received a master's degree in rehabilitation counseling from St. Cloud State University in 1973. He is an associate professor at Western Oregon State College and Director of the Regional Resource Center on Deafness. The son of deaf parents, Mr. Freeburg has been active in the field of deafness for 16 years. He has directed numerous in-service and preservice training programs for professionals serving deaf adolescents and young adults. Mr. Freeburg's research interests include professional training, utilization of assistive communication devices, and social integration of deaf students.

ROBERT GAYLORD-ROSS is a professor of special education and Coordinator of the Vocational Special Education Program at San Francisco State University. He earned his Ph.D. from Mississippi State University. A Fullbright Senior Research Fellow, Dr. Gaylord-Ross is co-author, with J. Holvoet, of *Strategies for Educating Students with Severe Handicaps* (Little, Brown, 1985), and editor of *Vocational Education for Persons with Handicaps* (Mayfield, 1988) and *Integration Strategies for Persons with Handicaps* (Paul H. Brookes, 1989). He has published in a number of journals, including *Journal of Applied Behavior Analysis* and *Behavior Therapy,* and has served on the editorial boards of *Career Development for Exceptional Individuals, Education and Training of the Mentally Retarded, Exceptional Children,* and *Journal of the Association for Persons with Severe Handicaps.*

THOMAS GUMPEL is a graduate student in the joint doctoral program in special education between San Francisco State University and the University of California, Berkeley. He also teaches mentally retarded adults attending a community college. He has conducted research on the measurement and training of social skills.

ANN TIEDEMANN HALVORSEN is the co-author and Training Coordinator of California's statewide systems-change grant for the integration of students with severe disabilities (1987–1992). She received her doctoral degree from the joint San Francisco State University/University of California, Berkeley program. She is a lecturer in the credential/master's program for teachers of students with severe disabilities at California State University, Hayward, and the author of several publications in the area of integration.

LAIRD W. HEAL is Professor of Special Education and Psychology at the University of Illinois at Urbana-Champaign. He was awarded his Ph.D. degree in psychology from the University of Wisconsin—Madison in 1964. Dr. Heal has served as an assistant and associate professor of psychology at George Peabody College in Nashville, Tennessee; as director of a project to evaluate a procedure adapted from the apparently successful program for habilitating cerebral palsied children at the Institute for Conductive Education in Budapest, Hungary; and as the Director of Research for the National Association of Retarded Citizens. Dr. Heal's research interest focuses on the deinstitutionalization movement, especially strategies and procedures for assessing cost-effectiveness of various residential alternatives for mentally retarded citizens. During the last ten years, Dr. Heal has published a book and a number of papers and contributed chapters dealing with deinstitutionalization research and ideology.

MARK MIZUKO received his Ph.D. in communication disorders from the University of Wisconsin—Madison. Currently he serves as an assistant professor of communication disorders at the University of Minnesota—Duluth. Dr. Mizuko's teaching responsibilities focus on the area of language acquisition assessment and intervention across the life span. His research interests focus on alternative and augmentative communication systems as they apply to a variety of handicapping conditions.

JENNIFER OLSON is an assistant professor and Coordinator of Early Childhood Programs in the Department of Counseling and Special Education at the University of Idaho. Dr. Olson received her Ph.D. in special education in 1981 from the University of Idaho. She has written several articles focused upon the application of family systems theory to early intervention for at-risk and handicapped young children. Additionally, she co-directs the Idaho National Outreach Project for Families with At-Risk and Handicapped Infants.

HYUN-SOOK PARK is the principal investigator of the Social Support Project at San Francisco State University, where she earned her Ph.D. in 1980. She has completed research and publications on the topic of social skill training. Dr. Park is currently investigating social skill and relationship intervention in work settings.

JOE REICHLE received his Ph.D. in communication disorders from the University of Wisconsin—Madison. He served for two years as a visiting assistant professor at the Center for Developmental Disabilities at the University of Vermont. He is currently an associate professor of communication disorders and educational psychology at the University of Minnesota. Dr. Reichle's teaching and research interests lie in the area of augmentative communication systems as they apply to persons with severe handicaps, and he directs master's, doctoral, and postdoctoral training programs in this area. Dr. Reichle also serves as a reviewer for a number of scholarly journals.

HOWARD ROTHMAN is a school psychologist for Santa Barbara County Schools and a licensed educational psychologist and marriage, family, and child counselor. He received a master's degree from the University of Southern California and is a doctoral candidate in special education at the University of California, Santa Barbara. As a former research psychologist, he helped develop and test intellectual assessment materials based on J. P. Guilford's Structure of the Intellect Model. He has lectured extensively on intellectual testing and the effects of test anxiety on performance. His current research interests include alternative forms of psychoeducational assessment, pupil study teams, and effects of special education placement on self-esteem.

WAYNE SAILOR is a professor of teacher education at San Francisco State University (SFSU). He coordinates programs for persons with severe disabilities at SFSU. He received his doctoral degree from the University of Kansas. He is past associate editor of the *Journal of Applied Behavior Analysis* and a member of the editorial board of the *Journal of the Association for Persons with Severe Handicaps*. Dr. Sailor currently directs a five-year research and technical assistance institute (1987–1992) concerned with the integration of students with severe disabilities into regular classrooms and schools. He is also site director of the SFSU site of the national Research and Training Center for Community-Referenced Behavior Management Technologies for Students with Severe Disabilities.

MELVYN I. SEMMEL is Professor of Special Education and Director of the Special Education Research Laboratory at the University of California, Santa Barbara. He received his doctorate from George Peabody College, Vanderbilt University. He has served as an associate professor and a senior research scientist at the Center for Language and Language Behavior, University of Michigan. He is the former director of the Center for Innovation in Teaching the Handicapped, Indiana University. He has published more than 125 articles, books, monographs, and research reports. He is a Fellow of the American Psychological Association (Division 15, 33) and the American Association on Mental Retardation. He is the 1988–89 Merrill Award Recipient from the Teacher Education Division of the Council for Exceptional Children. His research interests are policy issues related to individual differences in the schools, technology applications, information processing, and curriculum issues.

JOSEPH SENDELBAUGH received his doctorate in instruction from Northern Illinois University in 1977. He is an associate professor at Western Oregon State College and Director of the Rehabilitation Counseling Program in Deafness. The son of deaf parents, he has been employed as a teacher of deaf students in a residential school and as a vocational rehabilitation counselor. Dr. Sendelbaugh's research interests include assessment and evaluation of deaf students, functional skill training, and counseling interventions.

SHEPHERD SIEGEL is the Project Coordinator of the Career Ladder Program (CLP) at San Francisco State University, where he earned his Ph.D. CLP is a federal model demonstration program that provides transitional vocational services for youth with mild handicaps. Dr. Siegel has published a number of articles and chapters in this field.

JEFF SIGAFOOS is a doctoral candidate in educational psychology at the University of Minnesota and holds a behavior analyst certificate and master's degree in special education from the University of Minnesota.

HARVEY N. SWITZKY is a professor of educational psychology and special education in the Department of Educational Psychology, Counseling, and Special Education at Northern Illinois University, Dekalb. He received his Ph.D. degree in developmental psychology from Brown University in 1970. He has been an assistant professor of psychology in the Department of Psychology at George Peabody College for Teachers, and a scientist at the Institute on Mental Retardation and Intellectual Development, John F. Kennedy Center for Research on Education and Human Development, Nashville, Tennessee. Dr. Switzky's current research interests include the interrelationship between intelligence and personality, the influence of personality traits on learning and performance, cognitive modifiability, and learning potential assessment.

PHYLLIS TAPPE is a graduate student in the joint doctoral program in special education between San Francisco State University and the University of California, Berkeley. She is also a research associate on the Social Support Project. Previously, she was a teacher of students with learning disabilities and mental retardation.

Index